Cambridge studies in medieval life and thought

Edited by WALTER ULLMANN, LITT.D., F.B.A.
*Professor of Medieval History in the
University of Cambridge*

Third series, vol. 11

THE STAFFORDS, EARLS OF STAFFORD AND DUKES OF BUCKINGHAM
1394–1521

CAMBRIDGE STUDIES IN
MEDIEVAL LIFE AND THOUGHT

THIRD SERIES

THE STAFFORDS,
EARLS OF STAFFORD AND
DUKES OF BUCKINGHAM
1394-1521

CAROLE RAWCLIFFE

CAMBRIDGE UNIVERSITY PRESS
CAMBRIDGE
LONDON · NEW YORK · MELBOURNE

Published by the Syndics of the Cambridge University Press
The Pitt Building, Trumpington Street, Cambridge CB2 IRP
Bentley House, 200 Euston Road, London NWI 2DB
32 East 57th Street, New York, NY 10022, USA
296 Beaconsfield Parade, Middle Park, Melbourne 3206, Australia

© Cambridge University Press 1978

First published 1978

Printed in Great Britain by
The Eastern Press Limited
London and Reading

Library of Congress Cataloguing in Publication Data
Rawcliffe, Carole, 1946–
The Staffords: Earls of Stafford and Dukes of Buckingham, 1394–1521.
(Cambridge studies in medieval life and thought; 3d ser., v. 11.)
Includes bibliographical references and index.
1. Stafford family. 2. Great Britain – History – Lancaster and York, 1399–1485.
3. Great Britain – History – Tudors, 1485–1603. 4. Great Britain – Nobility.
I. Title. II. Series.
DA28.35.S77R37   929'.2'0941   77–5850
ISBN 0 521 21663 X

CONTENTS

MAP

TABLES

TO MY PARENTS

TO MY PARENTS

ACKNOWLEDGEMENTS

My thanks are due to the staff of all the libraries and record offices which I visited while writing this book. I am particularly grateful to Miss M. M. Condon of the Public Record Office, Lt Colonel J. Ingles, acting archivist to the Marquess of Bath at the time of my visits to Longleat House, and Mr F. B. Stitt of the Stafford County Record Office, who gave me much valuable assistance and cheerful encouragement during the early years of my research. It is impossible to acknowledge individually all those who have offered suggestions and help since I first began working on the Stafford family. Mr A. D. K. Hawkyard and Dr L. S. Woodger, my colleagues at the History of Parliament Trust, have been more than generous with references and information hitherto unknown to me; and I would also like to thank Miss E. A. Danbury, Dr R. I. Jack, Mr B. G. Owens, Mr H. Murray-Baillie, Dr R. S. Thomas and Dr R. Virgoe for their help in this respect. I owe a considerable debt to Mr T. B. Pugh both for his many suggested improvements to my Ph.D. thesis on the Staffords and for his advice on the interpretation of the first Duke of Buckingham's career. Professor Walter Ullmann has by his interest and guidance done much to render less arduous the task of converting a thesis into a book. I am also grateful to the staff of the Cambridge University Press for their assistance in preparing it for publication. My husband has read through and commented upon my text more times than he now cares to remember, and has had many pertinent criticisms to make in matters of presentation and style. Above all I am indebted to Dr Robin Jeffs, who first suggested the topic of my thesis some years ago. Since then he has read and discussed my work in all its stages and has made his own research readily available to me. Without his constant help and encouragement this book would never have been written.

February 1977   C. R.

ABBREVIATIONS

B.I.H.R.	*Bulletin of the Institute of Historical Research.*
B.J.R.L.	*Bulletin of the John Rylands Library.*
C.C.R.	*Calendar of Close Rolls.*
C.F.R.	*Calendar of Fine Rolls.*
Cal. Papal Regs.	*Calendar of Entries in the Papal Registers Relating to Great Britain and Ireland* (14 vols., H.M.S.O., 1894–1961).
C.P.R.	*Calendar of Patent Rolls.*
C.S.	Camden Society.
E.H.R.	*English Historical Review.*
Econ. H.R.	*Economic History Review.*
Foedera	*Foedera, Conventiones, Litterae et cuiuscunque Generis Acta Publica*, ed. T. Rymer (20 vols., The Hague, 1704–35).
G.E.C.	G. E. Cockayne, *The Complete Peerage*, ed. V. Gibbs and others (12 vols., 1910–59).
H.M.S.O.	Her Majesty's Stationery Office.
H.M.C.	Historical Manuscripts Commission.
L. & P. Henry VIII	*Letters and Papers, Foreign and Domestic, of the Reign of Henry VIII.*
N.L.W.	National Library of Wales.
P.L.	*The Paston Letters, 1422–1509*, ed J. Gairdner (4 vols., London, 1900–1).
P.C.C.	Probate Court of Canterbury.
P.P.C.	*Proceedings and Ordinances of the Privy Council*, ed. N. H. Nicholas (7 vols., R.C., 1843–7).
R.C.	Record Commission.
R.S.	Rolls Series.
Rot. Parl.	*Rotuli Parliamentorum*, ed. J. Strachey and others (6 vols., London, 1767–77).
State Papers Spanish	*Letters, Despatches and State Papers relating to the Negotiations between England and Spain* (vols. I, II and supplement, ed. G. A. Bergenroth, H.M.S.O., 1862–8).

Abbreviations

State Papers Venetian	*State Papers and Manuscripts relating to English Affairs, existing in the Archives and Collections of Venice* (vols. I to III, ed. R. Brown, H.M.S.O., 1864–9).
Statutes of the Realm	*Statutes of the Realm* (large folio), ed. A. Luders and others (11 vols., R.C., 1810–28).
T.R.H.S.	*Transactions of the Royal Historical Society.*
V.C.H.	*Victoria County History.*
W.A.M.	Westminster Abbey Muniments.
Year Book(s)	*Les Reports des cases en les ans des roys Edward V, Richard III, Henrie VII et Henri VIII* (London, 1679).

THE ABBREVIATION OF MANUSCRIPT SOURCES

Full details of classes of manuscripts in the British Library and the Public Record Office cited by number only in the text are given in the list of manuscript sources; references beginning D.641 and D.1721 are to documents in the Staffordshire County Record Office; all other locations are provided in the footnotes.

The Manors and larger properties occupied by Humphrey, first Duke of Buckingham, at Michaelmas, 1448. (Based on Longleat Ms. 6410.)

xiii

INTRODUCTION

The Staffords, Earls and Dukes of Buckingham, were among the richest and most powerful members of the later medieval English baronage; yet their great wealth and territorial resources, which they acquired in part through royal patronage, eventually brought about their downfall. From the early years of the fourteenth century until the death of the first Duke of Buckingham in 1460, the Staffords prospered in the service of the Crown. Their personal talents as soldiers and statesmen and their growing reserves of manpower were placed at the disposal of successive kings of England; in return they were elevated from relative obscurity to the highest rank of nobility.

The second Duke received no such favours from Edward IV, because the latter's insecurity on the throne made him innately suspicious of the Staffords' royal blood and their traditional expectations of a share in the business of government. A combination of frustration, fear and ambition perhaps led the Duke to support Richard of Gloucester, whose success in gaining the throne encouraged Buckingham himself to take part in an abortive *coup d'état* in October 1483. Although Henry VII reversed his attainder two years later the third Duke remained under constant suspicion as a potential rebel, and eventually went to the block in 1521 because of his failure to allay these fears.

The Staffords derived most of their income and almost all their influence from the ownership of land. Their place in national affairs was largely determined by their success as landlords and by their skill in exploiting every resource at their disposal. Like all medieval landowners they were concerned with efficient estate management and revenue collection, since their reputation as ' good lords ' or leaders of men depended largely upon the state of their finances and their ability to maintain a suitably impressive lifestyle. The survival of a large quantity of fifteenth- and early sixteenth-century records from the Stafford household and estates makes it possible to examine in detail not only how the three Dukes of Buckingham approached their administrative and financial problems, but also how these problems influenced their political behaviour.

The history of the Stafford archive is an interesting one. The third Duke began to order and classify his family papers many years before his death. Some of his father's manuscripts were destroyed during the rebellion of 1483 and the remainder were burnt by the Welsh supporters of Richard III two years later.[1] Estate records were negligently kept throughout Buckingham's minority; but there was a great corpus of evidence relating to the Staffords' eight receiverships from the late fourteenth century onwards, and these the Duke's officials set about sorting and numbering for purposes of litigation. They were stored, together with copies of his own estate accounts and business papers, in iron-bound chests, with plate locks, padlocks and iron bolts, in a specially built muniment room at his manor house at Thornbury. Three chests were removed to the Tower of London at the time of Buckingham's attainder, but, as a surviving contemporary catalogue shows, most of their contents were subsequently lost. Several other account rolls also found their way to the Tower, and are now in the Public Record Office.

Henry, Lord Stafford, continued his father's system for preserving records; he made many transcriptions and detailed lists of evidence concerning Buckingham's estates and titles. Most of the manuscripts he examined are not known to have survived, although his own notes, bound up into three so-called cartularies, give some idea of their scope. His son, Edward, was responsible for the compilation of an invaluable register *de rebus diversis*, which, together with Henry, Lord Stafford's letter book and two of his cartularies, a household book for 1508/9 and eight volumes of medieval and sixteenth-century estate records, eventually came into the hands of Stebbing Shaw, the Staffordshire antiquary. The second Lord Bagot acquired these volumes in

---

[1] For a more detailed account of the history of the Stafford manuscripts, their dispersal and present whereabouts, see C. Rawcliffe, 'The Papers of Edward, duke of Buckingham', *Journal of the Society of Archivists*, V (1976), pp. 294–300.

1820, and they now constitute a major part of the Bagot collection in the Staffordshire County Record Office.

The descendants of Henry, Lord Stafford, suffered many vicissitudes which led to a further dispersal of their family archive. Successive generations of Staffords managed, however, to retain a considerable number of medieval manuscripts and these were also recently deposited in the Staffordshire County Record Office. They represent the largest of several scattered deposits bearing upon the three Dukes of Buckingham and their estates, since they comprise over 300 account rolls, 200 court rolls and parts of court rolls, as well as several miscellaneous legal documents and administrative directives issued by the third Duke. The British Library Department of Manuscripts has acquired over the years many important records formerly belonging to the Staffords; but, except for the purchase in 1936 of a set of thirty account rolls and court rolls from the collection of W. A. Cogman, their provenance is largely unrecorded.

The most important collection of evidence for the affairs and finances of Humphrey, first Duke of Buckingham, is *The Redd Booke of Caures Castle*, a register of letters patent and general directives issued by the Duke and his ministers over the years 1434 to 1455. The original appears to have been lost, but a copy of it made between 1620 and 1648 by the Welsh genealogist Robert Vaughan of Hengwrt now belongs to the National Library of Wales.

As a result of the accidents of wardship and marriage some Stafford papers found their way into the archives of other landowners. The muniments of Lady Margaret Beaufort, the mother of Henry VII and the third Duke's guardian, now housed at Westminster Abbey, include two receiver general's accounts for the Stafford estates during the 1490s and an extensive survey of Buckingham's property undertaken over the years 1515 to 1518. The Howards obtained possession of some accounts at the time of the marriage of Thomas, third Duke of Norfolk, to one of Duke Edward's daughters; and the Marquesses of Bath inherited others as a result of the acquisition by their ancestor, Sir John Thynne, of the Staffords' lordship of Caus in 1576.

Taken as a whole, this widely-dispersed and incomplete collection of manuscripts still constitutes the largest and most comprehensive archive for any fifteenth- or early sixteenth-century English noble family. It provides an opportunity to examine in detail the organisation of a great estate and the changes which affected it over a period of more than one hundred and twenty years. Certain groups of manors and lordships, notably those in Staffordshire and Gloucestershire, are almost continuously documented, with near complete sets of accounts, court rolls and deeds for all but the decade 1475 to 1485. Less is known about other parts of the estates, but enough has survived in the form of receivers' accounts, valors and surveys to present a clear picture of the way in which the Staffords used their resources. Although the first two Dukes of Buckingham must inevitably remain shadowy figures in comparison with John of Gaunt (*d.* 1399), whose muniments form such a large and significant part of the medieval archives of the Duchy of Lancaster, their family papers are nevertheless the most important single source of information for the English baronage after 1400. As much is known about Gaunt as any member of the fifteenth-century nobility; but this ambitious son of Edward III, with his great retinue financed out of an income which may eventually have reached £20,000 a year, is not representative of the class as a whole. The loss of so many records concerning the administration and finances of Richard, Duke of York (*d.* 1460), the richest, if not the most efficient, landowner of his time, and the general paucity of evidence for other titled families of this period make the Staffords a particularly rewarding subject for study. The papers of the fifteenth- and early sixteenth-century Earls of Northumberland contain a quantity of manorial and central accounts, but the disappearance of all material relating to their household leaves a serious gap in our knowledge of the Percys' financial and domestic affairs.[2] In this respect their archive cannot be compared with that of the Staffords, which includes over twenty-five household accounts and day books for the period 1460 to 1521 alone. Although the last three Beauchamp Earls of Warwick left an impressive collection of estate and household accounts, valors and other documents,

---

[2] See J. M. W. Bean, *The Estates of the Percy Family 1416–1537* (Oxford, 1958), pp. 166–7 for a list of surviving Percy manuscripts between 1416 and 1537, and pp. 2–3 for a note on their limitations.

now as widely scattered as the Stafford papers, hardly anything is known of their estates after 1449, when they passed by marriage into the hands of Richard Neville, the Kingmaker.[3] This is all the more unfortunate because the Kingmaker's family muniments have been lost and his private affairs remain largely a matter of conjecture. Smaller collections and scattered groups of muniments have survived for other baronial houses, such as the Lords Grey of Ruthin, the Bourchiers, Lords Fitzwarren and Earls of Essex, the Talbot Earls of Shrewsbury and the Stanley Earls of Derby; but the lack of evidence imposes great limitations on any study of these houses.

Despite the comparative wealth of information at our disposal, a balanced history of the Staffords, dealing fully with each of the three Dukes of Buckingham and their finances, cannot now be written. The distribution of the source material is uneven: almost none survives for Duke Henry, whereas for Duke Edward there is a relative superabundance. So much in fact can be discerned about him that his equally celebrated but less well-documented ancestors inevitably suffer. He is perhaps the first English nobleman of whom a rounded character sketch can be attempted, and since he was such a driving force behind the reforms introduced on the Stafford estates during the sixteenth century, it is tempting to see him as a far greater innovator than he actually was. Certain parts of this book, especially those dealing with the Staffords' legal affairs and their exploitation of common law procedures for administrative ends, concentrate almost exclusively upon Duke Edward, not because he was necessarily the first of his line to employ such practices, but because he alone is known to have done so. Allowance should therefore be made for the date and limitations of the surviving evidence, which, if not properly assessed, tends to convey a distorted impression of developments on the Stafford estates.

The late K. B. McFarlane did much to alter our view of the place of the great nobleman in medieval society. The image of the violent, ungovernable warlord, so beloved by earlier generations, is now recognised to be false; we know that the English

---

[3] K. B. McFarlane, *The Nobility of Later Medieval England* (Oxford, 1973), p. 187, n. 2, lists the nine major deposits of Beauchamp family papers.

upper classes were not only better educated and politically more astute than had been supposed, but that they took a close personal interest in the control and management of their estates. Although outstanding for their wealth and the extent of their territorial possessions, the three Dukes of Buckingham were by no means atypical as landowners. They shared with their contemporaries a consuming desire ' to exploit every imagined right, to push every promising advantage to its limit'; nor were they alone in their insistence upon stringent economies at all levels of expenditure.[4] As they appear, more specialised studies of individuals and their families tend to underline similarities rather than differences in attitude. Mr T. B. Pugh's *The Marcher Lordships of South Wales 1415–1536* (Cardiff, 1963) has already made available much valuable information about the organisation of the Staffords' Welsh estates and their approach to the administration of justice in the Marches. He has drawn attention to the wider problems faced by Edward, third Duke of Buckingham, in his relations with the Crown, and in so doing has greatly contributed to our general understanding of the rôle and influence of the nobility in late medieval English society. My work owes much to both Mr McFarlane and Mr Pugh.

---

[4] *Ibid.*, p. 49. Mr McFarlane's researches into the Stafford family were unfinished when he died in 1966 and only a short paper based on them has been published (*ibid.*, pp. 201–212).

Chapter 1

THE RISE OF THE STAFFORD FAMILY
1343–1460

At the time of his attainder and execution in 1521, Edward Stafford, Duke of Buckingham, Earl of Stafford, Hereford and Northampton, Lord of Brecon and Holderness and heir general to both Edward III and Henry VI, held property worth over £6,000 a year gross. He and his ancestors had occupied many high offices, including the Constableships of England, Calais and France, and had served the Crown as councillors of state and captains of war. His estates were spread between Holderness in East Yorkshire and Newport in South Wales; he owned houses in Calais and possessed titles to lands in France and Ireland. Most of this great patrimony had been acquired in stages at the expense of other noble houses, which, being less fortunate than the Staffords, had failed to escape the disastrous consequences of attainder, dynastic failure and the accidents of war.

The early history of the Staffords was, however, undistinguished. Although the Norman knight Ralph de Tonei had been rewarded for his part in the conquest of England with a grant of more than one hundred confiscated manors, William I could never forget that Ralph's father had rebelled against him in Normandy, and had tempered his generosity with prudence by ensuring that these estates were scattered across England. Despite their claim to be titular lords of Stafford, Ralph's immediate descendants were prevented from controlling the town itself because they threatened to become too powerful along the Welsh March.[1] They were loyal by necessity rather than choice, for their slender finances and modest following placed an effective curb on their activities. Even so, the Staffords, as the de Toneis became known, proved themselves able men, whose military and adminis-

---

[1] T. J. Mazzinghi, 'Castle Church', *William Salt Archaeological Society*, VIII (1887), pp. 72–9; for a list of the various properties acquired by the Stafford family during the middle ages see Appendix A.

trative skill eventually earned them a place in national affairs. It also brought them titles and other marks of royal favour, including opportunities to make a number of highly advantageous marriages.

Ralph Stafford was the first of his line to achieve recognition both in England and France as a soldier, diplomat and statesman. The outbreak of the Hundred Years' War in 1338 provided him with a splendid opportunity for personal advancement which he exploited to the full. Then aged thirty-seven, with years of military experience in the Scottish wars and a strong position at court behind him, he was, from the onset of hostilities, among Edward III's most trusted captains and ambassadors. He received many rewards, of which the most outstanding was his creation as Earl of Stafford with an annuity of 1,000 marks in 1351.[2] Despite his loyal service during the wars with France, it is unlikely that such generosity would have been shown towards him had he not recently acquired the means of supporting an earldom. In 1347 Ralph and his heirs had been granted special livery of the Audley estates. The possessions of the childless Gilbert de Clare, Earl of Gloucester and Hereford, had been partitioned between his three surviving sisters in 1317. Margaret, the second sister, who was married to Hugh Audley, received the lordship of Newport in Wales and other property spread across the south of England, worth in all £2,314 a year.[3] The Audleys' only child, a daughter also named Margaret, was thus a most desirable commodity on the marriage market.

Shortly after the death of his first wife, Ralph Stafford led an armed raid on the Audleys' house at Thaxted and abducted the young Margaret.[4] With a potential income which was worth at least twenty times his own, and which was based on lands extending from Norfolk to the Welsh Marches, she was indeed a valuable prize. Far from disapproving of Ralph's second matrimonial venture, King Edward seems to have intervened to protect him from Hugh Audley's wrath; he may even have effected a rapprochement between Hugh and Ralph. By 1343, nine years

---

[2] *Cal. Charter Rolls*, vol. V p. 124.

[3] For a more detailed account of the partition see M. Altschul, *A Baronial Family in Medieval England: the Clares, 1217-1314* (Johns Hopkins' University Press, 1965), pp. 165-74.   [4] *C.P.R.*, 1334-8, p. 298.

TABLE I. *The early Staffords, 1038–1403*

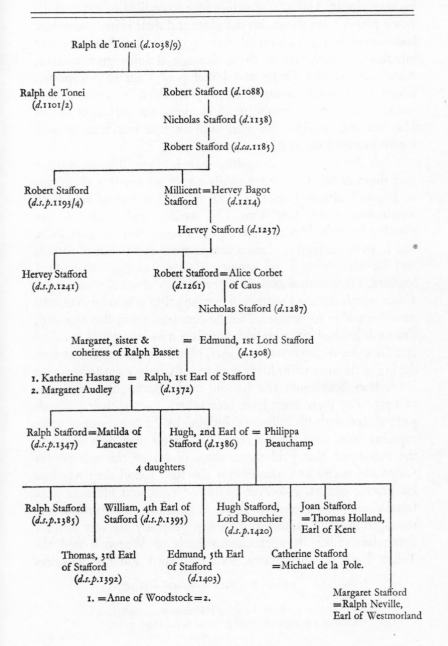

Ralph de Tonei (*d.*1038/9)

Ralph de Tonei (*d.*1101/2)

Robert Stafford (*d.*1088)

Nicholas Stafford (*d.*1138)

Robert Stafford (*d.ca.*1185)

Robert Stafford (*d.s.p.*1193/4)

Millicent Stafford = Hervey Bagot (*d.*1214)

Hervey Stafford (*d.*1237)

Hervey Stafford (*d.s.p.*1241)

Robert Stafford (*d.*1261) = Alice Corbet of Caus

Nicholas Stafford (*d.*1287)

Margaret, sister & coheiress of Ralph Basset = Edmund, 1st Lord Stafford (*d.*1308)

1. Katherine Hastang = Ralph, 1st Earl of Stafford
2. Margaret Audley = (*d.*1372)

Ralph Stafford (*d.s.p.*1347) = Matilda of Lancaster

Hugh, 2nd Earl of Stafford (*d.*1386) = Philippa Beauchamp

4 daughters

Ralph Stafford (*d.s.p.*1385)

William, 4th Earl of Stafford (*d.s.p.*1395)

Hugh Stafford, Lord Bourchier (*d.s.p.*1420)

Joan Stafford = Thomas Holland, Earl of Kent

Thomas, 3rd Earl of Stafford (*d.s.p.*1392)

Edmund, 5th Earl of Stafford (*d.*1403)

Catherine Stafford = Michael de la Pole.

1. = Anne of Woodstock = 2.

Margaret Stafford = Ralph Neville, Earl of Westmorland

after the marriage had taken place and some three years before his own death, Audley was sufficiently reconciled to settle all his wife's property on Ralph, his daughter and their heirs.[5] No sooner had they taken possession of these great estates than a second inheritance descended to them through Ralph's grandmother, Alice Corbet. The Castle and lordship of Caus in Shropshire, which was worth about £265 a year clear in 1401, greatly strengthened the Staffords' position along the turbulent Welsh Marches and provided the Earl with another recruiting ground for his private bodyguard.

Ralph Stafford died a wealthy man in 1372. The inquisition *post mortem* taken on his English estates set his annual income at £1,432,[6] although in fact after 1351 he seems to have been worth over twice this sum. The Audley and Corbet estates together brought him at least £3,350 a year; from his parents he had inherited a further £200 a year in rents and profits of justice; and he also enjoyed an annuity of 1,000 marks[7] as Earl of Stafford. He was thus assured of revenues of about £3,000 a year; a sum which during a successful campaigning season he may even have been able to double. That he benefited from the war with France is beyond question, although it is now impossible to calculate the value of the rewards, wages, plunder and ransoms he took during a lifetime of military service. His only recorded ransom is for Jean Boucicaut: this he sold to the Exchequer for £1,000 in 1353.[8] But there must have been others, even if their proceeds were shared with his followers. Judging by the behaviour of other captains, who were equally ready to defraud their own men and the exchequer that paid them, some of his official receipts for wages and necessary expenses may also have found their way into his private coffers. However badly the rank and file may have fared during the Hundred Years' War, those commanders who managed to avoid capture and ransom generally did very well for themselves. Like the Beauchamp Earls of Warwick and the Talbot Earls of Shrewsbury, Ralph Stafford and his successors

---

[5] *Ibid.*, 1343–5, pp. 140, 366, 384; *C.C.R.*, 1346–9, p. 347.
[6] C.135/230/62.
[7] The value of the mark was about two thirds of a pound (13s.4d.).
[8] *Issues of The Exchequer*, ed. J. Devon (R.C., 1847), p. 159.

owed their rising fortunes to the benefits of royal service and royal favour.[9]

Thanks to his wealth and connexions the first Earl was able to arrange good marriages for his children. His eldest son was betrothed to Matilda, the daughter of Henry of Grosmont, successively Earl of Derby and Duke of Lancaster, one of the most celebrated captains of the day. Matilda was heiress to the extensive Duchy of Lancaster estates, but her young husband died long before they descended to her.[10] Hugh, the Earl's second son and eventual heir, married the daughter of another noteworthy English commander, Thomas Beauchamp, Earl of Warwick. On succeeding to the earldom he began himself to play a prominent rôle in national affairs. Edward III's last years saw protests by the Commons against the conduct of the war with France and the continuous misuse of revenue; protests which culminated in the proceedings of the Good Parliament of 1376. Despite his connexions with the court, Hugh Stafford enjoyed great popularity, being nominated for membership of the newly enlarged royal council in that year. He was also among the ' sufficient men ' deemed suitable to advise the young Richard II, and served on many commissions, particularly those dealing with coastal defence and Scottish affairs.[11] But during Richard's Scottish expedition of 1385 his eldest son, Ralph, was killed in a brawl by the Earl of Huntingdon.[12] Deeply affected by his loss, and no doubt embittered by the King's failure to see justice done, the Earl made a pilgrimage to Jerusalem and died on the return journey in 1386. Before leaving he wisely took the precaution of making an extensive series of enfeoffments whereby most of his English estates were entrusted to friends and servants, so that although the next heir was a minor the Crown exercised wardship with very little of the property.[13]

[9] For a more general discussion of the English nobility and their approach to warfare see K. B. McFarlane, *The Nobility of Later Medieval England*, chapter II, *passim*.

[10] G.E.C., vol. VII p. 410.

[11] *Rot. Parl.*, vol. II pp. 322, 353; vol. III pp. 57, 73, 145.

[12] This dramatic incident, which threatened to disrupt the entire campaign, attracted a great deal of contemporary comment. See, for example, *Chroniques de Jean Froissart*, ed. S. Luce and others (14 vols., Société de l'Histoire de France, Paris, 1869-1966), vol. XI pp. 260-5; and *Polychronicon Ranulphi Higden*, ed. J. Lumby and C. Babington (9 vols., R.C., 1865-6), vol. IX p. 61.

[13] *C.P.R.*, 1377-81, p. 219; *op. cit.*, 1385-9, p. 364.

The third Earl, Thomas, was in fact old enough at the time of his father's death to take an active interest in the administration of his inheritance. He came of age in 1389 and married Anne, the daughter of Thomas of Woodstock, Duke of Gloucester, shortly afterwards. They had no children, so that on his early death in 1392 the earldom passed to Thomas's second brother, William. Gloucester took charge of the boy, who died only three years later aged seventeen; he was, however, allowed to keep the wardship and marriage of Thomas's third brother, Edmund, the fifth Earl of Stafford; and he immediately strengthened their relationship by marrying him to his widowed sister-in-law, Anne.[14] Almost all the property for which Edmund performed homage in 1400 had been administered by a group of councillors for an unbroken period of eighteen years. Largely as a result of their efforts, part of the Basset inheritance was secured for the Staffords after a long and costly legal battle with other claimants. Acquired piecemeal between the years 1391 and 1403, these new possessions in Norfolk and the Midlands were worth almost £200 a year. In addition to his own estates, the Earl acquired further property through his wife, but he did not live long enough to enjoy his increased income, being killed at the Battle of Shrewsbury in 1403. Now twice widowed, with the customary third of her two husbands' estates, the Countess Anne controlled over half the Stafford inheritance and was also a great landowner in her own right. Her successive marriages to the third and fifth Earls mark the final step in the Staffords' ascent to the upper reaches of the English nobility. From her father she had acquired a claim to the earldom of Buckingham and a title to property worth about £1,000 a year; soon after the death of her mother, Eleanor de Bohun, in 1399, she was recognised as sole heiress to half the de Bohun estates.

Humphrey de Bohun, Earl of Hereford, Essex and Northampton, died without issue in 1361. His lands and titles reverted to a nephew, who left two daughters: Eleanor, the elder, married Thomas of Woodstock, Duke of Gloucester, and when she came of age in 1380 the estates – save her mother's dower – were duly partitioned. Gloucester occupied the earldom of Essex in the right

[14] *C.F.R.*, 1391-9, p. 54; *C.P.R.*, 1396-9, pp. 376, 384.

12

TABLE II. *The de Bohun inheritance*

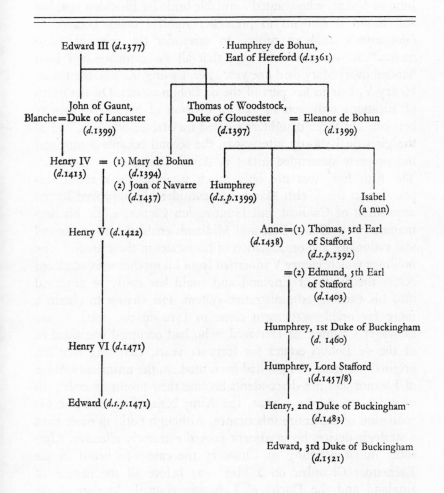

Edward III (*d.*1377)

Humphrey de Bohun, Earl of Hereford (*d.*1361)

Blanche = John of Gaunt, Duke of Lancaster (*d.*1399)

Thomas of Woodstock, Duke of Gloucester (*d.*1397) = Eleanor de Bohun (*d.*1399)

Henry IV (*d.*1413) = (1) Mary de Bohun (*d.*1394)

(2) Joan of Navarre (*d.*1437)

Humphrey (*d.s.p.*1399)

Isabel (a nun)

Henry V (*d.*1422)

Anne = (1) Thomas, 3rd Earl of Stafford (*d.*1438) (*d.s.p.*1392)

= (2) Edmund, 5th Earl of Stafford (*d.*1403)

Henry VI (*d.*1471)

Humphrey, 1st Duke of Buckingham (*d.* 1460)

Humphrey, Lord Stafford (*d.*1457/8)

Edward (*d.s.p.*1471)

Henry, 2nd Duke of Buckingham (*d.*1483)

Edward, 3rd Duke of Buckingham (*d.*1521)

of his wife, while enjoying the revenues due to her sister Mary, who was also his ward.[15] He virtually imprisoned the unfortunate girl at Pleshey in the hope that she would relinquish her share of the inheritance and enter a convent. She was finally rescued by John of Gaunt, who wanted a suitable bride for his eldest son, but still found it difficult to press her rightful claim because of Gloucester's stubborn refusal to surrender the relevant documents.[16] It was not until 1393 that all the evidence had been handed over; Mary died one year later, leaving her son, the future Henry V, heir to her part of the de Bohun estates. On the death of Eleanor's only son in 1399 a division of her own property between her three daughters seemed inevitable; however, one of the girls died shortly afterwards, the second became a nun and the property descended intact to Anne, Countess of Stafford.[17] The fifth Earl was not only much wealthier as a result; his position on the Welsh March was considerably improved by the acquisition of Caldicot and Huntingdon Castles, while his new manors in the South East and Midlands enabled him to expand and rationalise the organisation of his estates in these areas.[18] The holdings which Henry V inherited from his mother were scattered across the South of England and could less easily be absorbed into his existing administrative system. His chance to obtain a more favourable settlement came in 1419 on the death of the Dowager Countess of Hereford, who had occupied one third of of the de Bohun estates for forty-six years. Claiming that the original partition of 1380 had been made to the unfair advantage of Eleanor and her descendants because their profits exceeded his own by 100 marks a year, the King began litigation for the redivision of the entire inheritance. Although nothing more than a strategic device, his argument proved extremely effective. After some initial pleading in Chancery the case was heard in the Exchequer Chamber on 2 May 1421 before all the justices of England and the Duchy of Lancaster council. As part of the defence Anne's attorney argued that by first accepting Mary de

---

[15] *C.C.R.*, 1377–81, pp. 390–4, 410, 413–4, 439.

[16] N. Denholm-Young, *Seignorial Administration in England* (Oxford, 1937), p. 24; R. Somerville, *The Duchy of Lancaster* (2 vols., London, 1953–70), vol. I p. 68.

[17] G.E.C., vol. VI p. 475; *C.F.R.*, 1399–1405, pp. 70, 79, 99, 159.

[18] See D.L. 41/4/18 for a valor of the de Bohun estates held by the Staffords in 1412.

Bohun's purparty and then incorporating it into the Duchy of Lancaster both Henry V and his father had themselves ratified the arrangement.[19] Anne's case was a good one, but the Crown could not easily be defeated in a court of law, and Henry had marshalled all the legal aid at his disposal. A new partition was soon drawn up under the close supervision of the royal justices and entered on the Parliament Roll. Once his compact groups of lordships and manors had been annexed to the Duchy of Lancaster, King Henry permitted the Countess to enter her new estates, which, at an estimated £1,203 a year, were paradoxically worth at least £100 more than his own.[20]

Yet the Countess can hardly be said to have profited by the exchange, especially as she was made responsible for arrears of 3,000 marks due to the King from his former lordship of Brecon. It is more than likely that Henry engineered the second partition as a means of solving his financial problems in this area. Most of the deficit comprised unpaid fines and other judicial dues which proved very hard to collect: in July 1421 Anne agreed to pay off the debt, and probably had to assign revenues from one of her more law-abiding receiverships to do so.[21] Several other important issues were still to be settled, notably the division of £3,130 collected by crown officials from the Dowager Countess of Hereford's dower property between April 1419 and 1421.[22] Anne was entitled to half this sum, but despite all her efforts the money had not been paid eleven years later, when she was driven to petition parliament for redress. Although she finally decided to cut her losses and accept a compromise payment of 2,000 marks from Henry V's feoffees some months later, there is nothing to suggest that she was ever fully reimbursed or given adequate compensation for her heavy legal expenses.[23] Nor is this the only example of deliberate exploitation by the Crown. Since Eleanor de Bohun had outlived her sister Mary, she became the sole beneficiary of

---

[19] D.L. 41/7/5 (a contemporary transcription of the proceedings). King Henry had obtained statutory recognition that Mary de Bohun's estates were inheritable by his heirs, irrespective of their royal title, in 1414 (*Rot. Parl.*, vol. IV p. 46).

[20] *Ibid.*, p. 416.

[21] *P.P.C.*, vol. II p. 298.

[22] A valor of these estates was drawn up in July 1422, presumably with this purpose in mind (S.C.6/1117/4).

[23] *Rot. Parl.*, vol. IV p. 146; *C.C.R.*, 1429–35, p. 203.

certain provisions made by the Dowager Countess Joan. Yet these had been ignored when the dower lands were redivided, and Anne had lost property worth over £100 a year to which she alone possessed a title.[24] The partition of 1421 had further specified that any fees or advowsons held in gross should be shared between the two parties, but since it was difficult to determine exactly what revenues were involved here the arrangement remained open to practical abuse. Thus, whereas Anne claimed that a group of manors in and around Cantref Selyf belonged to the lordship of Brecon and were hers alone, the King argued that they did not and ought therefore to be partitioned. As an interim measure the land in question was let out at an annual farm of £73 to be shared between the rival claimants.[25] King Henry's lawyers were not slow to use the same delaying tactics as Thomas of Woodstock, whose retention of vital evidence had proved so obstructive thirty years before, and the Countess was only given access to the necessary muniments after an appeal to parliament. Once sure of a regular income from Cantref Selyf, the Crown also ignored her repeated requests for an inquiry into the question of ownership. The farm was renewed in 1423 and again, pending a decision, six years later, although Anne's share of the money remained unpaid for long periods.[26] She bequeathed this problem to her son, Humphrey, Duke of Buckingham, who in 1438 was given a token promise of half the receipts, together with permission to sue for possession at a later date.[27] That either he or the King could by then have made a profit from this unruly area seems, however, highly improbable: violence was rife, and the tenants went in constant fear of armed raiders and other ' mysgoverned persones ' from the Duke of York's retinue. Hardly any revenues were reaching the Exchequer by 1452, when the farmer was excused his arrears because of the ' grete rebelliows sterynges and disobeysaunces of the tenantes of the said maners '.[28] The second Duke's brief entry into the lordship and its recovery by his son in 1509 made little, if any, difference to their financial

[24] *Rot. Parl.*, vol. IV p. 176.   [25] *P.P.C.*, vol. II p. 294.
[26] *Rot. Parl.*, vol. IV p. 176; D.L. 28/4/11 fo. 31v; C.F.R., 1422–30, p. 33; C.P.R., 1422–9, p. 542; *Issues of the Exchequer*, p. 416.
[27] C.P.R., 1436–41, p. 233.
[28] E.28/77/45, 48; E.368/225, Hilary 31 Hen. VI, rot. 40–1.

position, although it naturally affected their relations with the Crown. Nor was it the only long-term problem raised by the repartition of 1421, for, as we shall see, future generations of Staffords had many reasons to question the terms of the second settlement.[29]

The Dowager's new purparty seemed at first to offer far greater opportunities for consolidation and expansion than the old. The castles and lordships of Hay, Huntingdon and Brecon, for example, promised to enhance the Staffords' growing authority in South Wales, although it soon became clear why Henry V had been so anxious to dispose of them. As in Cantref Selyf, a combination of local disorder and stubborn resistance on the part of the tenantry made efficient revenue collection impossible from the start. On the other hand, there were valuable new acquisitions in the home counties, the Midlands and the South West which helped to round off the family's extensive possessions south of the Humber. There was also an exchange of titles, so that Humphrey Stafford became heir to the two earldoms of Hereford and Northampton. A third earldom, that of Buckingham, came to him as part of his mother's inheritance from the Duke of Gloucester, through which she laid claim to both the lordship of Holderness in East Yorkshire and Oakham Castle with its appurtenances in Rutland. During the thirteenth century Holderness had boasted prosperous sheep farms and a model administration; two hundred years later its net annual profits could still rise above £700. Oakham in turn produced about £170 a year net, and constituted a welcome addition to the Staffords' estates in the East Midlands.[30] Anne's title dated back to her father's creation as Earl of Buckingham with an annuity of £1,000 in 1377. His fee was eventually to have been paid out of the revenues of these two lordships, but since Holderness had been granted to the Queen for life and Oakham was then in the joint possession of the Earl of Rutland and Joan, Dowager Countess of Hereford, he had to be content with a promise of the reversions in fee tail.[31] Although Henry IV hastened to annul the act of attainder which had been

---

[29] See pp. 30–2, 37–9.
[30] Denholm-Young, *op. cit.*, pp. 48–50; D.641/1/2/17 mm. 3, 21–2 (a valor of the Stafford estates for the year ending Michaelmas 1442).
[31] *C.P.R.*, 1388–92, p. 255; *op. cit.*, 1391–6, p. 504.

passed after Gloucester's judicial murder in 1397, Anne Stafford's claim to Holderness was conveniently forgotten and the lordship went as a reward to the King's own son, Thomas, Duke of Clarence. On the latter's death in 1421, Anne lost no time in petitioning for livery of her rightful inheritance. She was hardly more successful in this than in any of her other attempts to obtain justice, and cannot have enjoyed any revenues from the property until 1437 at the very earliest. Clarence's widow refused to surrender the lordship, even bringing a suit against the Countess, who was pronounced in default before the royal council in 1426.[32] A survey of her English lands for the year ending Michaelmas 1436 includes all her possessions save Holderness, although the inquisition *post mortem* taken on her Yorkshire estates two years later shows that she then held the lordship in chief.[33] It was only after pleading his case both in the Exchequer Chamber and the royal council that Duke Humphrey obtained entry there in 1439; the discovery and presentation of evidence proved a long and expensive business, but he was well served by skilful advisers and had many friends among his fellow-councillors. Thus, with the help of good lawyers and powerful connexions, Holderness finally became part of the Stafford estates.[34] The Countess Anne had experienced fewer difficulties in recovering the lordship of Oakham, since one third of it reverted to her directly as the Countess of Hereford's heir in 1419. Edward, Duke of York, contested her claim to the rest, but failed to establish a superior title.[35]

These new acquisitions, together with her share of the de Bohun inheritance and holdings as Dowager Countess of Stafford, made Anne perhaps the most wealthy woman in England. Even after land worth about £190 a year had been settled upon the sons of her third marriage to William Bourchier, Count of Eu, Humphrey, her eldest son, stood to inherit an annual income which, at £4,500 gross, was exactly three times greater than that already left to him by his father. The Dowager's death in 1438 placed him among the richest and most powerful landowners in

---

[32] S.C.8/142/7063; *P.P.C.*, vol. III pp. 209-10.
[33] S.C.11/816; C.139/93/44.
[34] D.1721/1/11 fo. 124 (a transcription of a ' lettre sent to Humfrey Duke of Buckynghame for the matter of Holdernes ffrom his servauntes Nicholas Poynts and Robert Whitgreave at London ').
[35] *C.F.R.*, 1413-22, pp. 286-8; *C.P.R.*, 1413-16, pp. 269-70.

England and made possible his creation as first Duke of Buckingham six years later.

His dukedom was also awarded in recognition of many years' loyal and continuous service to the Crown. This began with his first expedition to France while still a minor in 1420 and his admission to the royal council four years later.[36] Military and political affairs played a major part in his life, although he lacked the necessary qualities ever to become a great statesman or leader. Neither his attachment to Henry VI nor his remarkable diligence in public affairs proved an adequate substitute for natural ability. Indeed, despite his high standing among contemporaries, Buckingham was in many ways an unimaginative and unlikable man. The posthumous reputation accorded to him as a ' moderate ' rests largely upon his unwillingness to be drawn into the court party's quarrel with Richard of York and his partisans during the 1450s. Yet it can be argued that his decision to intervene on behalf of Henry VI hastened the outbreak of the Wars of the Roses. Against an obvious talent for dealing with his own estate staff must be set a harsh and often vindictive disposition, which, if the French sources are to be believed, manifested itself in his violent and offensive behaviour during the trial of Joan of Arc,[37] and continued to cloud his political judgement until he fell at the Battle of Northampton in 1460. Although he seems to have been generally respected at all levels of society, the Duke was not without enemies, many of whom had good reason to bear a grudge against him. Sir Baldwin Mountfort and his son, Sir Simon, for example, had been imprisoned by Buckingham until they agreed to sign away their title to property worth over £100 a year, and as a result of his implacable hostility towards them were unable to obtain redress for many years.[38]

From the time that he first began to play a part in national affairs Duke Humphrey seems deliberately to have avoided identi-

---

[36] *Henrici Quinti Angliae Regis Gesta*, ed. B. Williams (London, 1850), pp. 144, 279; *P.P.C.*, vol. III p. 143. He came of age in 1423 (*C.P.R.*, 1422–9, p. 75).

[37] Due allowance must be made for anti-English bias in this account of Buckingham's vicious attack on both Joan and one of her witnesses, although such outbursts were entirely in character (*Procès de Condamnation et de Réhabilitation de Jeanne d'Arc*, ed. J. Quicherat (5 vols., Paris, 1841–9), vol. III pp. 122, 140–1; I am grateful to Mr T. B. Pugh for drawing my attention to this reference).

[38] See p. 79.

fying himself with any political group. The early years of Henry VI's minority saw the rapid growth within the council of two mutually hostile factions, led respectively by Humphrey, Duke of Gloucester, and his uncle, Cardinal Beaufort. Buckingham could hardly ignore their intrigues, but he did not at first show any marked leaning towards either party. His marriage to Ann Neville, the fourth daughter of Ralph, Earl of Westmorland, by his second wife, Joan Beaufort, took place before 1424, and may have brought him closer to the Cardinal.[39] Yet, although he was prepared to defend Beaufort's ecclesiastical privileges, the Duke must at first have been attracted by Gloucester's demands for a more belligerent foreign policy. By 1432 he had held office as Constable of France, Governor of Paris and Lieutenant General of Normandy. As Captain of Belleme Castle and Count of Perche with a personal estate worth 800 marks a year, he also had a vested interest in the retention of English conquests abroad.[40] The defeats and withdrawals which followed the Duke of Bedford's death in 1435 perhaps convinced him that an honourable peace was to be preferred to the financial strain of a prolonged and unsuccessful war effort. The Cardinal pinned all his hopes upon Buckingham and the other distinguished ambassadors who met to negotiate with the French at Calais in 1439, but their proposals were rejected by the war party at home and the fighting dragged on.[41] Having previously refrained from any personal attack on the Duke of Gloucester, Buckingham took an active part in the show trial of his wife, Eleanor Cobham, for witchcraft in 1441. With Beaufort's enemies temporarily silenced, the peace initiative could be resumed.[42]

After his mother's death, Duke Humphrey's income exceeded £4,700 a year. Some of it went to offset his expenses as an ambassador, and there can be little doubt that his new wealth

---

[39] *Cal. Papal Regs.*, vol. VI p. 140.

[40] Jehan de Waurin, *Recueil des Croniques et Anchiennes Istories de la Grant Bretaigne . . .*, ed. W. Hardy (5 vols., R.S., 1864–91), vol. III p. 351; *The Chronicle of John Hardyng . . . with the Continuation by R. Grafton*, ed. H. Ellis (London, 1812), p. 398; *Letters and Papers Illustrative of the Wars of the English in France During the Reign of Henry VI*, ed. J. Stevenson (2 vols., R.S., 1861–4), vol. II, pt ii, p. 627.

[41] See C. T. Allmand, 'The Anglo-French Negotiations of 1439', *B.I.H.R.*, XL (1967).

[42] *An English Chronicle*, ed. J. S. Davies (C.S., 1st series vol. LXIV, 1856), p. 58.

was also partly responsible for his appointment as Constable of Calais in 1442. The soldiers there, who had not been paid for some time, were then on the verge of mutiny and it was evidently hoped that Buckingham would either use his personal influence to obtain preferential treatment in the Exchequer, or offset the deficit himself. Whatever contribution he may have made towards the garrison's upkeep was not quickly repaid, for on resigning the post eight years later he had still to recover over £19,395 in outstanding expenses.[43]

The Duke, absorbed in political affairs at home, rarely visited Calais. His first months in office coincided with yet another dispute over the conduct of the war in France, and the ensuing peace negotiations were not completed without much heated debate in the council. The settlement which King Henry and his most intimate advisers made with the French in 1445 provoked a violent public reaction when they became known, not only because of their outcome – the surrender of Maine – but even more because of their secrecy. His wife's death had rendered Gloucester politically harmless for the present, but while he lived he remained a threat to the King and his ministers as the leader to whom their critics might again turn. Buckingham had been involved in the peace negotiations; and as Constable of England he was responsible for the Duke of Gloucester's arrest – and possibly even his sudden death – in 1447. On the confiscation of the victim's estates he received the manor of Penshurst as his share of the spoils.[44]

The marriage contracts which he arranged for his children show Buckingham to have been strengthening his connexions at court. Two of his sons married into the Beaufort family; one daughter was betrothed to Aubrey de Vere, the Earl of Oxford's son, another to William, Viscount Beaumont, and a third to John, third Earl of Shrewsbury.[45] Charles VII's plans for a marriage

---

[43] *P.P.C.*, vol. V p. 203; *Rot. Parl.*, vol. V p. 206.

[44] *Letters and Papers Illustrative of the Wars of the English in France*, vol. I pp. 89–159; *An English Chronicle*, p. 63; *C.P.R.*, 1446–52, p. 45.

[45] Margaret, the daughter of Edmund, second Duke of Somerset, married Buckingham's eldest son in 1444 (N.L.W. Peniarth Ms. 280 fo. 34). According to G.E.C. vol. XII, pt. i, p. 48, her cousin, Margaret, Countess of Richmond, did not marry Henry Stafford until 1464; but Duke Humphrey's will makes it clear that they were already married by 10 July 1460 (P.C.C. Stockton 21). The other three weddings took place respectively in January 1443 (N.L.W. Peniarth Ms. 280 fo. 24), August 1452 (D.1721/1/1 fo. 359) and July 1458 (E.404/71/2/77).

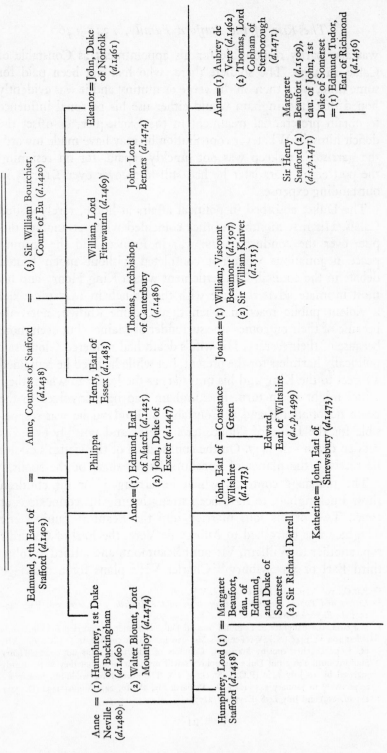

TABLE III. *The later Staffords, 1403–1521*

Edmund, 5th Earl of Stafford (*d.*1403) = Anne, Countess of Stafford (*d.*1438) = (3) Sir William Bourchier, Count of Eu (*d.*1420)

Anne = (1) Humphrey, 1st Duke of Buckingham (*d.*1460)
(2) Walter Blount, Lord Mountjoy (*d.*1474)
Anne Neville (*d.*1480)

Philippa

Anne = (1) Edmund, Earl of March (*d.*1425)
(2) John, Duke of Exeter (*d.*1447)

Henry, Earl of Essex (*d.*1483)

William, Lord Fitzwaurin (*d.*1469)

Thomas, Archbishop of Canterbury (*d.*1486)

Eleanor = John, Duke of Norfolk (*d.*1461)

John, Lord Berners (*d.*1474)

Humphrey, Lord (1) = Margaret Beaufort, dau. of Edmund, 2nd Duke of Somerset
Stafford (*d.*1458) (2) Sir Richard Darrell

John, Earl of Wiltshire (*d.*1473) = Constance Green

Joanna = (1) William, Viscount Beaumont (*d.*1507)
(2) Sir William Knivet (*d.*1515)

Ann = (1) Aubrey de Vere (*d.*1462)
(2) Thomas, Lord Cobham of Sterborough (*d.*1471)

Katherine = John, Earl of Shrewsbury (*d.*1473)

Edward, Earl of Wiltshire (*d.s.p.*1499)

Sir Henry Stafford (2) (*d.s.p.*1471)

Margaret (*d.*1509) = Beaufort (2), dau. of John, 1st Duke of Somerset = (1) Edmund Tudor, Earl of Richmond (*d.*1456)

22

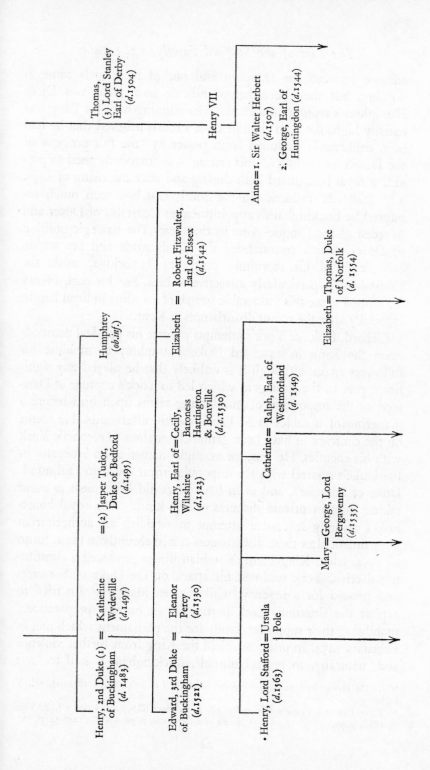

Henry, 2nd Duke (1) = Katherine
of Buckingham   Wydeville
(d. 1483)   (d. 1497)

=(2) Jasper Tudor,
Duke of Bedford
(d. 1495)

Thomas,
(3) Lord Stanley
Earl of Derby.
(d. 1504)

Henry VII

Edward, 3rd Duke = Eleanor
of Buckingham   Percy
(d. 1521).   (d. 1530)

Humphrey
(ob. inf.)

Elizabeth = Robert Fitzwalter,
            Earl of Essex
            (d. 1542)

Anne = 1. Sir Walter Herbert
         (d. 1507)

       2. George, Earl of
          Huntingdon (d. 1544)

Henry, Earl of = Cecily,
Wiltshire   Baroness
(d. 1523)   Hartington
                 & Bonville
                 (d. c. 1530)

• Henry, Lord Stafford = Ursula
(d. 1563)   Pole

Mary = George, Lord
        Bergavenny
        (d. 1535)

Catherine = Ralph, Earl of
            Westmorland
            (d. 1549)

Elizabeth = Thomas, Duke
            of Norfolk
            (d. 1554)

alliance between the Dauphin and one of these girls came to nothing, but they nevertheless indicate how great was Duke Humphrey's reputation abroad.[46] His standing with the King was equally high, for even though Cade's rebels believed that he had been deliberately excluded from power by ' the fals progeny of the Dewke of Suffolk ',[47] his retinue was frequently used to provide a royal bodyguard both during and after the rising of 1450. The Staffords' influence in the South East had been much enhanced by Buckingham's appointment as Constable of Dover and Warden of the Cinque Ports in that year. The strategic position of Dover, which commanded the Calais roads and lay within easy reach of his recruiting centre at Tonbridge, made the Constableship particularly attractive to him. For his part, Henry VI wished to see this vulnerable stretch of coastline in loyal hands, especially after the recent disturbances in Kent.

Richard, Duke of York's attempts to force his political demands upon the King in 1452 led Duke Humphrey to mobilise his followers again, although it is unlikely that he played any significant part in the stratagem which led to York's capture at Dartford or the imposition of humiliating terms upon him before a gathering of notables at St Paul's shortly afterwards. He seems on the contrary to have been genuinely anxious to reconcile York with his enemies. He was, for example, named as an arbitrator in the Duke's quarrel with the unpopular royal favourite, Edmund, Duke of Somerset, and as in later years did his utmost to avoid taking sides in private disputes of this kind.[48] The royal household's initially successful attempt to establish an authoritarian government after these disturbances ceased abruptly in the autumn of 1453, when King Henry's sudden illness produced a constitutional crisis. York resumed his attack on the Duke of Somerset and pressed for a regency, while Queen Margaret also tried to exploit the situation. Both parties began hurried preparations, mobilising their supporters ready for the parliament which met in February 1454. In order to shield the King from further violence and, naturally, to protect himself, Buckingham is said to have

---

[46] G. Du Fresne Beaucourt, *Histoire de Charles VII* (6 vols., Paris, 1881–91), vol. V p. 137.
[47] *Three Fifteenth Century Chronicles*, ed. J. Gairdner (C.S., 2nd series vol. XXVIII, 1880), p. 97. [48] *An English Chronicle*, p. 70; *C.C.R.*, 1447–54, p. 327.

ordered 2,000 liveries for his own men.[49] He and his half-brothers, Henry and Thomas Bourchier, were nevertheless prepared to support York during his tenure of the Protectorship. Duke Humphrey remained in London and was closely involved in the business of government: indeed, his record of attendance at council meetings throughout the 1450s is quite remarkable, given the general lack of enthusiasm displayed by most of his peers.[50] Even though he 'straungely conveied' the Duke of Somerset from prison in January 1455 and entered into recognizances on his behalf, Buckingham kept an open mind in his political dealings. His readiness to stand bail for another royal favourite, the Duke of Exeter, in 1454 is offset by an appearance among Lord Fauconberg's mainpernors – most of whom were Yorkist partisans – and a second, equally futile attempt to bring about an understanding between Somerset and York.[51] His conduct both before and after the first Battle of St Albans shows how difficult it was becoming for him to reconcile the dictates of loyalty with those of self-interest. Yet although he failed as a mediator, Duke Humphrey was at least able to help prolong the period of relative stability which followed York's second term as Protector.[52] This probably explains the growing antagonism shown towards him by Queen Margaret. His sudden retreat to Writtle ' noo thing well plesid, and sumwhat on easid of herte to his purpose' in April 1456 suggests that their relations were already strained. The dismissal of his two half-brothers from their offices served to widen the breach, which was common knowledge by October. The Queen in turn was incensed by Buckingham's intervention in her plot to arrest the Duke of York and clearly resented his continued presence at court.[53]

The outbreak of hostilities between Margaret's followers and the Yorkist lords in 1459 was almost certainly hastened by Duke

[49] *P.L.*, vol. I p. 265 (the news letter of John Stodeley, 19 Jan. 1450).

[50] *P.P.C.*, vol. VI pp. 175, 233; J. S. Roskell, ' The Problem of the Attendance of the Lords in Medieval Parliaments ', *B.I.H.R.*, XXIX (1956), p. 195.

[51] *Six Town Chronicles of England*, ed. R. Flenley (Oxford, 1911), p. 141; *Feodera*, vol. XI pp. 361–2; *C.C.R.*, 1454–61, pp. 49, 109, 287.

[52] For a more detailed account of Buckingham's conduct at this time see C. A. J. Armstrong, ' Politics and the Battle of St. Albans ', *B.I.H.R.*, XXIII (1960).

[53] *P.L.*, vol. I pp. 386 (John Bocking to John Paston, 8 May 1456), 408 (James Gresham to the same, 16 Oct. 1456).

Humphrey's decision to forget any personal animosity and support the Queen. His great retinue gave the court party a numerical advantage which made possible the crushing defeat of their enemies at Ludford in the same year. His services were amply rewarded by a grant of the property confiscated from York's wealthy chamberlain, Sir William Oldhall. These estates were rated for taxation at £369 a year in 1450 and were probably then worth more than twice this amount.[54] Although Oldhall's previous attainder, which lasted from 1453 to 1455, may well have had a serious long-term effect upon his finances, there can be little doubt that the award would over the years have compensated Duke Humphrey for the debts the Crown owed him. Sir William's lands were centered around the two Hertfordshire manors of Hunsdon and Eastwick; had the grant been effective, it would also have brought the Staffords his impressive new manor house at Hunsdon, which, according to William Worcester, had cost over 7,000 marks to build.[55] With a further promise of £300 to cover his military expenses, Buckingham was among the first to benefit from the acts of attainder passed by the Coventry Parliament in 1459. Loyalty to the Crown and a firm belief that Henry's enemies could be beaten no doubt influenced his course of action, although other motives probably counted for at least as much. Not enough is known about the state of Duke Humphrey's finances at this time to conclude that he was driven into the royal camp by the need to supplement an inadequate income. He may equally well have been under pressure from his more partisan retainers, who also expected to share in the profits of war.

At all events, his commitment to the cause of Henry VI was now complete. As warden of the Cinque Ports he was empowered to prepare the south-east coast against attack; he also took charge of the Duchess of York after her husband's flight to Ireland and is said to have treated her with great severity.[56] His interview

---

[54] *C.P.R.*, 1452–61, pp. 535, 548, 552, 571; E.359/29 m. 34 (I must thank Mr T. B. Pugh for this information about Oldhall's finances and for enlarging upon an interpretation of Buckingham's conduct put forward in his paper 'The Magnates, Knights and gentry', *Fifteenth-Century England*, ed. S. B. Chrimes and others (Manchester, 1972), pp. 106–7).

[55] *C.P.R.*, 1452–61, p. 103; William Worcester, *Itineraries*, ed. J. H. Harvey (Oxford, 1969), pp. 48–51.

[56] *C.P.R.*, 1452–61, pp. 525, 557, 564, 602, 611–2, 617; *Collections of a Citizen of London*, ed. J. Gairdner (C.S., 2nd series vol. XVII), p. 207.

with the Yorkist bishops before the Battle of Northampton took place in an atmosphere far removed from that at St Albans five years before. According to *An English Chronicle*, he would accept no compromise, threatening to kill the Earl of Warwick should he attempt an audience with King Henry.[57] Although the anonymous chronicler, a propagandist of the house of York and its supporters, was trying to present Warwick's actions in a favourable light, the Duke's outburst seems to reflect a long-standing and mutual antagonism between the two men. Warwick's persistent refusal to pay any rent for the manor of Drayton Basset, which he leased from the Staffords, cannot have improved their relations[58]; and if Buckingham had a personal quarrel to settle in 1459 it was more likely to have been with Richard Neville, Earl of Warwick, than with the Duke of York. Whatever plans for revenge he may have had ended abruptly on the battlefield. He was killed during an attack on the King's tent and was buried quietly at the Grey Friars, Northampton. Since his eldest son, Humphrey, Lord Stafford, had died of the plague in 1458, the Duke's lands and titles descended to his young grandson, Henry. For the second time in less than sixty years the Crown intervened to assert its rights of wardship and the Stafford family again faced the problem of a long minority.

---

[57] *Op. cit.*, p. 96.
[58] K. B. McFarlane, *The Nobility of Later Medieval England*, p. 223.

Chapter 2

THE SECOND AND THIRD DUKES OF
BUCKINGHAM, 1460–1521

When, on 28 February 1464, Edward IV purchased the wardship
and marriage of Henry, second Duke of Buckingham, from the
first Duke's executors, he may already have intended him as a
husband for Elizabeth Wydeville's younger sister, Katherine.[1]
The match took place some months before Henry and his brother
became members of the new Queen's household in August 1465,
and is said to have caused particular offence to Richard, Earl of
Warwick, and also to Buckingham himself in later life.[2] Whereas
the former probably regarded his own daughter, Isobel, as a more
suitable bride for the young Duke, the latter had less cause for
resentment. There is certainly no reason to believe that his subsequent hostility to the Wydevilles sprang from a sense of bitterness
at being forced to marry beneath him. Although no new estates
or titles came to him through his connexion with the Queen, he
was at least £3,000 richer as a result of the royal licences which
enabled him to enter his inheritance three years before coming of
age, and to recover the lordship of Cantref Selyf.[3] He had a more
genuine cause for complaint in his permanent exclusion from
power and the business of government: his duties at court were
purely ceremonial, while his official appointments, such as his
brief tenure of the High Stewardship of England for the Duke of
Clarence's trial, were largely formal.

Perhaps Duke Henry sought high office as a means of supple-
menting his own fixed income. He was clearly tired of playing
the courtier, and this on its own would have been sufficient reason

---

[1] *C.P.R.*, 1461–67, p. 298.
[2] Or so the Pseudo-William of Worcester believed (*Annales Rerum Anglicarum, Letters
and Papers Illustrative of the Wars of the English in France*, vol. II, pt ii, p. 785);
for a more balanced view of the marriage see J. Lander, ' Marriage and Politics in
the Fifteenth Century: the Nevilles and the Wydevilles ', *B.I.H.R.*, XXXVI (1963),
p. 135.
[3] *C.P.R.*, 1467–77, p. 367; *op. cit.*, 1476–85, p. 69.

for him to throw in his lot with Richard of Gloucester after Edward IV's death. The composition of the young King's retinue at Ludlow caused him grave concern, for the Wydevilles evidently intended to seize power at the first opportunity and had shown no desire to include him in their plans. Most of the information about Buckingham's military preparations during the spring and early summer of 1483 derives from chronicle sources and is not always reliable. Grafton reports that he had already promised ' a m^1. good felowes if need were ' to Gloucester before Edward V left for London on 24 April 1483, although no more than 300 Stafford retainers were present when the two Dukes met at Northampton five days later.[4] Their *coup* worked perfectly: within a few hours the Lords Grey and Rivers had been arrested and the King was in their hands. Confused rumours spread panic throughout the City of London, but Gloucester and Buckingham were soon able to reassure the populace by leaving most of their men outside the walls.[5]

Once he had been appointed protector, Richard set about the systematic elimination of any potential opponents, ably assisted by Duke Henry, who no doubt hoped to share his new ally's political ascendancy by making himself indispensable. He was allegedly the first to condemn Elizabeth Wydeville's ' womanishe forwardnesse ' in abusing the benefits of sanctuary, whence she had fled with Prince Richard. He also supervised investigations into the activities of Thomas Rotherham, the former Chancellor, John Morton, Bishop of Ely, and William, Lord Hastings, each of whom had owed their advancement to Edward IV and therefore fell under suspicion.[6] Even Richard's claim to the throne was made with Buckingham's full approval and encouragement. On 24 June the Duke used all his oratorical skill to convince the aldermen and citizens of London that Edward IV and his sons

---

4 *The Chronicle of John Hardyng*, p. 475; the respective merits of the chronicle sources for Richard's *coup d'état* and his subsequent relations with Duke Henry are discussed at length in A. Hanham, *Richard III and the Early Historians* (Oxford, 1975), pp. 4–15, 31–73, 129–30, 155–90.

5 Dominic Mancini, *The Usurpation of Richard III*, ed. C. A. J. Armstrong (Oxford, 1969), pp. 75–83.

6 Sir Thomas More, *The History of Richard III*, ed. R. S. Sylvester in *The Complete Works of St Thomas More* (5 vols., Yale University Press, 1963–), vol. II pp. 28, 90; Mancini, *op. cit.* pp. 89–93.

were illegitimate, but his virtuoso performance, ' soo well & eloquently uttyrd and w^t. soo angelyk a countenance ', failed to move an unwilling audience.[7] Fear of civil war rather than enthusiasm for Gloucester's cause finally prevailed upon the noblemen, knights and citizens who accompanied Duke Henry to Baynard's Castle and supported his petition for Richard to take the Crown.

The coronation was a personal triumph for Duke Henry, who, recently confirmed as Constable of England, made a magnificent progress through London at the head of a large entourage.[8] Both contemporary and later sources abound with references to his position as the most powerful subject in the land, for this was a time of great military activity with armed retainers flocking south *in numero terribili et inaudito*.[9] The fear that London would be occupied by a force of 20,000 men by the end of June was, of course, unwarranted, but Stafford liveries proliferated during the few weeks of Buckingham's personal ascendancy. Some of Lord Hastings' former adherents, opportunists to a man, had joined the Duke immediately after their leader's execution, and others must have followed this example. Never since the time of Warwick the Kingmaker, according to John Ross, had so many men worn a single badge.[10]

It is reasonable to assume that the Duke's invaluable support was from the outset conditional upon the award of both the Constableship and Henry V's share of the de Bohun inheritance, since he had apparently been trying for many years to obtain them from Edward IV. His title was a strong one: on the deaths of Henry VI and his only son in 1471, he had become the sole surviving heir to their half of these great estates. The property had, however already been confiscated by Edward IV, whose refusal to entertain Buckingham's petitions sprang not only from a reluctance to lose revenues worth over £1,000 a year but also from a real fear of the dynastic implications.[11] Instead of further-

---

[7] *The Great Chronicle of London*, ed. A. H. Thomas and I. D. Thornley (London, 1938), p. 232.

[8] *Edward Hall's Chronicle*, ed. H. Ellis (London, 1809), p. 375.

[9] *Historiae Croylandensis Continuatio*, ed. W. Fulman in *Rerum Anglicarum Scriptorum Veterum* (Oxford, 1684), vol. I pp. 565–6.

[10] *Stonor Letters and Papers, 1290–1483*, ed. C. L. Kingsford (C.S., 3rd series vols. XXIX & XXX, 1919), vol. XXX pp. 160–1; J. Ross, *Historia Regum Angliae*, ed. T. Hearne (Oxford, 1745), p. 216.

[11] More, *op. cit.*, p. 44; *Rot. Parl.*, vol. VI p. 478.

ing his aims, Duke Henry's attempt to emphasise his de Bohun –
and therefore royal – descent by assuming the arms of Thomas of
Woodstock [12] merely confirmed Edward's worst suspicions: had
he recognised the Duke as Henry VI's rightful heir he might well
have placed his own throne in jeopardy. Although he too must
have foreseen the dangers of meeting Buckingham's request,
Richard III was in no position to risk alienating his most powerful supporter. According to Sir Thomas More, an imaginative if
not always accurate historian of Richard's reign, the two men
agreed ' that the protectour should have the dukes aide to make
him king, & that the protectours onely lawful sonne, should mary
ye dukes daughter, and that the protectour should graunt him the
quiet possession of the Erledome of Hertford [sic], which he
claimed as his enheritance '.[13] The fact remains that on 13 July
1483 Duke Henry obtained the remaining de Bohun estates in
a grant which was to be endorsed by the first parliament of
the reign.[14] The military potential at his disposal in Wales and the
adjacent counties was, moreover, much increased as a result of the
many high offices which the grateful Richard granted to him. By
October 1483 he had not only been made Chief Justice and
Chamberlain of North and South Wales for life, but had also
obtained the Constableship, Stewardship and Receiver Generalship of all the crown lands there. His powers to raise men and
appoint officials extended into the Welsh estates of the Duchy of
Lancaster and the Earldom of March, where he exercised complete authority through the use of his own seal. Nor was this a
matter of empty titles. Orders were sent out enabling him to take
possession of castles and armaments throughout Wales, while the
promise of all other senior posts along the March as they fell
vacant substantially augmented his vast reserves of patronage.
Last, but not least, he was empowered to raise armed levies and
keep back the King's revenues in Dorset, Somerset and the
Marcher counties.[15] These overwhelming marks of royal favour
make it all the harder to understand Buckingham's sudden deci-

[12] H.M.C. *Sixth Report* (2 parts, H.M.S.O., 1877–8), pt i, p. 148.
[13] More, *op. cit.*, p. 44.
[14] D.1721/1/11 fos. 5–9 (a sixteenth-century transcription of the award).
[15] *Grants from the Crown During the Reign of Edward V*, ed. J. G. Nichols (C.S.,
1st series vol. LX, 1854), pp. 5, 12–13, 31–3, 36, 49.

sion to join forces with his aunt, Lady Margaret Beaufort, and a group of disgruntled Yorkists in a rebellion against the King. By agreeing to place Lady Margaret's son, Henry Tudor, on the throne, he perhaps hoped to conceal his own plans for a *coup d'état*. Other explanations are less convincing: it is certainly unrealistic to suppose that he acted out of a disinterested sense of loyalty or was motivated by the promptings of an uneasy conscience. More's belief in the persuasive influence of Bishop Morton, then a prisoner at Brecon Castle, sprang more from a desire to enhance the reputation of his former patron than from a concern for historical objectivity.[16] Morton may possibly have arranged for Reginald Bray, Lady Margaret's chief adviser, to visit Brecon and discuss the plan of campaign, but he can hardly have been involved in the earlier tentative advances made to the Duke as he travelled from London. The idea that Buckingham was stricken by remorse on hearing of the Princes' death at Richard's hands is hardly to be entertained; nor is there sufficient evidence that he was himself responsible for their murder. Far from recognising Henry Tudor's superior title, he seems to have regarded the young claimant as a pawn in his own manoeuvres to seize the throne. The possibility of some sudden disagreement between Buckingham and the King merits more serious consideration, but the reason for such an argument cannot be established with any degree of certainty. If a quarrel arose over the fate of Edward IV's two sons, Richard would obviously not wish this to be public knowledge, and would be likely to circulate a less incriminating explanation. The story that he deliberately withheld the de Bohun estates while accusing Duke Henry of secret treachery became the ' official ' version and was accepted without question by the time that Polydore Vergil came to write his History of England.[17] But relations between the King and his former ally cannot have been strained to breaking point, since the uprising took Richard completely by surprise.

A study of the outbreak and rapid collapse of Buckingham's rebellion shows that despite his apparent strength he could not rely on more than a handful of supporters. Strictly speaking, the

16 *Op. cit.*, pp. 90–3.
17 *Polydore Vergil's English History*, ed. H. Ellis (C.S., 1st series vol. XXX, 1844), p. 193; Hanham, *op. cit.*, p. 130.

rising should never have been given his name at all, since most of the strategy had already been worked out by members of the Tudor and Wydeville factions before he decided to take part. Of the ninety-seven insurgents subsequently attainted by parliament for treason, very few were associated with the Duke in any way. A. E. Conway's analysis of the Maidstone sector, for instance, reveals close connexions between the ringleaders and either the Wydevilles or Bishop Morton rather than with Duke Henry.[18] Only two of the Berkshire rebels appear to have had any reason for supporting him: both Sir William Berkeley and Sir John Harcourt were members of families traditionally loyal to the Staffords, although this factor alone is unlikely to have turned them against King Richard. Sir Nicholas Latimer, the Duke's chamberlain, who shared the command in Dorset with friends of Sir Reginald Bray, was clearly bound by close ties to his employer; on the other hand, the Exeter contingent had Buckingham's erstwhile enemy, Sir Thomas Grey, Marquess of Dorset, as its leader. It is always possible that several minor figures not listed in the parliament roll answered Duke Henry's summons, and that those who are named chose to follow him for reasons now unknown. Nevertheless, the surprising absence of any of his more prominent tenants or ministers among the insurgents attainted in November 1483 suggests a marked unwillingness on the part of his senior advisers to become involved in an act of open rebellion, especially against as formidable an adversary as Richard III.[19]

Five simultaneous risings were planned to take place across the South and West of England at the end of September. Nothing daunted by his complete lack of military experience, Buckingham undertook to march over the Welsh Border from Brecon, join the other rebels and defeat the King before he could mobilise an army. He was, however, prevented from crossing the Severn because of flooding, while his men, allegedly recruited ' against their wills and without any lust to fight ', abandoned him to his fate.[20] A final appeal to the gentry of Herefordshire proved fruitless. These miserable conditions, made worse by the appalling prospect of defeat, completely undermined what little morale

---

[18] *Archaeologia Cantiana*, XXXVII (1925), *passim*.

[19] *Rot. Parl.*, vol. VI pp. 245–7.

[20] Polydore Vergil, *op. cit.*, p. 195.

remained among the Duke's following. Nor could he depend upon the loyalty of his Welsh employees, whose first thought was to revenge themselves upon a harsh and inconsiderate master. Hardly had he left Brecon than the Vaughans of Tretower sacked the Castle and set fire to its contents:[21] if they, with a history of more than fifty years' continuous service to the Staffords, were so hostile to his plans, then the Duke's hopes of leading a successful rebellion from Wales were surely doomed from the start. It is significant that none of the chief conspirators known to have been at Brecon in October 1483 were Welshmen. Indeed, only three men (other than Duke Henry himself and Bishop Morton) were subsequently attainted for their involvement in that part of the rising. Neither Thomas Nandick, a Cambridge scholar described as an astrologer, nor John Rush, a merchant, can have provided Buckingham with much practical assistance. Sir William Knivet had probably assembled a number of armed retainers from his Norfolk estates, but there is no evidence that the natives of Brecon showed much enthusiasm for the cause. Duke Henry made no appeal to Welsh national sentiment, and never tried to win the respect or affection of his tenants. His great monopoly of offices had, moreover, been built up at the expense of many local figures, such as the Vaughans, the Kemys and William Herbert, second Earl of Pembroke, who were naturally anxious to recover their lost influence. That Richard III recognised his mistake in failing to cultivate this important element of Marcher society is clear from a series of awards made after the rising, when twenty-five annuities from the Crown's Welsh lordships and a number of posts on the forfeited Stafford estates were distributed among the local gentry.[22] Sir Thomas Vaughan's second raid on Brecon Castle, planned in 1486 as an act of vengeance against the new occupant, Jasper Tudor and his nephew, Henry VII, shows how effective Richard's new patronage had been.

Given his inability to inspire either loyalty or confidence among his retinue, it is hardly surprising that Buckingham should have

---

[21] D.1721/1/11 fos. 241–2 (a sixteenth-century account of the events following Buckingham's rebellion, reproduced in H. Owen and J. B. Blakeway, *A History of Shrewsbury* (2 vols., London, 1825), vol. I pp. 235–42).

[22] J. Gairdner, *Richard III* (Cambridge, 1898), Appendix IV; H. T. Evans, *Wales and the Wars of the Roses* (Cambridge, 1915), pp. 208–10.

searched in vain for help after his defeat. He went into hiding, but was betrayed by one of his own servants and summarily executed without trial at Salisbury on 2 November 1483. For many years he was regarded as the innocent victim of another's treachery, and as such provided the ballad-mongers with yet another variant on the theme of a great lord deceived by those whom he trusted most.

> The plaine old Duke, his life to save,
> Of his owne man did souccour crave;
> In hope that he would him releive
> That late much land to him did give.

> Base Banester this man was nam'd,
> By this vile deed for ever sham'd.
> ' It is ' quoth he ' a common thing
> To injure him that wrong'd his king '.

> Thus Banester his maister sold
> Unto his foe for hiere of gold,
> But marke his end, and rightly see
> The just reward of treachery.[23]

The Duke's five-year-old son was more fortunate, being helped to safety by a few loyal family retainers, despite the reward of 1,000 marks offered for his capture. The boy's mother, Katherine, Dowager Duchess of Buckingham, went as a captive to London, where she lived off a modest pension for the rest of Richard's brief reign.[24]

One of Henry VII's first acts on assuming the throne in 1485 was to reverse Buckingham's attainder and restore his widow's jointure. The rest of the Stafford estates were awarded to Henry's mother, Lady Margaret Beaufort, who also obtained custody of the young Duke and his brother. As with many other royal wards, their wealth and position was exploited to the full. Having tried unsuccessfully to arrange a marriage alliance between Duke Edward and the Duchess of Brittany, Henry VII finally allowed

---

23 Richard Johnson, ' A Crowne Garland of Golden Roses ', ed. W. Chappel in *Early English Poetry, Ballads and Popular Literature of the Middle Ages* (Percy Society, London, 1842); see H. E. Rollins, *Old English Ballads, 1553–1625* (Cambridge, 1920), pp. 349–50, for a discussion of other verses on this theme.
24 *C.P.R.*, 1476–85, p. 436.

the fourth Earl of Northumberland's executors to purchase Buckingham's marriage for £4,000 in 1490.[25] He had moreover deliberately set out to bind a number of his great nobles and other important public figures by heavy recognizances for debt. The reassertion of royal prerogatives enabled him to extort disproportionate sums from influential offenders and was used with great thoroughness to place these men financially and legally in his power. It was inevitable that Duke Edward, the richest and potentially the most dangerous of Henry's subjects, would fall victim to this policy. The bill of complaint which he addressed to the late King's executors in 1515 shows, despite certain exaggerations, how harshly and unfairly he had been treated. In order to meet the heavy fines imposed upon him because of his mother's remarriage without a royal licence in 1496 and his own early entry into his estates two years later, he had been driven to borrow money at considerable personal loss from a Lombard money lender.[26] Altogether he claimed to have been wrongfully charged with debts of £7,179 and to have lost over £3,554 in legal expenses and revenues withheld from him on his coming of age. His petition was rejected, for although Henry VIII had previously cancelled one bond for £400, he could not afford to be too generous.[27]

Even after Henry VII's death, Buckingham's position at court remained somewhat ambiguous. He was made a member of the royal council in November 1509 and clearly took a keen interest in affairs of state, but his voice carried no more weight with the new King than it had with the old. Whereas both were prepared to make political capital out of his love of ceremony and personal display, neither would admit him to their inner counsels. No matter how loyal he might strive to appear, Duke Edward's family history and nearness to the throne placed him under constant suspicion. Even after the birth of his second son, Henry VII's hopes of establishing a royal dynasty were threatened by Buckingham's very existence. When the King fell ill in 1499, for example,

[25] R. B. Wernham, *Before the Armada* (London, 1966), pp. 32–6; *State Papers Spanish*, vol. II nos. 25, 28; *Materials for a History of the Reign of Henry VII*, ed. W. W. Campbell (2 vols., R.S., 1873–7), vol. II p. 554.

[26] D.1721/1/1 fo. 378–9 (a sixteenth-century copy of the petition).

[27] *L. & P. Henry VIII*, vol. I, pt i, no. 357 (41).

the succession became a matter of debate in influential circles. Four years later the Treasurer of Calais made a formal deposition which records one such conversation between

> Many dyvers and grett personages, the whiche as at that tyme hapned to commune of the kynge oure master, and wat world shouldbe yf hys grace deperted, and hoo should have the rule in Inglond then. Some . . . spoke of my lorde of Buckyngham, that said that he wold be a ryall ruler, and so gave hym grett prees . . . but non of them . . . spake of my lorde prynce.[28]

As late as 1519 Sebastian Giustiniani, the Venetian ambassador, felt sure that Duke Edward would easily obtain the throne were Henry VIII to die without a son.[29]

Inevitably, Buckingham's attempts to recover the Constableship of England for himself and his descendants as the heirs of Humphrey de Bohun served to confirm these latent fears. The de Bohuns had always claimed that their three manors of Wheatenhurst, Haresfield and Newnham were held in return for service as Great Constable of England. This was in fact not so, but contemporaries seem to have accepted that tenure by grand serjeanty obtained in all three cases. Wheatenhurst had actually been acquired after the family became Constables; Haresfield was almost certainly held by knight service; and neither the partition of 1380 nor that of 1421 had anything to say on the matter, other than assigning the Constableship as a hereditary office.[30] Although the Countess Anne had been obliged to surrender Wheatenhurst in exchange for Haresfield and Newnham in 1421, she retained the title, which descended to her eldest son seventeen years later. It is interesting to note, however, that the Constableship was temporarily withheld from him by Henry VI, and that on his mother's death he merely received permission to sue for the office.[31] The question of feudal service was immaterial to Edward IV who made John Tiptoft, Earl of Worcester, and his brother-in-law, Anthony Wydeville, Earl Rivers, his Constables. Only after the accession of Richard III was the second Duke of Bucking-

28 *Letters and Papers Illustrative of the Reigns of Richard III and Henry VII*, ed. J. S. Gairdner (2 vols., R.S., 1861–3), vol. I p. 239.
29 *State Papers Venetian*, vol. III no. 1287.
30 J. H. Round, *Peerage and Pedigree* (2 vols., London, 1910), vol. I pp. 147–166.
31 *C.P.R.*, 1436–41, p. 233.

ham's title recognised, while his son was too young to act as Constable at the time of Henry VII's coronation. The next opportunity arose when Henry VIII was crowned in 1509, and Duke Edward duly petitioned for confirmation of his office. His evidence comprised a claim to be seised of the manors of Haresfield and Newnham which his ancestors had held by grand serjeanty as Constables of England.[32] After a long debate, during which King Henry's advisers attempted to prove that the office existed independently of any tenurial obligations and could be awarded only at the pleasure of the Crown, the council reached its decision. Buckingham won his case, and letters patent making him and his heirs Constables with all the usual fees and appurtenances were drafted at once. These were evidently not to Henry's liking, for the final enrolled version specified that the Constableship was to be awarded for one day only, and would become dormant after sunset on 23 June 1509.[33] Nothing short of permanent recognition, however, would satisfy the Duke, who felt with apparent justice that he had been deprived of his rightful office. He went before the council again five years later in a hearing which lasted for two terms and covered much of the evidence already considered during the first appeal.[34] Three aspects of his petition preoccupied those sitting in judgement. First, they were unanimous, though mistaken, in confirming that the Constableship could be reserved upon the feoffment of the three Gloucestershire manors. The second point under discussion concerned the employment of a deputy when the land was held by a woman, and was probably raised by the Crown in an attempt to prove that the office could no longer be regarded as hereditable once the property had been divided between female descendants. Since they could hardly ignore numerous examples to the contrary, the judges pronounced in Buckingham's favour. The partition of the de Bohun estates posed another question which Henry VIII's

[32] D.1721/1/11 fos. 133–50 (a sixteenth-century transcription of the proceedings).
[33] *L. & P. Henry VIII*, vol. 1, pt i, no. 94 (87, 89).
[34] The only primary sources for this case – besides a brief council memorandum (Landsdowne Ms. 639 fos. 70–2) – are J. Dyer, *Les Reports des Divers Selects Matters & Resolutions des Reverend Judges & Sages del Ley* (London, 1678), fo. 285b; and R. Keilway, *Reports d'Ascuns Cases Qui ont Evenues au Temps du Roy Henry VII et du Roy Henry VIII . . .* (London, 1688), fos. 170v–1. Their respective merits are compared by Round (*op. cit.*, vol. I pp. 150–1).

advisers turned to their advantage, arguing that because the third manor of Wheatenhurst was now held by the Crown, King Henry himself could lay claim to the Constableship. Once again the bench reached complete agreement, and found that although Duke Edward could be compelled at pleasure to fulfil his duties, the King in turn was quite free to excuse him. Justice Neville and his colleagues were clearly determined to prevent the Duke from obtaining office, and, on the grounds that it was ' very hault et dangerous & auxy very chargeable al Roy in fees ' to accept his petition, asked for a precise definition of the Constable's authority, together with a statement of his fees and perquisites.[35] Their argument that Duke Edward might acquire powers of arrest over the King himself was entirely specious, and can have been produced only as a last-ditch attempt to deny the validity of Buckingham's case. King Henry was, moreover, warned privately by his attorney general of the weakness of his own title to the remaining half of the de Bohun inheritance.[36]

Evidently there was by this time a growing apprehension lest Duke Edward should advance a wider claim not only to the estates but also the throne itself. It is hardly surprising that his suit for the Constableship met with such opposition, since it rekindled memories of his father's treason. A wiser man would have thought carefully before advertising his own descent from Edward III but the Duke was too impetuous to foresee the dangers involved. He even obtained a licence to endow Tewkesbury Abbey, the burial place of Henry VI's only son, with land worth £60 a year, and gave alms to the Abbey regularly throughout his lifetime.[37]

Henry VIII can hardly be blamed for putting a sinister interpretation upon activities of this kind, for in theory Buckingham was well placed to lead a conspiracy against the Tudors. His wife's brother, the fifth Earl of Northumberland, still commanded a sizeable following in the North, despite Henry VII's attempts to reduce his power there. By marrying first Sir Walter Herbert and then George Hastings, Earl of Huntingdon, the Duke's younger

[35] Dyer, *loc. cit.*
[36] Keilway, *op. cit.*, fo. 171.
[37] *L. & P. Henry VIII*, vol. 1, pt ii, no. 3226 (5).

sister, Anne, helped to build up the Staffords' influence along the Welsh March; indeed, in 1511 Buckingham was made steward of all the Earl's extensive property in Wales.[38] His three daughters were the wives of Thomas Howard, Earl of Surrey (later Duke of Norfolk), Ralph Neville, Earl of Westmorland, and George Neville, Lord Bergavenny; while his only son married Ursula Pole, whose mother, the Countess of Salisbury, eventually went to the block because of her royal blood. The last of these contracts had however been arranged through the good offices of no less an agent than Cardinal Wolsey, and took place in 1518 while Buckingham still enjoyed the King's particular favour.

Although there was apparently no lack of informers ready to fabricate reports of Buckingham's treason, neither Henry VIII nor the Cardinal considered it necessary to remove him as long as he remained quietly under their watchful eyes. The young King may well have felt a genuine attachment to his urbane and cultivated companion, whose love of letters was matched by an outstanding reputation for skill in the lists. If the two men occasionally quarrelled – as they did in 1510 because of Henry's brief liaison with Buckingham's sister [39] – their differences were soon forgotten in a round of festivities and ceremonial. Had he wished, the King could easily have exploited the discovery that Sir William Bulmer, a knight of the body, had been illegally retained by Duke Edward. The Duke is said to have expected savage reprisals – perhaps even death – but suffered nothing worse than a humiliating rebuke.[40] His brief period of disgrace was evidently over by March 1519, when Henry invited him to act as his champion in a royal tournament. Advancing years may explain Buckingham's reluctance to accept the offer, and he asked Wolsey to intervene on his behalf:

And forasmoche as I wolde be ryght loth to refuse to doo any thyng that should be at his [the King's] pleasure . . . for that I have allwey found his Highnes so goode and gracious lorde vnto me, and specially nowe at my last beyng with hym; and the rather through the ffavour of your goode Lordship . . . I am lothe and darr not be bolde to

[38] H.M.C. *Report on the Hastings Mss.* (4 vols., H.M.S.O., 1928–47), vol. I p. 307.
[39] *State Papers Spanish*, Supplement to vols. I and II pp. 39–40.
[40] K.B. 8/5 m. 5; for details of this case see pp. 99–100.

troble you withall, yut I shall hartyly desire youre goode lordsship as my speciall trust ys in you . . .[41]

Relations between Duke Edward and the Cardinal remained superficially smooth until the summer of 1519, if not later. It was then that Buckingham laid on a lavish entertainment for the court at his manor of Penshurst, and in so doing conveyed an exaggerated impression of wealth and power. Had they but known it, he and his friends were already being spied on by the Cardinal, who was under direct orders from King Henry himself to ' make good wache on the duke of Suffolke, on the duke of Bukyngham, on my lord off Northecomberland, on my lord off Darby, on my lord of Wylshere and on others whyche yow thynke suspecte . . .' [42] Foolishly, Duke Edward had chosen to criticise Wolsey's foreign policy, and thereby voiced his contemporaries' resentment over the loss of their traditional rôle in government. Many must have agreed privately with his complaint ' yt ye kyng wold gyft hys ffees, offices and rewardes rather to booyes yen to noble men ', but few were so outspoken.[43] Whatever doubts the King had begun to entertain about Buckingham's loyalty can only have been intensified by these periodic displays of intransigence.

Encouraged by a group of courtiers, including Duke Edward, Henry VIII had initially reacted against his father's cautious foreign policy and mounted a successful invasion of France in 1513. The complexities of European politics nonetheless caused him to seek peace and an alliance with the French; in this he followed the advice of Cardinal Wolsey against that of the Duke, who characteristically refused to modify his belligerent opinions. That both the Spanish and Venetian ambassadors should regard him as a friend and ally in their attempts to win support against the French was obviously a source of embarrassment to the Cardinal.[44] His bitter attacks on Wolsey's cherished scheme for a

---

41 *Original Letters Illustrative of English History*, ed. H. Ellis (3 series in 11 vols., London, 1824–46), 3rd series vol. 1 pp. 216–7. For a description of Duke Edward as a royal champion in his prime see S. Anglo, *An Introduction to the Great Tournament Roll of Westminster* (Oxford, 1968), pp. 34–40.   42 Add. Ms. 19398 fo. 644.

43 Harleian Ms. 283 fo. 70 (The Deposition of Robert Gilbert, the Duke's chancellor, 1521).

44 *State Papers Spanish*, vol. II p. 43; *L. & P. Henry VIII*, vol. 1, pt i, no. 476; *State Papers Venetian*, vol. II no. 117; Cottonian Ms. Galba B III fo. 327.

European peace grew more and more uncompromising. On being told of the interview which was planned to take place between King Henry and Francis I in 1520, he is said to have remarked ' that he did not know . . . what could be the cause of so great an expenditure of cash unless it was for the future spectacle of foolish speeches, or for a conference of trivialities . . .'.[45] Angry and disillusioned, the Duke retired soon afterwards to his newly built castle at Thornbury, where he remained aloof until his arrest for treason in April 1521. His sudden withdrawal from court was followed, in November 1520, by a request for permission to raise an armed bodyguard so that he could visit his Welsh lordships. This was enough to confirm the King's worst fears. The second Duke of Buckingham had planned to lead his rebellion from Wales in 1483, and history now seemed about to repeat itself. Duke Edward was quite genuinely afraid to face his Welsh tenants without a sizeable retinue, but his administrative problems must have appeared simply a front for more sinister activities.[46] Although perhaps necessary from a financial point of view, his projected tour of Newport and Brecon could not have been planned at a more inappropriate time. A number of his household staff and former employees were anxious to pay off old scores, and eagerly provided the Cardinal with incriminating evidence about their master. However popular he may have been as a ' bluff patriot ', Buckingham was intolerant and often wantonly vindictive towards his servants, many of whom went in constant fear of distraint or imprisonment.[47] Charles Knivet, for example, had been made a scapegoat for certain unpopular enclosures and evictions carried out by the Duke in the South East.[48] Wolsey's agents were easily able to exploit his sense of grievance, and soon had interesting developments to report:

And so, if it please your grace, of liklihode sume great matter there is, or elles is Charles a mervailous symple insolent body. Verray good pollecy it were to have the trouth knowen. The King that dead is . . .

[45] *The Anglica Historia of Polydore Vergil*, ed. D. Hay (C.S., 3rd series vol. LXXIV, 1950), p. 265.

[46] See p. 100 for the background to Buckingham's request.

[47] Many examples of the Duke's harsh behaviour may be found in chapter 9.

[48] I. S. Leadam, ' The Inquisition of 1517: Inclosures and Evictions ', *T.R.H.S.*, new series VI (1892), p. 190.

wold handle suche a cause circumspectly and with convenyent diligens for inveglyng, and yet not disclose it to the party . . . but kepe it to hym self, and alweies grope ferther.[49]

Other disgruntled employees were only too willing to provide the Cardinal with whatever he wanted to hear. Particularly damning evidence came from Edmund Dellacourt, Duke Edward's young confessor, and Robert Gilbert, his chancellor and confidant of twenty years' standing – both of whom were ideally placed to testify against him. Formal proceedings began on 13 May 1521, by which time Buckingham's guilt was already a foregone conclusion. Despite all Wolsey's efforts, the formal charges amounted to little more than hearsay. All manner of treasonous sentiments were attributed to the Duke on the basis of distorted and exaggerated reports of his conversations.[50] The Cardinal had nonetheless been careful to omit any adverse criticisms of his own foreign policy from the evidence presented in court, fearing to turn Buckingham into a popular martyr. Ludovico Spinelli, the Venetian Ambassador's secretary, observed how Duke Edward was sent for judgement ' under a strong escort of armed men, lest he should be rescued by his numerous following in London ', and went on to describe the scenes of universal grief as he mounted the block.[51] But apart from a brief outbreak of violence in the City, Buckingham's death provoked little open hostility. His friends and relatives among the English baronage were certainly quiescent, for no matter how much they may have opposed his judicial murder, they found it expedient to accept the verdict without question. Their pusillanimity had been a cause of great regret to Buckingham in his isolation, but only the most foolhardy were prepared to face the prospect of dynastic upheaval after years of relatively stable government.[52]

Predictably, the Cardinal hastened to make diplomatic propa-

49 S.P.1/22 fo. 57.
50 K.B. 8/5, *passim* (the record of Buckingham's trial); see M. Levine, ' The Fall of Edward, Duke of Buckingham ', *Tudor Men and Institutions*, ed. A. J. Flavin (Louisiana, 1972), pp. 31–48, for a fuller discussion of the evidence.
51 *State Papers Venetian*, vol. III no. 213.
52 Corporation of London R.O.; Repertory of the Court of Aldermen, vol. V fo. 204; K. B. McFarlane has already drawn attention to the Duke's complaint ' that it would do well enough if the noblemen durst break their minds together, but some of them mistrusteth, and feareth to break their minds together . . .' (' The Wars of the Roses ', *Proceedings of the British Academy*, L (1964), pp. 96–7).

ganda out of his rival's fall, which had aroused widespread comment in all the major courts of Europe. Yet, although he assured Francis I that Duke Edward had been removed for his opposition to a French alliance,[53] there is no real evidence, as was once believed, of a systematic attempt on Wolsey's part to isolate and destroy his most trenchant critic. Buckingham died because his pride and ambition made it impossible for him to accept the passive rôle of satellite and courtier which had been forced on so many of his peers. He had failed to convince the King that his wealth, territorial power and royal blood did not constitute a grave threat to the established order, and the penalty was death. In retrospect, the succession of blunders occasioned by Duke Edward's inability to appreciate the delicacy of his position can be seen to have led directly to Tower Hill.

[53] *L. & P. Henry VIII*, vol. III, pt ii, no. 1556.

Chapter 3

THE MANAGEMENT OF THE STAFFORD ESTATES, 1438–1521

Although the basic administrative methods common to most large estates were fairly uniform by the fifteenth century, no two families seem to have managed their property in the same way. Whereas each of the Duchy of Lancaster receiverships remained under the centralising influence of a receiver general, Richard, Duke of York's senior officials were rather more independent. Both the Staffords and the Beauchamp Earls of Warwick steered a middle course by employing a receiver general whose practical authority rarely extended beyond the areas under his personal control.[1] These differences were influenced by geographical considerations, which, in a large and scattered inheritance, tended to reinforce the individuality of each receiving area. The Earls of Stafford were certainly pragmatic. From 1384, if not earlier, their outlying lordships of Caus, Newport, Stafford and Tonbridge had been run separately. Brecon was added in 1421 and Holderness in 1439, leaving the receiver general with a 'central circuit' of farms and manors in the Midlands, the Home Counties and the South West. The amalgamation of Anne Stafford's estates with those of her son in 1438 made the creation of a seventh receivership based on Thornbury in Gloucestershire an administrative necessity.[2] The other receivers had ceased to supply their senior colleague with an annual statement of account long before this date, and the demands of Duke Humphrey's itinerant household tended to increase their autonomy. Money and supplies often worth more than £100 were handed over by the local receivers without any further authority. It was not uncommon for almost all the net profits of certain lordships to be spent on provisions,

---

[1] C. D. Ross and T. B. Pugh, 'Materials for the Study of Baronial Incomes in Fifteenth Century England', *Econ. H.R.*, 2nd series VI (1953), p. 190.

[2] The first surviving receiver's account for this year is dated Michaelmas 1440 (D.641/1/2/167).

45

while from remoter parts of the estates bills of credit or consignments of specie were sent directly to the Duke.

Each receiver had to shoulder heavy administrative and financial responsibilities. His duties were physically demanding, for the collection of revenues alone could entail weeks of continuous travel, often in unpleasant conditions. The routine business of estate management and the compilation of accounts might perhaps be left to a deputy, but the post was no sinecure. In an age notorious for its litigiousness, senior estate staff needed a sound working knowledge of the law. They were frequently called upon to represent their lord in any dealings with neighbouring landowners, and at the same time had to maintain discipline among their subordinates. Most appointments were made from the upper ranks of county society, since this class alone possessed the necessary training and skills. Although few of the first Duke's receivers were professional lawyers, almost all of them had served as commissioners of the peace; some became members of parliament, while others took up civic or royal posts either during or after their term of employment. During his thirty years as receiver general of the Stafford estates John Heton held many offices in his native Buckinghamshire, including those of sheriff, escheator and justice of the peace. The work involved did not interfere with his regular duties: on the contrary, the influence which he exercised as a landowner and shire knight served to strengthen his position and gained him the respect of subordinates and superiors alike.[3] He enjoyed Duke Humphrey's complete confidence and was given a number of important commissions, as in September 1444, when he travelled over eighty miles to Portsmouth for a meeting with the Duke of York.[4] Buckingham had already complained about the behaviour of York's retainers towards the tenants of Cantref Selyf, and this delicate matter was probably on the receiver general's agenda. Heton and his colleagues were, moreover, expected to mobilise their own servants when danger threatened, and some were no doubt appointed largely because of their personal following. The account rolls contain many references to prominent officials acting in a quasi-military capacity. Humphrey

---

[3] For details of his career see Appendix C Part I.
[4] D.641/1/2/18 m. 6 (his account for the year ending Michaelmas 1445).

Cotes, the receiver of Staffordshire, for example, assembled a force of mounted yeomen and led them to London himself at the time of Cade's rebellion in 1450; some months later his successor headed the sixty armed men who had been summoned at short notice to arrest that notorious law-breaker, Sir Thomas Malory.[5]

A particularly strong element of continuity was maintained when the receiver had already worked as his predecessor's assistant. Thomas Berkeley began his career as deputy to Nicholas Poyntz, receiver of the South Western estates, whom he succeeded in 1453. This receivership was divided into two parts, one of which was entrusted to Berkeley and his fellow deputy, John Wodeford. Their duties were onerous: they spent almost twelve weeks in the saddle when collecting the Michaelmas rents in 1443, and were also required to accompany the auditor on his tour of Buckingham's Hampshire manors.[6] Poyntz himself had to deal with a seemingly endless round of routine business. His itinerary after the annual audit at Michaelmas 1439, for instance, certainly left him with little time for anything else. No sooner had his accounts been examined than he was summoned to attend Duke Humphrey at Writtle in Essex; the late Dowager's creditors were awaiting payment and there were other problems – such as poaching in local parks and the supervision of repair work – which needed immediate attention. On his return to Thornbury, Poyntz made three separate inspections of the surrounding farms and manors, followed by a tour of the entire receivership for the collection of rents and the examination of his ministers' accounts. During quieter periods he seized the opportunity to negotiate entry fines and supervise the election of officials in the local courts.[7]

As his name implies, the receiver's primary function was to levy money from his employer's estates. Although it was understood that employees of all ranks would supplement their wages with bribes and any other perquisites which came their way, outright profiteering was another matter, and formal obligations for good behaviour were frequently taken from staff in respon-

---

[5] D.641/1/2/20 m. 3 (Heton's account for the year ending Michaelmas 1450), 57 m. 11 (Roger Draycote's account for the year ending Michaelmas 1451).

[6] D.641/1/2/171 m. 7v (Poyntz's account for the year ending Michaelmas 1444).

[7] D.641/1/2/167 m. 9.

sible positions. A standard procedure had evolved by 1450, when Thomas Vaughan was made receiver of Brecon. He and an impressive group of at least twelve ' sufficient persons ' were bound in sums equivalent to almost twice the lordship's anticipated revenues of about £1,060 a year.[8] Lesser officials made similar arrangements with their own receiver, who took either the property or the persons of his subordinates as surety before accounting on their behalf. In Wales, where arrears rose alarmingly and often went unpaid for years, a period of incarceration at Newport or Brecon Castles seemed the obvious deterrent; even the Constables themselves stood under pain of confiscation should their prisoners escape.[9]

The ministers appointed to administer Buckingham's Welsh Marcher lordships found it almost impossible to overcome the more general problem of violence and disorder. The countryside around Caus was so badly affected by outbreaks of lawlessness that in 1454 John Woderton, the receiver, hired a Welsh mercenary ' for kepyng my lorde's tenantes of the seid lordship from robery and pilage '. The situation was made worse by a protracted boundary dispute with the Duke of York, whose followers had carried off some of Duke Humphrey's tenants and imprisoned them in Montgomery Castle. Besides performing his normal duties – a difficult enough task in this troubled area – Woderton was also required to search out evidence in support of Buckingham's title and convey it personally to him in London.[10] This is by no means the only case of a receiver undertaking the type of work normally entrusted to professional lawyers. Sir Thomas Stanley's suit for the Staffords' manor of Bosley in Cheshire, for example, gave Humphrey Cotes a unique opportunity to display his legal talents. He attended the Chester Assizes regularly over a three-year period ending in 1446, and was present whenever Buckingham's counsel met to discuss their progress. The ambiguous nature of certain disbursements entered in Cotes' accounts at

---

[8] N.L.W. Peniarth Ms. 280 fo. 40.

[9] See, for example, S.C.6/924/23, *passim* (the accounts of the receiver of Newport and his ministers for the year ending Michaelmas 1448) and Longleat Ms. 3988, *passim* (the accounts of the receiver of Caus and his ministers for the year ending Michaelmas 1454).

[10] D.641/1/2/22 m. 6; Longleat Mss. 3988 m. 10v, 3847 m. 12v (his accounts for the years ending Michaelmas 1454, 1455 and 1458).

this time suggests that the delicate business of suborning witnesses could also be left in his capable hands. It is hardly surprising that Duke Humphrey relied upon him to safeguard his territorial interests when an inquisition *post mortem* was taken upon the Duke of Warwick's Staffordshire estates in 1445.[11]

Even when there was nothing else to preoccupy him, the receiver could exercise no more than a token supervision over most of the property entrusted to his care. This task lay with the manorial stewards, who were themselves answerable to a chief steward, usually with responsibility for the entire receivership. The regular holding of customary and seignorial courts was particularly important, not merely for financial or disciplinary reasons, but also as an essential part of the administrative machine. Ideally, every aspect of estate management then came under the steward's cognizance. Leases, entry fines and bills of sale were drawn up on his orders; he arranged for repairs, sanctioned reductions or increases in rent and was often called upon to suggest useful economies. There were, however, many abuses: negligence, corruption and sheer inefficiency sprang from the granting of stewardships as a type of annuity to senior personnel and liveried retainers. The worst effects of absenteeism were felt throughout the Welsh Marches and on the larger English manors, where the steward alone possessed sufficient authority to prevent malpractices. On becoming sub-receiver and steward of Macclesfield in 1460, John Savage was given almost complete autonomy in his dealings with the tenants and officials under him; he also agreed to live within the manor, but there is little likelihood that his promises were ever taken seriously.[12] The appointment of Thomas Arblaster, a Staffordshire man, as sheriff of Newport was certainly no more than a sinecure. His duties fell upon a series of subordinates, who were obliged to offer securities before taking on these additional responsibilities.[13] It is now impossible to tell exactly how harmful this system of patronage could be. A strong hand was needed to keep order in the Staffords' Marcher

---

11 D.641/1/2/54 mm. 9v–10, 55 m. 10, 56 m. 11 (Cotes' accounts for the years ending Michaelmas 1443, 1445 and 1446).

12 D.641/1/2/73 (Savage's indenture is endorsed on the bailiff of Macclesfield's account for the year ending Michaelmas 1462).

13 N.L.W. Peniarth Ms. 280 fo. 33.

lordships, especially as the native reeves and bailiffs were often unreliable. The tenants of Brecon regarded cattle-stealing as a legitimate source of income and protests about their ' grete roberies and pillages ' during the early 1450s eventually reached Duke Humphrey himself. ' For now it standeth upon ye poynt yt throw your labours & good accquitaylle all ye seid lo[rdshi]ps is like to stand in as good case as it hath done afore times ', he reminded Sir John Scudamore, the steward, who had done nothing to discipline the worst offenders. Possibly because of his indifference to local affairs Sir John was discharged from office and replaced by a Welshman on the advice of Buckingham's council some months later.[14] Yet although the lordship of Brecon could not be left in the hands of an absentee whose interests lay elsewhere, other stewardships in quieter areas continued to be used as a means of recruiting influential local gentry.

By the late thirteenth century most estate and household accounts were based on the long-established principle of individual liability. In accordance with this carefully balanced system of charge and discharge each official was responsible for the arrears of previous years as well as for the immediate issues of his manor or receivership. Any legitimate expenses were then deducted from the total charge, while overdue rents, unauthorised payments and cash in hand were all technically regarded as debts to be settled at the next audit. These safeguards were designed to protect the landlord from dishonest practices and tell us very little about actual profits. In order to calculate what clear revenues were potentially available, the auditors compiled a valor, or synthesis, of ministerial accounts by subtracting wages and other running costs from the current gross receipts. As a brief and essentially optimistic survey, a valor disguises arrears; nor does it record what proportion of the anticipated receipts was ever collected. The Staffords therefore compared real and ideal revenues annually by combining an abbreviated receiver's account, a brief valor and a more detailed list of uncollected rents in one document. Three such manuscripts have survived for the South Western estates during the 1450s and reveal a significant tendency

14 *Ibid.*, fo. 50.

towards profit-and-loss accountancy.[15] Effective reforms and realistic budgeting were clearly both impossible unless the auditors could provide comprehensive information of this kind.

All three Dukes of Buckingham were fortunate in their choice of financial advisers, many of whom remained in office for long periods and, like William Weldon, were professional men also employed by the Crown. Weldon began working for Duke Humphrey in 1435; five years later he became auditor general and kept his post until 1467, if not longer.[16] His duties as a royal auditor in Wales and Cheshire do not appear to have prevented him from undertaking the most routine tasks in person. In 1453, for example, he rode south from Staffordshire to hold a second court of audit in London; he then made a tour of the Duke's manors in Hampshire, Gloucestershire and Wiltshire, and after returning briefly to London moved across England from Holderness to Wales via the central circuit.[17] Despite his life of constant travel, Weldon also found time to audit Buckingham's accounts as Captain of Calais and Warden of the Cinque Ports; he was also frequently at hand to offer financial advice to various members of the Stafford family.

One of the auditor's main duties was to ensure that every possible source of income was being fully exploited. To do so he would search through old rentals, accounts and court rolls for evidence of unpaid debts or forgotten incidents. Except in Wales, the profits of seignorial justice were not great. Fines, tolls and forfeitures generally constituted less than 5% of the gross takings from each manor,[18] and although the Staffords cultivated every franchise in their possession, their goals were administrative rather than financial. Since Thornbury manor court met regularly every three or four weeks to deal with a considerable amount of business, the first Duke of Buckingham took the opportunity to issue general ordinances concerning the tenantry as a whole and the upkeep of their property.[19] These were designed to protect

---

[15] D.641/1/2/178 (partially destroyed), 179, 180.
[16] See Appendix C Part I.
[17] D.641/1/2/176 m. 8 (account of the receiver of Gloucestershire, Hampshire and Wiltshire for the year ending Michaelmas 1453).
[18] Two estate valors for the years ending Michaelmas 1442 (D.641/1/2/17) and 1448 (Longleat Ms. 6410) suggest that judicial dues usually fell far below this figure.
[19] There were, for instance, regulations concerning absenteeism, the damage done by

the entire community and may well have been drawn up after consultation with the villagers themselves. It was common for the Duke's officials to take advice on customary law from the most knowledgeable elders, who also met as an impromptu tribunal for the settlement of local disputes.[20] Anyone wishing to enter, alienate, exchange or enclose land held by custom of the manor had to pay for the privilege, while sanctions could always be brought against the difficult tenant who failed to repair his property or acted in an anti-social manner. The court rolls were therefore important because of the detailed evidence which they could provide about leases, entry fines and the transfer of property. This information went to make up a rental, which gave the auditor an independent means of establishing each minister's charge and the credibility of his petitions. Duke Humphrey himself saw the need for greater accuracy, and in 1443 instructed his senior auditor, the receiver general and the steward of Essex to form a commission *pour renoveller et refaire rentalles, custumaires et extentes*.[21]

Another potential source of profit, the feodary and honour courts, met under the direction of bailiff feodaries or stewards, who were responsible for the collection of feudal incidents from tenants holding by knight service. These irregular revenues were, however, becoming much harder to collect. The Duke's two feodary courts in Hampshire, Wiltshire and Gloucestershire, for example, rarely produced more than £5 a year above expenses, although as much as £168 had been raised in one year during the Dowager Countess's lifetime.[22] Tenure by knight service still entailed the payment of reliefs and other ' reasonable aids ', which were carefully listed and claimed whenever possible. Yet the Duke still found it difficult to enforce his rights, especially as many tenants evaded their feudal obligations by settling their property (and sometimes even their own children) on a group of feoffees. The cost of defending an action for wrongful distraint under

stray cattle and the holding of markets (D.641/1/4C/7 mm. 10v, 12, 34; Thornbury manor court rolls for the years 1438–50).

20 *Ibid.*, mm. 23v, 47–47v.

21 N.L.W. Peniarth Ms. 280 fo. 30.

22 D.641/1/2/161, 167–75 (accounts of the bailiff feodaries for the years ending 1413 and 1439–52), *passim*.

such circumstances could easily prove greater than the revenues at stake, and Buckingham learned to proceed with caution.[23]

Almost all the Staffords' demesnes had been farmed out by 1400, and, apart from small areas of pasture reserved for domestic use, were held either at will (on a yearly basis) or by leasehold (for a term of years). The occupants of customary or villein land did not always come from servile stock: on the contrary, it was as common for freeholders to farm *terra nativa* as it was for bondmen to take up freehold. As on other estates there are clear signs of a growing ' peasant aristocracy ', whose members were able to consolidate and enclose relatively large areas of farmland. It has been argued that the landowner suffered as a result of these changes, but contemporary economic circumstances did not work entirely to his disadvantage. The wealthy peasant could at least be relied upon to offer securities when he took on the lease of a manor. Duke Humphrey naturally wanted to obtain the most favourable terms not only for rents but also for conditions of tenure.[24] His larger manors usually went to either one farmer or a small group of tenants for periods ranging between three or four years and life; many leases were drawn up for a standard twelve years, but water mills were usually let for longer. Almost all such contracts included specific instructions for the upkeep of any buildings, closes or warrens taken on by the tenant, although the steward usually provided timber for the necessary repairs and sometimes agreed to accept a cut in rent. Mills in particular cost a great deal to maintain, and since they showed no profit while work was in progress, the Duke always covered himself by taking adequate security. Additional clauses about the replacement of livestock and the preservation of woodland appeared in a number of leases; it was also considered necessary to forbid intensive cultivation over the last two years of a tenancy. Certain farmers paid whatever tithes, taxes or feudal incidents had originally been borne by the landlord; some even provided hospitality for Buckingham's ministers.[25] Only a few estate and household staff were

---

[23] See, for example, D.641/1/2/271 (a bill of expenses for the defence of Buckingham's feodary in Oxfordshire against a writ of *replevin* brought by Sir Thomas Chetewood).

[24] As indeed did other landlords, such as the Archbishops of Canterbury (see F. R. H. Du Boulay, *The Lordship of Canterbury* (London, 1966), pp. 220–34).

[25] The accounts of the Duke's ten Warwickshire bailiffs for the year ending Michaelmas

accorded preferential treatment in the granting out of leases. Certain Welsh families were permitted to engross whole manors, but not many others enjoyed similar favours.[26] The bailiffs and other local officers who rented property from the Staffords would certainly have done so even had they not been his employees.

Duke Humphrey's involvement in political affairs prevented him from devoting much time to the management of his estates. He was well served by a number of loyal and talented officials, but some aspects of the administration were admittedly more inefficient than others. Absenteeism posed a major problem to all great landowners during the later middle ages, and continued to do so for as long as important posts were distributed among friends and retainers. It is less easy to explain why Buckingham was so apparently lax over the exploitation of certain casual sources of revenue, such as compulsory manumission, which seem to have been almost neglected until the early sixteenth century. So much more is known, however, about the third Duke of Buckingham's activities as a landlord that comparisons between him and his ancestors are essentially misleading. Nevertheless, Duke Humphrey's advisers were well aware of the need for efficiency and improvement.

The last Duke of Buckingham was responsible for many important changes on the Stafford estates, although the second half of the fifteenth century had seen a gradual tendency towards the centralised administrative system which he took to its logical conclusion. The Dowager Duchess Anne had retained control of all her late husband's English property until Duke Henry came of age, and even then enjoyed a lucrative jointure. Since she kept a small household which rarely moved outside the central circuit, her receivers began to send all their net profits directly to Kimbolton or Writtle. The posts of treasurer and receiver general were combined during the 1470s and there is enough evidence to suggest the growth of a single collecting agency.[27] The second

1444 (D.641/1/2/270, *passim*) contain several typical examples of leases for both manors and mills; so too do the returns from the South Western estates submitted two years later (D.641/1/2/172, *passim*).   [26] Pugh, *The Marcher Lordships*, pp. 165–6.
[27] Add. Ms. 29608 mm. 1, 3 (account of Thomas Garth, treasurer of the household 30 Sept. 1472 to 31 March 1474).

Duke favoured a more flexible organisation, but his receiver general still kept some overall financial responsibilities: for instance, every purchase was made and accounted for in his name by receivers particular who enjoyed little personal autonomy.[28] This situation may have changed after the Dowager's death in 1480; yet any move towards the old system of independent receiverships was checked first by the confiscation of the Stafford estates in 1483 and then by their division between Lady Margaret Beaufort and Jasper Tudor, Duke of Bedford, two years later. Bedford managed his wife's dower lands as a separate unit, and since she spent most of her time at Thornbury, this became the natural administrative centre for a complex of manors stretching between Newport and Kent. Lady Margaret placed her young ward's inheritance in the hands of a specially appointed receiver general. By directing all available clear receipts to one official she successfully curtailed all but the most essential local expenditure and provided Duke Edward with a model for his own reforms. He was probably also influenced by developments within the royal household, where the cofferer had assumed the direction of chamber finance. There was no longer any need for stores of money and provisions to be kept in every receivership, and Buckingham set out to bring surplus revenues under his personal control. From 1499 onwards substantial payments in cash and bills were made to William Cholmeley, his cofferer, from every part of the estates.[29] His attempts to streamline the administration were thorough and far-reaching: some were dictated by the requirements of a semi-permanent household; others sprang from a personal determination to improve efficiency and productivity at all levels.

It is now impossible to tell how great an innovator Duke Edward actually was, because the men who headed his administration held offices which are known to have existed in some form or another during the previous century. The surveyorship is a case in point: the first known appointment to this post dates from 1461, when Sir Thomas Burgh was given supervisory powers over all the Dowager Anne's estates, with a life annuity of 40

[28] D.641/1/2/26 (a receiver general's account for the period *ca.* Feb. 1476–May 1477).
[29] See pp. 89–90.

marks. Burgh's activities at court made it necessary for him to appoint a series of deputies, although his two successors, William Bedell and John Wingfield, were more conscientious. Small itinerant commissions accomplished a great deal under very trying circumstances, but there remained an obvious need for some officer to direct the systematic exploitation of territorial resources. Four experienced bureaucrats of proven ability acted as surveyors over the years 1499 to 1521. Among their duties were the imposition and collection of entry fines, the inspection of ministers' accounts and the sale of timber; they were also expected to draw up leases and deal with a wide variety of legal business.[30] Buckingham appears to have combined the surveyorship with the office of receiver general in or before 1514. Although this was only a temporary measure which probably depended for its success upon the skill and industry of Thomas Cade, it provides further evidence of the growing trend towards a more centralised administrative system. During Duke Humphrey's lifetime the receiver general had rarely intervened in the affairs of other receiverships, but from 1500 onwards he was called upon to undertake rigorous tours of inspection throughout the entire estates and report upon his findings.[31]

Buckingham was particularly anxious to place his stewards under constant surveillance, since it was through their negligence that his judicial rights had been allowed to lapse in many lordships. In 1504 the receiver general and an auditor were sent to make a detailed survey of the central circuit, with specific instructions for the removal of corrupt or inefficient under-stewards.[32] The problem of disciplining these men effectively was almost insurmountable, as a report made on the same area fourteen years later reveals. Absenteeism was not confined to the influential knights and gentlemen who held stewardships as sinecures. With deputies like the under-steward of Haverhill, who, as the receiver general caustically remarked, ' was at London, in the Tempyll,

---

30 See Appendix B for a list of surveyors. Examples of their activities may be found in S.C.6/Hen. VII 1076 m. 15 (account of the receiver of Kent and Surrey for the year ending Michaelmas 1506) and S.C.6/Hen. VII 1844 m. 2 (account of the receiver of Staffordshire for the year ending Michaelmas 1507).

31 D.641/1/2/201 m. 11 (account of the receiver of Gloucestershire, Hampshire and Wiltshire for the year ending Michaelmas 1500).

32 Pugh, *The Marcher Lordships*, p. 282.

and as it was sayd seke ',[33] there was nothing to prevent other landowners from enforcing their own seignorial privileges at Duke Edward's expense. The situation at Rothwell in Northamptonshire was even worse: its young and inexperienced bailiff had allowed valuable property to fall into decay, presumably because there was no resident steward to advise him. In the receiver general's own words:

I send to Buckyngham and to Oxford for Aschewell the Under Styward and he was at London; and for lacke of hymme and the cowett roollys Idyd kepe no cowrtte ther, wyche was to your grace a losse, ffor ther was dyvers off your tenantes that wold have taken up be copie bothe howssys and landes, wyche as yet remayne in your grace's handdes, ffor becawse the styward gyffe nott hyse attendans – that is not only by Aschewell, the Wnder Styward, but allso by all the wnder stywarddes thowrow your generall cyrcutte. Iff your grace shorttly gyffe not them in commawndment to attend your cowrtes every thre wekes, accordyng to the olde custome, yt wyll be to your losse . . . for there is no man that hasse wyll to sew to your cowrth or cowrthes, there accions hangyng so long ther, and no remedy ffor why ther is no cowrtes keptt.[34]

His recommendation that stewardships should be awarded only to 'men of substance' who could enter recognizances for the adequate performance of their duties was the logical extension of a scheme which Buckingham had already rationalised and improved. The bonds and securities demanded from all officers who had to render an account were rather higher and more consistent than in the previous century. Duke Edward's memorandum of 1504 ordered the immediate forfeiture of any minister in the central circuit whose payments fell more than eight weeks in arrears: since his reeves and bailiffs were already bound in sums exceeding their annual receipts, the Duke had, in theory, insured himself against the slightest loss.[35] At least two of his receivers general entered obligations worth £1,200 on taking up office; they also contracted to surrender their cash receipts at regular

---

[33] W.A.M. 5470 fo. 32 (a book of answers made by John Pickering, the receiver general, to Edward, Duke of Buckingham, *ca.* 1518–9; this Ms. is not foliated consecutively and the numbers given here count the first folio as 1, etc.).

[34] *Ibid.*, fo. 42v.

[35] Pugh, *The Marcher Lordships*, p. 282.

intervals and therefore took heavy security from their own subordinates.[36] Yet Buckingham's preference for the piecemeal –
albeit long-term – repayment of arrears instead of protracted
litigation meant that in practice forfeiture was a meaningless
threat to most of his local employees. Several charges were
brought against senior staff, but lesser officials usually managed
to avoid legal action. The escape of prisoners from Brecon Castle
in 1505 led Buckingham to claim bonds worth £300 from the
negligent keeper, whose debts were still unpaid fourteen years
later.[37] This example is typical of many others, and explains why
Duke Edward took such a keen interest in the appointment of
relatively minor officials. His commissioners were always on the
watch for 'talmen' and 'good payers' to act as stewards or
bailiffs, and to a certain extent their efforts were successful. A list
of office-holders on the Stafford estates made by the Crown in
1523 reflects very favourably upon Buckingham's choice of personnel. Paradoxically, his Welsh ministers were singled out for
particular praise as much for their 'great discretion' as their
ability to maintain law and order.[38] Extremes of good and bad
administration could well exist in relatively close proximity, and
Duke Edward's anxiety to correct abuses tends to obscure the fact
that by contemporary standards many of his employees were very
efficient. A gradual improvement in both discipline and finances
may perhaps be traced from the appointment of several highly
qualified clerics to responsible posts in the household and throughout the estates. They were not distracted by the political, legal or
mercantile interests which absorbed their lay colleagues, and could
moreover be rewarded at no additional cost from the Duke's
plentiful supply of benefices.

The third Duke was always prepared to help his more talented
employees, but few of them regarded him as either a kind or a
just lord. Some remained with him for long periods, but it is hard
to find many examples of the loyalty which Duke Humphrey
seems to have inspired among his receivers and household staff.
Seven different receivers general and at least sixteen auditors

[36] C.P.40/1024, Easter 11 Hen. VII, rot. 308v; 1027, Hilary 11 Hen. VIII, rot. 412v.
[37] S.C.6/Hen. VIII 4775 m. 9 (account of the receiver of Brecon for the year ending
Michaelmas 1519).
[38] S.P.1/29 fos. 170–80.

were appointed over the years 1498 to 1521. The death in 1511 of John Gunter, the most able and experienced of Buckingham's auditors, was a serious blow, since there was already very little continuity among his financial advisers. Gunter had worked for the Staffords since 1461 and had been a crown servant for many years: it may have been on his recommendation that the Duke made his other auditors individually responsible for smaller groups of manors assigned to them by a formal contract.[39] They now indented to deliver fair copies of every ministerial account for his personal scrutiny, and, being retained on a short-term basis, had to justify their continuation in office. Very few were reappointed; indeed, three eventually faced actions of account before the Court of Common Pleas.[40]

This preoccupation with the need for accurate record-keeping was more than justified, since large quantities of muniments had been destroyed in 1483 and even more valuable evidences had disappeared during the third Duke's minority. The effect of these losses was felt worst in the Marcher lordships, although accounts, court rolls and rentals had been badly kept throughout the estates. Duke Edward was only too well aware that his financial position could not be improved without the necessary paper-work, and on two occasions at least issued precise orders for the preservation and copying out of all important documents.[41] His auditors had meanwhile devised a short, tabulated form of account which made it possible to compare the amount and distribution of revenues from a manor or receivership over a fairly long period. Two such accounts have survived for the years Michaelmas 1498 to 1501, and were presumably compiled to reveal at a glance any marked changes in either income or expenditure after Duke Edward's coming of age.[42] It was less easy to recover missing records, as his bailiff feodaries found to their cost. Despite all their efforts ' t'inquier diligently for wardes, reliefs, instrucions, alienacions and other casualties ', feudal incidents fell uniformly into a

---

39 See Appendix B for a list of Duke Edward's auditors; Gunter's career is discussed more fully in Appendix C Part III.

40 C.P.40/1007, Trinity 6 Hen. VIII, rot. 466; 1012, Mich. 7 Hen. VIII, rot. 262, 588.

41 Pugh, *The Marcher Lordships*, pp. 248–9, 262–75, 283.

42 Eg. Roll 2198 (account of the receiver of Caus and his ministers); D.641/1/2/81 (account of the receiver of Staffordshire and his ministers).

steady decline. A great deal of time was therefore spent on the search for evidence which could be used in support of Buckingham's claims; by 1521, for example, it was possible to compile lists of knights' fees and their occupants in each receivership.[43] These were particularly useful in the hunt for wards, since the Duke's lawyers often had to defend his title against several other claimants – sometimes including the Crown.

On the whole, Buckingham was more successful in his exploitation of bondmen, although here again he was greatly hampered by the loss of court rolls and other muniments containing proof of serfdom. Although the commutation of labour services had lightened the burdens of villeinage, bondmen still possessed no rights in equity or the common law. They were chattels of a lord who could seize their goods and compel them to pay a heavy fine for manumission. The Thornbury court rolls refer to many small sums obtained through Duke Humphrey's rights over his unfree tenants, but although a few of these men were quite affluent, none ever appear to have had their goods confiscated. *The Redd Booke of Caures Castle* lists only eight manumissions on the entire Stafford estates between 1435 and 1455, while the second Duke of Buckingham seems largely to have ignored this potential source of revenue.[44] Villeinage was gradually allowed to lapse during the third Duke's minority, and his attempts to reintroduce it met with sullen opposition. His Welsh tenants were understandably reticent when interrogated by a special commission, but the search continued and in 1504 spread to the Midlands.[45] The reason for these persistent investigations becomes plain on examining the list of potential candidates for manumission submitted to Duke Edward by his receiver general in 1519. Although there were some villeins whose poverty made confiscation financially impractical, others seemed rich by any standards. The land of one Nottinghamshire bondman would have fetched £200 on the open market, while another villein in Langham was allegedly worth 200 marks a year.[46] K. B. McFarlane has already drawn attention

---

[43] E.36/150, *passim* (a survey of the Stafford estates made by Henry VIII's commissioners).

[44] D.641/1/2/4C/7 mm. 19–19v, 31v, 35, 43v, 45v, 57v, 64, 68v, 76–7; 4C/9 m. 31; N.L.W. Peniarth Ms. 280 fos. 16–17, 19, 25, 30, 35, 44, 47.

[45] Pugh, *The Marcher Lordships*, pp. 249, 285.   [46] W.A.M. 5470 fos. 46v, 47v.

to the infinite patience and low cunning shown by Buckingham's officers in seeking out ' concealed bondmen worth squeezing '; thanks to their efforts villeinage was revived on more than a score of English and Welsh manors, and on Duke Edward's death the royal surveyors found bondmen in Caus, Brecon, Holderness, Gloucestershire, Newport, Norfolk and the Midlands.[47] These men provided Buckingham with an irregular but not inconsiderable income. Pickering estimated that the unfree population of Rutland, Northamptonshire and Buckinghamshire was alone worth £523 and promised to ' disterne to the uttermost value of their substance '; nor was it uncommon for single individuals to offer fines of £40 or more for the restitution of their goods.[48]

Far greater sums were raised from the carefully managed sale of timber from the estates. Wood provided a type of credit which could be quickly realised during periods of extraordinary expenditure or financial embarrassment; it could otherwise be disposed of piecemeal, leased out to contractors or used locally for building. The Staffords had always regarded their forest land as a marketable commodity, and the first Duke's ministers were well able to drive a hard bargain. Nevertheless, it was Duke Edward who formulated a clear and consistent policy towards wood sales. He wanted long-term profits rather than quick returns and maintained strict controls over felling: even though the sale of timber in the central circuit between 1513 and 1515 alone fetched more than £413, reserves worth at least £5,200 were still untouched on the English estates in 1521.[49] Duke Edward dealt personally with a number of prospective purchasers, sending out commissioners to make sure that his instructions were followed to the letter. Tenants found guilty of ' light byhavyour making estrepe and wast in my lorde's woddes ' faced immediate eviction, while parkers and woodwards were obliged to enter heavy recognizances to cover such losses. Both practices had no doubt been introduced because of the heavy losses sustained during Duke

[47] *The Nobility of Later Medieval England*, pp. 224–6; E.36/150, *passim*.
[48] W.A.M. 5470 fos. 3v, 58v; Royal Ms. 7F XIV fo. 6v.
[49] D.1721/1/6 ' a booke of informacions gevyn by diverse my Lorde's grace's officers of divers Lordeshipes ' (*ca.* 1513–16; separate foliation from the rest of the volume) fo. 21; E.36/150, *passim*.

Edward's minority, when the Welsh forests in particular had been stripped of all saleable timber.[50]

Buckingham's energetic exploitation of feudal incidents and natural resources was matched by a characteristically determined attempt to increase his fixed landed income. By reducing the maximum period of leasehold tenancy to twenty-one years with options for renewal on the payment of an entry fine, he was able to increase rents at more frequent intervals.[51] Entry fines were first collected systematically on the Stafford estates during the early sixteenth century. Unlike the Percy Earls of Northumberland, Duke Edward did not adopt a fixed rate of fines, but chose to raise the highest possible amount in each individual case. It is impossible to compile a statistical analysis of the sums obtained, especially as a good deal of hard bargaining seems to have taken place after the Duke had invited offers from his prospective tenants. Although there was no lack of competition for agricultural property in the Midlands, many farmers simply refused to meet his excessive demands; others, fearing eviction in any case, simply neglected their farms. John Pickering tactfully tried to explain their grievances:

Sir, accordyng to my othe my conscience byndith me nothyng to conscile from your knowlege; therefore besechyng your grace to take no displeasour to me for my playnnes, for so it is, I have resoned both with certen of your tenantes and also with othir gentilmen and yomen for your fynes in every particuler place, and they have saide to me that they have no joye to offer to fyne, by the reason that thay stande ij or iij yere and nott fynysshed, whiche as they saye it is great los[s to them] and also a great hurt and decaye to your grace, for they s[ay that] they hadde it ensuerty they wolde do coste in reparacone, but because of unsuerty they willnott, and so they have answerid [to] me, and nott only one but all . . . therefore, as my thynk, hit shalbe necessary for your grace to take the fynes that byn resonable when they be offerid . . .[52]

[50] D.1721/1/6 'a booke of informacions, etc.' fo. 6v; Pugh, *The Marcher Lordships*, p. 248.

[51] Typical examples of such leases may be found in most ministerial accounts after 1498. See, for instance, Bibl. Harl. 1667 mm. 13v, 14 (local accounts from Kent and Surrey for the year ending Michaelmas 1512).

[52] W.A.M. 5470 fos. 57v–58.

The Duke also had to compromise over conditions of tenure. His father was probably the first of the Staffords to introduce into leases a clause threatening distraint for rents which fell more than three weeks into arrears, while the Dowager Duchess Katherine had taken obligations of £100 or more from her yeomen farmers.[53] Not all Duke Edward's tenants were prepared to commit themselves in this way and despite his insistence that they should pay for all repairs many refused to do so. Nevertheless, Pickering and his colleagues usually managed to negotiate terms which would have satisfied all but the most rapacious landlords.

The conversion of tenancies at will into copyhold was already well advanced on a number of estates when Duke Edward began to force these changes on his own customary tenants. Land which had previously been held on a yearly basis in return for a fixed and often unrealistic rent was now leased out for a few years on a competitive basis. In practice most copyholders enjoyed considerable security of tenure, although they faced the prospect of higher rents and entry fines whenever their copies were renewed. On his tour of the central circuit in 1518, John Pickering found that Buckingham's schemes had engendered a strange mixture of hostility and enthusiasm among the peasantry. Copyhold was firmly established in some areas, where his only task was to record future offers for Duke Edward's consideration. Several tenants welcomed the opportunity to consolidate their property, but the very poor, lacking both the capital and incentive for shrewd investment, remained staunchly conservative.[54] Yet few were prepared to offer prolonged resistance and Buckingham invariably got his own way. By 1519, for example, he had imposed entry fines worth £167 upon sixty-eight Staffordshire copyholders, and had leased out a large number of customary holdings across the Midlands.[55] His stubborn refusal to reduce rents or fines in the

---

53 D.641/1/2/77 m. 6v (account of the farmer of Tillington, Staffs., for the year ending Michaelmas 1489); D.641/1/2/259 mm. 2, 3v, 4v (local accounts from Essex for the year ending Michaelmas 1500).

54 W.A.M. 5470 fos. 14, 49, 57; B. J. Harris uses examples from Pickering's report to argue that collective strike action by the peasantry against the landlord had spread to the Stafford estates (' Landlords and Tenants in England in the later Middle Ages: The Buckingham Estates ', *Past and Present*, XLIII (1969), p. 147). It is, however, clear that resistance was confined to the lowest class of tenants, who saw no personal advantages in these changes.

55 D.641/1/2/96 mm. 2–3 (account of the receiver of Staffordshire for the year ending Michaelmas 1519).

face of economic hardship caused much bad feeling, particularly among the tenants of Newport, whose complaints were supported by his own councillors.

Although they were executed on a far more limited scale, Buckingham's plans for the enclosure of parkland aroused even greater antagonism. The second Duke is known to have enclosed a few small-holdings at Penshurst and 128 acres in the Dowlais area, but did not pursue a consistent policy in this respect.[56] Having established a semi-permanent household at Thornbury, his son embarked upon a far more ambitious project for the creation of ' a fayre parke hard by the castle '. It was begun in 1508 with the annexation of 300 acres of demesne and copyhold; two years later the Duke obtained permission from Henry VIII to impark a further 1,000 acres, but did nothing more until 1515 when he evicted a number of tenants at will.[57] These enclosures made Buckingham very unpopular and are said to have prejudiced his standing with the King: the royal commissioners sent out in 1517 to examine the effects of enclosure had nothing to say in his favour, but it is hard to accept I. S. Leadam's view that their findings were a determining factor in his fall.[58] Duke Edward saw no reason to modify a scheme which had been licensed by the King; over the next four years he more than doubled the size of a neighbouring deer park and enclosed a further 500 acres at Thornbury. The petitions and protests which reached Henry VIII in 1521 were occasioned by Buckingham's arbitrary refusal to compensate his tenants for the premature termination of their leases. Their chief grievance lay in the absence of proper remuneration rather than the evictions themselves, although these had apparently been carried out with characteristic ruthlessness.[59]

The enclosures at Thornbury were intended to provide ' fayr laundes for coursynge ' and deprived the Duke of valuable farm-

---

[56] D.641/1/2/255 m. 5 (account of the bailiff of Penshurst for the year ending Michaelmas 1477); Eg. Roll 2206 mm. 6–6v (account of the reeve of Dowlais for the year ending Michaelmas 1487).

[57] *The Itinerary of John Leland*, ed. L. Toulmin Smith (5 vols., London, 1906–10), vol. V p. 100; Leadam, *op. cit.*, pp. 188, 302–3; *L. & P. Henry VIII*, vol. I, pt ii, no. 546 (38).

[58] Leadam, *op. cit.*, p. 189.

[59] Leland, *op. cit.*, vol. V pp. 100–1; S.P.1/22 fos. 92–3 (the petition of the tenants of Thornbury to Sir John Dauncey). The royal commissioners of 1521 found ' great exclamacion for cloosing ynne of freehooldes and copy hooldes ' (E.36/150 fo. 4v).

land worth at least £50 a year. Apart from certain unspecified
' oppressions' which lost Charles Knivet his many offices in East
Anglia, there are few signs of any conscious attempts at intensive
arable or sheep farming on the Stafford estates. Henry VIII's
commissioners reported that a total of 131 acres of pasture had
been engrossed on four of Duke Edward's Yorkshire manors, but
his ancestors had always kept small breeding herds of sheep, cattle
and horses in the area around Brustwick.[60] Had he lived, the
Duke might have contemplated more sweeping changes in this
direction, for he was always receptive to ideas about improved
new agricultural methods.

Buckingham involved himself directly in every aspect of estate
management. Perhaps he followed the example of his father, who
was reputedly ' a sore and hard dealing man '; he shared with his
uncle, Lord Rivers, a shrewd and mercenary approach to the
running of his property.[61] His two great mentors, however, were
Lady Margaret Beaufort, in whose household he spent his forma-
tive years, and her steward, Reginald Bray, who remained a close
friend and trusted adviser in later life. He was well schooled in
the basic principles of Yorkist and Tudor administration and had
learned many hard lessons at the hands of Henry VII. This
experience was put to good account, although his obvious talents
were yoked to a harsh and acquisitive disposition. Like Henry VII,
' of nature assuredly he coveted to accumulate treasure; and was
a little poor in admiring riches '.[62]

---

[60] Leadam, *op. cit.*, pp. 286–9; in 1448 Duke Humphrey's Yorkshire demesnes had
supported over 2,600 sheep and a herd of cattle (D.641/1/2/19 m. 5v) and there was
still a stock keeper at Keyingham in 1521 (E.36/181 fo. 38).

[61] Lord Rivers was an extremely competent landlord, whose dealings do not always
reflect to his credit. His will, for example, reveals a conscience singularly well-
adjusted to the demands of self-interest (*Testamenta Vetusta*, ed. N. H. Nicholas
(2 vols., London, 1826), vol. I p. 334).

[62] Francis Bacon, *History of Henry VIII*, *The Works of Francis Bacon*, ed. J. Spedding
and others (14 vols., London, 1857–74), vol. VI p. 239.

Chapter 4

THE FIRST DUKE OF BUCKINGHAM'S
HOUSEHOLD AND RETINUE, 1438–1460

The first Duke of Buckingham's household was an itinerant body which accompanied him from one lordship to another as he toured the estates or executed official business. The Duke and his son, Humphrey, Lord Stafford, appear between them to have made fairly regular circuits of their property. Each receiving area boasted at least one large residence capable of accommodating the retinue with which they always travelled. The oldest and in many ways the most impressive of these was Stafford Castle, where Duke Humphrey kept a large stable with a resident staff of over forty yeomen and grooms. The Castle, dominating the town and its environs, provided an ideal recruiting centre and assembly point for his retainers in Cheshire, Staffordshire and the Welsh March. It had been built by Ralph Stafford in 1348 as a defence against the Welsh, and his choice of site continued to impress visitors long after the fortifications themselves had fallen into decay. As the crown commissioners sent to survey the Duke's estates in 1521 reported:

. . . The Castell standenth nigh a myle from the toune upon soo goodly an height that all the countrey may be seen XX[ti.] or XXX[ti.] myles aboute. An oon way a man may see to the Kynnge's lordship of Caurs in Wales XXX myles from thennes, and an other way to the Kynng's honour of Tutbury.[1]

Lord Stafford often visited the Castle with his own retainers during the 1440s and early 1450s, but the Duke evidently preferred his more comfortable seats at Writtle and Maxstoke. He obtained the latter in 1438 through an exchange with John, Lord Clinton. Maxstoke had a magnificent chapel, good stabling facili-

---

[1] E.36/150 fo. 58; D.1721/1/11 fo. 207 (a transcription of the indenture between Ralph Stafford and Ralph de Burcestre, mason, for the building of Stafford Castle, 13 Jan. 1348).

ties and a wide base court surrounded by domestic apartments; to it he added a massive iron gateway bearing the Stafford and Neville arms.[2] He stayed there when the court was at Coventry, and his receiver general and auditors made it their headquarters when they were working in the North Midlands. The manor of Writtle, with its fine timber buildings, lay but a short distance from London and could easily be provisioned from the central circuit. Anne, Dowager Duchess of Buckingham, continued to use the manor after her husband's death, and also spent a great deal of time at Kimbolton in Huntingdonshire. She enlarged the stables and added more spacious living quarters, so that even in 1521 after years of neglect it appeared ' a right goodly lodging conteyned in little roome withynne a moote, well and compendiously trussed togader in due and convenient proporcion '.[3]

Tonbridge Castle was particularly important to Duke Humphrey, since it gave him a stronghold in Kent, within easy reach of both London and Dover. As an active member of Henry VI's council with official commitments in Normandy, Calais and later the Cinque Ports, he needed such a base. Henry VIII's commissioners pronounced it ' the strongest forteres and moste like unto a castell of any other that the (third) Duke hadde in Englande or Wales '.[4] The buildings were by this time somewhat dilapidated, as Duke Edward had allowed most of his residences to fall into decay. Not even the first Duke made the fullest possible use of all his property. During his youth he had occasionally passed a few weeks at the two strong Marcher castles of Brecon and Newport, but the buildings – and, indeed, the lordships themselves – were sadly neglected from the 1440s onwards. The castles of Caus, Hay, Huntingdon and Bronllys, once so prominent along the Welsh Border, were similarly allowed to collapse into ' colde, ruynous and decaid ' heaps of rubble.[5] The third Duke of Buck-

---

[2] *Ibid.*, fos. 271–4 (a transcription of the indenture between Buckingham and Lord Clinton, 16 May 1438); see W. Dugdale, *The Antiquities of Warwickshire* (2 vols., London, 1730), vol. II p. 995 for a description of Maxstoke.

[3] E.36/150 fo. 27.

[4] *Ibid.*, fo. 13; during the fifteenth century the Castle accommodated large numbers of yeomen and grooms on a semi-permanent basis (D.641/1/2/231 m. 5, 233B m. 12; accounts of the receiver of Kent and Surrey for the years ending Michaelmas 1430 and 1446).

[5] E.36/150 fos. 23v, 50; Pugh, *The Marcher Lordships*, p. 247.

ingham is generally associated with Thornbury, but the earlier Staffords had all recognised its attractions. The manor was an ideal stopping place on journeys between London and the Welsh March; there was an ample supply of agricultural produce from its flourishing demesne farms and luxury goods could easily be purchased in Bristol. The three Dukes also kept at least one residence in London, which they rented from the Abbots of Sawtry.[6] A good deal of business was transacted there by the council, while a semi-permanent treasury and exchequer dealt with routine administrative affairs. The beautiful setting of Penshurst manor in Kent appealed more to the third Duke than to the first, but both men found it very convenient when in London. They also resided at Bletchingley in Surrey from time to time.

The Stafford household appears to have been run on a fairly rigid hierarchical basis. Contemporary accounting methods demanded that artificial distinctions be drawn between separate departments; yet although formal accounts and memoranda tell us a great deal about administrative theory, the workings of a great household were in practice undoubtedly much simpler and less systematic. Most great noblemen had long ceased to maintain the large, expensive and often unmanageable establishments of former days. *The Black Book of the Household of Edward IV*, for example, stipulated that a ducal entourage ought ideally to comprise no more than 240 persons, including forty gentlemen, eighty yeomen and a variety of lesser attendants.[7] The figures quoted in this type of ordinance are never entirely reliable, but they provide useful information about the reforms and economies which seemed most important to professional administrators. It is unlikely that the Staffords ever maintained a permanent following of this size. Duke Humphrey chose to travel with a small riding household augmented by local reserves of tenants and retainers: the great household, being a larger and more complex machine, could not move about so easily and tended to base itself on the Duke's principal residences. Domestic servants were paid by the receiver general, whose accounts list the wages of staff in both

---

[6] D.641/1/2/18 m. 6; N.L.W. Peniarth Ms. 280 fo. 46.
[7] *The Household of Edward IV, The Black Book and the Ordinances of 1478*, ed. A. R. Myers (Manchester, 1959), p. 90.

establishments. In 1439 the riding household consisted of fifty-six attendants, the majority of whom were either pages or yeomen; it is uncertain how many people Buckingham employed altogether at this time, but there were 107 clerks, chaplains, officials, ladies and menial servants on his payroll in 1450. The expansion which took place over the next seven years may well have been influenced by external political events. Twenty-two additional appointments had been made by 1457, giving a full complement of seventeen esquires and gentlemen, twelve senior and thirty-nine lesser yeomen, thirty-eight pages, four chaplains, a herald, fifteen waiting women and a small clerical staff. Almost all the new recruits were men of some social standing, who could be called upon for military support at times of crisis.[8]

Very little is known about either the cost or the organisation of Duke Humphrey's great and itinerant households. Separate accounts were kept by both bodies, which were financed from a variety of sources during the fifteenth century. Only one account appears to have survived for his itinerant household, but since it is largely concerned with preparations for the Calais peace conference of 1439 it cannot be considered representative.[9] The great household is rather better documented, but even with three complete treasurers' accounts (for the years ending Michaelmas 1444, 1453 and 1455) many questions are still unanswered.[10] References exist, for instance, to a cofferer, although his place in the administrative system remains obscure. The same is true of John Hely, Buckingham's secretary; his only recorded appearance is in a diplomatic context, but his duties may well have extended to domestic affairs.[11] Both cofferer and secretary occupied important positions in the third Duke's household and it seems reasonable to suppose that their offices were then already well established.

The early fifteenth century saw a growing tendency towards specialisation within the household. During Earl Edmund's life-

---

[8] D.641/1/2/15 m. 6; 21 m. 7; 23 m. 6 (receiver general's accounts for the years ending Michaelmas 1439, 1450 and 1457).

[9] Eg. Roll 2208 (account of the clerk of the itinerant household from 17 Oct. 1438 to 5 Oct. 1439).

[10] *Compota Domestica Familiarum de Buckingham et D'Angoulême*, ed. W. B. D. D. Turnbull (Roxburghe Club, Edinburgh, 1836), pp. 2–22; D.641/1/3/4; Eg. Roll 2209.

[11] *Compota Domestica*, p. 9; *Letters and Papers Illustrative of the Wars of the English in France*, vol. I p. 101.

time three officers – the treasurer, chamberlain and steward – acted as purveyors and paymasters: the receiver general accounted on their behalf, but there was no single channel for the purchase of supplies.[12] The Dowager Countess Anne referred all questions of household finance first to a treasurer and then to her steward, Sir Roger Aston, an extremely capable and experienced administrator who had been one of the late Earl's retainers. He probably left office to further his career in local government and the service of the Crown during the 1420s, when control of the money and provisions assigned for domestic use reverted to the treasurer.[13] Duke Humphrey retained this system, and although his chamberlain made occasional purchases for the foreign household, no attempt was ever made to limit the treasurer's overall authority. It cannot have been easy to maintain even a semblance of order among the liveried retainers, henchmen and menial servants who made up the great household: as at court, the steward gradually began to assume responsibility for disciplinary affairs, while his colleague, the controller, supervised the smooth running of each department. The third Duke of Buckingham's controllers were very influential men, although their fifteenth-century predecessors remain anonymous.

Individual accounts were kept for the four main household offices of kitchen, pantry, cellar and chamber. It was the treasurer's task to prepare a composite statement of expenditure on all these departments. Current practice required that all payments in kind made from the estates and all sums of money sent directly to any creditors by the local receivers should be set down in precise figures as his personal charge. He was then obliged to show exactly how this sum had been allocated: his claims to have delivered specific provisions to a particular department could then be checked against the detailed inventory of household goods which was always endorsed on these returns, while any cash or goods not accounted for were automatically carried over as arrears.

[12] D.641/1/2/6 m. 9 (the receiver general's account for the year ending Michaelmas 1401).

[13] D.641/1/2/7–9 (the receiver general's accounts for the years ending Michaelmas 1407, 1409 and 1410) and 12 (his account for the year ending Michaelmas 1431, which shows that Richard Donham, the Dowager's treasurer, had by then assumed control of household finances).

He was also expected to produce a full list of the tradesmen and merchants who were still awaiting payment. No examples of the day books from which most of this information was derived are available before 1465, but it is nevertheless clear that the treasurer's final account was an attempt to provide a comprehensive analysis of material from a variety of different sources.

Financial skill and administrative ability were evidently the sole requirements of a good treasurer. The long and distinguished career of William Wistowe, for instance, an obscure clerk who rose to occupy this office for over twenty years, certainly owed nothing to wealth, rank or influence. Having proved himself in the demanding post of clerk to Buckingham's ʰoreign household, he was promoted to the treasurership before 1441, and the Duke with characteristic foresight increased his salary soon afterwards. Wistowe's last years were spent as steward to Sir Henry Stafford and the Countess of Richmond, an appointment probably made on the recommendation of Sir Henry's mother, the Dowager Duchess Anne.[14] Many other senior personnel held office for long periods, having first gained valuable experience in subordinate posts. By agreeing to serve the sons or widow of their first employer they helped to maintain continuity where it was most needed – at the very centre of the administrative system.

Yet the household was not a self-contained unit kept separate from the estates. Receivers, auditors and stewards, together with members of the domestic staff, made decisions affecting all types of business. Whatever its drawbacks, a peripatetic establishment was at least able to preserve strong local ties by moving from one lordship to another. This process was encouraged by Duke Humphrey's shrewd choice of men like the Hexstall brothers, whose family connexions could be used to advantage. Three of the brothers settled in the Dover area, having moved south from Staffordshire before 1438. It was then that William Hexstall became receiver of Kent and Surrey, continuing to collect Buckingham's rents and support his retinue at Tonbridge for the next twenty years. The household travelled through Kent at frequent

---

14 See Appendix B for details of Wistowe's various appointments. He died in *ca.* Feb. 1470, at which time he was in charge of Sir Henry Stafford's domestic establishment (W.A.M. 12187; an account for Sir Henry's household for the period 13 Aug. 1469 to 7 June 1470).

intervals, and brought Hexstall in close contact with his brother, Henry, who assumed the joint posts of chamberlain, larderer and general purveyor in or before 1445. Thomas Hexstall, the third brother, began his professional career with a clerkship in the foreign household, but was subsequently made receiver of the Duke's revenues as Constable of Dover.[15] His influence in the town grew accordingly: indeed, he eventually became mayor and was several times returned as a local man by the burgesses to parliament.[16] Although Buckingham must have foreseen the dangers of placing too much authority in the hands of one family, he was even more anxious to strengthen his hand in an area where he could rely on few local sympathies. The Hexstalls were ambitious, for they and others like them had discovered that the best opportunities for advancement lay in the service of a great magnate. This is why they joined the Duke; and it is perhaps a mark of the latter's ability to satisfy the ambitions of his employees that so many professional administrators wore his livery for life and were succeeded in office by their own sons or brothers. K. B. McFarlane has already drawn attention to 'the marked heredi-tary character' of the private bureaucracies built up by great landowners such as the Staffords and the Beauchamp Earls of Warwick, and has also shown how common it was for genera-tions of the same family to administer an estate despite changes in ownership.[17] Other followers were drawn by more superficial attractions; for them the household sought to advertise in unmis-takable terms the wealth, power and influence of the Staffords. Financial profit and efficiency were never ends in themselves; they merely helped to provide a setting against which Duke Humphrey could act out his rôle as a good lord and patron.

Although the first Duke of Buckingham's affinity is compara-tively well documented, it is impossible to discover exactly how

15 The Hexstalls' various offices are listed in Appendix B. Thomas Hexstall was respon-sible for Buckingham's finances as Constable of Dover and Warden of the Cinque Ports from at least 14 Sep. 1454 to 14 June 1460 (D.641/1/2/22 m. 9-2/238).

16 *History of Parliament. Biographies of the Members of the Commons House, 1439-1509*, ed. J. C. Wedgwood (H.M.S.O., 1936), p. 449; see U. Lambert, *Bletchingley* (2 vols., London, 1921), vol. I chapter VIII, *passim*, for a more detailed if occasion-ally inaccurate history of the Hexstall family.

17 *The Nobility of Later Medieval England*, pp. 140-1.

many supporters he could call upon at any given time. The recruitment of all but domestic servants by indenture was made illegal in 1390; men were still retained in this way, but a growing number accepted sinecures or loosely-worded annuities in order to remain within the law. In practice it made no real difference how a money fee was awarded; nor did the recipient necessarily feel any obligation to honour his side of the bargain. Indeed, personal ties were usually the most effective guarantee of personal loyalty.

Two valors for the years ending Michaelmas 1442 and 1448 contain comprehensive lists of all the annuities charged upon Duke Humphrey's landed income. They can be used in conjunction with the surviving estate accounts and *The Redd Booke of Caures Castell* to make an almost complete survey of his retinue during the 1440s.[18] Its cost was surprisingly modest. In 1442, for example, he spent no more than £565.14s.0d. on fees, including his wife's allowance of £100. Three annuities totalling £40 had still to be paid, but even then less than one seventh (and excluding awards made to members of his family less than one ninth) of his *net* income was accounted for.[19] The eighty-three annuitants who were not his close relatives fall into three main groups: knights; esquires; and a cross-section of lawyers, yeomen and domestic staff. At least five (and probably seven) of the eight knights listed in 1442 were bound by formal indentures; each had contracted to serve the Duke for life, in peace as in war, and provide him with specific numbers of men as required.[20] Their promises of loyalty were in fact little more than empty formulae. Even the yeomen farmers of Staffordshire were prepared to risk the Duke's displeasure by accepting other liveries;[21] while knights and esquires, who had so much more to offer, commonly pledged themselves to four or five lords at once with no other thought than material gain.[22] Sixteen esquires are known to have entered into military

---

[18] A list of the men and women known to have taken fees from Duke Humphrey over this period may be found in Appendix D part I.   [19] D.641/1/2/17 m. 2v.

[20] The terms of the more important contracts entered in Buckingham's register are discussed in A. Compton Reeves, ' Some of Humphrey Stafford's Military Indentures ', *Nottingham Medieval Studies*, XVI (1972), pp. 80-7.

[21] D.641/1/2/57 m. 11 (account of the receiver of Staffordshire for the year ending Michaelmas 1451).

[22] Sir Humphrey Stafford of Grafton is a case in point: he took fees worth £71 a year from eight different lords – including Duke Humphrey, his kinsman, who paid him an annuity of 40 marks (McFarlane, *op. cit.*, pp. 108-9).

indentures; the other ten were either estate stewards, or councillors, or gentlemen of local standing. Not all the Duke's annuitants were well-born: a surprising number of fees were used to supplement the salaries of men and women occupying relatively humble positions in the household. Thus, for instance, the third group of annuitants was more miscellaneous. It includes three ladies-in-waiting, a carpenter, six musicians, two heralds and a group of yeomen. The latter were probably expected to take up arms on Duke Humphrey's behalf, since their awards were conditional upon continuous ' good service ' – a suitably nebulous phrase which admitted a variety of interpretations. Twelve lawyers, most of whom had been retained by at least one other lord, each drew a standard payment of £2 a year in return for their counsel. Even at this late date, Duke Humphrey continued to pay the fees of two Staffordshire yeomen retained by his father in the previous century and also awarded pensions to some of his mother's old servants.

The retinue remained virtually unchanged over the next six years. The annuity list for 1447–8 records a total expenditure of £585.9s.1d. on eighty-four persons (including the Duchess and Sir John Bourchier, Buckingham's half-brother).[23] There are no signs of the rapid changes in allegiance which affected so many great affinities. Only two of the knights listed in 1442 are missing from the second valor: one, Sir Griffith Vaughan, had died, while the other, Sir Edward Grey, now Baron Ferrers of Groby, had terminated his formal association with the Staffords. Since his younger brother, Robert Grey, was retained as an esquire at 20 marks a year in 1445–6, relations between the Staffords and the Greys must have remained friendly. Four of Duke Humphrey's esquires had received knighthoods by this time, although their fees were not increased. Six left him altogether between 1442 and 1447; four of them had contracted to serve for life, but the others were not ostensibly bound by any such restrictions. Among their successors were John Constable, the son of one of Buckingham's most powerful knights, John Trevelyan, an extremely influential esquire of the body to Henry VI, and two prominent members of the ducal household. As in 1442, twenty-six esquires were

[23] Longleat Ms. 6410, m. 2v.

retained in all. The legal element of the council was also kept up to strength: five lawyers, including the Duke's attorney at the Exchequer, disappeared from the payroll and were replaced by six others, all of whom possessed the highest qualifications. Many councillors were appointed on a short-term basis and there is no reason to question Buckingham's standing with members of the legal fraternity because of these changes. There are also some new names among the personal attendants, servants and yeomen, but on the whole the general picture is one of permanence and stability.

These two valors do not provide a definitive list of the first Duke's retainers during the 1440s. At least eleven additional fees granted out in the previous decade or between 1442 and 1447 are recorded elsewhere. Two of the recipients were esquires with size-able estates along the Welsh March; there were also four lawyers, whose advice was presumably required for one or two specific cases. It is also possible that Buckingham paid some of his fol-lowers with money advanced to him by the Crown. Other noble-men certainly obtained financial support of this kind. For example, Richard Beauchamp, Earl of Warwick, spent only a small part of his own income on retaining, because most of the men who accompanied him abroad were on royal pay. Buckingham was Constable of Calais for just over eight years and had ample oppor-tunity to garrison the town with Stafford retainers, yet there is no evidence to suggest that he did so.[24] Nor were his wages paid regularly enough to leave a cash surplus for expenditure at home. On becoming Constable of Dover he granted £10 a year to William Fiennes, Lord Saye and Sele, who undertook to answer the Duke's summons with his own 'competent fellowship'. Fiennes' capture and prohibitive ransom by the French in 1453 probably brought this arrangement to an end, and it proved too costly to replace him.[25]

Since from 1450 onwards the ducal affinity was summoned with increasing regularity and often formed part of the royal bodyguard, one might expect the Duke to have retained more

24 Only one of the 120 soldiers on the muster roll for Duke Humphrey's visit to Calais in 1447 – Richard Culpepper – appears to have had any connexion with the Staffords: he had been retained at £5 a year in 1440 (E.101/54/8; D.641/1/2/233A m. 11).

25 N.L.W. Peniarth Ms. 280 fo. 49; G.E.C., vol. II p. 482 note e.

men for military purposes. The account rolls, however, present a rather different picture. The eight annuities charged upon Buckingham's Warwickshire manors in 1443 had been almost halved by 1457, and the receiver of Staffordshire recorded a steady reduction in fees, which fell from nineteen to fourteen over the years 1445 to 1458. Only one new retainer was paid from the South Western estates throughout this period.[26] The information obtained from these fragmented sources is totally inadequate for purposes of statistical analysis, but we do know that at least twenty-six new fees were distributed after 1448, together with an allowance of £40 a year settled by Duke Humphrey upon his eldest son.[27] Three knights and four esquires indented to assist the Staffords with their own men, while Buckingham's physician, six councillors, a lady-in-waiting and the keeper of Calais Castle were also retained by written contracts. None of the latter can have provided any military support, although the eight other gentlemen and yeomen whose letters patent have survived were no doubt expected to do so. These figures probably represent only a proportion of the total number of annuities paid out by Buckingham during the 1450s, but there is still no reason to suppose that he began to retain men on the scale of the Percy Earls of Northumberland. By 1461 the third Earl's expenditure on fees and regular wages accounted for between one third and one half of his gross landed income and was the greatest single charge upon it. The salary of £2,500 a year paid to him as Warden of the East March helped to offset part of this heavy burden and it may be argued that such a large following was essential for keeping the peace along the border: yet the Earl seems to have been far more anxious to recruit in the South, setting aside almost all the revenues from his Sussex estates for this purpose.[28] After 1455, the worsening political climate encouraged many landowners to make preparations for their own defence, but few, including the great Duke of Buckingham, felt it necessary to

---

[26] D.641/1/2/56 mm. 10–10v, 62 mm. 11–11v (the receiver of Staffordshire's accounts for the years ending Michaelmas 1446 and 1458); 173 m. 8v, 180 m. 1 (the receiver of Gloucester, Hampshire and Wiltshire's accounts for the years ending Michaelmas 1447 and 1459); 270, *passim*, and S.C.6/1040/15 (accounts of the Duke's Warwickshire bailiffs for the years ending Michaelmas 1444 and 1457).

[27] See Appendix D part I (c).

[28] J. M. W. Bean, *The Estates of the Percy Family* (Oxford, 1958), pp. 93–6, 106.

spend so much on retaining. Perhaps experience had by then taught Duke Humphrey that the indiscriminate granting out of annuities was simply not worthwhile.

It has been suggested earlier that one of Duke Humphrey's reasons for taking up arms in 1459 may well have been the need to provide for his more ambitious supporters. His financial difficulties during the late 1450s were not serious enough to cause defections from his retinue, although expenditure on the household alone was beginning to pose a very real problem. Even he could not rely on the loyalty of men who looked to him for the regular payment of their fees and the prospect of other rich rewards. Buckingham was nonetheless always sure of support at a local level. Most of his yeoman farmers, tenants and estate staff wore the Stafford livery because of long-established personal connexions and a tradition of service handed down from one generation to another. The same methods of recruitment obtained in peace as in war, although there was naturally a more pronounced sense of urgency during periods of unrest. Each receiver dispatched messengers to the knights, esquires and yeomen whose services were needed, warning them to prepare for more specific instructions. The order to stand by in defensible array seems, for instance, to have been issued throughout the estates at the time of Cade's rebellion. Inspired no doubt by a fear of the mob, John Heton purchased 103 lb of gunpowder to defend Maxstoke Castle, while the receiver of Brecon spent the summer ' a bidyng for ye sauf garde of ye Castell, be me Lorde's comaundement '.[29] According to *Bale's Chronicle*, the Duke and Lord Rivers entered London on 12 June 1450 ' with greet power of people in lyveries with veends and arraied for war '.[30] Unfortunately, nothing is known of the preparations which were made at Tonbridge Castle, although a force of yeomen had travelled south from Staffordshire by the end of May.[31] In the following September Buckingham joined the court at Kenilworth with another ' greet feles-

---

29 D.641/1/2/20 m. 1; 21 m. 7.
30 *Six Town Chronicles*, p. 129.
31 Humphrey Cotes claimed expenses of £17.10s.0d. incurred by 74 retainers, whom he had led from Stafford to London in May and June 1450 (D.641/1/2/20 m. 3). The cost of stabling and providing for Buckingham's men at Tonbridge over the year ending Michaelmas 1455 exceeded £130, above a payment of £30 made to the men who had fought at St Albans (D.641/1/2/22 m. 7v).

ship', no doubt recruited from his estates, and remained in attendance upon King Henry for a year. He then provided 'a grete and notable noumbre of personnes' to escort the King on his journey into Kent, probably for the session of *oyer* and *terminer* held at Tonbridge at the end of June 1451 upon Richard Lennard, one of the self-confessed murderers of William de la Pole, Duke of Suffolk. The Duke had previously been named as a commissioner to examine Lennard and his accomplice, Thomas Smith, although his presence with Henry VI at Tonbridge was as much an exercise in royal propaganda as an attempt to bring the murderers to justice.[32]

In the absence of a national peace-keeping force, the great landowners were often called upon to deal with local outbreaks of violence and organised crime. As a justice of *oyer* and *terminer* during the Lombard riots of 1456, for example, Duke Humphrey found it necessary to use his own men to restore order in the City of London.[33] But the speed and efficiency with which he executed an earlier commission to arrest Sir Thomas Malory in 1451 betray a rather less impartial sense of justice. Sir Thomas had already tried to murder him, and the Duke was out for revenge.[34] The armed tenants and retainers who enforced the law on these occasions were summoned on an entirely *ad hoc* basis, meeting Duke Humphrey or his representatives at a convenient place and returning home as soon as their orders had been fulfilled. They were also expected to stage an impressive reception whenever members of Buckingham's family arrived in the area, although the promise of lavish hospitality and perhaps even a personal interview with the Duke himself clearly made such an effort worthwhile. These tours of inspection provided the opportunity for public displays of the Staffords' wealth and power; they confirmed Buckingham's standing in the eyes of his followers and strengthened the corporate spirit of his affinity.

---

[32] R. Virgoe, 'The Death of William de la Pole, Duke of Suffolk', *B.J.R.L.*, XLVII (1965), pp. 501–2; *C.R.P.*, 1446–52, p. 475; E.404/68/77 (the Duke received £400 in expenses).

[33] R. Flenley, 'London and Foreign Merchants in the Reign of Henry VI', *E.H.R.*, XXV (1910), pp. 650–2.

[34] A. C. Baugh's article 'Documenting Sir Thomas Malory', *Speculum*, VIII (1933), contains a full account of Malory's feud with the Duke of Buckingham, while P. J. C. Field, 'Sir Thomas Malory, M.P.', *B.I.H.R.*, XLVII (1974), sets out to correct some earlier misconceptions about Malory's career.

Some of the Duke's friends and well-wishers were bound to him by ties less tangible than the receipt of a money fee. Success in most aspects of later medieval life depended largely upon the ' good lordship ' or assistance of a social superior, whose support was regarded as a commodity to be bought or sold according to the current market price. Patronage might take the form of gifts, offices, or help in some private dispute; other less concrete rewards lay in the status which such a relationship bestowed upon the client. The lord who failed to uphold this system soon lost his followers to more powerful rivals, since it was easy to attract even the most influential men by exploiting their ambitions. The Staffords seldom intervened directly in their retainers' affairs, but when they did so it was with telling effect. Sir William Mountfort of Coleshill in Arden, the wealthiest knight in Warwickshire, spent his early years with Richard, Earl of Warwick, but on the latter's death in 1438 he grew closer to the Staffords. He had married twice: first Margaret Pecche, by whom he had five sons, and secondly Joan de Aldewiche, who persuaded him to disinherit his other children in favour of their own son, Sir Edmund. In order to release the manors which were already settled upon Sir Baldwin, his eldest son and heir, he made Buckingham one of his feoffees, ' so that when Sir Baldwin made his claim thereunto, the Duke through his greatness so terrified him with threats, that he forced him solemnly to disclaim the former intail [and] . . . to procure . . . his brothers of the whole blood, under their hands and seals to do the like '.[35] As prisoners in two of Duke Humphrey's strongest castles, Sir Baldwin and his son had no alternative but to sign away all their legal rights to the family estates, hand over any relevant documents and disclaim all knowledge of previous settlements to their advantage. Sir Edmund, who was carver to Henry VI, had formidable allies in James, Earl of Wiltshire, and the Queen, but, despite the very real danger of further retribution, Sir Baldwin brought his case before an independent tribunal after his father's death in 1452. Two of the arbitrators were related to Buckingham, and both seem to have

---

[35] Dugdale, *Warwickshire*, vol. 11 pp. 1009–12. The author refers only to Sir William's manors of Ilmingdon, Coleshill and Ramenham, although other property at Kingshurst, Kingsford and Ullenhall was also at stake (*C.C.R.*, 1454–61, p. 364; *op. cit.*, 1468–70, no. 1326).

used their influence to secure an unfavourable award.[36] Sir Baldwin recovered one manor, but the rest of his inheritance remained with his half-brother, who settled it upon three of the Duke's most trusted advisers.[37] Sir Edmund was an extremely powerful man with many friends at court and a substantial local following, and Buckingham was clearly as eager to enlist his support as Edmund and his followers were to find an effective patron. It is hardly surprising to discover that Sir Baldwin joined the Duke of York during the 1450s; following his half-brother's example, he named the Earls of March, Pembroke and Warwick as his feoffees. They in turn proved to be good lords, for on Buckingham's death all the Mountfort estates were restored to him.[38] Sir Edmund went into exile, but returned before 1475 to join the second Duke's household. He died an affluent country gentleman, having spent his last years as chamberlain and estate steward to the Dowager Duchess Katherine.[39] Sir Baldwin's son, Simon, likewise refused to follow the dictates of political opportunism, and took part in Perkin Warbeck's conspiracy against Henry VII: among his judges was Edward, third Duke of Buckingham.[40]

It was in the interests of both parties that Duke Humphrey's servants and retainers should have their own careers and connexions. Robert Whitgreve, a lawyer who was returned as member of parliament for Stafford on twenty-four separate occasions, still continued to serve the Duke in various positions of great trust for over twenty years, and was rewarded with the first (and for want of evidence only) grant of arms ever made by him to an employee.[41] As a teller of the Exchequer he was certainly well placed to watch over Buckingham's financial affairs, and could, of course, supervise the presentation of his appeals or petitions to

---

[36] The opposition to Sir Baldwin was indeed great, as can be seen from a series of MSS. relating to the manor of Ramenham, which reverted to Joan Mountfort on her husband's death. Among her feoffees were Henry VI, Duke Humphrey, the Duke of Somerset and the Earl of Wiltshire (W.A.M. 4532, 4538, 4542, 4555).

[37] *C.C.R.*, 1454–61, pp. 185, 364–5; Dugdale, *Warwickshire*, vol. II p. 1009; Sir Baldwin was also forced to deny that he had ever settled any property upon either the Earl of Warwick (*C.C.R.*, 1454–61, p. 185), or his son, Simon, with remainders to the Earls of March, Pembroke and Warwick (*ibid.*, p. 36; see also *C.C.R.*, 1468–76, no. 1326).

[38] Dugdale, *Warwickshire*, vol. II pp. 1010–11; *C.P.R.*, 1461–7, p. 75.

[39] See Appendix B.

[40] *Rot. Parl.*, vol. VI pp. 492, 503.

[41] D.1721/1/1 fo. 391v (a later copy of this grant).

Parliament. Whitgreve was a professional administrator of the highest calibre, whose impressive parliamentary record owed little, if anything, to his association with the Duke. He and many others like him enjoyed a personal prestige which makes it extremely difficult to measure the effects or extent of Buckingham's political patronage with any degree of certainty. Over the years 1400 to 1521 at least ninety-three of the Staffords' annuitants and senior personnel sat in the Commons, although there is no evidence of any attempt to build up a faction there. On the contrary, some of these men placed their loyalty to the Dukes of Buckingham well below their other affiliations; Sir Thomas Burgh, for instance, was a crown servant, while William Burley, his neighbour on the March, who took the fees of a number of great landowners, supported the Duke of York. Both men were experienced politicians and could choose their own lords on their own terms. It would be absurd to suppose that Nicholas Ashton, a justice of the Common Pleas and a parliamentary figure of some standing, was elected on Duke Humphrey's orders simply because he occupied one of his stewardships: a lawyer in his position could usually expect to make a large collection of such offices.[42]

Even in Staffordshire, where the first Duke's influence was strongest, the local gentry seem to have been free from all but the subtlest forms of outside intervention.[43] This was partly a matter of tact and diplomacy on Buckingham's part: although some members may well have been put forward at his request, he was careful not to offend local sensibilities by insisting upon the return of outsiders. Thus, once William Hexstall had gone to live in Kent, he ceased to represent the borough of Stafford and became the member for Bletchingley.[44] Certain local families, such as the Astons, Erdswycks and Vernons, who had already come to dominate Staffordshire during Duke Humphrey's minority, simply donned the Stafford livery and continued as before to serve as shire knights. Successive generations of Whit-

---

[42] The posts held by these men are listed in Appendix B.

[43] J. C. Wedgwood, *A Parliamentary History of Stafford* (2 vols., for the William Salt Genealogical Society, 1917–18), vol. I, intro. p. xlvi; see K. B. McFarlane, 'Parliament and Bastard Feudalism', *T.R.H.S.*, 4th series XXVI (1944), for some examples of the Duke of Norfolk's difficulties in this respect.

[44] Wedgwood, *A Parliamentary History of Stafford*, vol. I p. 208.

greves, Harper and Barber were also known and respected by the inhabitants of Stafford. In 1453, when the King was beginning to reassert his authority over the Commons, William Barber and his son John were both returned for the borough: it is quite likely that Buckingham used his influence in favour of these two loyal household officers, but their election was nonetheless certain. In sessions when his own business as Constable of Calais or Dover came before parliament, Duke Humphrey must have been reassured by the presence of his two councillors, Robert Whitgreve and William Cumberford, among the Commons, but the burgesses of Stafford were no less anxious that their interests should be represented by these very capable men. The evidence in favour of political management is therefore purely circumstantial; far from imposing their own wishes upon an unwilling electorate, Duke Humphrey and his descendants were generally happy to accept whoever might be returned. Had this not been so, each minority would have seen a dramatic change in the choice of members, for no matter how skilfully a steward or receiver might deploy the patronage at his disposal, he lacked both the authority and incentive for successful management. As it was, the same names continued to dominate the political scene.[45]

Certain seats were nevertheless regarded as personal property in Buckingham's gift. The electors of Bletchingley in particular were often obliged to accept placemen with few local connexions. Thomas Hexstall, for example, was still young and inexperienced when he first entered the Commons in 1447, although his brother, William, the next member for Bletchingley, was already well known there. Duke Humphrey wanted to assist these two promising employees and thereby bestowed upon them a mark of favour worth far more than the most generous annuity. John Andrews, who represented the borough in 1449, had by then spent the best part of his life as attorney general to the Staffords and his election was perhaps a reward for many past services.[46] On the whole, parliamentary patronage tended to benefit the client rather than his good lord.

The same is true of presentations to livings or religious offices.

[45] *Ibid.*, pp. 257–65.
[46] For details of Andrews' career see Appendix C part I.

In principle, the award of a benefice to some enterprising clergy-man differed little from any other type of retainer. The Lords Grey of Ruthin used their twenty advowsons to advance the careers of younger sons, reward senior estate staff, and provide for the relatives of trustworthy local employees.[47] Despite the number of benefices at his disposal, the first Duke of Bucking-ham adopted a far less utilitarian approach, probably because his half-brother, Thomas Bourchier, who became Archbishop of Canterbury in 1454, was better able to provide for any needy relatives. According to his inquisition *post mortem* of 1460, Duke Humphrey possessed twenty-two advowsons, six of which allowed him to appoint the heads of religious houses. His register lists presentations to a further twenty-two churches, two chapels, two priories and a chantry over the years 1435 to 1455 alone. Margaret Audley's inheritance brought the Staffords twenty-five new bene-fices and other foundations, including eight abbeys and churches not named in either of these two documents; the de Bohun parti-tion of 1421 also refers to an unspecified number of ' avouesons & autres choses '. It seems likely, therefore, that Buckingham laid claim to *at least* fifty-seven major livings; he also employed several clerics as chaplains and confessors.[48] Thirty-nine awards of bene-fices and five licences allowing convents to elect their own superiors are recorded in *The Redd Booke of Caures Castell*. Only four of the recipients appear to have had any close connexions with the Duke. His physician was made parson of Southill in 1452, while Henry Hexstall occupied a rich living at Chipstead until his ordination as vicar of Bletchingley – a town which had already returned two of his brothers to Parliament. John Woder-ton had preceded Hexstall at Chipstead before taking up a bene-fice worth 40 marks a year at Tilbrook in 1441. One of the few clergymen to hold a senior administrative post at this time, Woderton was receiver of Caus for thirteen years and acquired a second, more local living at Worthen in 1453. The papal dispen-sation which made this possible refers to him as Duke Hum-phrey's chaplain and points to an unmistakable case of good

[47] R. I. Jack, ' The Ecclesiastical Patronage Exercised by a Baronial Family in the Later Middle Ages ', *Journal of Religious History*, III (1964/5), pp. 275–95.

[48] C.139/180/59; N.L.W. Peniarth Ms. 280, *passim*; C.47/9/23; *Rot. Parl.*, vol. IV p. 138.

83

service rewarded.[49] His kinsman, Walter Woderton, was likewise made incumbent of Cowden on the resignation of its former occupant in 1449.[50] Buckingham's private chaplains also did well for themselves. In 1454 Robert Toppyng, a friar preacher, at that time confessor to the ducal household, acquired a dispensation to hold any single benefice and was probably given one of the Duke's advowsons. His successor, Philip Water, the rector of Stackpole Elidor, certainly made the most of his appointment. With approval from Rome, Water took up a second living at Kingsbury, which gave him an average annual income of £44; eleven years later Buckingham endorsed yet another petition for his commensal chaplain to be allowed three separate prebends.[51] These examples are somewhat exceptional. By and large, Duke Humphrey seems to have adopted a policy of *laissez-faire* in his dealings as an ecclesiastical patron. His was a conventional piety. Although his bequests to the family foundations at Pleshey and Maxstoke were more than generous, he is known to have made only two modest grants of land and money to the Church during his lifetime.[52] There is certainly nothing to suggest that he shared his mother's interest in the affairs of neighbouring religious houses. The Dowager Countess of Stafford had given many costly vestments and pieces of plate to her great friend and confidant, John Wynch, the Prior of Llanthony, and was also a notable benefactress to the College of Pleshey, which her father had founded in 1393.[53]

As one of the richest and most powerful men in England, Duke Humphrey commanded immense reserves of patronage. It was unnecessary for him to spend heavily on retaining while so many of his estate and household staff were themselves good lords to scores of tenants and retainers. Certain offices, particularly stewardships, were used to attract the best lawyers and most influential country gentlemen, while he was also in a position to

---

[49] N.L.W. Peniarth Ms. 280 fos. 15, 19, 20, 52, 56; *Cal. Papal Regs.*, vol. X p. 151.

[50] N.L.W. Peniarth Ms. 280 fo. 47.

[51] *Cal. Papal Regs.*, vol. X pp. 15, 148, vol. XI p. 539.

[52] P.C.C. Stockton 21; *C.P.R.*, 1446–52, pp. 180, 557.

[53] C.115/A3/K2/6682 (the Register of John Wynch, Prior of Llanthony by Gloucester, 1408–1436), *passim*; *C.P.R.*, 1452–61, p. 153; *A Collection of All the Wills now known to be Extant of the Kings and Queens of England from William I to Henry VII*, ed. J. Nichols (Society of Antiquaries, London, 1780), pp. 278–81.

advance the careers of the young administrators who entered his service without wealth or connexions. Except in times of war, Buckingham had little need to display his military power: the name of Stafford was generally enough to achieve what he wanted, and for this reason the full extent of his influence as a lord and patron must remain incompletely defined.

Chapter 5

CHANGES IN THE DUCAL LIFESTYLE,

1460–1521

The modifications of administrative procedure which took place during the third Duke of Buckingham's lifetime were not confined to his estates. As we have already seen, the transition towards a more sedentary household provided a great impetus for reform, and also brought about a number of striking changes in the size and composition of the Stafford retinue.[1] Duke Edward, his servants and modest following established themselves at Thornbury; they spent long periods in London and the surrounding manors, but never travelled north and because of local hostility did not dare to visit Wales. The rebuilding of Thornbury Castle – the major undertaking of Duke Edward's later years – was seriously begun in 1511 and still remained unfinished when he was beheaded. His plans, however, were near enough completion to confirm all Henry VIII's worst suspicions, and it is easy to see how these fears were generated. Most of the Staffords' larger manors and all their castles contained ' service lodgings ', but when completed those at Thornbury would in size have surpassed them all.[2] Three courts intended to house retainers were partly built by 1518; they stood apart from the other servants' quarters so that armed men could be mustered quickly in emergencies. Two large turreted gate houses, emblazoned with the family arms, crests and mottoes, also served as a tangible manifestation of the Duke's unrivalled position in the South West. The defences were to have been strengthened by a deep moat, gunports and a massive portcullis, while the armoury was already stocked with three pieces of ordnance. Yet, although the new manor assumed a forbidding aspect with ' gates and toures in it Castelle

[1] See pp. 54–5.
[2] M. Wood, *The English Mediaeval House* (London, 1965), pp. 235–41. I must also thank Mr A. K. Hawkyard for providing me with additional information about Duke Edward's building works.

lyke ',[3] there can be no doubt that Buckingham's first concern
was to build himself a magnificent retreat where he could live in
style and comfort. His preference for a more settled way of life
combined with a strict sense of economy led him to neglect all
but a few of the other residences which he had inherited. The
manor of Bletchingley was greatly enlarged to provide a stopping-
place for the household on its visits to London, so that in 1521 it
appeared 'newly and properly built with many good lodgings
and houses of offices '.[4] The manors of Penshurst in Kent and
Red Rose in London were also kept in good repair, but little, if
anything, was spent elsewhere. Thornbury's administrative, geographical and aesthetic qualities had seized the Duke's imagina-
tion, and for many years he was preoccupied with this grandiose
architectural venture at the expense of less exciting projects.

Duke Edward was not the first of his line to abandon the
peripatetic existence led by most of the fifteenth-century nobility.
Even after her second marriage to Walter Blount, Lord Mountjoy,
the Dowager Duchess Anne remained firmly attached to her
favourite houses at Writtle and Kimbolton, while Edward IV's
gift of the life tenancy of ' an Inne called Hungerforde's place '
proved useful on her annual visits to London.[5] Her retinue was
predictably both small and functional. In 1466, for example, her
annual domestic wage bill came to no more than £66 although
this figure does not include payments to grooms, ladies or clerical
staff. Seven years later the receiver general anticipated an overall
expenditure of £133 on salaries, which suggests an establishment
of about sixty persons.[6] It is unlikely that Duke Henry would

[3] Leland, *op. cit.*, vol. V p. 100. Historians disagree over Thornbury's capacity to
withstand a state of siege. W. Douglas Simpson describes it as ' the final manifestation of the fortified house of the over-mighty subject, designed to accommodate his
array of armed retainers ', although his estimate of Buckingham's military strength
is based upon a misreading of very limited evidence ('Bastard Feudalism and the
Later Castles ', *Antiquaries Journal*, XXVI (1946), pp. 163–70). K. B. McFarlane,
on the other hand, believed Thornbury to be nothing more than a magnificent
showplace without adequate defences (*The Nobility of Later Medieval England*,
p. 209). But this would only have been the case during full-scale warfare, as parts
of the building were certainly strong enough to resist minor assaults.

[4] E.36/150 fo. 16; D.641/1/3/6 m. 2 (the secretary's account for the period 28 Mar.
1499 to 12 Mar. 1507); E.36/220 fo. 3v (the cofferer's account for the period 30 Sept.
1520 to 30 Apr. 1521).

[5] *C.P.R.*, 1461–67, p. 196; *Rot. Parl.*, vol. V p. 523.

[6] Add. Mss. 34213 fos. 20, 58v, 125 (a day book for the Dowager's household for the
period 1 Apr. 1465 to 31 Mar. 1466) and 29608 m. 2.

have been content with such a small household, yet his frequent journeys between London and Brecon were made with an unimpressive enough company. Considering the lawless state of the Marches at this time, the escort of sixty-six liveried retainers which accompanied him in 1476 does not seem excessive.[7] The size and cost of his household remain a matter of conjecture: the number of staff engaged as domestic servants during the spring and summer of 1483 must have increased dramatically, as must the expense of providing food and wages for the motley crowd of opportunists attracted by his rising fortunes. On the other hand, there is no reason to suppose that the second Duke of Buckingham was any less able to maintain a balanced budget than his son, about whom so much more is known.

Duke Edward's love of ostentatious display was in no way incompatible with the desire for economy and efficiency characteristic of all his financial dealings. His immediate entourage was larger and costlier than the first Duke's, but it consumed a far smaller proportion of his landed income and was probably better managed. An ' approved and renewed ' household roll, compiled at some point between 1511 and 1514, records that Buckingham and his family required a staff of 225, at an annual cost of £650 in fees and wages.[8] These men and women made up the great household; eighty-six of them were assigned to the Duchess Eleanor and 130 to the Duke, who usually chose rather less than half this number to ride with him on long journeys. Not everyone was in attendance at the same time. According to two treasurer's accounts for the year ending 31 March 1504, only 130 people were then receiving board wages. Continuous arrivals and departures are also noted among the gentlemen, yeomen and pages who attended Duke Edward at Thornbury during the winter of 1508/9, although there were rarely more than 150 servants in residence at once.[9] Shortly before his death in 1521 Buckingham is known to have kept a permanent following of

---

[7] D.641/1/2/26 m. 4.

[8] E.101/518/5, pt i (this Ms. is undated, but internal evidence shows it to have been compiled between 1511 and 1514).

[9] D.641/1/3/8 m. 3; Add. Roll 40859B (respectively the treasurer's full and declared accounts for the year ending 31 Mar. 1504); D.1721/1/5, *passim* (a household book for the period 5 Nov. 1508 to 22 Mar. 1509. Extracts from this Ms. have been published by J. Gage in *Archaeologia*, XXV (1834), pp. 330–9).

148,[10] so it seems reasonable to regard the ' approved and renewed ' household roll as a memorandum drawn up to show the
maximum rather than the customary size of his household. This
is borne out by two wardrobers' accounts for the years ending
31 March 1516 and 1517, which record the purchase of cloth for
eighty-three and eighty-seven liveries respectively to be worn by
domestic employees.[11] Not all of Buckingham's servants wore his
colours, but these figures do not convey the impression of a large
or a wasteful establishment.

The redirection of surplus revenues from the receiverships to an
administrative centre at Thornbury had a far-reaching effect upon
the reorganisation of Buckingham's household. As officer in
charge of the receipt and distribution of these clear profits, the
cofferer enjoyed a particularly important position with great
responsibilities. Yet William Cholmeley, who occupied the post
for at least eighteen years, appears to have come from the yeoman
class and was certainly appointed on personal merit alone. Unlike
the receiver general or the senior auditors, Cholmeley did not
travel about the estates. Large sums of money were collected and
reallocated in his name by agents, while he remained under the
Duke's surveillance at Thornbury. His annual accounts were
checked with painstaking thoroughness: one for the months
January to September 1508 bears Duke Edward's signature at the
top and bottom of every page to show that the cash totals had
been examined by him for errors or signs of dishonesty.[12] Such a
procedure was not, as in some households, an empty formality,
since Buckingham was known personally to sanction or disallow
items of expenditure in this way. The crown auditor appointed
to go through certain household accounts for the period 1500–
1503 found, for instance, that Duke Edward had ' figured every
lef and every side of lef ' of one day-book in an attempt to discover
if his secretary was guilty of embezzlement.[13] Almost all of
Cholmeley's disbursements were made directly from the estates

10 Longleat Ms. 457 (a check list of household personnel compiled after the marriage
of Henry, Lord Stafford, in 1519).

11 E.101/631/20 m. 18v; D.641/1/3/9 m. 31v (the first of these Mss. is incomplete).

12 S.P.1/22 fos. 61–84, *passim*.

13 E.101/529/2(2) (a fragment of the unnamed auditor's report to the Star Chamber,
after 1509; I am grateful to Miss M. Condon for drawing my attention to this Ms.).

to the wardrober and the treasurer, while sums raised on credit, together with other extraordinary revenues, were managed separately by Robert Gilbert, the chancellor and keeper of the privy purse. A distinguished Oxford scholar and former lecturer in sophistry who could turn his hand to any type of business, he supervised the complex negotiations and legal technicalities involved in large-scale borrowing. A fragment of his account for the months July to October 1519 shows that he had successfully raised over £2,344 within a matter of weeks. Some of this money went straight into Buckingham's private ' casket ', but most of it was assigned to the cofferer for household expenses.[14] Although it is possible to speak in very general terms of two financial departments within the great household, neither was rigidly defined. This was partly because of Gilbert's wide-ranging administrative responsibilities, which gave him a freedom of action not enjoyed by his other senior colleagues. The previous chancellor, Sir Richard Sackville, had pursued an independent career in the service of the Crown and was prevented by a variety of official commitments from exploiting his position to the full. His ambitious successor permitted no such distractions, and within a few years of assuming the chancellorship in 1500 had made himself the Duke's most trusted agent and confidant, standing surety for his debts and bringing legal actions on his behalf. Delicate matters which required tactful handling were invariably entrusted to this eloquent sophist. The task of obtaining Wolsey's permission for an armed escort to accompany Duke Edward on his projected tour of the Welsh Marcher lordships was but one difficult assignment among many: others ranged from the enforcement of discipline in the household to important property transactions.[15] When necessary, Gilbert's assistant, the almoner, could be left to arrange small loans, and on at least one occasion he represented the Duke himself on a local commission of enquiry.[16]

Throughout the later middle ages the increasing complexity of estate and household management had demanded an ever growing

14 Royal Ms. 14B XXXV D fos. 1–2v.

15 Cottonian Ms. Titus B1 fos. 171–4 (a letter of instructions sent to Gilbert by the Duke, 26 Nov. 1520); for details of Gilbert's career see Appendix C, part IV.

16 *L. & P. Henry VIII*, vol. 1, pt ii, no. 3173. Details of the career of George Poley, the Duke's Almoner, may be found in Appendix C, part IV.

and more specialised staff. A number of fifteenth-century landowners, including Richard Beauchamp, Earl of Warwick, and
Sir John Fastolf, assigned their private correspondence and miscel-
laneous paperwork to secretaries; Edward IV adopted a similar
policy within the royal household and his example was soon
followed on most other great estates.[17] Unlike many of his colleagues, Thomas Lucas, the Duke of Bedford's secretary, did not
take up service with the Staffords after his employer's death, but
recommended one of his protégés, a clerk named John Russell,
for promotion. Russell's account for his eight years in office shows
exactly how varied a secretary's duties could be. He not only saw
to the drawing up of recognizances, writs and letters patent in the
Exchequer, but also purchased jewellery for the wardrobe, super-
intended building work and paid annuities.[18] He and his successors toured the estates collecting revenues, examining accounts
and acting as agents for the cofferer; they left a resident staff of
four clerks behind at Thornbury to deal with routine book-
keeping and returned for conferences with their employer at frequent intervals. By relieving his receivers particular of these and
other responsibilities the Duke no doubt hoped to exercise far
greater control over expenditure. His indignation at Russell's
persistent failure to render an acceptable account is therefore
understandable, although, as we shall see, the malicious way in
which he then hounded his former secretary was out of all proportion to the offence.[19] Being acquainted at first hand with the
driving force of self-interest, Duke Edward was not inclined to be
over-generous in his assessment of human nature. The secretary's
clandestine marriage and his attempts to provide for a needy
family confirmed Buckingham in the belief that clergymen without dependants were infinitely more trustworthy as employees.
Russell's two successors, Laurence Stubbes and Thomas Mos-
croft, had both taken orders. Stubbes was not without worldly
ambition, and left the Duke's service in 1515 to work for Thomas
Wolsey, who was then Archbishop of York; but Moscroff had

---

[17] C. D. Ross, ' The Estates and Finances of Richard Beauchamp, Earl of Warwick ',
Dugdale Occasional Papers, XII (1956), p. 14; K. B. McFarlane, *The Nobility of
Later Medieval England*, p. 44.

[18] D.641/1/3/6, *passim*.

[19] See pp. 166–7.

been sent to Oxford at Buckingham's expense and relied completely upon his patron's generosity.[20]

Despite these new additions to the official hierarchy, the long-established posts of treasurer, steward and controller remained virtually unchanged. If anything, the duties involved were more strictly defined by Duke Edward than they had been during the second half of the fifteenth century. The Dowager Duchess Anne, for example, had given John Heton almost unlimited authority by making him both steward of her household and receiver general. So successful was this experiment that on Heton's resignation Thomas Garth, an extremely able administrator, was allowed to combine the two posts of treasurer and receiver general.[21] The second Duke of Buckingham seems to have shared his grandmother's empirical approach, and although his less settled way of life made such a degree of centralisation impossible, the financial and administrative responsibilities vested in his steward, Sir Edmund Mountfort, were considerable.[22] As befitted their growing authority, the Staffords' treasurers and stewards during this period tended to come from a rather higher social class than their predecessors. Richard Pole, who was a wealthy landowner in his own right, acted as both receiver of Gloucestershire and steward to the Dowager Duchess Katherine, being retained in the latter post by Duke Edward at an annual fee of £30. Few of Buckingham's other senior personnel were as loyal as he: most were younger, more ambitious men, intent on furthering their own careers. This was certainly true of Sir Humphrey Bannaster, whose appointment to the treasurership followed a brief period in the less demanding post of controller. As an experienced official with a sound knowledge of conciliar and judicial business, he was sure of a place in any great household. His decision to join the Duke of Suffolk proved a wise one, which enabled him to play a leading rôle in the civic government of Calais and established his useful connexion with Henry VIII's sister, the Duchess. Since he could no longer hope for sustained periods of administrative continuity, Buckingham set out to exploit the diverse talents of his ministers while they remained

[20] See Appendix C, part IV for details of their careers.
[21] See Appendix B.   [22] D.641/1/2/26 mm. 5–7.

with him. Sir Robert Turberville, a lawyer with many years' service in local government to his credit, was a typical product of this utilitarian system. His rapid translation from the treasurership to the stewardship of the household and thence to the post of receiver general over the years 1502 to 1503 may well have been necessitated by staffing problems similar to those already observed on the estates.[23]

Although it was fairly common for noblemen to store surplus revenues as well as plate, jewellery and clothing in their wardrobes, the Staffords never made full use of this particular department. Until about 1500 the receivers general and particular financed and accounted for most of the keeper's purchases; after this date the money for clothing the entire household came from both the coffers and the privy purse. Duke Edward delighted in his reputation as ' Ung Paris ou ung Hector de Troye sur son cheval ',[24] and seized upon each public appearance as an opportunity to surpass earlier sartorial triumphs. His magnificent costume for the wedding of Prince Arthur and Katherine of Aragon in 1501 was said to have been worth £1,500; four days later he entered the lists with a brilliant display of pageantry designed to overwhelm the most casual observer.[25] Henry VIII's meeting with the Emperor Maximilian at Ardres in 1513 saw the brief fulfilment of Buckingham's hopes for English conquests abroad, and on this occasion he appeared resplendent in purple satin ' his apparell and his barde full of Antelopes and swannes of fyne gold bullion and full of spangyls and littell belles of gold meruelous costly & pleasāt to behold '.[26] Despite his protests about the cost of Henry VIII's second visit to France seven years later, the Duke was determined to outshine all the other noblemen present at the Field of the Cloth of Gold. Expenditure on the wardrobe alone rose by over £2,500 in 1520, although this figure includes the cost of equipping an escort of five chaplains and 140 men, as well as providing Duke Edward's more elaborate

[23] The careers of Pole, Bannaster and Turberville are documented in Appendix C, part IV.
[24] Robert Macquereau, *Histoire Générale De L'Europe Depuis La Naissance De Charle-Quint, Jusqu'au Cinq Juin MDXXVII* (Louvain, 1765), p. 79.
[25] *The Great Chronicle of London*, pp. 311, 313.
[26] *Edward Hall's Chronicle*, p. 544.

costume.[27] The activities of Thomas Bridges, who became keeper of the wardrobe in 1515, are very well documented and probably differed very little from those of his fifteenth-century predecessors. Like the treasurer he was answerable for a number of sub-departments, and kept a day-book in which he recorded purchases ranging from padlocks to Flemish tapestries.[28] His enrolled account for the clothing and equipment supplied to various retainers and members of the household over the year ending 31 March 1517 covers twenty yards of parchment: every item of expenditure, however small, was set down in detail and there is nothing to suggest that Buckingham's careful budgeting stopped short in matters of dress. Gifts of gold cloth and velvet were made to a few senior personnel and lawyers, but the overall picture is of a cut-back in unnecessary spending.[29]

Notwithstanding his general carefulness in money matters, Duke Edward took great pleasure in providing extremely lavish and spectacular displays of hospitality. As K. B. McFarlane has already pointed out, these accounted for no more than a very small proportion of his income, although his posthumous reputation as ' bounteous Buckingham, the mirror of all courtesy' was well deserved.[30] Minstrels and other entertainers were always welcome at Thornbury. His own group of singers and resident instru-mentalists was supplemented from time to time by performers from other great households: during the Christmas festivities of 1508, for example, at least forty-one musicians and a company of players were called upon to amuse the gathering. A Welsh harpist, an Irish poet, gypsies and royal choristers all shared Duke Edward's largesse; so did the friars, scholars and preachers whom his piety and love of learning attracted to his household.[31] Having himself received an extremely good education, he set out to pro-vide the best possible tuition for the boys who joined his establish-ment as choristers and henchmen. Standards must have been high, for in 1521 Robert Brook, ' scoler of Oxford and nowe

---

[27] J. G. Russell, *The Field of the Cloth of Gold* (London, 1969), p. 191; the ward-rober's accounts are analysed more fully on p. 135.

[28] Longleat Misc. Ms. XIII (this day book for the year ending 30 Sept. 1517 is the only one of a series known to have survived).

[29] D.641/1/3/9.

[30] *The Nobility of Later Medieval England*, pp. 208–9.

[31] D.1721/1/5 fos. 45–6; S.P.1/22 fos. 61–84, *passim*; E.36/220, *passim*.

admitted scolemaister to the said Duke's Hinxmen and Wardis ', obtained a yearly allowance so that he could continue with his own academic career.[32] The wardrober was instructed to give each child a primer and a Latin grammar, while works by authors such as Terence, Sulpicius and Isidore of Seville were used as basic texts for study. Devotional books, romances and commentaries on English law may also have been made available from the Duke's own library, which seems to have been quite large. In 1516 alone he bought at least six books for himself and seven for his son. The young Lord Stafford's reading matter was largely religious, although it also included works on architecture and French history; Buckingham evidently preferred tales of chivalry, turning to legal studies and the ever popular *de Consolatione Philosophiae* of Boethius in his more serious moments.[33] Seventy-four of the books catalogued at Stafford Castle in 1556 were published before Duke Edward's death, and most of these had probably been acquired on his orders from presses throughout Europe. They range from Ramon Lull's *Arbor Scientiae* and other practical treatises on cosmology, natural history, medicine and theology to texts by the early fathers, biblical commentaries and recent editions of the classics.[34] This catholic choice of titles is in many ways a reflection of literary tastes among the upper ranks of contemporary society, for the Duke was certainly not unique in his love of learning and was not the first of the Staffords to derive pleasure from the ownership of books.

Anne Stafford's correspondence with the Prior of Llanthony shows her to have been a serious and well-educated woman: the books bequeathed to her by her mother out of the great de Bohun collection and the evidence of literacy in the will which she herself made in 1428 both confirm this impression. The first Duke's widow was also something of a bibliophile, whose bequest of ' a boke of English of Legenda Sanctorum, a boke of ffrensh called

---

[32] E.36/220 fo. 10v.

[33] E.101/631/20, dorse, *passim*; D.641/1/3/9, dorse, *passim*. Although no books were bought for her at this time, the Duke's wife, Eleanor Percy, was apparently a woman of letters. She could at least turn her hand to poetry, and one of her verses, possibly in autograph, is inscribed in a contemporary book of hours (Arundel Ms. 318).

[34] This list is bound in the back of Lord Stafford's letter book (D.1721/1/10) and covers 13 closely written folios. A few titles are noted in the H.M.C.'s *Fourth Report* (2 parts, H.M.S.O., 1874), pt i, p. 328.

Lukan, an other boke of ffrensh of the pistell and Gaspelles and a prymmer with calpes of silver and gilt covered with purpull velvett' to Lady Margaret Beaufort suggests that the two women followed the same scholarly pursuits.[35] Between them Duke Edward and his son acquired a number of books from the presses of Wynkin de Worde, who had been Lady Margaret's printer for over fifteen years. It was he who published one of Buckingham's commissions – a translation of the popular romance *The Story of Helyas, Knight of the Swan*, made by Robert Copland from the French edition of 1504.[36] The Duke's interest in this work was not only scholarly but personal, for in common with many great European families, his de Bohun ancestors had claimed their descent from Godfrey de Bouillon, who, according to legend, was Sir Helyas' grandson. *The Story of Helyas* may indeed be regarded as yet further propaganda in Buckingham's suit for the Constableship of England, but not all his acts of patronage were so calculated.

Despite his ruthlessness in other respects, Duke Edward was always sympathetic towards the penurious clerks and students who turned to him for help. On being told by his friend and confessor, the Carthusian monk Nicholas Hopkins, of a poor child who wished to enter holy orders, he immediately adopted the boy and found him a good tutor.[37] Both the chancellor's and the cofferer's accounts contain many examples of his generosity towards members of the lower clergy, as well as his obvious pleasure in the company of their superiors. Even after leaving her household, Buckingham seems to have remained very much under the influence of Lady Margaret Beaufort. It was allegedly at her request that he granted thirty-one acres of land in Bumpstead Helion, Essex, to Queens' College, Cambridge, in 1505, besides discussing the possibility of other settlements with the college

---

[35] K. B. McFarlane, *The Nobility of Later Medieval England*, pp. 236, 241; P.C.C. Logge 2 (the will of Anne, Duchess of Buckingham, proved 31 Oct. 1480).

[36] The first English edition ' translated out of frensshe into englysshe at thynstygacyon of the puyssant et illustryous Prynce, lorde Edwarde Duke of Buckyngham . . .' appeared in 1512 (Facsimile edition, published by the Grolier Club, New York, 1901); for the background to this legend see Sir A. Wagner, ' The Swan Badge and the Swan Knight ', *Archaeologia*, XCVII (1959).

[37] S.P.1/22 fo. 41; the boy was probably ' our scoler Fraunceys ', for whom the chancellor made many purchases in 1519 (Royal Ms. 14B XXXV D fos. 2–2v, 13–14v).

authorities at this time.[38] He was also a benefactor of both Christ's College, Cambridge, and St Paul's School, London; the extent of these two endowments remains unknown, although the second probably resulted from his association with John Colet, the Dean of St Paul's. Colet appears among the inner circle of friends and councillors who acted as his feoffees between the years 1513 and 1515, and had already won the respect of many learned patrons.[39] The Duke's confirmation in 1508 of a grant of land made to Merton College, Oxford, by his ancestors serves as a reminder that earlier generations of the Stafford family had also taken an active interest in education.[40] Although it was for many years believed to be his own foundation, Buckingham (now Magdalene) College, Cambridge, owed its name to his father. The college was originally set up in 1428 as a refuge for Benedictine monks tempted from their studies by the worldly attractions of the town. Duke Henry is said to have financed its earliest brick buildings and some of the work on the chapel, but there is no contemporary evidence for this since all the college records as well as his own accounts have been lost. The tradition that Edward, Duke of Buckingham, studied at the college also remains unsubstantiated, as does the belief that he built the great hall there in 1519. Historians of the college have always described him as one of its earliest and most liberal benefactors, though their only primary source seems to be a brief entry in the Old Book of Magdalene College made several years after the Duke's death. His trumpeters visited Cambridge at the time of the hall's completion, but again there are no references in any of his surviving muniments to expenditure on the college.[41]

---

[38] W. G. Searle, 'The History of the Queen's College of St Margaret and St Bernard in the University of Cambridge, 1446–1560', *Cambridge Antiquarian Society*, IX (1867), p. 250.

[39] According to Add. Ms. 36542 fo. 98, one of the muniment chests at Thornbury in 1520 contained 'my lordi's licence for mortising of landis gyven to Marten College in Oxford and to Criste's college in Cambridge and to the gramer scole by powle's Churche in London '; Colet's association with the Duke is established in C.P.40/1003, Easter 4/5 Hen. VIII, rot. 441–2v, 445–6, 448–9v, 453, 458, and Corporation of London R.O., Husting Book II (1506–37) fos. 117–8; he also tried to arbitrate during Buckingham's dispute with his secretary, John Russell (STA CHA2/23/111, 26/386).

[40] Add. Ms. 36542 fo. 98; ' *Registrum Annalium Collegii Mertonensis, 1483–1521* ', ed. H. E. Salter, *Oxford Historical Society*, LXXVI (1921), pp. 354, 362.

[41] J. B. Mullinger, *The University of Cambridge, from the Royal Injunctions of 1535 to the Accession of Charles I* (Cambridge, 1884), p. 64; C. H. Cooper, *Annals of*

Rather more is known about Duke Edward's relations with the Church, towards which he was both a generous and exacting patron. In August 1514 he obtained permission to found a college at Thornbury and endow it with land worth up to £300 a year. He also planned to settle an annual income of £60 upon Tewkesbury Abbey, although by honouring the burial place of Edward, Prince of Wales, Henry VI's son, he no doubt hoped to advertise his own Lancastrian connexions.[42] It should not be supposed, however, that Buckingham lacked genuine religious feeling. He took his responsibilities towards the Church very seriously, and arranged many visits to neighbouring houses, such as Keynsham Abbey, when he was at Thornbury. His senior officials were similarly instructed to investigate any rumours of indiscipline or corruption in the Staffords' less accessible foundations. John Pickering's detailed report on the Prior of Maxstoke's colourful lifestyle provides a good illustration of the importance which Buckingham attached to these matters. The canons of Maxstoke begged him to sit in judgement upon their venal superior, while the sheriff of Warwickshire recognised that nothing could be done until the Duke's advice and opinion had been sought.[43] The outcome of this particular affair is not recorded, although the full extent of Buckingham's influence in lay and ecclesiastical circles alike can be seen from the way in which he dealt with the disturbances at Kingswood Abbey, Gloucestershire, in 1517. The replacement of the old abbot by a royal nominee had provoked a full-scale riot, during which a number of important local figures, resentful of these reforms, launched an attack on the Abbey buildings. Duke Edward immediately sent a token force of retainers to restore order and the new incumbent met with no more overt opposition. His enemies, among whom were two of the Duke's employees, openly admitted that ' the displeasure of my lorde's grace ' was a more potent deterrent than five hundred men.[44]

Cambridge (5 vols., Cambridge, 1842–1908), vol. I p. 302; The Old Book of Magdalene College fo. iv (I am grateful to the College Librarian, Mr D. Pepys-Whiteley, for making this Ms. available to me, and for providing information about the records in his care).

[42] *L. & P. Henry VIII*, vol. I, pt ii, no. 3226 (3, 5).   [43] W.A.M. 5470 fo. 48.

[44] *L. & P. Henry VIII*, vol. I, pt ii, no. 3173; STA CHA2/17/259, 19/305, 20/7, 24/67, 25/203 and S.P.1/22 fos. 95–5v (depositions concerning these riots).

There were, however, very few occasions on which Buckingham ever had to support the power of his name with the force of arms. For most of the time he was escorted by a small band of liveried servants and he never attempted to retain men on the scale that his great-grandfather, the first Duke, had done. He was nevertheless always viewed as a potential military threat by the Crown because of his father's rôle in the events of 1483. Although the collapse of the October rising provided incontestable proof of the Staffords' failure to inspire either the affection or loyalty of the families upon whose support their power was based, the mere fact that a rebellion had taken place was enough to cast a long shadow over Duke Edward's relations with the house of Tudor. Both Henry VII and his son, fearing some attempt upon their royal title, were innately suspicious not only of Buckingham but of the English baronage as a whole. Both monarchs sought to impose further restrictions on retaining through the introduction of new and stricter legislation and the widespread use of repressive proclamations. While recognising the importance of private retinues, which provided the Crown with an army in wartime and a means of keeping order during periods of unrest, they sought to limit the occasions when men could be raised and armed by their more powerful subjects. Henry VIII's estimate of the third Duke's military potential was far wide of the mark, although his suspicions were not entirely unjustified. In 1519 Sir William Bulmer, an able soldier who had distinguished himself during the Flodden campaign, was brought before the Star Chamber on a charge of accepting and wearing the Stafford livery while serving as a member of the royal household. The King is said to have remarked ' That he would none of his seruauntes should hang on another mannes sleue, and that he was aswel able to maintein him as the duke of Buckingham, and that what might be thought of his departyng and what myght bee supposed by ye duke's retaining, he would not then declare.' [45] Bulmer's case was little more than a set-piece, intended to prove the seriousness with which King Henry regarded illegal retaining; even so, it has

---

[45] *Edward Hall's Chronicle*, p. 599; Bulmer's military career is described in M. H. Dodds and R. Dodds, *The Pilgrimage of Grace 1536–1537 and the Exeter Conspiracy 1538* (2 vols., Cambridge, 1915), vol. I p. 37.

been described as one of the major events leading to Buckingham's downfall in 1521, and raises the question of his real – or supposed – threat to the Crown.[46] There is certainly nothing in the surviving wardrober's accounts to support the allegation that Duke Edward had been suborning other members of the royal guard with costly gifts of gold cloth and liveries. But although all the evidence points to a policy of stringent economy where retaining and the distribution of rewards was concerned, it is easy to see how Buckingham's family history, together with a number of ill-considered actions on his part, could arouse Henry VIII's mistrust. The building of Thornbury, the lavish entertainment provided for the court at Penshurst in 1519 and Buckingham's continuous references to his de Bohun ancestry were all bound to alarm the King. So too was his request in November 1520 for permission to recruit an armed bodyguard for protection during his proposed visit to Wales. Even more extortionate and oppressive than his father, he experienced insurmountable difficulties in administering the Marcher lordships from Thornbury, but did not dare to cross the Welsh border without an escort. 'We kanne not to be ther for our suerty wyth out iij or iiij hundred men ', he argued; ' and though we shal have them of our owne officers and tenants, yet many of them shalbe our gentylmen's servauntes of small stature.' [47] The memory of the 1483 rising remained fixed in the King's mind: Buckingham was refused his licence and within a matter of weeks Wolsey and his agents were searching for evidence to use at the Duke's trial. Even had he wished to do so, however, Duke Edward could not possibly have led a successful rebellion from Wales: the local population was deeply hostile, and, like his father, he lacked the necessary military background. As a young man he had helped to disperse the forces of Perkin Warbeck, but his only other experience of warfare was in 1513, when he headed a contingent of 550 soldiers during Henry VIII's invasion of France. Although full of praise for his magnificent appearance, the chroniclers are uniformly reticent about his conduct in the field; according to John Taylor, who kept a diary of

---

[46] W. H. Durham, jr, for example, believes that Duke Edward stood condemned in Henry VIII's eyes from this time onwards (' Wolsey's Rule of the King's Whole Council ', *American History Review*, XLIX (1944), p. 655).

[47] Cottonian Ms. Titus B1 fo. 174.

the campaign, he seems to have been partly responsible for a failure to protect the English supply lines from the enemy.[48]

There are, moreover, clear signs of a marked change in the composition of Duke Edward's retinue, which seems to have been far smaller than that of either the first or second Dukes of Buckingham. The introduction of a centralised administrative system after 1499 naturally affected the way in which extraordinary expenses, such as annuities, were met. A dramatic fall in the number of fees paid out by each receiver cannot in itself be regarded as more than one inevitable result of these sweeping changes, but in this case neither the cofferer nor the chancellor appears to have assumed the office of ducal paymaster. Some annuities were still paid locally on the production of letters patent and these may well represent the sum total of Buckingham's expenditure on retaining. In 1502, for instance, the receiver of Kent and Surrey claimed an allowance for the payment of five annuities, three of which continued until the Duke's death nineteen years later.[49] The number of fees recorded in the Gloucestershire accounts rose from one to nine over the same period, while fourteen men and women obtained annual pensions from the central circuit in 1521.[50] The royal commissioners sent to report on the late Duke's estate staff in 1523 also noted the names of twenty-six annuitants whose fees came to £145.17s.0d. Although this list was made almost two years after Buckingham died, there only seems to be one significant omission – that of Robert Turberville; it includes six doctors, lawyers and scholars, the same number of household staff, two heralds and three officers holding minor posts on the estates.[51] Of the remainder, Sir Thomas Woodstock, Sir Edward Neville (both of whom had been given stewardships by the Duke), William Norris and Sir John Grey might conceivably have provided him with military support, but there is

---

[48] E.405/79 fo. 32v; E.101/56/25 fo. 87–9v; *L. & P. Henry VIII*, vol. 1, pt ii, no. 2391.

[49] D.641/1/2/235 m. 1, S.C.6/Hen. VIII 5797 m. 3 (his accounts for the years ending Michaelmas 1503 and Michaelmas 1521); for a list of annuities paid by Duke Edward see Appendix D, part II.

[50] S.C.6/Hen. VII 1075 m. 12v, Hen. VIII 5819 mm. 4v–5 (accounts of the receiver of Gloucestershire, Hampshire and Wiltshire for the year ending Michaelmas 1502 and a two-year period ending at Michaelmas 1521); S.C.6/Hen. VIII 5841 mm. 4v–5 (account of the receiver general for the year ending Michaelmas 1521).

[51] S.P.1/29, fo. 180.

nothing to suggest that they had ever entered into any formal undertaking to do so. Nor do any of the references to fees and annuities occurring in the local receivers' accounts contain any mention of specific obligations.

Paradoxically Duke Edward continued to grant stewardships as supplementary annuities even though attempting at the same time to prevent absenteeism on the estates. Most of the recipients were either relatives by marriage or lawyers: the former could always have been approached for help in times of crisis, irrespective of the payment of a money fee, while the latter were cultivated for their professional skills alone. Neither took their duties very seriously. In 1501, for example, Richard Empson was made steward of the Staffords' Northamptonshire estates on the under-standing that his work could be done by a deputy.[52] Deputies must also have been engaged by the Earls of Northumberland and Shrewsbury, Sir Andrew Windsor, Sir John Seymour, John Brooke and Walter Luke, all of whom held stewardships at the time of Buckingham's death.[53] It is less likely, however, that members of the Duke's immediate family were ever permitted to discharge the obligations of office so lightly. From 1500, if not before, Henry Stafford, Earl of Wiltshire, had been actively involved in the administration of his brother's Marcher lordships and was an obvious choice as steward of both Newport and Brecon. The appointment of Henry, Lord Stafford, the Duke's eighteen-year-old son, as chief steward of all the family estates in 1519 must surely indicate that he was already beginning to receive a serious training in administrative affairs.[54]

The nature of Buckingham's household and the membership of his following alike reflect certain basic changes in the great magnates' rôle as patrons and their attitude towards retaining in general. Their desire for a more civilised way of living manifested itself in many ways, the chief of which was an increased expen-diture on building and domestic improvements, usually offset by economies in other quarters. The sixteenth-century landowner looked to bricks and mortar rather than a great train of liveried

---

[52] S.C.6/Hen. VII 455 m. 3 (the bailiff of Rothwell's account for the year ending Michaelmas 1506).

[53] See Appendix B for a list of these offices.

[54] D.1721/1/1 fo. 382 (a later transcript of Buckingham's grant to his son).

attendants to express his wealth and position. Less than a century after the first Duke of Buckingham had provided Henry VI with a regular bodyguard of armed men, the last turned, partly of his own accord and partly through force of circumstance, to the patronage of scholars, lawyers and clergymen. Because of the more stable times in which they lived, and because of the stricter controls exercised over retaining, he and his contemporaries began to forsake their ancestors' martial habits in favour of less exacting and more cultivated pursuits. The spread of humanism and with it the growing interest shown by the upper classes in practical education undoubtedly encouraged him to do so. If not ahead of his time, Duke Edward was clearly among the first English noblemen to whom the term ' renaissance aristocrat ' can properly be applied.

Chapter 6

THE FINANCES OF THE STAFFORDS,

1400–1473

The economic position of the later medieval nobility has long been a matter of debate. But recent research into the finances of individual families clearly shows that the astute and resourceful landlord could usually overcome such problems as falling property values or opposition from local tenantry by showing resilience and adaptability in the face of changing circumstances. Whereas Richard, Duke of York, appears to have been a very poor administrator, other great landowners, both lay and ecclesiastical, were able to avoid any serious loss of revenue because they managed their estates efficiently. It would, however, be unwise to hold any landowner entirely responsible for his own success or failure. A regular income composed largely of rents and entry fines became less attractive once the purchasing power of that income began to fall; this could in part be offset by the careful husbanding of available resources, but if, like Richard Beauchamp, Earl of Warwick, or Richard, Duke of York, a landlord spent long periods abroad, the results of a lack of personal control soon become apparent.[1] Despite frequent visits to France in the 1420s and 1430s Humphrey, first Duke of Buckingham, was able to maintain a fairly tight hold over the direction of his affairs, since he was fortunate in the loyal and skilful officials who advised him. Of far greater consequence for Buckingham and his descendants were the financial and administrative effects of the three long minorities which beset the house of Stafford during the fifteenth century. Even when they finally came of age, the first two Dukes did not obtain full possession of their estates: Anne, Dowager Countess of Stafford, retained some of her late husband's richest and most conveniently situated manors until

[1] The importance – and generally high quality – of direct supervision by the landlord was emphasised by K. B. McFarlane in the third of his Ford lectures of 1953 (*The Nobility of Later Medieval England*, pp. 41–60).

Duke Humphrey was thirty-six, and the latter's widow in turn enjoyed a sizeable jointure for seven years after her grandson entered into his inheritance. Both men undoubtedly resented the financial restrictions placed upon them by the longevity of these formidable women, but neither had any reason to complain of the way in which the dower properties were being run. Far from exploiting their share of the family estates, the two dowagers showed themselves equally zealous in the drive for administrative efficiency. The most harmful consequence of these minorities lay rather in the reversion of certain lucrative holdings to the Crown. In 1460 only the two Welsh lordships of Newport and Brecon passed out of the family's immediate control, but this was nonetheless unfortunate, for the Staffords already found it extremely difficult to exercise their authority in Wales, and were owed large sums of money by tenants and ministers alike. Arguably, the greatest problem facing all three Dukes of Buckingham was that of raising more than a fraction of the Welsh revenues which, in theory, comprised over one third of their annual income. Other financial difficulties arose over the years, but none lasted so long or had such protracted effects.

THE STAFFORD ESTATES FROM 1400 TO 1438

Almost all the Staffords' agricultural property was in the hands of tenant farmers by 1401, the date of the first full extant valor of their estates. Earl Edmund's English and Welsh possessions were at this time grouped into six major administrative units, which later became independent receiverships and remained virtually unchanged for the next century.[2] The receiver general was directly responsible for a central circuit of twenty-eight farms and manors spread across eleven of the wealthiest counties in the Midlands and East Anglia. His clear annual receipts, valued at £826 in 1401, consisted largely of rents, fines and customary dues; casual revenues from wood sales, parkland and other irregular sources were less predictable, but could usually be relied upon to give at least £150 a year. The sixteen manors and more scattered holdings in the South West which had originally formed part of the

[2] D.641/1/2/6, *passim*.

great Clare inheritance were equally productive, lying as they did in one of the most fertile areas of England. Until the Dowager Countess Anne's death in 1438 they were also administered by the receiver general; his anticipated clear annual revenues from Gloucestershire, Hampshire and Wiltshire exceeded £387 at the beginning of the fifteenth century. As in the central circuit, a high proportion of this sum came from tenant farmers, although the profits of seignorial justice and commuted labour services were comparatively high. This was in marked contrast to the South East, particularly Kent, where most of the peasants were customarily regarded as freeholders and had never performed boon works of any kind. In both Kent and Surrey, the Staffords' smaller, but nonetheless lucrative, demesne farms were leased out *in toto* to single tenants, while the complex judicial and fiscal rights attendant upon the possession of Tonbridge Castle were exercised by a number of bailiffs. Expenditure on annuities, repairs and other immediate charges consumed almost one third of the lordship's net receipts, which stood at £452 in 1401. Profits from the fifth Earl's Staffordshire estates were also lower than usual, since land worth £40 a year had been settled upon his younger brother, Hugh, Lord Bourchier.[3] This left him with about £87 a year above what had already been spent on running the large and well-equipped stables at Stafford. The proportion of revenues spent here on building work was, however, far lower than that assigned to maintain Caus Castle in a permanently defensible state against the Welsh. Worth less than £57 a year clear in 1401, the lordship of Caus, with its areas of dense woodland and relatively poor villein farmers, was not only the least productive part of the Stafford estates, but also one of the most difficult to keep in order. Violence had always been endemic along the March, but the Earl's financial difficulties were a more recent phenomenon. In 1391 the two lordships of Caus and Newport had provided the Staffords with over one third of their landed income. Ten years later they accounted for less than one quarter, and had by then entered a period of long-term economic decline which Glyn Dŵr's rebellion in 1403 made irreversible.[4] Yet, despite this steady drop in clear revenues, Newport remained extremely wealthy until the

[3] W. Dugdale, *The Baronage of England* (2 vols., London, 1675), vol. I p. 173.
[4] Pugh, *The Marcher Lordships*, p. 151; *V.C.H. Shropshire*, vol. VIII pp. 316–22.

rising; profits derived from the administration of justice were high, and even after local expenses had been met Earl Edmund expected to receive about £410 from his local officials over the year ending Michaelmas 1401.

At this time his entire inheritance bore a valuation of over £2,967 a year gross and almost £2,429 a year net (including annuities).[5] A comparison between these estimates – for an estate valor can never be regarded as anything more than a statement of potential revenues – and the receiver general's current account shows that the Earl was sure of £1,987 a year from the estates, once an additional £115 had been spent on local expenses and approximately £107 on annuities. Even allowing for his considerable outlay on preparations for Henry IV's expeditions to Scotland and Wales, he was still well able to live within what appears to have been a carefully planned budget.[6] The same is true of the Dowager Countess Anne, who, from 1403 until her death thirty-five years later, occupied over half the Stafford estates, together with her own share of the de Bohun inheritance. In 1408/9, for example, her third husband, Sir William Bourchier, received over £1,160 from these properties, above the £510 set aside for household expenses, fees and legal costs by the receiver general.[7] Evidence of slowly mounting arrearages over the years 1406 to 1411 does not detract from an overall impression of financial stability. The only real losses sustained during this period were in the lordship of Newport, which ought to have brought the Dowager approximately £133 a year net but which in 1407 still produced nothing ' because of the rebellion '.[8] This seems to have been a temporary set-back, for in the following year Edward, Duke of York, agreed to farm Anne's share of the lordship at an annual rent of £100, and on his death in 1415 she herself took on a lease of that part of Newport which had reverted to the Crown. By 1430, however, Duke Humphrey had either purchased or been given her dower properties there: this suggests that she had by then despaired of effecting any immediate reforms.[9]

Although the redivision of the de Bohun inheritance in 1421 ought to have made no difference to the Dowager's landed income, she and her descendants had every reason to regret the

[5] D.641/1/2/6 m. 8v. [6] *Ibid.*, mm. 8v–9. [7] D.641/1/2/8.
[8] D.641/1/2/7. [9] Pugh, *The Marcher Lordships*, pp. 151–2.

acquisition of Brecon, Huntington, Talgarth and Hay – all Marcher lordships which could never be made to realise their full potential. This was no new problem, and may indeed have been a major factor in influencing Henry V to demand an exchange. There had already been complaints about mismanagement in the Brecon area, and although Glyn Dŵr's rebellion undoubtedly created serious problems for the King's officials, stagnation had set in well before the fifteenth century.[10] The four lordships, subsequently entrusted to a single receiver, were said to be worth £372 a year in 1421, but the Dowager cannot have seen more than half this sum. Henry V had demanded that she pay off the arrears of 300 marks which had accumulated before the partition, and this, together with the receiver's inability to raise more than a small proportion of current judicial dues and rents, meant that almost all her clear profits were assigned in advance. These losses were fortunately offset elsewhere, notably in Rutland, where rents and casual profits left to the Countess by her father, Thomas of Woodstock, generally exceeded £200 a year, clear of all reprises.[11] Moreover, on Sir William Bourchier's death in 1425, the Countess received a dower of eight manors in Suffolk and Essex worth almost £185 a year gross. She assigned approximately half this sum to her second son, Henry Bourchier, Earl of Essex, but she was still sure of at least £60 a year once local expenses had been met.[12] The situation in England was in every way more helpful. Between 1430 and 1435 the receiver general's annual receipts (excluding revenues paid directly to the Countess from Stafford-shire and Caus) rose from £1,639 to £1,744, of which all but a minimal sum was delivered either to the coffers or to the treasurer of the household.[13] According to a valor compiled at Michaelmas 1435, *all* the Countess Anne's English estates were worth an estimated £2,187 a year gross and £1,880 clear including sums assigned for the payment of annuities. The narrow margin between real and potential receipts owed a great deal to careful

---

[10] W. Rees, *South Wales and the March, 1284–1415, A Social and Agrarian Study* (Oxford, 1924), pp. 109, 243–57; R. R. Davies, ' Baronial Accounts, Incomes and Arrears in the Later Middle Ages ', *Econ. H.R.*, XXI (1968), pp. 223–7.
[11] See pp. 11–17.
[12] Longleat Mss. 345, 455 (accounts of the receiver of Suffolk and Essex for the period *ca.* Jan. 1425 to Michaelmas 1438; I am grateful to Dr Linda Woodger for drawing my attention to these documents). [13] D.641/1/2/12–14.

management at all levels; but the gradual decline in clear profits from the Welsh Marcher lordships was no less a product of absenteeism and local maladministration.

DUKE HUMPHREY'S LANDED INCOME FROM 1422 TO 1460

The Crown derived comparatively little profit from Duke Humphrey's long minority. Over half the Stafford estates were in the Dowager's hands, and the lordship of Tonbridge had reverted as a feudal tenure to the Archbishops of Canterbury. In all, the rents and manors settled by Henry IV upon his wife, Joan of Navarre, produced little more than £204 a year; these, together with the wardship and marriage of the young heir, remained in her hands until her temporary forfeiture in 1419 and she appears to have exploited her position to the full.[14] Duke Humphrey had particular occasion to complain about the spoliation of his Staffordshire estates, although the death of his uncle, Hugh, Lord Bourchier, in 1420 brought him the reversion of more efficiently run property worth £204 in the North Midlands.[15] Even so, while the Dowager lived Buckingham must have found it difficult to keep within the limited income at his disposal. Worth at most about £1,260 a year, the estates which he inherited in 1422 cannot have produced enough to support the cost of his growing household and retinue, and it was fortunate for him that substantial profits could still be made out of the war with France. The County of Perche, granted to him together with the Captaincy of Bellesme in 1431, was valued at 800 marks a year,[16] and he must also have enriched himself with plunder, ransoms and the perquisites of office while abroad during the 1430s. Nor was the Crown's generosity confined to France: the land and rents in four English counties settled upon Buckingham by Henry VI in May 1438 gave him an additional £150 a year, and although most of this property had been regranted or resumed by 1455, he had already benefited considerably from the award.[17]

---

[14] *C.P.R.*, 1399–1405, p. 239; *C.C.R.*, 1402–5, p. 260; *C.P.R.*, 1401–5, pp. 328, 347, 476; *op. cit.*, 1408–13, p. 38.

[15] *C.F.R.*, 1413–22, p. 326; see also p. 106 above.

[16] This figure is given in an estate valor for the year ending Michaelmas 1448 (Longleat Ms. 6410 m. 21), but probably represents a far earlier assessment.

[17] See Appendix A.

The financial side of Duke Humphrey's military and diplomatic affairs was managed by a treasurer of wars, who appears never to have become involved in any other aspect of his employer's activities.[18] Since none of the treasurer's accounts are now extant, it is impossible to tell how heavily he relied upon contributions from the estates; whatever money reached him from this source was evidently being paid through the coffers, for none of Buckingham's receivers ever dealt with him directly. Their duty was to provide cash or produce for the itinerant household, pay off whatever annuities had been assigned from particular manors, and deliver any remaining revenues to Duke Humphrey himself. The latter's finances improved considerably on the Dowager's death in 1438, which not only released property worth about £1,800 a year net but also gave him a claim to the lordship of Holderness. This fertile area of East Yorkshire could usually be relied on to show a clear annual profit of at least £600, made up largely of rents from twenty-eight manors and demesne farms. It was also at this time that Buckingham's estates in the South West, greatly enlarged by the addition of the Dowager's de Bohun manors, were hived off to form a separate receivership.[19] The full effect of these new acquisitions may be seen from two complete estate valors, the first compiled at Michaelmas 1442, the second six years later.[20] An analysis of these documents reveals the following information about Duke Humphrey's anticipated annual revenues:

TABLE IV. *Two Estate Valors of 1442 and 1448*

	Mich. 1441/2	Mich. 1447/8
Gross receipts	£6,004	£6,411
Running costs	£1,140	£1,110
Dead rents	£ 148	£ 167
Annuities paid locally	£ 167	£ 114
Clear receipts	£4,549	£5,020

[18] Indeed, only one reference to John Woodhouse, the occupant of this post in 1443, has survived (N.L.W. Peniarth Ms. 280 fo. 24).
[19] See p. 45.
[20] D.641/1/2/17; Longleat Ms. 6410.

How far do these figures reflect the true state of Duke Humphrey's income during the 1440s? The apparent rise in clear receipts by about £470 over the years 1441 to 1448 was in part the result of greater productivity and more efficient administration, although the accession of Penshurst and its appurtenances in 1447 increased Buckingham's rental by at least £26 a year net.[21] He had also inherited a modest estate from his aunt Joan Stafford in 1442, but these scattered rents and feudal profits are not listed in any account rolls.[22] On the whole, the two valors convey a rather misleading impression of Buckingham's financial position, in so far as certain parts of the estates – notably the lordship of Cantref Selyf in Wales and the County of Perche in France – cannot have produced what was expected of them.[23]

There was, in fact, a marked discrepancy between real and potential revenues in certain receiverships and a strong correlation in others. Although the receiver general was no longer responsible for the South Western estates, his charge included the two crown manors of Atherstone and Weedon Beck, granted to Buckingham for life in 1438, and property in Suffolk purchased by the Duke two years later.[24] Together, these produced about £130 a year during the 1440s and were thus able to compensate for unpaid revenues elsewhere. Arrearages were rising annually by £100 or more in the central circuit throughout this period, but the fault lay almost solely with the royal officials who were supposed to hand over Duke Humphrey's various annuities, and was not an administrative one. Even so, the clear receipts of £1,276 recorded by John Heton at Michaelmas 1450 were a good £550 lower than those anticipated in the valor of 1448; and although these receipts had risen to £1,411 by 1457, the amount of wastage and evasion at a local level was evidently quite great.[25] The South Western estates are almost continuously documented throughout the fifteenth century and it is possible to build up a more detailed picture of the financial situation there. At first the ostensively dramatic rise and fall in the receiver's arrears between 1439 and 1460 was nothing more than a cyclical phenomenon, but gradually

[21] See Appendix A; Penshurst was said to be worth this sum in the valor of 1499 (D.641/1/2/27 m. 10).

[22] G.E.C., vol. VII pp. 156–9; C.139/109/36.

[23] See pp. 14, 16–17.

[24] See Appendix A.

[25] D.641/1/2/21, 23.

the problem grew more serious. A detailed list of outstanding debts compiled in September 1459 shows clearly enough that the £564 owed by Thomas Berkeley and his subordinates was far in excess of their theoretical, let alone real, annual profits. The latter could differ by over £250 from one year to another, but nevertheless did not fall below £418 after 1452.[26] It was then still possible to offset long-term economic and organisational difficulties by careful management, and while this situation continued Buckingham had no immediate cause for concern. This was also the case in Staffordshire, where from 1450 onwards arrearages accounted for more than two thirds of the receiver's total charge. Rising from £79 in 1440 to £235 in 1459, this deficit was partly made up of expenditure awaiting the Duke's formal acquittance, but most of it comprised ' real ' debts, often written off years before. Paradoxically, clear receipts remained fairly constant, enabling the receiver to spend an average of about £200 a year on household provisions and Buckingham's retinue in the North Midlands.[27] Given the almost perpetual state of disorder along the Welsh March, returns from the nearby lordship of Caus were even more promising. Again, a fairly steady increase in arrearages between 1444 and 1458 had not produced a corresponding fall in profits; on the contrary, these rose noticeably over the same period and stood at an unprecedented £99 in 1458. The two receiverships of Staffordshire and Caus were jointly valued at £400 a year clear in 1448, although between them they are never known to have produced more than £337 a year during Duke Humphrey's lifetime. He could, however, derive some satisfaction from the fact that neither area had begun to show serious signs of financial decline.[28]

Information about Holderness, the most productive of the Staffords' English lordships, is very meagre indeed. Only one receiver's account has survived to supplement the estate valors made during the 1440s; it may well record exceptionally high receipts. Less than half of the £424 in hand at Michaelmas 1448 comprised arrears in the true sense, since a number of payments

---

[26] D.641/1/2/19 m. 3, 20 m. 4, 22 m. 3, 167–8, 170–1, 173–6, 178–80, *passim*.
[27] D.641/1/2/19 m. 4, 20 m. 3, 54–60, 62, *passim*.
[28] Longleat Mss. 3847, 3988–9, 4010; D.641/1/2/19 m. 5, 20 m. 2, 22 m. 6.

had not yet been allowed by the auditor. It was, moreover, possible to raise the entire £737 anticipated in clear revenues from Holderness at that time – an achievement which testifies to the administrative efficiency of the local staff, but which may never have been repeated.[29] The loss of all but two complete returns from Kent and Surrey renders equally unsafe any generalisations about Buckingham's revenues from the South East, especially as both arrearages and building costs could fluctuate by over £40 from year to year.[30] Yet, here again, the valor of 1448 proved remarkably accurate: at £243, clear annual profits fell only £2 below the estimated total, although significant economies had been made in the receiver's immediate expenditure.

Whatever satisfaction Duke Humphrey may have derived from the relative stability of his English revenues clearly did not extend across the border into Wales, where the problem of unpaid rents and judicial dues, already acute in his mother's day, had assumed serious proportions. Arrears in the receivership of Brecon alone had reached the alarming total of £2,453 by Michaelmas 1454 and showed every sign of continuing to rise at an even higher rate.[31] Hardly any of the fine of 2,000 marks granted to Duke Humphrey for redeeming the Great Sessions in 1450 was paid over the next four years; indeed, by forgoing his right to hold the Brecon Sessions in 1453, and again in 1454, Buckingham tacitly admitted his inability to deal with a worsening financial situation. Although said to be worth £1,014 a year in 1448, net receipts from the Brecon area reached only £823 at that time, and had sunk below £232 two years later.[32] Even allowing for considerable variations in the receiver's annual takings, the overall picture was far from reassuring. Returns from Newport over the same period reveal a similar ' waning of the lord's authority '. This, rather than any single economic factor, was mainly responsible both for the backlog of over £786 in overdue rents and fines recorded by the receiver in 1457 and for his failure to raise more than two thirds of the clear profits expected from him during the previous decade. The decline of Newport as a trading centre and the existence of several unoccupied or unprofitable holdings naturally added to

---

[29] D.641/1/2/19 m. 5. [30] *Ibid.*, m. 7, 22 m. 7.
[31] *Ibid.*, m. 2.
[32] Pugh, *The Marcher Lordships*, pp. 175–6; D.641/1/2/19 m. 1, 20 m. 1.

the receiver's difficulties, but the basic problem lay in the unwillingness of the tenantry, both rich and poor, to comply with
Duke Humphrey's fiscal and judicial demands.[33] Had the Duke
not relied upon these two Welsh receiverships to provide over a
third of his landed income this deplorable situation might not
have been so bad; as it was, the intransigence of the local tenantry
began seriously to undermine his ability to live within his means.

Buckingham was not alone in experiencing grave difficulties in
the management of his Marcher lordships. Richard, Duke of
York's property in Wales and along the Welsh Border was said
to be worth £4,195 a year gross at Michaelmas 1443. Expenditure
on fees, wages and repairs accounted for almost £1,316 of this
sum, which left the Duke with anticipated clear receipts of
£2,879. Arrears from the previous year stood at over £3,692,
however, and although York's receiver general eventually
managed to recover £1,000 of the £3,536 still overdue at Michaelmas 1443, most of the deficit comprised long-standing debts owed
by his subordinates. Over £867 of the Duke of York's Welsh
income was made up of fines, gifts and tallages, and these casual
receipts must have been the first to fall into arrears. This was
certainly the case on the Welsh estates of the Duchy of Lancaster,
where the proportion of extraordinary to order revenues was far
higher than that in any of its English lordships. Despite their
highly efficient approach to administrative problems the Duchy
officials still found it extremely hard to prevent a steady fall in
profits.[34]

It would have required additional revenues in the order of
£500 a year to compensate Buckingham for losses in Wales, but
although the English estates showed signs of increased productivity during the late 1450s such a large sum was not forthcoming.
Moreover, whereas the valors of 1442 and 1448 implausibly record
a rise of 100% in receipts from the lordship of Perche, the real
value of this property was already falling because of English
reverses in France. Whatever net profits were still available seem

---

[33] Pugh, *The Marcher Lordships*, pp. 169, 175; S.C.6/924/23–5; D.641/1/2/22 m. 1.

[34] S.C.11/818, *passim* (a valor of the Duke of York's property in the Marches, Herefordshire, Shropshire and Staffordshire for the year ending Michaelmas 1443); Davies,
op. cit., pp. 221–5.

to have been spent locally on defence, and it may even have been necessary to subsidise the garrison at Bellesme from England.[35]

Lack of information now makes it impossible to give precise details of Buckingham's landed income in any given year, but enough is known about each of the eight receiverships during the late 1440s to provide a fairly accurate impression of his finances at this time. The available evidence, already considered in some detail by Mr Pugh, suggests that Duke Humphrey cannot have raised more than £3,700 net over the year ending Michaelmas 1448.[36] He then expected the Stafford estates to yield over £5,000, an unduly optimistic figure which bore little relation to the true state of his affairs. Although clearly aware of this very real deficit, the Duke continued to base his expenditure on anticipated rather than actual profits. He could not avoid doing so, for certain necessary expenses – notably those incurred during his Captaincy of Calais and later while he was Warden of the Cinque Ports – rendered ineffective whatever economies he was able to make elsewhere. It is, moreover, unlikely that the cost of providing King Henry with a bodyguard during the early 1450s was offset by the single payment of £400 made to him in 1454; and his share of the spoils after the royal victory at Ludford five years later came too late materially to affect his financial position.[37]

DUKE HUMPHREY'S EXPENDITURE FROM 1422 TO 1460

Whereas the amount spent on fees and annuities did not alter significantly during this period, Buckingham's domestic expenses were rising steadily from year to year. He had, after all, to maintain certain standards of hospitality and display, and could not afford to lose his reputation as a ' good lord '. Exactly how great a proportion of his income was assigned to the household remains unknown: the three surviving accounts of the treasurer of the great household do not list purchases made for Humphrey, Lord Stafford's establishment when it toured the northern receiver-

---

[35] In 1445, for example, Matthew Gough was made bailiff of Perche and captain of Bellesme with an annuity of £20 and the promise of wages for himself and 39 men (N.L.W. Peniarth Ms. 280 fo. 36).

[36] Pugh, *The Marcher Lordships*, pp. 176–8.

[37] E.404/68/97; see p. 26.

ships, nor do they show what was spent on Buckingham's itinerant or 'riding' household. Since both bodies were provisioned directly from the estates, it would require far more local evidence than is now available to give a clear idea of the revenues they consumed. Only one account remains for Duke Humphrey's itinerant household; it records a total outlay of £897 between 17 October 1438 and 5 October 1439, but it cannot be regarded as typical because of the unusually heavy costs occasioned by his visits to France at this time.[38] Not even the treasurer's own accounts, analysed below, give a complete picture of expenditure on the great household, because the fees and wages of domestic staff, which rose from about £218 to £300 a year between 1449 and 1457, were paid by the receiver general.[39]

TABLE V. *Three Accounts for the Great Household, 1443–1455*[40]

	Mich. 1443/4	Mich. 1452/3	Mich. 1454/5
Arrears	—	—	—
Receipts	£1,648	£1,992	£2,219
Purchases and other payments	£1,849	£2,111	£1,933
	£201 overspent	£119 overspent + £150 overspent in 1451/2	£286 in hand

The treasurer sometimes found it difficult to manage without anticipating future revenues, although he does not seem to have done so on a large scale. That he could end his account at Michaelmas 1455 with £286 in hand is less reassuring than at first appears, since Duke Humphrey had for some time during these years been in attendance upon the King, and would have spent heavily on both his itinerant household and retinue.

The few surviving references to purchases of cloth, armour and

38 Eg. Roll 2208.
39 D.641/1/2/21 m. 7; 23 m. 6.
40 Turnbull, *op. cit.*, pp. 2–22; D.641/1/3/4; Eg. Roll 2209.

saddlery made by the receiver general give only the vaguest idea of how Buckingham's wardrobe was organised, and tell us nothing about its finances. The third Duke's wardrober needed about £2,500 a year to equip a household of over 150 persons; his great grandfather may reasonably be supposed to have required at least half this sum. Thus, at a conservative estimate, Duke Humphrey's routine annual expenditure cannot have fallen much below £4,000 during the late 1440s and had probably risen to a minimum of £4,400 by the end of the following decade. This figure takes no account of any possible increase in the number of fees and annuities awarded by Duke Humphrey from 1450 onwards; but there is no evidence to suggest that the cost of his retinue ever rose much above £560 a year.[41] By this date, how- ever, his real annual income was already approximately £300 short of the amount required to meet all these regular charges.

The additional expenses which he incurred while Constable of Calais came therefore as a particularly heavy burden on an over- strained budget. Able though he was, Buckingham secured the Constableship more because of his wealth and influence in the Exchequer than because of any personal qualities of leadership. The Crown no doubt hoped that in the case of economic failure or delays at home, he would use his own revenues to pay the garrison's wages; and indeed his first action on assuming office in 1442 was to intercede on behalf of the unpaid and near-mutinous soldiery.[42] Despite its promise of 1,000 marks, to be raised before Easter 1443, the Government owed him £5,000 by the following June, and fell even further into arrears as a result of the King's desperate shortage of money. Being powerless himself to raise the necessary funds until parliament had met to consider the whole question of how Calais should be financed, Henry VI could only approach his ' right trusty and welbeloved cousin ' for one advance after another.[43] In the event, parliament's scheme for bypassing the Exchequer and supplying the treasurer of Calais directly from the royal customs proved unacceptable; prests for wages and provisions remained so inadequate that in 1445 Buckingham

[41] See pp. 73–7.
[42] *P.P.C.*, vol. V p. 207.
[43] *C.P.R.*, 1441–6, p. 128; *P.P.C.*, vol. V p. 285; *Letters and Papers Illustrative of the Wars of the English in France*, vol. I pp. 492–3.

obtained the farm of Hammes, Sandgate and the Skevinage of Calais in part repayment of these mounting debts. The initial grant was for ten years, but when in December 1450 he gave up both the farm and the Constableship itself, the Government owed him £19,395.[44] In theory, Duke Humphrey had managed to negotiate a prompt and ostensively workable means of recovering this money. He received a parliamentary award of customs and subsidies ' comyng and growyng of all manere goodes and merchandises' shipped through Sandwich; as from February 1451 a second assignment was made to him from the tolls levied on English wool exports.[45] Nevertheless, although Buckingham enjoyed the rare privilege of appointing his own collectors, these revenues were much sought after by other royal creditors, and it was here, in the struggle for preference, that his influence could be used to the greatest advantage. He petitioned successfully to be exempted from a number of grants and enactments (including two acts of resumption) concerning the royal customs, so that by Michaelmas 1454 at least £8,198 of the original debt had been recovered. Two years later, the last of these provisions, addressed to the customers of Sandwich, was made on Duke Humphrey's behalf, which suggests that he had then recovered or, more probably, agreed to forgo any outstanding arrears.[46] Unless some alternative form of reimbursement had been arranged before this date his potential losses may have exceeded £11,000, although there is no way of telling whether or not the Duke made exaggerated claims upon the Exchequer. Other English captains were quite prepared to do so, by alleging that they had paid wages which, in fact, were still overdue.[47]

Although it carried far lighter financial responsibilities than Buckingham's previous appointment, the Constableship of Dover and Wardenship of the Cinque Ports, which he purchased from Lord Saye and Sele in 1450, proved yet another drain on his resources. Whereas the Government made every effort to repay

---

[44] G. L. Harriss, ' The Struggle for Calais ', *E.H.R.*, LXXV (1960), p. 33; *C.F.R.*, 1445–52, p. 115; E.101/54/12; *Rot. Parl.*, vol. V p. 206.   [45] E.101/54/12.

[46] *Rot. Parl.*, vol. V pp. 209, 219, 233, 245–7, 264, 297, 308; *C.P.R.*, 1446–52, pp. 323, 377; N.L.W. Peniarth Ms. 280 fo. 48; E.356/20 fos. 40–40v; *C.C.R.*, 1454–61, pp. 22, 152.

[47] See, for example, K. B. McFarlane, ' The Investment of Sir John Fastolf's Profits of War ', *T.R.H.S.*, 5th series VII (1957), p. 93.

former captains of Calais, the various assignments of £300 a year intended for the Cinque Ports soon fell into arrears and were even harder to recover. Eventually, during the Hilary term of 1457, Duke Humphrey began an action for debt against the sheriff of Hampshire, who then owed him over £267, only to find that Queen Margaret's annual pension of £100 from that county was being paid at his expense.[48] The necessary revenues were simply not available, as can be seen from the accounts compiled by Thomas Hexstall, receiver of Buckingham's fees as warden. Almost all of the £1,262 outstanding in June 1460 comprised unpaid farms and customs, which had proved impossible to collect over the previous ten years.[49] Meanwhile, Duke Humphrey was still obliged to maintain adequate defences in an area of great strategic importance. Some wages and expenses must have been met out of his own coffers, if only on a temporary basis; during the previous decade an annual advance of about £250 would have proved no more than a slight strain upon his income, but he now had many additional costs to meet, not least being those of finding suitable wives and husbands for six of his children.

The marriage of Joan Stafford with William, son and heir of John, Viscount Beaumont, in 1452 cost the Duke £1,533, together with a total payment of £350 for his daughter's upkeep in Beaumont's household.[50] He managed to pay off the second sum with very little trouble, but found it very difficult to raise the annual instalments of the larger debt. As he explained soon after the contract had been drawn up:

In gode faith brother, it is so with me at this tyme I have but easy stuffe of money withinne me, for so meche as the seison of the yer is not yet growen, so that I may not plese youre seid gode brotherhode, as God knoweth my will and entent were to do, and I had it.[51]

His payments to Beaumont ceased completely in 1457, and it was left to his executors, and eventually his grandson, the second Duke, to repay the £442 still outstanding then. Buckingham also made provision in his will for the surrender of a portion worth

[48] D.641/1/1/6/3 (a sixteenth-century transcript of the proceedings).
[49] D.641/1/2/22 m. 9, 236–8; E.101/54/17.
[50] D.1721/1/1 fo. 395, a copy of an account for the payment of Joan Stafford's marriage portion, compiled after 16 Aug. 1459.
[51] *P.L.*, vol. I p. 61; Duke Humphrey to Viscount Beaumont, undated.

£1,000 which had been settled upon Katherine Stafford on her marriage to John, Earl of Shrewsbury, in 1458.[52] The Duke's unforeseen death two years later released him from what would have been an equally heavy financial burden. He had by then promised to make an estate of land worth 400 marks a year to his son, John, whose young wife, Constance Green, joined the ducal household in 1458 and remained, with her retinue, as an additional charge upon his domestic budget.[53] The financial arrangements made by John, Earl of Oxford, and Duke Humphrey on the betrothal of their two children in 1443 are now unknown, although the Earl's son obviously commanded a high price on the marriage market. The same is true of Margaret Beaufort, the only daughter and heiress of the second Duke of Somerset, whom Buckingham obtained as a bride for his eldest son. Her cousin Margaret later married the younger Henry Stafford, although the couple did not benefit materially until the Duke's death.

That Buckingham wished to be buried ' withoute any sumptous coostes or charges ' may reflect an unusual degree of piety on his part, although the state of his finances at this time hardly allowed for a magnificent funeral. One of his first concerns was to make provision for the payment of various debts by instructing his executors to sell property worth at least £45 a year clear, and by making available to them the revenues of Holderness and other lucrative farms in the South of England, which were already in the hands of his trusted advisers.[54] It is now impossible to calculate how much he owed his various creditors, since the task of repaying them lay with the Dowager, whose domestic expenses can rarely be distinguished from her disbursements as an executrix. Nonetheless, the question remains: was Duke Humphrey driven to adopt a more extreme loyalist position because of economic as well as political factors? His senior

[52] P.C.C. Stockton 21.

[53] Northants, R.O. SS 4254 (indenture between Duke Humphrey and Henry Green, esquire, 19 Jan. 1458).

[54] P.C.C. Stockton 21; Duke Humphrey made provision for the sale of the manor of Macclesfield and other land in Cheshire (worth £7 a year clear in 1456; D.641/1/2/73), the manors of Aston, Bridgnorth and other land in Shropshire (worth about £12 a year clear in 1448; Longleat Ms. 6410 mm. 10–11), the lordship of Talgarth (valued, optimistically, at £26 a year clear in 1448; *ibid.*, m. 17) and the manor of Little Perendon, Essex (no valuation available). Talgarth was never sold but by 1518 had long ceased to show a clear profit (S.C.6/Hen. VIII 4775 m. 2).

employees and annuitants may have advocated such a course, especially if they could not always rely upon the regular payment of their fees and wages. A reward of confiscated property from some great estate would have helped to solve Buckingham's most pressing problems, and in this respect his position was remarkably akin to that of Richard, Duke of York. The latter could rarely collect more than three quarters of a landed income worth about £4,500 a year and had also despaired of recovering the enormous sums due to him as a former officer and creditor of the Crown.[55] Yet the analogy is in many ways a misleading one. York's rash behaviour and extravagance during the 1450s worsened an acute state of indebtedness which extensive borrowing and land sales could hardly alleviate, but Buckingham showed himself to be a competent landowner whose financial position, however difficult, did not force him to take such extreme measures. Indeed, although Duke Humphrey lived above his income and consequently fell into debt, he could no doubt have pursued the same lifestyle without unduly stringent economies for many years to come. He certainly enjoyed excellent credit, and so far as is known was never driven to dispose of either land or personal effects during his lifetime.

THE STAFFORD ESTATES FROM 1460 TO 1473

The financial consequences of Duke Henry's long minority, which lasted from his grandfather's death in July 1460 until January 1473, were by no means as serious as might at first be supposed. Since the Dowager Duchess Anne obtained immediate possession of her jointure, took livery of Holderness in 1461 and was given custody of her late husband's other English property by Edward IV, the administration of all but the two Welsh receiverships remained virtually unchanged.[56] Land worth 800 marks a year had been settled upon two of the Dowager's younger sons, but these losses were partly offset in February 1464 by Edward IV's

55 R. A. Griffiths, 'Duke Richard of York's Intentions in 1450 and the Origins of the Wars of the Roses', *Journal of Medieval History*, I (1975), pp. 194–6; J. T. Rosenthal, 'The Estates and Finances of Richard, Duke of York (1411–60)', *Studies in Medieval and Renaissance History* (Nebraska), II (1965), *passim*.

56 *C.P.R.*, 1452–61, p. 639; *op. cit.*, 1461–7, p. 24; *C.F.R.*, 1452–61, p. 284.

readiness to forgo the annual farm of £262 (itself reduced from an initial £380), which Anne had been paying into the Exchequer as keeper of the Stafford estates held by the Crown. In return for what was effectively a concession of more than £1,830, she surrendered all her rights to the marriage and wardship of the young Duke.[57] Her net income rose accordingly, although there were other less obvious reasons for the gradual increase in profits recorded during the late 1460s. Even after her marriage to Walter Blount, Lord Mountjoy, the Dowager maintained a smaller and more centralised household; this proved cheaper to run and placed less of an immediate financial burden on the outlying receiver-ships. It would also appear that greater control was being exercised upon expenditure at a purely local level. Over the finan-cial year ending Michaelmas 1467, for example, the receiver general raised all but £37 of the £950 laid to his charge, delivered £627 to the Dowager's coffers and spent a further £91 on annui-ties.[58] Bearing in mind that rents worth over £300 had been assigned to John and Henry Stafford from the Midlands and that the sub-receiver of Norfolk was then accounting separately for property worth about £60 a year net, there are clear signs of increased productivity throughout the central circuit. This was also true of the South Western estates, for although six manors worth over £109 a year had been granted to Sir Henry Stafford and his wife by the late Duke, an average of about £256 was still being paid to the Dowager during the 1460s. Running costs were kept at a minimum, and for once it was possible to contain the problem of arrearages. Indeed, most of the sums recorded as 'cash in hand', particularly during the months after Bucking-ham's death, were no more than expenses awaiting his widow's approval.[59] Again, whereas the accounts of the receiver of Stafford-shire convey a superficial impression of mounting indebtedness, at least two thirds of the £335 which he owed by Michaelmas 1470 comprised valid payments made on Anne's behalf but not yet authorised by her. Thus, even though cash profits appear at first glance to have fallen slightly since the previous decade, the

[57] *Ibid.*, 1461–71, pp. 11, 62; *C.P.R.*, 1461–7, p. 298. Anne and her second husband were, however, obliged to pay for 'the support and finding' of Duke Henry during Henry VI's readeption (E.404/75/1/2).

[58] D.641/1/2/25.　　　　　　　　　　　　　　[59] D.641/1/2/181–2, 185, 187, 189.

overall situation was in fact more favourable.[60] Not enough is known about the three receiverships of Kent and Surrey, Caus, and Holderness during this period to permit more than a few generalisations on the state of their finances, but here also available revenues seem to have been administered with the modicum of wastage. Accounts have survived from both Holderness and Caus for the year ending Michaelmas 1473; these postdate Duke Henry's entry into his immediate inheritance, but show clearly enough that contumacious debts did not yet consume more than a small part of potential profits. In Holderness, for example, the receiver obtained his final *quietus* a mere six months after being pronounced £224 in arrears, having previously raised over £514 for the Dowager's immediate use.[61]

There is clearly insufficient evidence for a detailed analysis of Anne's income during the 1460s, but with so many instances of efficient management at a relatively high level, it seems reasonable to accept the findings of a valor drawn up at Michaelmas 1473.[62] Her jointure alone was then said to be worth about £1,245 a year net (after the deduction of running costs and dead rents in the order of £496), although this figure does not include revenues from Kent, which probably brought an additional £90 a year or more. Even allowing for a fairly significant discrepancy between real and anticipated revenues, her average annual income during the previous year may well have exceeded £2,000 net; if this was in fact so, the Staffords' six English receiverships were evidently producing rather more than they had done at the time of Duke Humphrey's death. As we have already seen, the Dowager's household with its permanent staff of about sixty could be run on a far lower budget. Together the great and itinerant households cost no more than £1,616 over an eighteen-month period ending in March 1474, while expenditure on domestic wages accounted for a mere £133 during the previous year.[63] The treasurer was apparently able to retain considerable sums of money at the end of each accounting period; and since the Dowager then had no

---

[60] D.641/1/2/63, 65, 68–9, 71.   [61] Add. Ch. 22644–5.
[62] Add. Ms. 29608 m. 2.
[63] *Ibid.*, m. 1. The Dowager spent less than £783 on provisions for her great household over the financial year ending 31 Sept. 1463, but she had not then remarried (Turnbull, *op. cit.*, pp. 43–54).

other heavy commitments, this cash surplus may indeed be taken as evidence of her well-ordered finances.

Fear of a foreign invasion aimed at the Welsh coast and the prospect of a Lancastrian rising there led Edward IV to place the Staffords' Marcher lordships in the hands of his two strongest and hitherto most loyal supporters. Richard, Earl of Warwick, obtained the receiverships of Newport and Brecon in November 1460, but was obliged to surrender the latter soon afterwards; William, Lord Herbert, whose devotion to the Yorkist cause also demanded an appropriate reward, had assumed control of the administration by September 1461, and continued to occupy this part of Duke Henry's inheritance until his own death eight years later.[64] As a Welshman with estates along the March, Herbert was able to exercise close personal supervision over the collection of judicial dues, and for the first time in many years the lordship of Newport began to realise its full potential. Between 1465 and 1468 his net annual profits stood at about £358 – above the annual farm of £100 a year which he was paying into the Exchequer. By the simple expedient of imprisoning any recalcitrant officials in Newport Castle, he also managed to clear a substantial backlog of unpaid debts and effectively prevented the accumulation of new ones.[65] This remarkable display of administrative efficiency contrasts sharply with the returns made for Brecon and its appurtenances by John Milewater, receiver general of Edward IV's Welsh revenues. There is no record of any money ever having been paid to the Earl of Warwick; indeed, once an annual assignment of 500 marks for the upkeep of Duke Henry and his younger brother had been made upon the receivership of Brecon in 1464 and increased by a further £100 one year later, there was nothing left to account for. Even before this date net profits barely exceeded an average of £176 a year, while arrearages had risen to over £463 by Michaelmas 1465.[66] As the first Duke had found to his cost, this problem could never be solved by an absentee landlord, and if Milewater, the experienced royal administrator, gave up the unequal struggle, there was little hope for Duke Henry, who took livery of his depleted inheritance in January 1473.

[64] *C.F.R.*, 1452–61, p. 287; *C.P.R.*, 1461–7, p. 13; Pugh, *The Marcher Lordships*, p. 240.   [65] *Ibid.*, pp. 179–80.
[66] *C.P.R.*, 1461–7, pp. 324, 463–4; S.C.6/1305/15, 1157/9 m. 2, 11 m. 1, 12 m. 1.

Chapter 7

THE FINANCES OF THE STAFFORDS,
1473–1521

The almost total loss of material concerning the Stafford estates between 1473 and 1483 makes it impossible even to speculate about the size of Duke Henry's income. That he benefited financially from the Duchess Anne's death in 1480 goes without question, for she had until then retained as her dower the most productive English lordships, leaving Buckingham to face the problems of administration in Wales. He had nevertheless been fortunate in gaining entry to the customary two thirds of his inheritance in January 1473, some six years before actually coming of age. While still a minor he had also obtained possession of land worth an annual 400 marks which was due to him in reversion from the late Sir Henry Stafford.[1] Finally, in 1478, Edward IV relinquished his claim to the lordship of Cantref Selyf in favour of Duke Henry, although it is unlikely that the latter derived any profit from the award. Very little is known of the Marcher estates during this period. Frequent visits to Brecon Castle did not enhance Buckingham's popularity among the Welsh, nor could he rely upon the unqualified support of his senior administrators; these two factors may well have intensified a decline in revenues, with which, as a young and inexperienced landlord, he was ill equipped to deal. Between them the receiverships of Newport and Brecon produced no more than £429 of the £1,419 available to Duke Henry in clear revenues over the period Michaelmas 1476 to *ca.* 23 May 1478. Yet although the receiver general began his account with arrears of almost £720, he was able to discharge over two thirds of this debt, while his predecessor obtained further warrants for outstanding expenses of £1,457.[2] It cannot have been easy for Buckingham to live within this tight

---

[1] *C.P.R.*, 1467–76, p. 298.

[2] D.641/1/2/26, *passim*.

budget, especially as the revenues from eleven of his more profitable English manors had been set aside for the payment of Joan, Viscountess Beaumont's dower in 1474 and were still being assigned for this purpose six years later.[3] Indeed, there is no means of telling exactly what proportion of Buckingham's total expenditure the receiver general was in fact able to meet. His recorded outlay of £89 on fees and rewards to household servants, for example, must surely represent only a part of the domestic wage bill; nor do we know how much the great household cost at this time. No other revenues were evidently then available, and if the Stafford estates could not produce enough for him to live on, then Duke Henry must have run into debt. Perhaps the additional £1,200 a year which came to him on the Dowager's death was not enough to compensate for an overexpenditure of several years; but even if his finances had reached a state of equilibrium by 1483, the Duke's decision to join Gloucester's *coup d'état* was clearly influenced by the prospect of some rich reward. He may well have been promised revenues worth £1,084 a year from the remaining de Bohun estates, since these, together with other generous gifts, were his within a few weeks of Richard's coronation. Yet the cost of maintaining a larger and even more splendid household, swollen by numerous armed retainers, undoubtedly offset whatever financial benefits accrued from his association with the new King, and could have been a determining factor behind his own attempt on the throne.

THE STAFFORD ESTATES FROM 1483 TO 1498

Having settled an allowance of 200 marks a year upon the Dowager Duchess Katherine, and having made provision for the payment of her late husband's debts, Richard III began to distribute lands and offices from the Stafford estates among his supporters.[4] The division of spoils was fortunately short-lived: Henry Tudor's first parliament made haste to repeal the act of attainder passed against Buckingham in 1483, and restored to the Dowager a jointure valued at 1,000 marks a year. Her marriage to the

---

[3] *Ibid.*, mm. 1–3; P.C.C. Logge 2.
[4] *C.P.R.*, 1476–85, pp. 436, 497–8; Appendix B, *passim*.

King's uncle, Jasper, Duke of Bedford, presumably influenced both the size and rapidity of this award, which comprised property in East Anglia, Kent, the Midlands, Gloucestershire and Newport, and was worth far more than the official estimate placed upon it. The removal in 1495 of a clause permitting Duke Edward to contest the settlement once he came of age suggests that it was fully expected to promote ' great uncerteinte and troble ' between mother and son.[5]

The Dowager's net annual income can rarely have fallen below £1,000 and may well have been far higher. Bedford treated her estates as a separate unit, thus making it possible to introduce a more centralised and economical administrative system. The four sub-receivers whom he appointed to supervise her share of the central circuit, for instance, were able to keep a close watch on local expenditure, and in 1496 delivered over £483 to the receiver general for Katherine's immediate use.[6] Net profits from the Staffords' Gloucestershire estates appear to have fallen slightly since the previous minority, but an average of £255 a year was still available between 1485 and 1494 once modest running costs had been met.[7] No returns have survived from the receivership of Kent and Surrey during this period; and because the Dowager had only part of the family property there, a comparison with later returns is somewhat misleading. Allowing both for this and for the last Duke's improved system of revenue collection, it seems that about £180 (but no more than £200) a year net reached her coffers from the South East. The lordship of Newport, again beset by the same administrative problems as earlier, hardly produced much more while it was in Katherine's hands. This part of the Stafford estates had been given to her as a means of strengthening Bedford's influence in Wales, although the local tenantry were no more amenable to his authority than to that of the first and second Dukes of Buckingham before him. The receiver's total charge at Michaelmas 1487 came to £440, but included unpaid fines of £85, £68 claimed by the Crown and almost £125 in straightforward arrears.[8] A second account, compiled three

5 *Rot. Parl.*, vol. VI pp. 284, 471.
6 S.C.6/Hen. VII 1842.
7 D.641/1/2/192–9, *passim.*
8 Eg. Roll 2206 m. 14.

years after Bedford's death, suggests that this mounting deficit had been cleared; on the other hand, the practice of cancelling any overdue debts when a receivership changed hands may well have forced his widow to accept a considerable loss of revenue.[9] Certainly, her net profits at that time amounted to less than £167.

Despite his heavy expenditure on a large and costly household, Bedford does not seem to have exploited his wife's estates in order to raise maximum immediate profits at the expense of the future heir. Wholesale negligence did far more damage than outright venality, especially in the lordship of Newport, where seignorial rights were allowed to lapse and ' gret and yn maner extreme wast and distruccion' was done in the forests of Machen.[10] It is unlikely that Bedford ordered the sale of this valuable timber, which was probably removed by the staff and local inhabitants. Nor can he be entirely blamed for the existence of dishonest officials and the absence of effective supervision. Even Margaret, Countess of Richmond, the King's mother and keeper of the remaining Stafford estates, found it impossible to exercise her authority in Wales. Net profits from the receivership of Brecon had risen appreciably by 1496, but nothing could be done to improve administrative standards there. The receiver general and John Gunter, one of Henry VII's most experienced auditors, visited Brecon in May 1494 with specific instructions for the collection of debts, but made little headway in the face of opposition from below.[11] Lady Margaret's unprecedented decision to write off a long-standing deficit of £2,095 two years later shows what little hope remained of recovering the money before Duke Edward came of age.[12] Her failure to effect any improvements in Wales is all the more remarkable when compared with her skilful and efficient management of the Staffords' English estates. Nonetheless, although the receiver general was being paid an average of

[9] N.L.W. Tredegar Park Ms. 147 mm. 10–10v.

[10] Pugh, *The Marcher Lordships*, 266; for a discussion of Jasper Tudor's finances see R. S. Thomas, 'The Political Career, Estates and "connection" of Jasper Tudor, Earl of Pembroke and Duke of Bedford' (unpublished Ph.D. thesis, Univ. Coll. Swansea, 1971).

[11] S.C.6/Hen. VII 1652 m. 5v (account of the receiver of Brecon for the year ending Michaelmas 1494).

[12] Eg. Roll 2193 m. 6 (account of the receiver of Brecon for the year ending Michaelmas 1496).

about £1,384 from England and Wales during the late 1480s and took delivery of £1,876 over the year ending Michaelmas 1496, it was not always possible for him to maintain a balanced budget.[13] This was because Henry VII had pre-empted £1,000 a year from his mother's share of the Stafford inheritance for expenditure on the royal household, leaving her to support Duke Edward and his younger brother at an annual cost of 500 marks.[14] Once these two permanent charges had been met, very little remained for such necessities as fees, wages and legal expenses, which were kept at a minimum. The last Duke had many reasons for gratitude towards his guardian, not least being her concern to husband all the revenues available from his estates and render more effective the way in which they were levied. There is no evidence of any deliberate spoliation or wastage at any level during her thirteen years' tenure of the young Duke's patrimony.

DUKE EDWARD'S LANDED INCOME FROM 1498 TO 1521

Buckingham obtained custody of his entire inheritance in 1498 while still technically a minor. Whatever sorrow he may have felt on his mother's early death some months before was no doubt assuaged by the prospect of lands and rents worth an additional £1,000 a year. Other property in the South West reverted to him when Duke Humphrey's grandson, the childless Earl of Wiltshire, died in 1499.[15] From the very beginning, therefore, he was able to implement sweeping reforms throughout the entire estates – reforms which were clearly based upon the same principles of centralisation and economy adopted by Lady Margaret and her ministers. All senior estate staff were now no more than financial agents acting on the cofferer's behalf. At Michaelmas 1502, for example, the receiver general delivered almost £1,432 to the coffers, above an additional £158 in expenditure awaiting the ducal warrant.[16] These remarkably high payments, far in excess of net profits recorded during the first Duke's lifetime, were made possible by a dramatic reduction in running costs and local

---

13 W.A.M. 32348–9 (accounts of Lady Margaret's receivers general for the years Michaelmas 1485–88 and 1495–6).

14 *Rot. Parl.*, vol. VI p. 299; C.66/564 m. 5.

15 *C.C.R.*, 1485–1500, nos. 1219–20.   16 D.641/1/2/28.

expenses. Indeed, the central circuit was said to produce over £1,728 a year net at the time of Buckingham's death in 1521. A comparison between this assessment and actual deliveries to the coffers then made by the receiver general suggests that it was impossible to raise much more than half the anticipated amount; but since large sums of money had been retained locally during the confused period after Duke Edward's execution, the original estimate may not have been too wide of the mark.[17] Six manors worth approximately £344 a year had also been sold some months before, although no allowance was made for a corresponding drop in revenues.

Returns from the South Western estates showed a marked improvement, again because of more effective administrative techniques rather than greater agricultural productivity. Buckingham's presence at Thornbury acted as a spur to greater efficiency. Net profits averaged about £440 annually during the period after his first entry, and had it not been for an outlay of £190 on building works in 1504, they would have reached the unprecedented total of £853 for that year alone.[18] Again, the apparent discrepancy of £200 between real and potential receipts in 1521 was due almost solely to the problems of revenue collection usually encountered when a receivership changed hands. The manors in Gloucestershire, Hampshire and Wiltshire were then valued at £502 a year net – a figure barely £30 in excess of deliveries made to the cofferer from this area some years before.[19] The more distant English lordships were also benefiting from closer supervision. Cash receipts from Staffordshire rose steadily from £256 to £387 over the years 1497 to 1512; and even in 1519, when there was considerable local resistance to the imposition of higher entry fines, Buckingham recovered about £342 net in rents and profits of justice from his tenants.[20] Only once, in 1451, had the first Duke managed to raise more than £300 from the same receivership, although returns from the nearby lordship of Caus were

---

[17] E.36/181 fos. 2–26 (a valor of the Stafford estates for the year ending Michaelmas 1521); S.C.6/Hen. VIII 5841.

[18] D.641/1/2/200–2, 204; Add. Roll 26873.

[19] E.36/181 fos. 45–51; S.C.6/Hen. VIII 5819; Longleat Ms. 6415 m. 1 (a cofferer's account for the year ending 31 Mar. 1515).

[20] D.641/1/2/79–81, 83–4, 88, 96; S.C.6/Hen. VII 1844, Hen. VIII 5803.

evidently somewhat higher during his lifetime. Net profits had always fluctuated dramatically, but at less than £45 a year, Duke Edward's average receipts fell far short of the £75 anticipated in the valor of 1521.[21] These losses were amply compensated for elsewhere. The receivership of Kent and Surrey was valued at £334 a year net in 1499, and produced all but £6 of this sum seven years later. It was in fact worth rather more, for payments of £249 then listed among the receiver's arrearages were nothing more than routine expenses awaiting Buckingham's warrant. A second account, drawn up at Michaelmas 1521, gives an even more misleading impression of indebtedness, this time because of the retention and late delivery of revenues which took place after Duke Edward's execution.[22] There is certainly no evidence of any long-term financial difficulties here, or in any of the other English receiverships. Although gross receipts from Holderness fell by approximately £200 between 1448 and 1521, Buckingham managed to cut running costs in an attempt to offset this decline. At least three quarters of the net receipts of £604 anticipated by the crown commissioners in 1521 seem to have been reaching the coffers during the previous decade. The local estate staff delivered £492 to the receiver in 1508, which probably left him with about £460 for delivery to the coffers; but there is no means of telling if this figure represents a reliable average. Over the year ending Michaelmas 1515, for example, the cofferer obtained cash and bonds worth £702 from Holderness; the receiver may well have been paying off some old debts, but his achievement is no less remarkable for that.[23]

Once again, it was in Wales that the twin problems of mal-administration and mounting arrearages combined to thwart Buckingham's plans for reform. Attempts to revive old seignorial rights and privileges merely strengthened local resistance, while Henry VII's insistence upon the payment of £1,646 in miscel-laneous judicial dues outstanding from the time of Duke Edward's minority must have consumed the equivalent of three years' revenue from Newport and Brecon. King Henry's ' gift ' of the

21 Eg. Rolls 2198, 2200; Longleat Mss. 3701, 3990; E.36/181 fos. 31–4.
22 D.641/1/2/27 mm. 9v–12v (a valor of part of the Stafford estates for the year ending Michaelmas 1499); S.C.6/Hen. VII 1076 mm. 14–16; Hen. VIII 5795.
23 D.641/1/2/27 mm. 1–4v; S.C.6/Hen. VII 1029, *passim*; Longleat Ms. 6415 m. 2.

lordship of Cantref Selyf cost the Duke a further £1,000 in 1509, although it is extremely unlikely that the property in question could even have fetched one third of this sum on the open market.[24] These additional charges came at a particularly unfortunate time, for arrears were building up faster than ever before. Respited, or temporary, debts charged to the receiver of Brecon at Michaelmas 1519 accounted for about £7,770 of the £28,569 euphemistically described as ' cash in hand '. The rest of this sum was made up of fines, forfeits and tallages, some of which had been unpaid since the time of Buckingham's first entry.[25] The lordship of Brecon can rarely have produced more than half the £981 expected from it in 1521, and so great was Duke Edward's concern at the state of his finances there that in 1520 he had begun serious preparations for a tour of the Marches. The problem of arrearages was far less acute at Newport, since the time-lag between initial expenditure and final acquittal was responsible for a significant proportion of the receiver's debts. In 1512, for instance, the staff and tenants petitioned to be excused a joint deficit of £691 which had grown up over the previous twelve years because of the delay in clearing local expenditure. Unpaid rents and fines in the order of £843 had still to be collected, however, and they threatened to remain overdue for an indefinite period.[26] The residents of Newport would not pay the fines demanded of them for redeeming the Great Sessions and this single act of resistance was alone responsible for over half the receiver's debts. Although Buckingham could console himself with the fact that net profits were over £100 higher than they had been during the 1440s, he was really no nearer to enforcing his authority in Wales than the first Duke had been before him.

Despite his lack of success in the Marcher lordships, Duke Edward had many real achievements to his credit. Comparisons with earlier valors are often misleading, but there are clear signs

[24] D.1721/1/1 fos. 378v–9; the lordship produced £15 clear over the year ending Michaelmas 1519 (S.C.6/Hen. VIII 4775 m. lv); although it was fairly common for the vendor to ask about twenty times the annual net value of agricultural property, the amount paid naturally varied according to circumstances. Whereas Buckingham was able to sell land in the Midlands and South at a rather higher rate (see p. 141), he could not have hoped to strike such advantageous bargains in Wales.

[25] S.C.6/Hen. VIII 4775.

[26] Eg. Roll 2207.

of a substantial reduction in running costs, which had consumed about £1,280 a year during the 1440s.[27] According to the royal commissioners' assessment, they stood at £743 in 1521, and would have left almost £4,906 in hand, above all reprises: that is to say net profits were at least 30% higher than they had been seventy years before. There may well have been an even more striking improvement, for this valor, compiled in a period of administrative change and uncertainty, anticipated rather lower takings than those actually recorded by the cofferer in his account for the year ending Michaelmas 1515. Almost £5,053 of his total charge then comprised payments from senior estate staff, while a further £571 was made available to him in loans and assignments from Buckingham's privy purse. William Cholmeley needed only a fraction of this second sum to balance his books, and was left with a cash surplus of £507 when all his expenses had been met.[28] A second account for the seven months before Duke Edward's arrest conveys the same impression of a substantial income skilfully deployed through careful management. The revenues of £2,839 paid into the coffers between 1 October 1520 and 30 April 1521 were almost as high as Duke Humphrey's *annual* receipts during the early 1450s.[29]

DUKE EDWARD'S EXPENDITURE FROM 1498 TO 1521

From 1500 onwards, the great and itinerant households were financed by the cofferer, presumably with the intention of cutting down on unnecessary expenses. Despite the amount of available evidence it is hard to calculate the exact cost of these two bodies. Combined accounts for the year ending Michaelmas 1504 provide a detailed record of purchases and other current charges, but may possibly omit a significant part of the domestic wage bill. The great household cost £1,673 at this time, while £210 and £178 were spent on Lord Stafford's separate establishment and Duke Edward's riding household respectively. The treasurer invariably retained large sums of money from year to year, and on this occasion closed his account with £243 in hand.[30] A book of pur

---

[27] E.36/181, *passim*.
[28] Longleat Ms. 6415, *passim*.
[29] E.36/220, *passim*.
[30] Add. Ms. 40859B.

chases made for the great household between 31 March 1506 and
1 April 1507 records a total outlay of £1,370 on wages and provisions, including sums assigned for the upkeep of Buckingham's
retinue in London throughout the summer of 1506. There are no
references, however, to expenditure on the administrative and
domestic staff who remained behind at Thornbury, and in this
respect the account is incomplete.[31] Henry VIII's visit to Penshurst in August 1519 and his meeting with Francis I at the Field
of the Cloth of Gold in the following year both proved extremely
expensive for Duke Edward. According to three brief but comprehensive household accounts enrolled over the period 1 October
1517 to 30 September 1520, an extra £1,000 was spent on hospitality for the court (Table VI).

Whereas keepers of the wardrobe had previously received both
goods and money directly from a number of different sources,
they now dealt almost exclusively with the cofferer. Thomas
Bridges, who served as keeper from 1515, appears to have been
entrusted with far larger quantities of cloth and other commodi-
ties than were needed in any one year, which explains why such

TABLE VI. *Three Accounts for the Great and Itinerant Households, 1517–20*

(Royal Ms. 14B XXXV B mm. 3–4)

	1 Oct. 1517– 30 Sept. 1518	1 Oct. 1518– 30 Sept. 1519	1 Oct. 1519– 30 Sept. 1520
Receipts			
Goods/cash in hand	£ 432	£ 519	£ 432
Current charge	£2,822	£3,674	£3,216
Total	£3,254	£4,193	£3,648
Expenditure			
Itinerant household	£ 423	£ 552	£ 331
Fees & wages	£ 340	£ 346	£ 403
Provisions, etc.	£1,972	£2,863	£2,273
Total	£2,735	£3,761	£3,007
Goods/cash in hand	£ 519	£ 432	£ 641

[31] Longleat Misc. Ms. XII fos. 30–1, 68–9, 123v–4v.

comparatively large sums of money (the cash value of these goods) were charged to him at the beginning of each new account.

Even though it could exceed £2,400 Duke Edward's annual expenditure on the wardrobe was by no means excessive, given that it sufficed to clothe and equip his family and all his domestic servants. The increased cost of robes, armour and supplies for the ducal retinue in France placed a particularly heavy burden upon the keeper, whose additional outlay of more than £2,000 in 1520 was largely financed by a series of short-term loans.

TABLE VII. *The Wardrober's Declared Accounts, 1516–20*[32]

	31 Mar. 1516–31 Mar. 1517	30 Sept. 1517–30 Sept. 1518	30 Sept. 1518–30 Sept. 1519	30 Sept. 1519–30 Sept. 1520
Cash/goods in hand	£ 48	£ 304	£ 448	£ 526
Current receipts	£1,034	£2,558	£2,664	£4,490
Total	£1,082	£2,862	£3,112	£5,016
Expenditure	£1,023	£2,414	£2,586	£4,200
Cash/goods in hand	£ 59	£ 448	£ 526	£ 816

Although the household and wardrobe were the main continuous charges upon Duke Edward's income, two other major items of expenditure accounted for a sizeable proportion of his resources over the years. The business of finding suitable husbands for his three daughters was a costly one, especially as he hoped in this way to extend his political influence. On 9 July 1509 he bought the wardship and marriage of Ralph, Earl of Westmorland, whom he had chosen for his eldest daughter, Elizabeth.[33] Shortly before their formal betrothal, Thomas, Lord Howard, a more powerful and potentially richer candidate, asked Buckingham for the girl's hand, and much against her will she was

---

[32] D.641/1/3/9 mm. 1–5; Royal Ms. 14B XXXV C mm. 2–4.
[33] *L. & P. Henry VIII*, vol. I, pt ii, no. 1156; the purchase price is unknown, although Buckingham received an allowance of £50 a year for the boy's upkeep (Longleat Ms. 6415 m. 3).

obliged to marry him. Howard appears to have been the sole beneficiary of the marriage contract, for whereas Duke Edward had paid him 2,000 marks at the time of the wedding in 1512, he consistently failed to honour his financial obligations, and even deprived his wife of her jewellery and other possessions.[34] Had the Duke lived he might have behaved otherwise, but the Stafford connexion was no longer of any use to him after 1521. The young Earl of Westmorland meanwhile remained in Buckingham's custody, and being too valuable a prize to let out of the family was married to Katherine, the Duke's second daughter. The size of her dowry remains unknown, although it cannot have been much less than that settled upon her elder sister. The marriage of Mary Stafford to George, Lord Bergavenny, in June 1519 cost her father *at least* 2,000 marks, although the immediate burden was somewhat lightened by Bergavenny's evident willingness to postpone the date of payment.[35] Understandably, the Duke sought to recoup his losses by negotiating the best possible contract for his son and heir, Henry, Lord Stafford. At Wolsey's suggestion he approached the Earl of Shrewsbury, who had daughters of marriageable age, but made such exorbitant demands that the Earl was forced to decline his offer.[36] The terms finally accepted by Margaret, Countess of Salisbury, on the marriage of her daughter to Henry Stafford in 1518 may represent a compromise on Buckingham's part; even so, he had every reason to congratulate himself on driving a hard bargain. Ursula Pole brought with her a dowry of 3,000 marks, payable in regular instalments over the next six years, together with the promise of a further 1,000 marks should her mother recover certain property from the Crown. Besides undertaking to meet any incidental expenses – which included the cost of the wedding celebrations – the Countess also agreed to settle an estate worth 700 marks a year upon the couple. Buckingham for his part was to make them sure of a further £500 a year, but had not even begun to make the necessary arrangements by the time of his death.[37]

---

[34] Cottonian Ms. Titus B1 fo. 390.

[35] Royal Mss. 14B XXXV A9, 10 (creditors' rolls drawn up by Buckingham in 1520).

[36] *L. & P. Henry VIII*, vol. II, pt i, nos. 1893, 1970.

[37] H.M.C. *Seventh Report* (2 vols., H.M.S.O., 1879), vol. I p. 584; *Report on the Hastings Mss.*, vol. I p. 308.

He was no less anxious that his illegitimate daughter should do well for herself, and planned her betrothal to Thomas Fitzgerald, the Earl of Kildare's son and heir, whose wardship and marriage he purchased from the Crown in 1519.[38] Because of his father's imprisonment under suspicion of treason, the young child had been entrusted to a series of guardians – two of whom, Thomas Dudley and Thomas Dowcra, the Prior of the Order of St John of Jerusalem in England, insisted upon adequate compensation for their lost revenues. Thus, in addition to the £200 demanded by Henry VIII, the Duke had also to buy out Dudley's interest at an agreed price of £97 and make good the Prior's claims. He owed Dowcra 200 marks in March 1520, which means that altogether he had spent over £430 on a match destined never to take place.[39] It had cost him at least £4,766 to marry off all four daughters, but against this must be set the £2,000 which he expected to receive from the Countess of Salisbury by Christmas 1524. Only his early death made the balance so unfavourable.

The conversion of Thornbury manor into a semi-fortified country seat was Buckingham's most conspicuous item of expenditure. We do not know exactly how much his grandiose schemes cost, but the royal commissioners' description of work completed by 1521 and a later survey made in 1582 both suggest an outlay of several thousand pounds on the building alone.[40] Although some fairly extensive repairs had been done before the foundations of the great gatehouse were laid in 1511, this seems to mark the start of Duke Edward's rebuilding programme. Three years later the cofferer dispatched £823 *pro novis edificiis et reparacionibus manerii de Thornbury*, at which date the house itself was almost finished; and in January 1521 he paid for a final inspection of the walls and roofing.[41] The state apartments, hall, chapel and private chambers were all then in use, but most of the store rooms and lodgings set around an outer court remained incomplete, as did the massive gatehouse leading to them. Work on this part of the

---

[38] *L. & P. Hen. VIII*, vol. III, pt i, no. 497; Royal Ms. 14B XXXV A2 (a creditors' roll drawn up by Duke Edward on 31 May 1518).

[39] Royal Mss. 7F XIV fo. 4 (a book of receipts and payments by the Chancellor from 1 Oct. 1518 to 31 Sept. 1519); 14B XXXV A10.

[40] E.36/150 fos. 4 (19)–4v; Stowe Ms. 795 fo. 59 *et seq*.

[41] Longleat Ms. 6415 m. 7; E.36/220 fo. 16.

building halted abruptly in about 1519, when supplies of fine quality stone either ran out or proved too expensive. In view of the unusually high cost of running both the household and the wardrobe at this time, it was only natural that Buckingham should effect temporary economies elsewhere. There is certainly no reason to believe that he lacked either the capital or credit to continue with his plans, since other landowners, such as Henry, ninth Earl of Northumberland, are known to have spent freely on similar ventures in the face of far more pressing financial obligations.[42] Few residences of this size were completed over a successive period of years, and the Duke may well have chosen to suspend operations while absent at court and in France. The fact remains, however, that by Christmas 1520 his chief concern was to repay the creditors who had advanced him large sums of money over the previous two years.

Duke Edward's *optimum* expenditure stood at about £5,500 a year during the period Michaelmas 1514 to Michaelmas 1518. The household and wardrobe together consumed no more than £4,200 of Cholmeley's annual receipts, above an average outlay of about £1,000 a year on work at Thornbury and other extra-ordinary payments. Even if he was not living exactly within his income, Buckingham was quite clearly able to balance his accounts by raising a few modest short-term loans. In 1519, however, he required an additional £1,500 to pay for Henry VIII's entertainment at Penshurst, and in the following year he spent *at least* £3,000 on his visit to France. As one of the richest men in England with a reputation for great shrewdness in business affairs, he found it easy to obtain credit, but was thus forced to pledge future revenues for many years ahead. Not all his debts were so straightforward, or of such a recent date. Shortly after coming of age in 1498, Duke Edward had been faced with successive demands for fines and damages of £7,200 claimed by the Crown, and even though Henry VIII had allowed him to recover a bond for £400 in 1509, there was no question of any further exemptions. According to a royal memorandum compiled in 1514, £3,769 of the original debt (or perhaps even a new one) remained

---

[42] G. R. Batho, 'The Finances of an Elizabethan Nobleman; Henry Percy, Ninth Earl of Northumberland', *Econ. H.R.*, 2nd series, IX (1956–7), pp. 446–8.

payable in annual instalments of 500 marks.[43] The first entry in
' A credytors rolle made off my nowne hand of all such summys
of mone that I, Edward Duke off Buckyngham dothe owe unto
the last daye of May anno X Regis Henrici Octavi [1518] '
records a greatly reduced debt to the Crown of £1,322; but by
September 1520 Henry and his agents had obtained bonds from
the Duke for three separate sums totalling £2,855. Political as
well as financial considerations made the King unwilling to grant
him a final *quietus*, although it is worth pointing out that
Buckingham owed considerably less than many other noblemen,
including his own brother.[44]

The Duke's other debts came to about £600 on 31 May 1518.
He had borrowed a further £1,077 by the following December
and in January 1519 noted that £2,428 was ' payable bytwene thys
and Crystmes '.[45] If we deduct the £1,322 then owed to the King,
it appears that most of his creditors were men whose demands
would have been met as a matter of routine out of the domestic
budget. A memorandum dated March 1519 shows how Duke
Edward planned to set aside £7,300 over the next five years for
such a purpose.[46] Again, only part of this sum can be described as
an additional charge upon his income, since merchants and tradesmen were often prepared to wait for some time before the settlement of their accounts. These short-term advances, upon which
every great landowner relied to some extent, were quite different
from formal loans repayable with interest over a set period of
years. The cofferer seems to have managed quite well without the
latter kind of financial assistance until 1519 when Robert Gilbert,
Buckingham's chancellor, raised over £2,937 on his behalf. In all,
Gilbert delivered £3,135 to his colleague during the summer of
that year, largely in order to pay for the festivities at Penshurst.[47]
Some of the money had doubtless been borrowed to tide Duke
Edward over until the Michaelmas audit, but enough was still
owing in March 1520 seriously to upset all his earlier calculations.
He then acknowledged eighteen separate obligations for the repay-

---

43 D.1721/1/1 fos. 378v–9; *L. & P. Henry VIII*, vol. I, pt i, no. 357 (41); S.P.1/9
fo. 180v.

44 Royal Mss. 14B XXXV A2, 11; *L. & P. Henry VIII*, vol. III, pt i, no. 1153.

45 Royal Mss. 14B XXXV A2, 4, 5.

46 *Ibid.*, 14B XXXV D.   47 *Ibid.*, 7F XIV fos. 1–19, *passim*.

ment of £6,949, about £795 of which was already overdue.[48] Because he had not then completed an entry for ' merchants and tradespeople ' his debts cannot be estimated in their entirety, and it is only for the latter part of 1520 that the full extent of these commitments becomes known. An undated creditors' roll, attributable on the grounds of internal evidence to some point between June and December of that year, bears the clear total of £10,535 in Buckingham's own hand. Approximately £3,730 had been raised over the previous half-year as a result of unforeseen expenses arising from Duke Edward's unwilling attendance upon the King in France.[49]

Despite the apparent size of his debts, Buckingham owed no more than the equivalent of two years' clear landed income; contemporaries did not regard borrowing on this scale as excessively risky and credit was still readily available to him. He had nonetheless to make repayments at the rate of £2,800 a year, and understandably sought to ease this heavy burden in a variety of ways. In November 1520, Robert Gilbert was dispatched to appease Buckingham's more influential creditors by offering them further securities in return for easier terms, while the Duke began to put pressure on those who owed him money.[50] He had always kept a list of such debts, but found that others were no less anxious to postpone the date of reckoning than he was himself. John, Lord Berners, for example, had entered recognizances for the payment of £1,200 some six years before; he could not meet these obligations and there was no way for Duke Edward to force him without recourse to the cumbersome machinery of the law.[51] Some alternative source of revenue had to be made available quickly, and since he was naturally unwilling to negotiate any more formal loans, Buckingham arranged for the sale of property on the open market. Although hastened by a pressing need to augment his landed income, his decision to dispose of manors worth about £195 a year net was quite clearly in line with earlier plans for streamlining organisation of the Stafford estates. Like many other

[48] *Ibid.*, 14B XXXV A10.
[49] *Ibid.*, 14B XXXV A9.
[50] Cottonian Ms. Titus B1 fo. 171v.
[51] Royal Ms. 14B XXXV A1 (Buckingham's list of debts owed to him at 30 Sept. 1516); Cottonian Ms. Titus B1 fo. 171v.

landowners he recognised the administrative advantages which could be gained from selling off outlying or unproductive blocs of land; the quest for greater efficiency had already led him to investigate the possibility of certain exchanges, so that holdings of this kind could be replaced by farmland nearer to the main receiving centres. The valor of 1521 records an earlier agreement with Lord Berners, whereby the Duke had surrendered seven scattered farms in Kent and Surrey, the Oxfordshire manor of Stratton Audley and land on the periphery of the South Western estates in return for unspecified agricultural property – probably in Essex, where most of Berners' patrimony lay.[52] A number of tenements in Southwark had also gone as part of a larger but now undocumented exchange with the Duke of Suffolk.[53] On the other hand, Robert, Lord Willoughby de Brooke, was not so easily convinced by his neighbour's persuasive arguments, especially as the lordship of Caliland, which Buckingham hoped to exchange for more accessible farmland near Thornbury, had so evidently suffered from neglect over the years. For once the Duke's characteristically devious approach, with veiled allusions to ' grete offers ' from other interested parties, proved unsuccessful.[54] Experience had taught him to behave circumspectly where property transactions were concerned, for in 1506 he had handed over the manor of Leo's Hall, Suffolk, in return for Sir Thomas Lucas' estates at Helion, only to find that he had been ' ylle and untrowly defamed to ye yerly losse of a xj li or a bove be syde waves and straves with oder adwantages '.[55]

Buckingham had every reason, however, to congratulate himself on the results of his land sales during the spring of 1520. These raised £4,546, partly in immediate cash payments – a figure somewhat greater than the actual value of the property concerned. On 16 May Sir William Compton, a royal favourite, bought four Warwickshire manors worth £80 a year for £1,640, and it is possible that terms for an exchange involving Beaverstone Castle

---

[52] E.36/181 fos. 24, 43–4, 49.

[53] *Ibid.*, fo. 43.

[54] Cottonian Ms. Titus B1 fo. 172; Caliland had declined in value from £17 to £13 a year, net, between 1442 and 1521. At the time of Buckingham's death unpaid rents exceeded £53 (D.641/1/2/17 m. 7; E.36/181 fo. 25; S.C.6/Hen. VIII 5841 m. 7v).

[55] John Gage, *The History and Antiquities of Suffolk: Thingoe Hundred* (London, 1838), p. 92; W.A.M. 5470 fo. 33.

in Gloucestershire were also discussed at this time.[56] Making a
virtue of necessity, Duke Edward had chosen to part with land
on the very perimeter of the central circuit and thus rationalise
an unduly large and disparate administrative unit. He had no such
reasons for selling either Colston Basset, the most profitable of his
Nottinghamshire manors, or farmland at Hengrave in Suffolk,
and drove a hard bargain over the purchase price with the London
merchant, Sir Thomas Kitson. On 20 May 1520, the latter agreed
to pay £2,000 at once for the two properties and deliver a further
£340 to Buckingham on his arrival at Calais a month later.[57]
Although he was clearly unwilling to offer as much as 850 marks
for the manor of Ratcliffe on Soar, also in Nottinghamshire, Sir
Richard Sacheverell finally committed himself in February 1520.
His reluctance to proceed with the sale is understandable in view
of the dilapidated state of the manor house and buildings, which
would have cost a considerable amount to repair. Sir Richard had
originally made a generous offer for the leasehold of Colston
Basset, but for some unknown reason chose to return the Duke's
indentures and acquire the less productive holding outright.[58]
For his part, Buckingham had done well to cut his losses and dispose of property unlikely to attract a reliable tenant. Nonetheless,
it is hard to believe that a landlord of his proven ability could not
have effected the necessary improvements himself, or that, under
happier financial circumstances, some less drastic way of reducing
the central circuit to manageable proportions could not have been
found. Duke Edward's alleged desire ' to see ye tyme yt Sir William Compton shuld be glad to lett hym have ye land ayen yt
he had sold hym ' suggests clearly enough that he would have
preferred to keep the Stafford estates intact.[59]

Events during the summers of 1519 and 1520 undoubtedly
placed a severe strain on Buckingham's income, but his problems
were neither unique nor insuperable. The fifth Earl of Northumberland, for example, was obliged to borrow on an equally
large scale during this period, yet almost all his debts had been
cleared when he died in 1527.[60] There is no reason to suppose that,

---

[56] *Statutes of the Realm*, vol. III pp. 271–3; Cottonian Ms. Titus B1 fo. 173v.
[57] *Statutes of the Realm*, vol. III pp. 273–6.
[58] *Ibid.*, p. 276; W.A.M. 5470 fos. 47v, 57v.   [59] Harleian Ms. 283 fo. 70.
[60] J. M. W. Bean, *The Estates of the Percy Family* (Oxford, 1958), pp. 141–2.

had he lived, Duke Edward would not likewise have restored his finances to a state of equilibrium. The chance survival of so many lists of creditors from his last two years tends to direct attention away from the financial skill which he had displayed over two decades. To infer, as does K. B. McFarlane, that Buckingham's sudden dependence upon ' gulls and money lenders ' was a sign of imminent bankruptcy is quite unwarranted. For a landowner of his great wealth to owe the equivalent of two years' net revenue was hardly ' financial ruin '; the fact that Duke Edward took serious measures to repay his debts before they did indeed reach unmanageable proportions surely indicates his determination to avoid such an outcome.[61] A far more serious threat to his continued prosperity – one not mentioned by McFarlane – lay in the problem of mounting arrearages in the Welsh Marcher lordships. As Buckingham knew only too well, one third of the unpaid debts owed by the tenants of Brecon alone would have sufficed to meet all his obligations, and it was in the hope of collecting some of this money that he planned to visit Wales in November 1520. Whether or not he would have succeeded must remain a matter of speculation; but it is reasonable to suppose that his major preoccupation was, and would have continued to be, the long-term problem of effective administration in Wales rather than the temporary embarrassment of debts whose eventual repayment was well within his capabilities.

---

[61] *The Nobility of Later Medieval England*, pp. 209–10.

Chapter 8

THE STAFFORDS AND THEIR COUNCIL

Every great landowner relied heavily upon an inner circle of administrative staff, lawyers and influential retainers to whom he could turn for advice and help in the running of his estates and the conduct of his business affairs. The Staffords had particular need of a council to supervise the organisation of their large household and eight scattered receiverships; but whereas the first Duke of Buckingham was evidently content to leave all but the most important decisions to the senior personnel and legal advisers who made up his council, the third Duke had more ambitious plans for this long-established and versatile institution.

Very little is known about the work and composition of magnate councils during the fifteenth century, although it seems that these advisory and executive bodies differed from the better documented Duchy of Lancaster council only in the more limited scope of their judicial powers. The Duchy council met regularly in London to debate financial, administrative and legal matters, while smaller commissions travelled around the estates.[1] This was a fairly general practice which often caused friction at a local level and sometimes led to more serious disagreements over the interpretation of franchises. Contemporary sources reveal a deep-seated antagonism towards baronial councils: in 1391, for example, the Commons complained that the nobility was encroaching upon questions of tenure and real estate which ought properly to have been settled at common law.[2] Sir John Fortescue, writing more than half a century later, was chiefly critical of the way in which certain councillors abused a position of trust to advance their own interests, often by manipulating the very lord they were supposed

---

[1] R. S. Somerville, ' The Duchy of Lancaster Council and the Court of the Duchy Chamber ', *T.R.H.S.*, 4th series XXIII (1941), pp. 159–77.
[2] *Rot. Parl.*, vol. III p. 285.

to serve.[3] It is tempting to see in these attacks evidence of a gradual growth in the practical powers of both councils and councillors, but this would be hard to prove. Dr Levett's general-isations on the subject are based on her discovery of oppressive methods, including the introduction of practices of Roman law on the estates of St Albans Abbey, and have now been dismissed as largely unrepresentative. Anomalies of this kind may have obtained at St Albans, where civil lawyers were frequently in attendance, but there is no recorded instance of such arbitrary conduct by secular landlords.[4] The Staffords were certainly un-willing to interfere with the administration of justice in their manorial courts: an almost complete set of court rolls for Thorn-bury manor, where their tenants continued to perform suit of court regularly throughout the fifteenth and sixteenth centuries, contains only one passing reference to the council, which had little direct contact with the Gloucestershire peasantry.[5] Not even Duke Edward, preoccupied as he was with the enforcement of his legal rights, found it necessary to go beyond a strict interpretation of customary practice and the common law.

The council was essentially an extension or representative of the lord himself, and as such was responsible to him for the successful management of his affairs. This explains why, from the thirteenth century onwards, if not before, bureaucrats and lawyers had come to dominate what was originally a consultative body composed of a nobleman's chief vassals and peers. The growing complexity of large-scale administration made it impossible for any landlord, however astute, to supervise all his business interests in person. In an age notorious for its litigiousness, few property owners could hope to escape having to go to law during their lifetimes, and most regarded the law as nothing more than a tool to be exploited by the rich and powerful. No transaction involving the sale, enfeoffment or disposal of property could safely be completed without expert advice, and for this reason professional lawyers

---

[3] *The Governance of England*, ed. C. Plummer (Oxford, 1885), p. 145.

[4] A. D. Levett, *Studies in Manorial History* (Oxford, 1938), pp. 21–40; for a correc-tive to her views see K. B. McFarlane, *The Nobility of Later Medieval England*, p. 214.

[5] D.641/1/4C/7 m. 55; one of the parties in a property suit had agreed to submit his evidence to ' the counsellors learned in the law ' for their opinion before the court met on 9 Feb. 1447.

began to play an increasingly important rôle outside the courts as feoffees, executors and trustees. Families like the Staffords, who possessed extensive judicial rights in Wales, also commissioned many of their legal staff as justices itinerant to hold sessions in the Marcher lordships, usually in the company of other senior administrative personnel.

The activities and procedure of the Staffords' council are comparatively well documented, although it is still difficult to establish precise details of membership. Unlike certain types of indenture and letter patent which have survived among the Duchy of Lancaster archives, those issued by the three Dukes of Buckingham do not always specify an obligation to give counsel even when one is known to have existed.[6] Whereas a lawyer was invariably retained *pro consilio suo*, administrative staff did not enter a formal agreement of this kind, and it is only through brief entries in local account rolls – usually among the foreign expenses claimed by a receiver or his bailiffs – that their involvement in conciliar business comes to light. Some lawyers served continuously over long periods, while others were hired to deal with specific cases or complicated property transactions. The first Duke of Buckingham paid regular fees to at least twenty-nine lawyers between 1438 and 1460; thirteen estate and household employees are known to have sat with them over the same period, although this figure clearly represents a very small proportion of the total membership.[7] A further twenty-eight senior officials and influential country gentlemen whose names appear on the letters patent appointing justices itinerant to the Brecon Sessions during the 1440s almost certainly advised on wider questions of policy and administration. Some local receivers, notably Nicholas Poyntz, John Scudamore and John Jorce, were sent out on tours of inspection from time to time, and it seems reasonable to suppose that they attended council meetings together with the receiver general and the treasurer of the household, if only in an official capacity. Duke Humphrey's half-brothers, the Bourchiers, and his more powerful tenants and retainers were probably present when particularly important matters came under discussion; just as the

6 Somerville, *The Duchy of Lancaster*, vol. I p. 81.
7 For the names and brief biographical details of councillors retained between 1423 and 1521 see Appendix C.

nobility expected to confer with the Crown on matters of state, so the gentry were anxious to acquire the authority and prestige which the rank of councillor to a great lord bestowed upon them.

The Dowager Duchess Anne kept a far smaller council than her first husband, but as the widow of an eminent Lancastrian with large and scattered estates in her personal custody, she set out to enlist the support of prominent Yorkist lawyers and courtiers like Sir Thomas Burgh and William, Lord Hastings. These men were far too involved in their own highly successful careers to take more than a passing interest in her affairs, and, as ever, the routine business of administration was supervised by a group of ten or twenty experienced personnel and semi-resident lawyers. Many of them had worked for the late Duke and some probably joined his grandson who, being less than twenty at the time of his first entry in 1473, had great need of capable advisers. The little evidence which has survived about Duke Henry's council does not suggest that it differed in any way from the established pattern. Apart from his step-father, Sir Richard Darrell, the ten justices itinerant chosen to preside over the Great Sessions at Newport in 1476 were either lawyers or senior employees. A small staff of attorneys based at Westminster looked after Buckingham's litigation in the royal courts and his dealings with the Exchequer, while a coterie of trusted retainers, including Sir Nicholas Latimer and Sir William Knivet, helped to execute his complex political manoeuvres during the summer of 1483. These two men were the only members of Duke Henry's immediate circle to play an active part in the October rebellion, and, as we have seen earlier, it may well be that the rest of his councillors had already chosen to dissociate themselves from this foolhardy venture.

As might be expected, the last Duke was quick to recognise his council's great potential as a supervisory and reforming body. He retained at least fifteen lawyers on a regular basis from 1498 until his death, and also engaged a number of attorneys and temporary counsel to represent him at Westminster. A bare minimum of twenty-two senior officials were also made councillors, but by 1520 membership seems to have been on an *ad hoc* basis dependent upon residence at Thornbury. No lawyers attended the two formal council meetings held there in the autumn of that year, although the most important household staff, the receiver general and the master of the works were all present.[8] Perhaps these high-ranking personnel comprised a ' privy ' or inner council which met separately to debate questions of policy. Such a body, designed as a type of standing committee to deal with financial and administrative problems, is known to have existed during the fifteenth century. The ministers who assembled at Maxstoke Castle in 1443, for instance, could offer suggestions based on years of collective experience: the auditor general was on hand to give specialist advice, while others had spent years on the Stafford estates in positions of great authority.[9] The wording of certain petitions presented to Duke Edward in 1516 confirms that the ' councel lerned ' was by then regarded as a separate department to which legal matters were automatically addressed.[10]

The factor of distance prevented the council from meeting regularly, and, from the late fourteenth century until the building of Thornbury by Duke Edward, only the lawyers resident in London for most of the year could plan their movements with any degree of certainty. This is why so much routine business was left unattended for comparatively long periods; officials of all ranks had to obtain the council's approval for any unusual disbursements, and the resulting flood of petitions could clearly not receive the immediate attention of a peripatetic body which met only at intervals. The ever-increasing backlog of relatively unimportant appeals brought by reeves, bailiffs and tenants throughout the estates made it necessary to observe a strict sense of priority. A typical example of this is to be found in the returns for the manor of Stafford during the time of Duke Edward's minority. The Master of the Hospital of St John at Stafford claimed rents worth 2s.4d. a year which had been granted to his predecessor by the first Duke of Buckingham. The local receiver suggested an appeal to the royal council, but since the matter was so trivial, it was decided to wait until the young Duke came of age. Thus an entry in the accounts presented at Michaelmas 1498 records the

8 See p. 151.
9 D.641/1/2/54 m. 10.
10 D.1721/1/6 ' a book of informacions, etc.', *passim*.

postponement of any final decision until *ista dicta materia per parte domini et eciam per parte dicti magistri meliori modo examinetur per consilium domini in lege.* Twelve years later the bailiff of Stafford was still petitioning to be excused the same 2s.4d., and probably continued to do so until Buckingham's death in 1521.[11] Here the sum remained constant, but in many cases arrears mounted steadily because the council had still to sanction a regular item of expenditure. From 1460 onwards, for instance, the Prior of Bridgnorth received an annual rent of 3s.4d. from one of the Duchess Anne's tenant farmers, yet, since the auditor refused to ratify these payments until the Prior's evidence had been examined by the council, they were automatically entered as a cumulative debt at the foot of every account for the next sixteen years.[12] Other ministers were more fortunate. The bailiffs of Haresfield, Gloucestershire, who often had difficulty in raising their annual farm because of flooding, obtained generous concessions without any trouble, as did other staff and tenants offering reasonable proof of bad harvests, disease or local disorder. Robberies were common, especially in Wales, and the council seems to have been sympathetic towards men like Nicholas Corbet, the bailiff of Worthen, whose possessions were stolen in 1500. Corbet successfully claimed an allowance of 40s. to make good his losses and two years later obtained a formal acquittance from Duke Edward's commissioners in session at Newport Castle.[13]

On the whole, the council managed to uphold a relatively high standard of administrative efficiency, for although certain delays were unavoidable, every effort was made to deal promptly with cases of corruption or incompetence wherever they might occur. It appears that during the fifteenth century the general audit for receivers in the Midlands and South of England was held before a full session of the council meeting in London. As in 1428, when the receiver of Kent and Surrey set out with one of Duke Hum-

---

11 D.641/1/2/78 m. lv; 80 m. lv; S.C.6/Hen. VIII 5803 m. 1 (accounts of the bailiffs of Stafford for a four-year period ending at Michaelmas 1498, and the years ending Michaelmas 1499 and 1510 respectively).

12 D.641/1/2/75 m. 2 (account of the farmer of Bridgnorth for the year ending Michaelmas 1476).

13 D.641/1/2/162 m. 7; 163 m. 7 (accounts of the bailiff of Haresfield for the years ending Michaelmas 1434 and 1435 respectively); Longleat Ms. 3701 m. 12v (account of the receiver of Caus for the year ending Michaelmas 1502).

phrey's auditors to discuss his expenses *cum magno consilio domini*, most senior personnel made annual visits to the capital, bringing with them their own and their subordinates' accounts for examination.[14] The last Duke of Buckingham clearly empowered his council to act as a supreme court of audit with authority to overrule the decisions of individual ministers. When, in 1502, the bailiff of Haresfield was charged with concealing receipts of £8.15s.5d., his activities were investigated by an auditor who then submitted a mass of evidence for further scrutiny *coram consilium domini*. Another official was even refused an acquittance for his wages until he too had appeared before the court to justify his case, and there are many similar instances of the council intervening to settle financial questions of this kind.[15]

Because of the cost and inconvenience of litigation, defaulting tenants and employees posed an almost insoluble problem to the great landowner, who often consulted his lawyers before approaching particularly influential debtors. It was clearly inadvisable to demand arrears of rent from the Earl of Warwick in 1450 ' withoute ye advise of my Lorde's counceille ',[16] although during Duke Edward's lifetime, if not before, great trouble was taken over the collection of quite trivial sums. On one occasion in 1511, Robert Gilbert and Thomas Jubbes, the Duke's most senior councillors, compiled a detailed memorandum about a heriot worth no more than 7s.4d.; this was intended not only for the village bailiff, but for the auditor general, who had been afraid to act without more precise instructions from above. Indeed, judging by the strange assortment of problems and appeals referred to the council, nothing, however insignificant, seems to have escaped its attention. In May 1516 one clerk even noted down a ' remembraunce to be made to my lorde's counsell when they goo unto Staffordshir that ther be a restraynt made that ther goo no cartes through Maudeley Park ', although by this date there are clear signs of an attempt to deal quickly with routine matters according to a prearranged agenda.[17]

---

[14] D.641/1/2/231 m. 9.
[15] D.641/1/2/202 m. 9 (account of the bailiff of Haresfield for the year ending Michaelmas 1502).
[16] D.641/1/2/20 m. 3.
[17] D.641/1/2/92 m. 6 (account of the bailiff of Darlaston for the year ending Michaelmas 1516); D.1721/1/6 ' a booke of informacions, etc.' fo. 10v.

Very little is known about the procedure adopted at council meetings and no accounts or indentures have survived to show how many ancillary staff were employed as messengers and copyists. Among the evidence collected by Cardinal Wolsey for use at Buckingham's trial is a description of two sessions of the Duke's 'privy' council held at Thornbury in October 1520, which suggests that it met regularly and got through a considerable amount of paperwork. On the first occasion Duke Edward

. . . sent commaundement to hys counseyll than beyng att hys manour off Thornebury thatt aftur dyner they shoulde be in aredynes to gyff hys grace attendauns wythe sytche instruccyons and odur remmembraunces as they hadd concernynge the ordur off hys landys aswell in hys circute generall as particulare; att whytche tyme hys sayd counseyll, that ys to wytt, Mastur Thomas Wotton, Deane of hys chapell, M[aster] George Poley, his Almoner, Doctour Jenyns, his Surveyor Particuler, Mastur Thomas Moscroff, his Cownsellour in Fysyke, M[aster] John Dalacourt, his Chapleyn, and Thomas Cade, clerke, his Receyvour Generall, gaff hys sayd grace attendauns. And whan they wer by hys sayd commaundement broght in to hys presence, he commaundement [sic] theym to sytt downe att the borde; and than syttinge he sayd to hys sayd cownseyll ' I commaunded yow to brynge your bokys wythe yow '. Wherunto awnswer was made by hys sayd Surveyour and Receyvour ' so we have done '.[18]

Buckingham then announced his plans for a pilgrimage to Jerusalem and the setting up of a commission to run the estates while he was abroad. It is interesting to note that all the councillors then present were clergymen raised to high office by the Duke as a means of improving administrative standards. Not all of them were above suspicion, however, and one of their number had apparently broken the strict rule of confidentiality binding upon members of the council:

. . . the sayd Duke at a nodur season, syttynge in hys cownseyll, . . . reasond wythe hys cownseyll that ytt was very nessessary for hym to take hys journey into Walles for the orduringe of hys lordchyps ther, and for the admynestracyon off iustice, and sayd he hadd made sute to the Kynge's hyghnes for hys licence soo to doo. Wytche he sayd he had opteynyd, yett neverthelas he nedyd nott so to make sute . . .

18 S.P.1/22 fo. 58.

saynge also thatt he had befor debatyd the same amongest his cownseyll, and the same was publysched and knawne in the Kynge's cowrt
befor the commynge thedur off sytche his cownselours as he sent for
to sew to the Kynge's hyghnes and to his cownsell for hys sayd
licence. And [he] sayd thatt he knew nott whom he schulde mistruste
to have disclosed thatt, except only his sayd Receyvour Thomas Cade
for thatt he was nye unto Syr William Compton, whytche hadd rull
abowtt Burforde, wher hys same Receyvour ys vicar.[19]

It was only natural that the Duke's chief advisers should
become involved in his private affairs. A few trusted servants
were used as envoys carrying messages to and from the court,
while others frequently entered recognizances or went surety on
his behalf. Thus, for example, between the years 1512 and 1514
many of Buckingham's councillors first acted as plaintiffs in a
series of collusive suits brought to free almost all his inheritance
from pre-existing entails, and then became his feoffees.[20] In many
cases the enfeoffment to use was regarded as a purely formal
undertaking, although experience had taught the three Dukes of
Buckingham how necessary it was to make careful provision for
the settlement of their property. Like their ancestors, the Earls of
Stafford, they chose the ablest lawyers and officials as executors
and feoffees, thus strengthening the hands of those best suited to
assume control over the estates should the next heir succeed as a
minor. Evidence from the previous century reveals how the
council had grown in size and authority as a result of the problems created by a succession of minorities. During the 1390s – an
unsettled decade which saw the early deaths of both the third and
fourth Earls of Stafford – a group of senior officials and lawyers
took the entire administration into their own hands. It was
through their efforts that a number of important transactions,
such as the marriage of Joan Stafford to the Earl of Kent's eldest
son and the recovery at law of the Bassett inheritance, were
brought to a successful conclusion.[21] The council played an equally
crucial rôle during the three long minorities which beset the

---

[19] *Ibid.*
[20] Richard and John Brooke, Thomas Cade, Thomas Jubbes, Robert Gilbert and John
Scott were among those most frequently named in this respect; see Appendix C.
[21] D.641/1/2/4, 5 (receiver general's accounts for the years ending Michaelmas 1391
and 1394).

Stafford family during the fifteenth century; indeed, it was largely responsible for maintaining such a marked degree of administrative continuity throughout the period. Each dowager relied heavily upon the nucleus of loyal retainers who remained to assist her, and in turn died leaving her estates in the custody of a few trusted advisers. On the death of Anne, Dowager Countess of Stafford, in 1438, John Harper, Thomas Willoughby, John Andrews and other members of her council automatically joined Duke Humphrey, while she herself had confirmed most of her late husband's appointments some thirty-five years before. The first Duke's widow left an equally valuable legacy of administrative and legal staff to her grandson; many of the latter's councillors continued to serve the Dowager Duchess Katherine and her second husband, Jasper Tudor, and some, like Sir William Knivet and Sir Edmund Mountfort, eventually became the last Duke's ministers.

Although it spent long periods in London, which was a semi-permanent centre for its operations during the fifteenth century, the council often split up into small groups or commissions. These could be sent to any part of the estates at relatively short notice and little expense. It was common for two or three councillors, who between them possessed a sound knowledge of law and administration, to work closely with the resident staff of each receivership. Besides dealing with local complaints and petitions, they were empowered to impose entry fines, raise or lower rents and collect outstanding debts. Not all their decisions met with approval; a group of councillors touring the Stowe area in 1446 were somewhat critical of the over-generous leases drawn up by their predecessors, and, as we have already seen, there was a marked difference of opinion between Duke Edward and his advisers over the rate of entry fines to be enforced in the same lordship.[22] He nevertheless made particular use of these itinerant commissions, seeing them as a means of tightening his hold over the running of the estates, and with one notable exception his efforts appear to have been rewarded. In 1506, for example, the controller and the treasurer of the household rode from London

---

[22] S.C.6/924/25 m. 4v (account of the approver of Stowe for the year ending Michaelmas 1457); see p. 64.

to Penshurst, where they spent fifteen days with Buckingham and his auditor general for an unusually thorough examination of accounts. Senior domestic staff were always available to offer practical help in financial matters, and may even have acted collectively as a court of audit.[23]

Conciliar commissions were particularly necessary in Wales, where an unfortunate combination of circumstances for which the second and third Dukes of Buckingham were largely to blame conspired to thwart any attempts at effective estate management. Having been left to their own devices during Duke Edward's minority, the tenantry were understandably resentful of his attempts to reimpose customary obligations and collect outstanding revenues. This problem was intensified by the incompetence, indifference and in some cases the outright hostility of many Welsh employees; frequent tours of inspection seemed the best solution, although they in turn generated so much discontent that by 1520 the council despaired of raising the great backlog of arrears. Never before had such serious financial and administrative difficulties been experienced along the March. The Earls of Stafford had spent long periods in Wales during the fourteenth century and do not appear to have been at all unpopular there. Duke Humphrey often crossed the Welsh border as a young man; at Michaelmas 1425 he and a number of councillors went to Newport for the annual audit and returned two years later to confirm the borough charters.[24] Again, in 1433, he was present at an enquiry into the King's possessions at Newport and saw to the collection of dues which had lapsed during his minority.[25] All these matters were debated by a mixed assembly of local staff, gentry and retainers, who continued to deal with Buckingham's representatives once his involvement in Welsh affairs had given way to more pressing commitments at home and abroad. Any vestiges of loyalty towards the Staffords had demonstrably

[23] S.C.Hen. VII 1076 m. 15.

[24] D.641/1/2/241 (account of the receiver of Caus for the year ending Michaelmas 1424); O. Morgan, 'Early Charters of the Borough of Newport in Wentloog', *Archaeologia*, XLVIII (1885), pt ii, pp. 431–55.

[25] In June of that year the coroner of Wentloog was excused rents from land which, *per veram examinacionem inde habitam coram domino et consilio suo apud castrum de Newport*, were shown not to belong to the Staffords (S.C.6/924/23 m. 6; account of the coroner for the year ending Michaelmas 1448).

vanished long before Duke Edward's coming of age in 1497, which explains why he immediately began to transfer power from the resident staff to certain members of the council. A number of small commissions toured the Marches at regular intervals over the next twenty-five years in a vain attempt to recover outstanding debts and enforce the Duke's judicial rights. Among the justices itinerant sent to preside over the Great Sessions of Newport and Brecon were commonly three or four senior officials and lawyers who would afterwards make a general circuit of the area, examining accounts and attending to any other extraordinary business. In 1511, for instance, the controller of the household, the receiver general and John Seintgeorge, the most experienced of Buckingham's auditors, spent five months in Wales with the express purpose of harassing any persistent defaulters. They were no more successful than the commissioners who had tried to negotiate a rate of fines for redeeming the Great Sessions at Brecon two years before, since this practice had merely hardened local opinion against the Duke and created further administrative problems for his overworked advisers.[26] The system of taking bonds for good behaviour from the inhabitants of the Marcher lordships also proved increasingly difficult to enforce, and it is hard to see what Buckingham could have done to avoid Henry VIII's charges of ' default and negligence ' in this respect.[27] The council was zealous enough in making estate staff and other employees offer heavy securities, although the long list of unpaid fines and pledges in almost every receiver's account for this period shows how often the penalty of forfeiture was avoided.[28]

Duke Edward's failure to effect improvements in his Welsh receiverships was certainly not due to a lack of effort on his part. Conciliar commissions were planned with great thoroughness and carried with them the Duke's own written memoranda. Two such sets of instructions have survived to illustrate the scope and importance of these enquiries; another insight into the careful

[26] S.C.6/Hen. VIII 4775 mm. 6v–7v.
[27] T. B. Pugh, *The Marcher Lordships*, pp. 245–6, and ' The Indenture of the Marches between Henry VII and Edward Stafford, Duke of Buckingham ', *E.H.R.*, LXXI (1956), pp. 140–1.
[28] See, for instance, Eg. Roll 2195 mm. 9–9v (account of the receiver of Bronllys, Cantref Selyf, Penkelly and Alexanderstown for the year ending Michaelmas 1517) and S.C.6/4775 mm. 9–9v.

organisation of estate business is provided by a small 'booke of informations' which records complaints and petitions addressed to Buckingham and his council between May 1516 and November 1518.[29] Tenants and staff alike were encouraged to report any cases of corruption or inefficiency, while other questions were referred directly to the 'councel lerned'. The Duke was frequently troubled by rival claims to his property and expected all his employees to inform him of any local disputes which might end in litigation. It was standard practice for the receiver general and his colleagues to collect evidence about wards, bondmen and uncooperative tenants so that the council could take prompt action against them should the usual techniques of persuasion prove unsuccessful. The strong-minded Lady Barrington, who would ' not be rowled nalder be keper nor baylory but too doo as it plese here ', refused to be overawed by her more powerful neighbour; [30] but most of the Duke's adversaries at law hoped to reach more amicable settlements. In 1509, for example, John Pickering informed his employer that the Abbot of Ramsey, who had enclosed some of the Staffords' farmland at Walton, was

contente att any time yt my lorde's grace shall commawnd any off his lerned councell to send hymm word or commawnd hymm; he wilbe ther in a redynes with his evidences and his lerned councell and to refourme all suche wronges as shalbe thought be your grace's cowncell . . . Wher thoroughe he will make a large amendes, iff any suche can be proved, for in no wyse he will nott have you his hevy lorde . . .[31]

The council was occasionally called upon to provide independent arbitration in property disputes involving the three Dukes of Buckingham, and seems to have displayed a surprising impartiality in reaching its decisions. Thus in 1519 the third Duke with uncharacteristic generosity agreed to compensate Sir Edward Chamberlain's lost claim to the manor of Penshurst. ' We have caused youre hole tytle to be examyned by our Councell ', he wrote, ' by whos advise we ar content to allowe you a convenable recompense, which we do not somuch for doubte of youre title,

29 T. B. Pugh, *The Marcher Lordships*, pp. 262–75, 281–6; D.1721/1/6.
30 W.A.M. 5470 fo. 15v.
31 *Ibid.*, fo. 43.

as forr that we sett more by a frende than enny profitt or comodi-
tie . . .' There is no evidence, however, that Buckingham's pious
sentiments were ever translated into hard cash.[32]

Lawyers and administrative staff with legal training were indispensable in cases of this type, and at times played a crucial rôle
in the history of the Stafford inheritance. One such occasion arose
in 1421, when the Dowager Countess Anne was forced to accept
a redivision of the de Bohun estates. She obtained formal seisin of
the property awarded to her on 3 July, but because of the many
obstacles placed in her way was obliged to remain in London with
her advisers throughout the summer. After some debate it was
agreed that two royal officers and two members of the Stafford
council should divide the relevant administrative and legal records
between them. Anne's representatives, John Fray and Robert
Frampton (who both eventually became Barons of the Exchequer),
supervised matters with characteristic efficiency;[33] yet despite
their personal qualities they were severely hampered by the
Crown's determination to profit from the new partition and were
chiefly employed in drawing up a series of complaints and petitions on the Countess's behalf. Duke Humphrey was better able
to protect his territorial interests, as can be seen from his struggle
with Sir Thomas Stanley for the ownership of Bosley Manor in
Cheshire. The case was first heard at the Chester Assizes in the
Trinity term of 1443 and dragged on for three years until
Stanley's failure to appear caused him to be non-suited.[34] If the
disbursements made by Humphrey Cotes, then receiver of Staffordshire, are any guide, Buckingham was extremely anxious to
secure the manor. In 1442 Robert Whitgreve, a lawyer with considerable local influence, visited Bosley, where he and his messengers spent almost £11 in incidental expenses. The relatives of
Ralph Macclesfield, who had originally settled Bosley on the
Duke, shared another handsome reward of £10, and one of their
number was entertained at Stafford – perhaps as an unwilling
guest.[35] Once Buckingham realised that his suit was likely to drag

---

[32] *Original Letters Illustrative of English History*, 3rd series, vol. I p. 213.
[33] D.L.28/4/11 fo. 31v; both Frampton and Fray stood high in the Countess's favour
and were chosen to act as her executors (*Testamenta Vetusta*, vol. I p. 238).
[34] Chester 29/149 rot. 16–16v; 151 rot. 24.
[35] D.641/1/2/54 mm. 9–10.

on for some time, he enlisted a number of distinguished legal advisers to help with the case. Both William Cumberford and Ralph Pole were no doubt involved from the very beginning; Thomas Dencalf, the third new member of the council learned, acted as their attorney, and four of the most talented common lawyers then practising at Westminster were recruited over the next three years.[36] Several councillors visited Chester with a large following of armed yeomen to hear the justices' final verdict in 1446, and John Andrews, Buckingham's attorney general, arrived soon afterwards. A constant stream of letters and memoranda was meanwhile exchanged between the absent Duke and his representatives, who proceeded to negotiate a settlement with Sir Thomas after obtaining seisin of the manor in court. Long delays and the prospect of heavy financial losses probably hastened this compromise solution, which enabled the Stanleys to recover Bosley on terms favourable to the Duke.[37]

Since most of the Staffords' legal business was transacted in London, a few members of the 'councel lerned' remained at Westminster to represent their interests at the Exchequer and in the common law courts. From 1384, if not before, the receiver general had paid out fees to nine lawyers, including an advocate and two royal justices in the court of common pleas; seven years later, the clerk of the rolls, a remembrancer of the Exchequer and two serjeants-at-law also drew regular annuities from the estates.[38] Further specialist appointments were made during the early fifteenth century, when great landowners, litigious and acquisitive almost without exception, began to compete seriously for the services of able and experienced lawyers. Elizabeth's Wydeville's council with its attorney general, eight Exchequer officials and staff of trained lawyers was perhaps slightly larger than most magnate councils, but nevertheless offers a typical example of the increasingly important rôle played by legal advisers in private administration.[39] This is not to suggest that the majority of lawyers

---

[36] Piers Ardern and Walter Moyll were both retained in 1443; Robert Danby joined them one year later and Thomas Burgoyne in 1446 (see Appendix C).

[37] D.641/1/2/56 m. 11.

[38] D.641/1/2/1 (the receiver general's account for the year ending Michaelmas 1384) and 4.

[39] A. R. Myers, 'The Household of Queen Elizabeth Woodville, 1466–7', *B.J.R.L.*, L (1967–8), pp. 214–5, 456–62.

took their obligations any more seriously than other retainers drawing a money fee. The phenomenon of ' good lordship ' produced exactly the same effect on the legal profession as it did upon the ambitious knights and esquires who accepted annuities and wages from any influential person ready to offer them. Every nobleman sought to obtain preferential, if not openly partial, treatment at law by giving pensions and gifts to judges, lawyers and government employees, while the latter were never slow to accept any number of ill-concealed bribes from rival clients. Once they had been awarded an annual fee, Duke Humphrey's legal advisers became *ipso facto* members of his council, although many of them had little time for routine business since their first loyalties lay elsewhere. William Burley, an extremely capable lawyer and experienced parliamentarian, had, for example, already established strong personal connections with the Dukes of Suffolk and Gloucester and the Earl of Shrewsbury before taking up office as steward of the lordship of Caus in 1442. He was at the same time employed as steward of Montgomery by the Duke of York, who had previously retained him as a councillor at an exceptionally high fee of 20 marks a year, and who commanded his ultimate allegiance.[40] In common with most of the lawyers employed by Duke Humphrey, Burley had also proved himself in the service of the Crown. Indeed, most of his colleagues on the Stafford council owed their elevation to the bench and their advancement in local government to years spent in humbler posts on the Duchy of Lancaster estates. Only a few of their number, notably Richard Whitgreve, Thomas Littleton, William Cumberford and Thomas Arblaster, can in any sense be regarded as essentially permanent members of Buckingham's immediate circle; it was they who dealt with more mundane problems of law and administration, generally under the direction of an attorney general.

John Andrews, the first known holder of this office, was appointed by the Dowager Countess Anne in 1431 to take charge of matters arising from the dispute over the de Bohun inheritance, and soon turned his attention to the management of her other

---

[40] See Appendix C.

property. When she died, he joined Duke Humphrey's household at a far higher salary and with increased responsibilities, not only supervising all the legal and financial aspects of the Duke's two appointments as Constable of Calais and Warden of the Cinque Ports, but also taking charge of any litigation to reach the central courts at Westminster.[41] He occasionally appeared there in person, but most pleading was done by John Holme, whom Buckingham had initially retained in 1440 ' to dele for him in al pleas and suites in ye Exchequer as well for him as yt her to be moved ', and subsequently engaged on a far wider basis. Whether or not Holme continued to promote the interests of his former patron on becoming a Baron of the Exchequer in 1446 is a matter of conjecture, but Duke Humphrey was no doubt anxious to keep up the connexion, if only as a means of recovering his unpaid expenses from the Crown.

The office of attorney general seems to have become something of a sinecure during the second Duke's lifetime. In 1476, for instance, it was held by Richard Isham, a very successful lawyer whose services were much in demand. Although both he and Roger Townshend, Buckingham's attorney in the King's Bench, Common Pleas and Exchequer of Pleas were formally included among the Duke's feoffees, there is nothing to suggest that either man played any part in the running of the estates. Very little is known about Duke Henry's relations with other members of the legal profession, but he could evidently call upon the ablest lawyers of the day to assist him. Of these, William Hussey was particularly distinguished, rising to become Chief Justice of the King's Bench during his time as adviser to the Dowager Duchess Anne and her grandson.

It was, however, the last Duke of Buckingham who earned a particular reputation as the friend and patron of lawyers. The account of his trial in the *Year Book* of 1521 ends on an unusually personal note, introduced by one who had cause to regret his untimely death. ' Dieu a son aime graunt mercy ', wrote the anonymous author, ' car il fuit tresnoble prince & prudent, &

---

[41] See Appendices B and C for further information about the advocates and attorneys general employed by the Staffords during the fifteenth and early sixteenth centuries.

mirrour de tout curtesy '.[42] The cynic might argue that Buckingham's popularity in legal circles was solely due to the great quantity of business brought by him before the courts, but his interest in the practice and theory of law was quite genuine, and he was anxious to advance the careers of promising young advocates. He certainly appears to have enjoyed far more cordial relations with lawyers, some of whom served him well for many years, than with his constantly changing administrative personnel. A striking element of continuity was maintained among the Duke's staff at Westminster. John Carter directed all his numerous suits in the Exchequer of Pleas for at least fourteen years, and continued to advise the three attorneys who replaced him officially in 1512. Although the records do not always mention counsel by name, most of Buckingham's litigation in the common pleas was undertaken by John Cowper, who also appeared on behalf of various senior household and estate officials suing their subordinates for debt. John Scott, the Duke's attorney general, proved an equally capable servant and gradually came to acquire far more authority than any of his predecessors. Perhaps Buckingham was influenced by the example of his uncle, Earl Rivers, whose attorney general was entrusted with many important commissions, besides directing the overall finances and administration of his employer's estates.[43] Scott's duties were equally diverse; so much so that in 1502 he was able to act as receiver of Kent and Surrey until a permanent replacement could be found for the late occupant of this post. He spent much of his time collecting revenues from the outlying receiverships, particularly in Wales, and also took delivery of the not inconsiderable fines and damages awarded to the Duke at law. His task was no doubt made easier by the grant, in 1513, of the office of Chief Baron of the Exchequer in reversion, and by his personal influence in the field of local government. Understandably enough, Scott's appearances in court were confined to difficult or important suits, such as that

---

[42] *Year Book*, Easter 13 Henry VIII, fo. 12. This posthumous tribute is quoted by Dr E. W. Ives in his Ph.D. thesis ' Some Aspects of the Legal Profession in the Late Fifteenth and Early Sixteenth Centuries ' (London University, 1955), p. 381, and I am grateful to the author for permission to cite his work.

[43] E. W. Ives, ' Andrew Dymmock and the Papers of Antony, Earl Rivers, 1482–3 ', *B.I.H.R.*, XLI (1968), pp. 216–25.

brought by Duke Edward against his own brother over the settlement made on the latter's marriage, which took place between 1503 and 1505. Buckingham deeply regretted having promised to settle an estate on Lord Henry's wife and heirs male, and in order to secure the immediate reversion of the property insisted that it should be regarded as a jointure, tenable only by the couple themselves. The judges' verdict remains unknown, but Scott acquitted himself well.[44] Indeed, he always showed great skill as an advocate, presenting Duke Edward's suit for the Constableship of England in 1509, and almost certainly conducting a similar appeal before a panel of justices and royal councillors five years later.[45] One of the most talented and industrious of the Duke's advisers, ' our trusty councelour John Scott ' was often sent with gifts and messages to court, which itself is a sure sign of his standing in the official hierarchy. His successor, Christopher Hales, also rose from relatively obscurity to a position of trust, and thereby laid the foundations of an outstanding legal career, becoming successively the King's solicitor and attorney general, and finally holding office as Master of the Rolls. Hale's activities are less well documented, although they probably followed the established pattern; some of his duties may have been shared with John Jennings, the surveyor general, a doctor of laws and advocate in the Court of Arches, and others within the small group of lawyers who met regularly at Thornbury to discuss Buckingham's legal affairs.

As one whose reading matter included Littleton's *Tenures* and contemporary works on statute law, Duke Edward evidently enjoyed the contact which these meetings gave him with the finer legal minds of the age, but his first thought was to exploit all the available talent at his disposal. This was how the council, which had always been a powerful and active body, finally achieved its full administrative and judicial potential. The remarkable similarity between executive methods employed on both the Stafford and crown estates at this time suggests that many of Buckingham's were modelled upon the procedure of the court of general surveyors; although his own council was theoretically unable to

---

[44] *Year Book*, Michaelmas 20 Henry VII, fos. 10–11.
[45] See p. 37.

imprison tenants or demand written evidence from them, it was no less concerned to search out defaulters and take obligations from all classes of men than its royal counterpart.[46] Neither body was recognised as a court of law, yet both employed techniques far in advance of anything then available to litigants at Westminster and were alike the product of a single-minded attempt to achieve financial and administrative efficiency.

[46] B. P. Wolffe, *The Crown Lands* (London, 1970), pp. 73–6.

Chapter 9

THE STAFFORDS AND THE COMMON LAW

Chronicle sources for the late fifteenth and early sixteenth centuries and the colourful language of the legal records themselves paint a tempting picture for the unwary eye: the English upper classes were, it might appear, indefatigable protagonists in a ceaseless round of land disputes, trampling roughshod over the finer principles of the common law. The cost of litigation, the protracted delays once a case reached the courts, and the importance of powerful connexions naturally worked to the rich man's advantage, although wealth, rank and influence could seldom be guaranteed to hasten the cumbersome process of judgement. It is surprising to discover exactly how often the last Duke of Buckingham withdrew quite important suits from the Court of Common Pleas simply because of evasive tactics on the part of his adversaries. If he, the most powerful – and almost certainly the most litigious – magnate of his day, could but rarely manipulate the law to his own satisfaction, the effects of clientage cannot have been so bad. Indeed, both he and his contemporaries were mostly concerned with cases of debt and trespass which for the lawyers in their service amounted to little more than routine paperwork.[1] A good deal of secret diplomacy must inevitably have gone on behind the scenes, but there are few signs of overt corruption.

From the time of his coming of age in March 1498 until his death twenty-three years later, Duke Edward began at least 128 separate actions in the Courts of the King's Bench and Common Pleas.[2] Twenty-two of these cases were terminated abruptly on his

---

[1] For a general discussion of the problems facing the medieval litigant see M. Hastings, *The Court of Common Pleas in Fifteenth Century England* (Cornell University Press, 1947), Chapter XV, *passim*.

[2] All the actions known to have been brought by the last Duke of Buckingham in both the Courts of the King's Bench and Common Pleas are listed in Appendix E, to which reference should be made for details of the cases discussed in this chapter.

death in April 1521, but only six of the remaining 106 are known to have reached a successful conclusion. The senior household staff who together brought a further forty-three suits for debt on Buckingham's behalf recovered through the courts only £5 of the £4,811 which they alleged was owing to them. This explains why settlement by private arbitration was so popular as an alternative means of redress. The Duke clearly set little store by Chief Justice Fortescue's strictures on the need to avoid ' hasty proceedure ',[3] but seems to have been powerless when faced with the long delays inherent in the English legal system. So far as he was concerned, a lawsuit might serve as a threat, and perhaps had a certain amount of nuisance value, but was obviously neither the quickest nor the most efficient way of obtaining justice. His utilitarian approach to the common law is reflected in the large number of suits – seventy-four in all – removed by him from the courts after less than one year. Only sixteen cases dragged on for more than seven years, and most of these were comparatively trivial; major suits for debt or actions against employees could not be left in this way, especially as the threat of outlawry, once an effective means of bringing the defendant to court, no longer carried any real weight.

The most striking feature of Duke Edward's litigation in the Court of Common Pleas is the number of cases concerning ministers of all ranks. He was without doubt a harsh master to dishonest or inefficient servants, and, given his own way, would have dispensed entirely with the courts by bringing all offenders before his own council. Certain employees bound themselves in heavy sums to accept arbitration by this somewhat partial body, although at least one, Henry Fowke, a yeoman of the stables accused of trespass, had second thoughts and was sued both for his original offence and subsequent default. Many other cases, particularly actions of account involving large amounts of money, were almost always heard first by the Duke's own court of audit simply because unnecessary delays could result in lost revenues. The auditors themselves were especially vulnerable once Buckingham's campaign for the proper enrolment of records was under way. John St George and Edward Edgar [4] were sued for damages

---

3 *De Laudibus Legum Angliae*, ed. S. B. Chrimes (Cambridge, 1942), p. 133.
4 The Duke also began a suit against Edgar in Chancery (C.1/441/2).

of 1,000 marks and £200 respectively as a result of their negligent book-keeping, while John Buttys, a former colleague, was called upon to surrender the pledges of 200 marks which he had offered at the time of his appointment as auditor of the Norfolk area.

Senior officials in the household were subject to a close personal scrutiny which extended to their private finances and domestic affairs. A petition addressed to the Star Chamber by John Russell, the Duke's secretary, clearly illustrates how unscrupulous and vindictive Buckingham could be to those who he believed had wronged him. Russell had allegedly failed to account for receipts of almost £5,900 during his seven years in office and was summoned before the ducal council to explain himself. Although he may have been rather careless over his accounts, Russell evidently expected to be cleared of any more serious charges. Having entered bonds in the order of £2,000 as a guarantee of his willingness to attend a final audit, he met with nothing but obstruction and harassment. Despite all evidence to the contrary Buckingham insisted that his former servant had embezzled over £3,300. Rather than weaken his position by recourse to common law, whose slow processes tended to favour the defendant, Duke Edward submitted the case to private arbitration, and when this failed seized Russell's estates into his own hands as a final act of vengeance. It was at this point, nine years after the proceedings had begun, that Russell appealed to the Star Chamber. Duke Edward's sly references to ' knowledge and informacion made unto hym, howe that the seid Russell did were in his garmentes and apparell as fyne velvet and silke in his doblettes & jaketes, and cloth in his gownes and oder as the Duke [himself] did, and also did ryde with his doble horses, founde his nedy fader, moder and bretherne, and of pore bodies kept theym as gentillfolkes in their countres, which were tofore ryght pore and nedy ', carried little weight with those who met to try the case. The independent auditor appointed to examine all the relevant accounts, day books and indentures expressed surprise at the unwillingness of Buckingham's auditors to accept most of Russell's petitions and found that over £1,013 had, moreover, been wrongfully laid to his charge.[5] The final verdict is unknown, but Russell's subsequent

[5] STA CHA 2/23/111, 26/386 (respectively Russell's petition and Duke Edward's reply) and E.101/529/2.

rise as a crown servant and administrator suggests that the young Henry VIII had already taken Buckingham's measure.[6] Other instances of arbitrary behaviour come readily to hand, for the Duke was intolerant of delay and often tried to circumvent the law. Not content with the substantial obligations which he had taken from his auditor, John St George, during the course of another legal battle, he had the unfortunate man imprisoned in Gloucester Castle on the pretext that warrants for his arrest had already been issued. A strongly worded royal writ secured the prisoner's release some months later, and St George himself began an action for wrongful arrest against Duke Edward in the Court of Common Pleas.[7] Yet even he, with his catalogue of grievances, was either forced or persuaded to abandon his case, and presumably take whatever compensation Buckingham saw fit to offer.

Not every employee was prepared to accept the Duke's interpretation of justice, although many found it hard to escape his surveillance. In November 1520, for example, he sent Robert Gilbert to arrest two chaplains for leaving his service without permission, and had but a short time before confiscated the goods of Elizabeth Knivet, a lady in waiting, because of some unspecified misdemeanour on her part.[8] This particular injustice, as well as other personal wrongs suffered during his years with the Duke, led her kinsman, Charles Knivet, to testify against Buckingham in 1521; and another lady in waiting, Margaret Gedding, had already revenged herself by providing Wolsey with evidence against her former employer.[9] Neither Robert Gilbert nor Edmund Dellacourt, the other key witness at Buckingham's trial, had any such obvious motives for betraying their master, although the household had by this time become such a hotbed of fear and suspicion that none of its members can have felt themselves entirely secure.

Between the Easter term of 1507 and the Michaelmas term of 1519 Buckingham had sued no less than three of his treasurers, three receivers general, two wardrobers, one of his almoners and

---

[6] See Appendix C part IV for details of Russell's career.
[7] C.P.40/1013, Hilary 7 Hen. VIII, rot. 505v.
[8] Cottonian Ms. Titus B1 fo. 172v; *L. & P. Henry VIII*, vol. III, pt i, no. 1288 (10).
[9] Cottonian Ms. Titus B1 fo. 173.

the keeper of his jewels. The majority were taken to court because of some failure, real or imagined, to fulfil the terms laid down in their contracts of employment. Both Thomas Cade and John Pickering, for example, were said to have forfeited bonds in the order of £1,200 which they had entered on assuming office. They were clearly being sued for inefficiency rather than theft, for Cade kept his post until the Duke's death, with every apparent mark of favour. So too did five of the other senior personnel noted above, and even Richard Mynors, who faced eight separate actions for debts totalling £1,562, is known to have remained in service for at least three years after his first summons to court. Hardly one to forgive and forget, Duke Edward may well have used the law as a means of tightening his hold over recalcitrant employees. Two courses were open to him: sometimes the threat of protracted legal action alone served its purpose, but in most cases he no doubt preferred to offer a private settlement which was conditional upon the surrender of even heavier sureties. He could thus bring both financial and legal pressure to bear upon those who had displeased him, and was at the same time spared the cost of further litigation. His calculated approach to the law – in all probability modelled upon that of Henry VII – was far more than the expression of some personal idiosyncrasy. It was a vital part of his policy for the improvement of administrative standards, and as such was geared to serve practical ends rather than abstract principles of justice. His task required draconian measures similar to those employed with varying degrees of success by a number of reforming landlords before him. The ' cruel and vengible ' Sir John Fastolf had frequently employed the two weapons of legal action and imprisonment in his fight against inefficiency, deriving considerable personal satisfaction, if not always a significant rise in profits, from his many law suits.[10]

The need to set a stern example to junior personnel also ranked high in Buckingham's order of priorities, and although he could not sue every defaulting bailiff on his estates, a few local staff were singled out, almost at random, to submit to the full rigours of the law. Some were luckier than others. Whereas Richard Sumpter, the bailiff of Macclesfield, suffered both imprisonment

[10] K. B. McFarlane, ' The Investment of Sir John Fastolf's Profits of War ', pp. 111–3.

and forfeiture because of his debts,[11] several minor officials managed to postpone the day of reckoning for years by manipulating the machinery of the common law. Duke Edward's long and unsuccessful suit against Jankyn ap Thomas Havard and his five mainpernors shows how easily an employer could be prevented from enforcing his contracts through the courts. Jankyn was made constable of Brecon Castle in 1509, having offered personal sureties of £20, together with an additional £200 which he and his friends had raised as pledges of his good behaviour in office. The Duke's attempts to recover these bonds nine years later were doomed to failure, since the six defendants chose to place themselves outside the law rather than answer his summons. They had little to fear from the slow and largely ineffectual process of outlawry, which in at least four cases had not been completed by the time of Buckingham's death. Successive delays in the delivery of writs and the summoning of juries here and elsewhere made it extremely difficult for the Duke to press any suit forward.

On the whole, he preferred to leave actions of this kind to senior estate and household staff, declaring them personally responsible for the debts of any tradesmen or subordinates, and thus saving himself the cost and inconvenience of further litigation. Between Hilary 1502 and Michaelmas 1520 his treasurers, auditors and other high ranking officials sued at least eighty-seven different persons in the course of forty-three cases brought before the Court of Common Pleas. Presumably the main aim was to secure a private agreement, for over three quarters of these cases were withdrawn abruptly after one or two terms and only one – for the recovery of a mere £5 – ever came before a jury. Because they had to answer to the Duke for any irregularities, members of the court of audit showed no mercy towards defaulters, and could not afford to be too scrupulous where matters of personal conduct were concerned. John Wheeler, a deputy receiver general, had, for instance, been cheated of £8 by one of his bailiffs, but was nonetheless ordered to produce the money immediately after the Michaelmas audit of 1514. Despite his repeated and well-documented protests of innocence, Wheeler was dispatched to New-

---

[11] S.C.6/Hen. VIII 5803 m. 9.

gate until the debt had been paid.[12] That others managed to escape for years while owing far larger sums of money must have heightened his sense of grievance, although his only means of redress lay through the singularly ineffectual machinery of the King's Bench.

Buckingham's treatment of his own staff may be explained, if not excused, in terms of administrative policy, but it is less easy to justify his uncompromising and often wantonly malicious behaviour towards men and women from all levels of society. He showed a single-minded and almost obsessive determination to get his own way, using the law only when other, less creditable methods failed. The Welsh tenantry in particular suffered from a near continuous series of abuses occasioned by Duke Edward's exploitation of his judicial rights as a Marcher landlord. Refusing to accept Henry VIII's decrees for the reform of customary services in the lordship of Penkelly, he imprisoned two of the men who had resisted him as a warning to any other independent spirits.[13] The same fate befell twelve leading residents of the manor of Holton, to which Buckingham laid claim during the course of a property dispute with Walter Vaughan. His suit had been two years before the courts when, in despair of recovering the manor by legal means, he sent a body of armed men to seize it and Vaughan's partisans by force. His prisoners remained for some time in Newport Castle 'contrarie to a letter to hym dyrected by the Kyngy's Councell of that partys', and were eventually driven to petition the Court of Star Chamber for their release.[14] These two cases not only provide further evidence of Duke Edward's contempt for the law, but also show him to have been a thoroughly disruptive influence along the March. The successful enforcement of law and order in Wales depended upon a close cooperation between the great landowners and the Crown, and was inevitably frustrated by Duke Edward's refusal to administer justice with an unbiased hand. When, in November 1520, another member of the prolific Vaughan family was sent for trial at Brecon, Cardinal Wolsey saw fit to issue a solemn warning. 'And foralsmuche as . . . the said William Vaughan

[12] K.B.27/1012, Trinity 6 Hen. VIII, rot. 61; 1013, Mich. 6 Hen. VIII, rot. 28.
[13] Pugh, *The Marcher Lordships*, pp. 133–8; STA CHA 2/21/115.
[14] STA CHA 2/19/223.

alledgith against the said Duke's officers parcialite ', ran his instructions, ' it is also ordred that the said Duke's officers only shall
not sitte upon the same Vaughan, but also the Kinge's Commissioners . . . And over, that the same Vaughan may be indifferently
handled and truely according to his desyre, setting aparte all
rancour, malice or parcialite and withoute delaies unreasonable.' [15]

It is possible to cite many other instances of that besetting sense
of grievance which tended to distort Buckingham's judgement
and was so clearly a matter of concern in high places. The most
interesting, both in terms of the personalities involved and the
complexity of the legal proceedings, brought Duke Edward into
direct confrontation with Sir Thomas Lucas, Henry VII's solicitor
general. Their disagreement dated from November 1499, when
Lucas was alleged to have cheated the Duke of two valuable
wards and their inheritance by falsifying an inquisition *post
mortem*. Buckingham's previous experience as a royal ward had
made him innately suspicious of any such inquiries, and his decision to sue Sir Thomas for fraud may not have been totally
unjustified. Had he remained within the law all might have been
well, but soon after the first hearing before the justices of the
King's Bench in 1510 he embarked upon a more extreme course
of action by seizing two of Lucas's manors in Norfolk. The doubtful title which he advanced hardly served to conceal what had by
now become a single-minded desire for revenge. His dislike of
Sir Thomas was clearly intensified by the latter's involvement in
an earlier exchange of manors which had robbed the Staffords of
more than £11 a year.[16] He was, moreover, unused to meeting
such stubborn resistance from those whom he took to law; and
this, a matter of self-conceit, probably explains why he began a
separate action of slander against Lucas in the Michaelmas term
of 1512, alleging him to be in contempt of the statute *de Scandalis
Magnatum* of 1394. If, as was argued, Lucas had accused Duke

---

[15] S.P.1/21 fos. 125–6. This was not the first occasion on which Buckingham fell
under suspicion: the royal council minutes for 12 April 1514 record that the Master
of the Rolls himself was to examine certain of Duke Edward's witnesses because of
serious objections put forward by the defendant Llewelyn ap Morgan (Landsdowne
Ms. 639 fo. 92). The latter had been receiver of Brecon until Michaelmas 1512, when
he left office with an unpaid deficit of £64. The case, which is otherwise undocumented, may have concerned these debts.

[16] See p. 141.

Edward of trying to suborn the jury and, incidentally, of having 'no more conscience than a dogge', then Lucas could claim that he had spoken under extreme provocation. His attempts to recover Colehall and Risby, the manors which Buckingham had usurped, had met with nothing but delays and evasions, and continued to do so until 1519 when he once more laid his case before the Duke:

Your grace by faust informacyon and upon untrue surmise, made by one William Payne, that the premises should be parcel of your manor of Hengrave . . . commanded entry to be made unto the same to your use. It pleased your Highness at your last being at Oxford . . . to have my title heard before your counsel at your manor, called the Red Rose, in London; and for that purpose ye sent for the said Payne to bring afore you such evidence and writings as he could to justify the said surmise; that Payne did not . . . but secretly stole away . . . [and] . . . that from his delay and your Highness being departed from Thornbury, nine years had elapsed, and no entry had been made by your orator . . . and that my Lord of Canterbury had moved your Highness, and that ye answered him ye are well contented to hear his suit; and if any default be, it rested in ye orator that he did not call upon your counsel . . .[17]

It is easy to see why Sir Thomas was so manifestly unwilling to accept private arbitration in the other two cases, although the courts themselves were not immune from Buckingham's far-reaching influence. The fine of £60 imposed upon Lucas for slander at the Suffolk Assizes in 1513 may well have owed something to Duke Edward's manipulation of the local jury. Lucas certainly believed so, and appealed to the King's Bench for a traverse. Accusations of bias were commonly used to obstruct the course of justice, but this particular one apparently had some justification. Buckingham owned extensive property in East Anglia, and was therefore in a position to labour the sheriff in his choice of jury. Evidence of his attempts to do so was brought by Lucas into the King's Bench, although he was eventually nonsuited because of his failure to appear in court after seven successive adjournments.[18] Why the Duke should then have appealed to

[17] J. Gage, *The History and Antiquities of Hengrave in Suffolk* (London, 1822), pp. 100–1. The original petition is not known to have survived.
[18] K.B.27/1009, Mich. 5 Hen. VIII, rot. 19v; 1010, Hilary 5 Hen. VIII, rot. 38–8a.

172

the Star Chamber for further damages remains a complete mystery.[19] The Star Chamber, with its great concern for the enforcement of law and order, was far more likely to prove hostile towards him, if only because of his previous attempts to pervert the law. He seems, moreover, either to have ignored, or even to have been totally unaware of, the possible consequences of bringing such a private vendetta before ministers of the Crown. Lucas had already been cleared of any imputations of fraud by the King's Bench in 1513; the case of slander had also been settled at common law, and it was only Duke Edward's ' ynward great grugge' which kept the dispute alive. We do not know if it ever ended, although we may be reasonably sure of its effects upon Buckingham's already unenviable reputation.

Always harsh and often unjust in his treatment of defaulting employees, Duke Edward showed himself equally ruthless towards other debtors. No less than sixty-three persons were sued by him in the Common Pleas for debts ranging from 63*s.*11*d.* to 500 marks. He hoped to recover a total of at least £3,854, but was successful in only one case, which brought him £8 from two tenants. Other settlements were no doubt made out of court, for the majority of cases disappear suddenly from the records after two or three terms. Most of these hinged upon the debtors' alleged failure to implement some form of written obligation, usually for a standard sum of either £40 or £100 offered as security on behalf of various merchants and officials. The Duke's interpretation of what constituted a broken contract was jesuitical to a degree, as the mainpernors of his brother-in-law, Sir Walter Herbert, found to their cost. At the time of his marriage to Lady Anne Stafford in 1499, Herbert undertook to settle specific property worth 300 marks a year upon her as a jointure. A series of enfeoffments, deeds and indentures drawn up by members of the Herbert family over the next six years show that Sir William had amply fulfilled his promises by the time of his death; [20] he had, however, conveyed certain manors not mentioned in the original settlement, and

---

19 Neither his appeal nor any details of its contents are known to have survived. John Bruce cites this suit as an example of Buckingham's vindictiveness (' The History of the Star Chamber ', *Archaeologia*, XXVIII (1834), p. 374); it is also noted, somewhat briefly, by R. Compton in his discussion of actions for slander (*L'Authorite et Iurisdiction des Courts de la Maiestie de la Roygne* . . . (London, 1594), fo. 13b).

20 C.C.R., 1500–9, nos. 496, 509.

because of this, a mere technicality, Buckingham felt justified in suing those who stood surety for him. Sir Edward Darrell, for example, was declared to have forfeited bonds worth 500 marks, although after five years of delays and postponements in the Common Pleas Duke Edward apparently agreed to settle out of court. Perhaps for once he felt unsure of his case and recognised that any compromise would work to his advantage.

It is now impossible to tell how often the Duke's litigation ended thus. None of the seventy-two persons sued by him for trespass, or the forty-five others accused of theft, ever found themselves before a jury; nor was he any more successful in obtaining redress from a smaller group of fifteen men and women whom he believed to have infringed his rights as a landlord. The expedient of bringing suits for trespass before the justices of both the King's Bench and the Common Pleas resulted in nothing more than additional legal expenses and was abandoned as a futile exercise after 1507. Experience must surely have taught the Duke that there was no way of circumventing or speeding up common law procedure, yet he persisted in spite of these difficulties. His attitude was wholly in character; and it set him apart from the majority of his contemporaries, whose appearances in court were few and far between. An analysis of the cases brought by members of the English baronage in the Common Pleas over a three-year period ending at Michaelmas 1515 (table VIII) confirms Buckingham's reputation for litigiousness – a reputation evidently shared and perhaps even surpassed by his brother-in-law, Henry Percy, fifth Earl of Northumberland.

Whereas the majority of litigants considered here were involved solely in a few minor cases of debt and trespass, Duke Edward and the Earl alone concerned themselves with the collection of outstanding arrears and the punishment of unsatisfactory officials. That they should do so was partly a matter of personal interest in the running of their estates, although it should not be forgotten that both men were landowners on a far larger scale than most, and therefore encountered a wider range of administrative and financial problems. With his modest inheritance and mere handful of employees, Lord Fitzwarren, for example, had neither the resources nor the incentive to emulate Duke Edward; Henry

TABLE VIII. *Cases brought by members of the English baronage in the Common Pleas between Hilary 1513 and Michaelmas 1515*

(C.P. 40/1001–12, *passim*)

	Trespass	Debt	Cases vs. Officers	Property and feudal rights	Theft	Total
Thomas, Earl of Arundel	–	3	–	–	–	3
John, Lord Berners	–	–	–	1	–	1
Robert, Lord Brooke	2	–	1	1	–	4
Edward, Duke of Buckingham	5	11	6	4	–	26
George, Lord Bergavenny	4	3	1	1	–	9
Archbishop of Canterbury	4	1	–	–	–	5
Thomas, Lord Cobham	3	–	–	–	–	3
Thomas, Lord Dacre	6	3	1	3	–	13
Thomas, Lord Darcy	3	3	–	1	2	9
Katherine, Countess of Devon	11	–	–	1	–	12
Edward, Lord Dudley	4	1	–	–	–	5
Henry, Earl of Essex	1	–	–	–	–	1
Walter, Lord Ferrers	1	–	–	–	–	1
Robert, Lord Fitzwalter	1	–	–	2	–	3
John, Lord Fitzwarren	3	1	–	–	1	5
Charles Herbert (Earl of Worcester)	1	2	–	–	–	3
Thomas Howard (Earl of Surrey)	–	3	–	2	–	5
Queen Katherine	3	2	1	–	–	6
Richard, Earl of Kent	3	1	–	–	1	5
Richard, Lord Latimer	–	1	–	1	–	2
William, Lord Mountjoy	1	2	–	1	–	4
Henry, Earl of Northumberland	7	12	9	4	2	34
Thomas, Earl of Ormonde	–	1	–	2	–	3
John, Earl of Oxford	–	2	–	–	–	2
George, Earl of Shrewsbury	1	2	–	–	1	4
Charles, Duke of Suffolk	1	–	–	–	–	1
Thomas, Earl of Surrey	1	10	–	–	1	12
William, Lord Willoughby	–	–	–	–	1	1
Henry, Earl of Wiltshire	–	1	–	1	1	3
Archbishop of York	5	4	–	–	–	9

Percy, on the other hand, shared his enthusiasm for litigation and proved an equally harsh master to those who served him. Nine members of his staff faced actions of account during the period under review,[21] although none had been bound in such heavy sums as those demanded by Duke Edward of his officials. Nor does the Earl appear to have brought as many suits for the recovery of sums pledged as security to him in formal obligations. Three persistent debtors had apparently retained 100 marks each outstanding on a joint bond, while John Willoughby and his wife were said to owe 1,000 marks between them;[22] but these four cases alone concerned forfeited bonds. However, Buckingham and the Earl were alike unable to avoid the constraints imposed upon them by the leisurely workings of the English judicial system, and seem both to have used the threat of legal action more as a positive manifestation of their displeasure than as a direct means of obtaining redress.

Buckingham was most active as a litigant in the Exchequer of Pleas, where his cases appeared every year with monotonous regularity. In this court complaints were heard against crown officers who had failed to discharge payments sanctioned by royal warrant. Duke Edward, as the recipient of an annuity of £40 assigned on the farm of Bedfordshire and Buckinghamshire for the upkeep of his dukedom and three annuities of £20 similarly assigned on the farms of Staffordshire, Herefordshire and Northamptonshire in respect of his comital titles, became involved in almost continuous litigation because his fees were not regularly paid. All three Dukes of Buckingham experienced considerable difficulties in recovering their annuities, but Duke Edward's persistence in going to law because of this was not matched by his predecessors. Between 1498 and 1521 he made at least thirty-one separate appeals to the Barons of the Exchequer, and surprisingly obtained a favourable hearing in all but eight.[23] Each suit was

---

[21] The most senior of whom, John Turner, was an auditor charged with failing to declare his accounts for a period of eight years (C.P.40/1001, Mich. 4 Hen. VIII, rot. 430).

[22] C.P.40/1006, Easter 6 Hen. VIII, rot. 25; 1008, Mich. 6 Hen. VIII, rot. 469v.

[23] E.13/178 mm. 13-16v; 179 mm. 4-4v; 180 mm. 3, 8-10v, 18-19v, 22-3; 181 mm. 19-9v, 44-4v, 48-8v; 182 mm. 28-29v; 183 mm. 10-12v; 184 mm. 3-4v; 185 mm. 13-3v; 189 mm. 9-10v, 29-9v; 190 mm. 2-2v; 193 mm. 5-5v, 18-8v; 194 mm. 14-4v; 195 mm. 3-3v; 198 mm. 2-2v, 25-5v; 199 mm. 4-4v, 21-1v.

brought against the sheriffs or former sheriffs of those counties whence his fee was assigned, and he laid claim to arrears in excess of £988. Working on the assumption that delays were inevitable, he would agitate for payment as soon as his attorneys had presented his letters patent at the Exchequer. Speed was essential: further litigation often followed the court's initial ruling, and it could take several years for the Duke to recover even part of his debts. In 1501, for instance, Richard Burton, the sheriff of Northamptonshire, was sued for £20 outstanding on the previous year's annuity. Duke Edward won the case, but when his attorney arrived to collect the money, the necessary writs had not been issued. Burton's successor appeared in court during the Trinity term of 1502 to explain that he could only raise goods worth £5, and was ordered to make good the deficit at the first opportunity. Buckingham meanwhile waited in vain until 1504, when he asked for an official writ to hasten the confiscation. Yet as long as each successive sheriff continued to exploit Burton's alleged insolvency nothing else could be done, and more than three quarters of the original debt had to be written off.[24] Problems of this kind were not uncommon, although Duke Edward showed characteristic determination in overcoming them. Not so his father, who made only one attempt to recover money from the Crown – this was in 1474, shortly after his official coming of age – and thereafter allowed arrears to build up at the rate of almost £50 a year.[25] Only eleven rolls survive for the Exchequer of Pleas during Henry VI's reign, thus making it impossible to tell how often the first Duke of Buckingham sought redress from this quarter. Unpaid fees accounted for £1,000 of the receiver general's deficit at Michaelmas 1457, however, which suggests that any such attempts were singularly unsuccessful.[26] Perhaps he was prepared to forgo the money out of loyalty to the Crown and sympathy for King Henry's financial difficulties; at all events, he showed no real enthusiasm for litigation. This was true of his affairs as a whole, for of the Staffords only Duke Edward had frequent recourse to the law.

The comparative infrequency of the second Duke's appearances

---

[24] E.13/180 mm. 18–19v.
[25] E.13/160 mm. 11–1v; D.641/1/2/26 m. 7.
[26] D.641/1/2/23 mm. 9v–10.

in court is particularly striking, given his position as a great land-owner. During the last three years of his life, for example, he brought no more than six suits in the Common Pleas and none in the King's Bench.[27] Only one man was sued for debt, and there were no proceedings against unsatisfactory officials. Duke Humphrey's record is not much more impressive, since his chief concern was to collect modest debts and punish trespassers in his parks. Forty-two of the fifty-seven persons sued by him between 1449 and 1451 were common poachers,[28] while a further eight – all members of the Ferrers' affinity – had evidently conspired to assault him.[29] An incident recorded in a King's Bench indictment of 1451 admits a more sinister interpretation, however. In the previous year a band of armed men, said to number one hundred and ' covered with long beards and painted on their faces with black charcoal, calling themselves servants of the queen of the fairies, intending their names should not be known ', carried off a considerable quantity of game from the Duke's park at Penshurst. One of the leaders of a conspiracy in Kent some months before had also been known as ' a servant of the queen of the fairies ', and there can be little doubt that some, if not all, of these men were his erstwhile followers.[30] Yet these few examples cannot be taken as evidence of mounting disorder on the Stafford estates: on the contrary, during this, one of the most turbulent periods of the fifteenth century, Buckingham had no other business before the King's Bench where cases of riot and disorder were commonly heard. The general pattern of his litigation hardly changed over the years 1456 to 1460. Sixteen of the twenty-three suits which he began during this period were for debt, but none of the sums involved exceeded £40 and some were very small indeed. Only one case seems to have hinged upon the forfeiture of a written

27 C.P.40/875, Hilary 20 Ed. IV, rot. 176; 878, Mich. 21 Ed. IV, rot. 281; 879, Hilary 21 Ed. IV, rot. 307v, 438v; 881, Trinity 22 Ed. IV, rot. 230; 882, Mich. 22 Ed. IV, rot. 416.

28 C.P.40/752, Hilary 27 Hen. VI, rot. 155; 753, Easter 27 Hen. VI, rot. 414v; 762, Trinity 29 Hen. VI, rot. 350v.

29 C.P.40/761, Easter 29 Hen. VI, rot. 284; 758, Trinity 28 Hen. VI, rot. 154; the Duke also brought six actions for debt (759, Mich. 29 Hen. VI, rot. 259; 761, Easter 29 Hen. VI, rot. 298; 763, Mich. 30 Hen. VI, rot. 286v, 463, 517, 605), and one short-lived action of account (756, Easter 28 Hen. VI, rot. 25).

30 R. Virgoe, ' Some Ancient Indictments in the King's Bench referring to Kent, 1450–1452 ', *Kent Records*, XVIII (1964), pp. 254–5.

bond, while most of the others were brought against recalcitrant tenant farmers who had fallen behind with their rents.[31] Duke Humphrey's lack of success in court is borne out by his surviving estate accounts, which record the very same arrearages years after his death. The executors of a bailiff named Birde, who had owed the Duke £3.10s. in 1435, were still charged with the same debt at Michaelmas 1461, as was Thomas Mitchell of Milton, whose deficit of £12 dated from 1449 if not before.[32] Thomas Berkley, receiver of the South Western estates, joined Buckingham in taking legal action against seven persistent debtors from the Gloucestershire area, although this attempt to clear off a mounting backlog of arrears was also thwarted by delays and technicalities.[33] Other equally futile attempts at debt collection were made in the lordship of Tonbridge and throughout the central circuit, but circumstances again conspired to prevent a smooth passage through the courts.

In one respect, however, the first Duke of Buckingham was more litigious than his descendants, if only because the political situation worked to his advantage. The disgrace and partial forfeiture of Queen Joan (Henry IV's widow) made it possible for him to bring at least five suits against her and her tenant farmers for exploiting the Stafford estates during his long minority.[34] The second Duke was certainly in no position to sue either the Crown or his grandmother for similar negligence, although it would appear from the latter's persistence in reclaiming debts through the courts that her policy towards staff and tenants alike was more than severe. Between 1473 and 1476, for instance, the Dowager Duchess Anne attempted to recover over £456 from twenty-three people, some of whom had almost certainly entered bonds for the payment of quite considerable sums.[35] Lady Margaret Beaufort, Duke Edward's guardian,

---

31 C.P.40/780-97, *passim*; since numbers 783-4, 787-8, 790, 793 and 796 are now unfit for production, it is quite likely that the Duke was involved in other actions at this time.

32 C.P.40/781, Easter 34 Hen. VI, rot. 340; 791, Mich. 37 Hen. VI, rot. 62; D.641/1/2/181 m. 10v.

33 C.P.40/791, Mich. 37 Hen. VI, rot. 62, 71v; the receiver's deficit accounted for over one third of his total charge by Michaelmas 1459, and was in part made up of debts claimed unsuccessfully in the courts (D.641/1/2/180 m. 1).

34 C.P.40/650, Trinity 1 Hen. VI, rot. 252; 654, Trinity 2 Hen. VI, rot. 43-3v, 56.

35 C.P.40/847, Trinity 13 Ed. IV, rot. 75, 76v, 331v; 849, Hilary 13 Ed. IV, rot. 100;

proved equally zealous in the pursuit of her ward's less satisfactory tenants, bringing no fewer than twenty-eight suits for debt in an attempt to settle £215 in overdue arrearages before the young man came of age.[36] Yet even she, the King's mother, found it expedient to withdraw most of these cases after one or two preliminary hearings, and is not known to have recovered any of the money owed to her.

Only once, during his protracted disagreement with Sir Baldwin Mountfort, does Duke Humphrey appear to have used the law as an instrument for the pursuit of private vendettas. On this occasion he and his friends brought two actions of assault against their unfortunate victim, whose disinheritance at Buckingham's hands marked the beginnings of a bitter feud.[37] Even here, however, his decision to sue may be easily justified, if not excused, and there are few signs of the vindictiveness and rapacity which characterise the last Duke's approach to litigation. Perhaps Duke Humphrey had less need to invoke the law and could rely on threats alone. The Welsh antiquary Theophilus Jones believed that many of his tenants were made bankrupt ' through the mere terror of unequal litigation ', and recalls the legend originally set down in Thomas's *History of Welsh Heroes*, of how one of these men escaped from Gloucester gaol after three years' imprisonment without trial.[38] Clearly, if the Duke had few compunctions over the arrest of Sir Baldwin Mountfort and his sons, his treatment of the Welsh peasantry may well have been so harsh as to make it quite unnecessary for him to take them to law.

The three Dukes' legal jurisdiction along the Marches and their position as the lords of many manorial courts gave them sufficient power to deal with all but the most persistent offenders. It was a different matter with cases which went before the common law courts or equity: here they could not rely upon a favourable judgement and in most cases seem eventually to have

856, Mich. 15 Ed. IV, rot. 215, 251v, 461v. Proceedings were also begun against a few poachers and local miscreants (854, Easter 15 Ed. IV, rot. 404v; 856, Mich. 15 Ed. IV, rot. 456v; 857, Hilary 15 Ed. IV, rot. 388).

[36] C.P.40/944, Easter 13 Hen. VII, rot. 33; 945 Trinity 13 Hen. VII, rot. 27v, 28, 362, 371v.

[37] C.P.40/789, Easter 36 Hen. VI, rot. 134; 792, Hilary 37 Hen. VI, rot. 394.

[38] *A History of the County of Brecknock*, enlarged by Sir Joseph Russell Burley (4 vols., Brecon, 1909–30), vol. I p. 105 and Harleian Ms. 4181 fo. 81; the connexion between these two works is discussed in Pugh, *The Marcher Lordships*, p. 240n.

placed their grievances before private arbitration. Historians have commonly and perhaps naturally assumed that magnates of great standing and authority could influence the courts for their own purposes, but this was so only to a limited extent. The inability of the last Duke of Buckingham to bring most of his suits to a conclusion leads one to question how the majority of litigants fared in their dealings with the law. Indeed, it is doubtful whether recourse to legal action was by this time regarded as much more than a form of pressure designed to hasten some private settlement.

CONCLUSION

The sudden and dramatic fall of Edward, Duke of Buckingham, the greatest nobleman in England, inevitably made a lasting impression upon his contemporaries. Sir Thomas More, who had himself been rewarded with property from the confiscated Stafford estates, was clearly thinking of Buckingham's disgrace when he later came to write these lines on the subject of envy:

> If it so were that thou knewest a great Duke, kepyng so great estate and princely port in his howse, that you being a ryght meane manne, haddest in thyne heart great enuy thereat, and specially at some special daye, in which he kepeth for the mariage of his chylde, a great honorable court aboue other times, if thou beyng thereat, and the syght of the rialty and honoure shewed hym of all the county about resorting to hym . . . if thou sholdest sodeinly be surely aduertised, yt for secret treason lately detected to the King he shold undoubtedly be taken the morow his courte al broken up, his goodes ceased, his wife put out, his children dysherited, himselfe caste in prison, broughte furth & arrayned, the matter out of question & he should be condemned, his cote armour reuersed, his gilt spurres hewen of his heles, himself hanged drawen and quartered, howe thinkeste thou by thy fayth amyd thyne enuy, shouldeste thou not sodaynly chaunge into pity? [1]

The shock felt by many English noblemen and courtiers at Buckingham's end was rendered less severe by Henry VIII's shrewdly calculated distribution of offices and land from his inheritance. Although he wisely kept the Duke's Welsh Marcher lordships in his own hands, he used most of the English estates for purposes of patronage. Duke Edward's widow, Eleanor, was confirmed in a jointure comprising lands and rents in Northamptonshire, Wiltshire, and Newport worth 2,000 marks a year, while her son,

[1] *The workes of Sir Thomas More Knyght, sometyme Lord Chaunccellor of England, wrytten by him in the Englysh tonge*, ed. William Rastell (London, 1557), fo. 86.

182

Henry, obtained possession of the two less lucrative receiverships of Caus and Staffordshire – save for the Castle and manor of Stafford, which he did not recover until 1531.[2] A further seventy-one persons were excepted from the act of attainder passed against Buckingham in 1523. Eleven appointments and grants of property previously made by the late Duke were confirmed by Henry VIII, who disposed of a further sixty-five farms, townships and manors together with the sub-receivership of Norfolk, and nominated at least forty-three new office-holders throughout the Stafford estates. Most of these grants were quite modest, for only nine persons received more than two manors and few made a significant profit. A handful of royal favourites were, however, shown particular generosity: Sir Thomas Boleyn and his son, George, for example, engrossed no less than sixteen offices in the lordship of Tonbridge; three manors worth over £77 a year clear went to Richard Jerningham; other courtiers, including Sir Henry Guildford, Sir Gilbert Tailboys, Sir Nicholas Carew and Sir Richard Neville, each secured one of the late Duke's larger and more lucrative manors.[3]

Henry VIII recognised the wisdom of giving a share of the spoils to the great magnates who had meekly accepted Buckingham's fall. The Dukes of Norfolk and Suffolk, Thomas, Marquess of Dorset, and the Earls of Essex, Surrey, Devonshire, Northumberland, Worcester and Shrewsbury kept whatever sinecures they had enjoyed in the past, and were rewarded with additional grants of land. The Duke of Norfolk and Duke Edward's son-in-law, Thomas, Earl of Surrey, shared property worth almost £100 a year from the sub-receivership of Norfolk; and a considerable part of the Staffords' estates in Suffolk was handed over to the King's sister Mary, who held it as a jointure with her husband, Charles, Duke of Suffolk. As the new owner of three of Buckingham's most productive Warwickshire manors, the Marquess of Dorset was at least £63 a year richer than before, while Henry, Earl of Essex, could expect at least £131 a year clear from the property in Somerset and Essex awarded to him.

It was not avarice alone which made the leading members of

---

[2] *Statutes of the Realm*, vol. III pp. 267–70; *L. & P. Henry VIII*, vol. V no. 364 (29).
[3] *Statutes of the Realm*, vol. III pp. 246–58, *passim*.

the English baronage ready to accept Duke Edward's disgrace and forfeiture. Henry VII and his son had over the years been so successful in establishing a court nobility dependent upon royal favour that by 1521 the likelihood of sustained and organised resistance from the upper ranks of English society was indeed remote. That Henry VII deliberately set out to restrict the power and independence of his most eminent subjects is now beyond question. This was done through the calculated exploitation of all the legal and fiscal devices at his disposal, and one by one individual noblemen were brought under his personal control. His two chief weapons – the recognizance and the act of attainder – were used with consummate skill: by 1509 at least one adult member of almost every noble family in England was in some way bound to the King, either as a debtor or as the former victim of an act of attainder, and was thus dependent upon Henry's good will for the restitution of his inheritance.[4] The career of Thomas Howard, Earl of Surrey and Duke of Norfolk, provides a particularly striking example of Henry's ability to manipulate a potentially ' over mighty subject' once he had gained control of his estates. Both Thomas and his father, John, Duke of Norfolk, had fought for Richard III at Bosworth and were duly attainted in the first parliament of the new reign. Norfolk died in battle, but his son was wounded and taken prisoner. The latter's obvious talents and ambition for high office seem to have made an impression on the King, who pardoned him and in 1489 restored his earldom and part of his inheritance. The Earl nevertheless had to work hard to retain Henry's favour, and it was only gradually that his other estates were given back to him. Not until 1514 – one year after his defeat of the Scots at Flodden and thirteen years after his appointment as Treasurer of England – was he created Duke of Norfolk; and even then his family fortunes had not been fully restored. He died in 1524, having bought back only part of the property given to others by Henry VII after the forfeiture of the Howard estates, and having been forced to accept the permanent loss of all Richard III's grants to his father. He had, however, been actively

---

[4] See J. R. Lander, ' Bonds, coercion and fear: Henry VII and the peerage', in *Florilegium Historiale: Essays presented to Wallace K. Ferguson*, ed. J. G. Rowe and W. H. Stockdale (Toronto, 1971), *passim*, for a fuller discussion of the various cases cited here.

and successfully involved in the business of government and in warfare, and in this respect enjoyed marks of favour denied to most of his titled contemporaries.

The third Duke of Buckingham was not alone in feeling bitterness and indignation at Henry's attempts to turn the nobility into satellites and courtiers whose function was to act as vehicles for royal propaganda rather than as ministers of state. Certain members of the baronage were perhaps too untrustworthy or too unreliable to occupy a high position. John, Lord Zouche, George, Lord Bergavenny, and Thomas, Earl of Dorset, for example, had each behaved in such a way as to warrant their exclusion from power. The severe financial penalties imposed upon them in the form of heavy recognizances for debt and the enforced settlement of valuable property upon royal trustees not only rendered them completely harmless, but also made them amenable to the King's every wish. His wish invariably brought them to court, where, like Richard, Earl of Kent, they could be kept under his watchful eye. The Earl was perhaps the most unfortunate of Henry VII's victims, for as well as being forced to make over all his property to the Crown as security for the repayment of a ' debt' of almost £4,500, he was obliged to attend daily upon the King and suffer the indignity of the appointment of a royal official to supervise his household. Admittedly, Kent was something of a prodigal, but he had done nothing to deserve such harsh treatment, which led to his impoverishment and the eventual bankruptcy of his house. Other noblemen who had far more reason to expect preferment were equally disappointed. Henry Percy, fifth Earl of Northumberland, was given a sharp reminder of the delicacy of his position in 1505, when he was condemned to pay a fine of £10,000 for abducting a royal ward. The terms were subsequently modified in the Earl's favour, but he too lived in fear that the King might suddenly make him honour the crippling obligations into which he had been forced to enter. Henry VIII cancelled what remained of Northumberland's debt, but continued to watch over him, seizing every opportunity to reduce his influence in the North and keep him at court.

Similar pressures were also brought to bear on Edward, Duke of Buckingham, the richest and potentially the most dangerous subject in England. Although he had no alternative but to reverse the attainder passed on Duke Edward's father in 1483, Henry VII managed to extort large sums of money from the Stafford estates by exploiting his rights of marriage and wardship.[5] Even more galling for the Duke was the refusal by the Tudors to admit him to their inner counsels: he was bitter at being denied the high office to which he felt his wealth and status entitled him, and unlike his contemporaries made no attempt to conceal his growing discontent. However strongly individual lords may have resented their loss of personal freedom, few were prepared even to contemplate the possibility of an open rebellion. By the time of Buckingham's death in 1521 the nobility as a class had undoubtedly been weakened and its resolution undermined. The lack of positive reaction to his fall is symptomatic of the subservience to which Tudor policy had reduced the English baronage. Henry VII and his son had so effectively destroyed their sense of solidarity, while offering the nation more stable government than it had previously known, that without jeopardising their throne they could deal firmly with a recalcitrant like Duke Edward.

Henry VII was not the first English monarch to attempt the creation of a court nobility, nor was he the first to arouse the antagonism of the Staffords for doing so. Without doubt one of the main reasons behind Duke Henry's decision to throw in his lot with Richard of Gloucester on the death of Edward IV was his hostility towards the latter's *protégés*, whom he felt to have usurped a place that was rightly his. The Queen's relatives in particular were extremely unpopular among the longer-established noble families. Their rapid rise from relatively humble origins made them many enemies in a class particularly sensitive to precise distinctions of birth. Moreover, as Dr Ross has recently shown, the political influence of the Wydevilles, derived from their closeness to the King and their predominance in the royal household, was a genuine cause for alarm to those living outside the charmed circle of the court.[6] Whereas Henry VII sought to turn his great lords into courtiers, King Edward surrounded himself with a largely *parvenu* nobility, which he had elevated from the ranks

[5] See pp. 35-6.
[6] C. D. Ross, *Edward IV* (London, 1975), pp. 97-101.

of county society and used as a means of strengthening his personal rule. Although he never attempted either to weaken or control the baronage as a whole, and was indeed even prepared to bolster the local authority of certain lords, Edward IV bestowed his patronage in such a way as to create a division between 'the court' and 'the country'. Henry, Duke of Buckingham, had better reason than most to bear a grudge against the King's new favourites. As a great Marcher landowner, he could not but resent the authority given to the Queen's brother, Anthony, Earl Rivers, in Wales, especially as he himself had been excluded from all commissions of the peace outside Staffordshire. Not only his unfulfilled political ambitions but also an awareness of his own social superiority nourished his hatred of the new nobility. During the course of his reign Edward IV created or revived no less than thirty-five peerage titles, the majority of which were conferred before 1471.[7] The Queen's grasping relatives, as well as many former supporters of the house of York, did particularly well for themselves; and it is easy to see how Buckingham, with his great estates and royal blood, should feel personally affronted by the ennoblement of Elizabeth Wydeville's son, Thomas Grey, Earl of Huntingdon and Marquess of Dorset, and by the excessive favour shown to her five brothers. Her father, Richard Wydeville, Earl Rivers, had been raised to the peerage during the previous reign, but was no more popular than his children. He was abused in 1460 by the Earl of Warwick and other prominent Yorkists for his low birth and presumptuous behaviour on the grounds that he had been 'made by maryage, and also made Lord, and that it was not his parte to have swyche langage of Lords, beyng of the Kyngs blood'.[8]

Although Henry VI never ceased to recognise his dependence upon the prestige and authority of Humphrey, first Duke of Buckingham, there can be little doubt that his lavish distribution of titles among men of greatly inferior status caused the Duke considerable dismay, and was perhaps one reason for his strained relations with the court party during the late 1450s. Like the

[7] T. B. Pugh, 'The magnates, knights and gentry', pp. 116–7.
[8] Ross, *op. cit.*, p. 90, citing *P.L.*, vol. I p. 506 (William Paston to John Paston, 28 Jan. 1460). Rivers had married Jacquetta de Luxembourg, widow of John, Duke of Bedford, in 1436/7.

young Edward IV, King Henry showed a marked lack of political foresight in his use of patronage. He created over twenty-five new titles between 1436 and 1461, and also made many promotions within the existing baronage. The new rank of viscount was, for example, bestowed on John, Lord Beaumont, in 1440, and that of marquess reintroduced in 1444 as a reward for William de la Pole, Earl of Suffolk. The first Earl, a favourite of Richard II, had been contemptuously dismissed as '*vir plus aptus mercimoniis quam militiae*', an opinion which many held of his grandson, the much-hated fourth Earl.[9] Although the de la Poles had benefited greatly from Richard's generosity, they never recovered financially from the first Earl's forfeiture in 1387, and William was certainly not rich enough in his own right to support himself in the style of either a marquess or, after his second promotion in 1447, a duke. Success as a courtier secured his place on embassies and commissions and brought him many important offices with great reserves of patronage attached. One by one his supporters were themselves raised to the peerage and began to build up their own networks of clientage. Sir John Stourton (created Lord Stourton in 1448), Sir John Beauchamp (created Lord Beauchamp of Powick in 1447), and Sir James Fiennes (created Lord Saye and Sele in 1447) were all among ' the fals progeny of the Dewke of Suffolke ', vilified – and in Fiennes' case actually murdered – by Cade's rebels in 1450. So too was Sir Ralph Boteler, an influential member of the royal household, who received the Barony of Sudeley with an annuity of 200 marks in 1441 and subsequently accumulated an impressive collection of offices. His Castle of Sudeley in Gloucestershire was built out of ' spoyles gotten in France ' and the fees and perquisites which after 1440 were his for the asking.[10]

Richard, Duke of York, the heir male of Edward III and one of the richest landowners in England, felt himself particularly threatened by the rise of these ambitious placemen. York's many sympathisers complained of his exclusion from office and begged the King ' Also to take about his person the myghte prynce, the

9 Pugh, *op. cit.*, p. 95; G.E.C., vol. XII, pt i, p. 443.

10 K. B. McFarlane, *The Nobility of Later Medieval England*, pp. 181–2; G.E.C., vol. XII, pt ii, pp. 419–21; Leland, *op. cit.*, vol. II p. 56.

Duke of Exceter, the Duke of Bokyngham, the Duke of Nor-
ffolke, and his trewe erlys and barons of his lond '.[11]

Henry VI had no intention of limiting the authority of such a
loyal and committed supporter as Humphrey, Duke of Buckingham, but nevertheless showed himself remarkably insensitive to
the Duke's great sense of family pride. Buckingham's claim to be
accorded precedence over all newly created dukes not of the blood
royal brought him into conflict with the twenty-year-old Henry
Beauchamp, whose dukedom, awarded in 1445, was allowed to
rank above his own. Although he was the son of the great captain,
Richard, Earl of Warwick, and enjoyed an estimated income of
about £4,900 a year, Beauchamp had less royal blood in his veins
than Buckingham, and, being a mere youth, could not match
the Duke's reputation as a soldier and statesman.[12] The precedence question was finally settled by parliament, which decided
that ' one of the sayd Dukes shulde have the premynens and sytt
above the other an hole yeare and then that other above him and
all the next yeare aftyre . . .'[13] Warwick's early death without
heirs male terminated this *ad hoc* arrangement, and Duke Humphrey secured a grant of special precedence. Even though his
position was now assured, Buckingham cannot have welcomed
the creation of the upstart William de la Pole as Duke of Suffolk,
and may indeed have felt that a dukedom was too high an honour
for the unpopular courtier Edmund Beaufort, a grandson of John
of Gaunt and his mistress, Katherine Swynford.

The history of the Staffords during the fifteenth and early sixteenth centuries illustrates the gradual decline in the political
power of the great landowning families which dominated the
English baronage at the beginning of this period. Henry VI's
attempts to bolster his authority through the inflation of honours
and the creation of a court nobility inevitably lessened even if it
did not undermine the control exercised by men like Humphrey,
Duke of Buckingham, over affairs of state. The second Duke
suffered far more from the withdrawal and redirection of royal

[11] *Three Fifteenth Century Chronicles*, p. 97.
[12] See K. B. McFarlane, *op. cit.*, pp. 187–201 for further information about the Beau-
champs' finances.
[13] D.1721/1/1 fo. 384b (a sixteenth-century transcription of the settlement).

Conclusion

patronage, while the third was the victim of a conscious plan to curb the aristocracy as a class. In the history of their time the Staffords played a large, but strangely negative part. Unwilling to accept what they were ultimately powerless to resist, they were cast as the representatives of an old order giving way to a new.

Appendix A

THE STAFFORD ESTATES

1. *Property Held by Robert Stafford in 1086*

Lincolnshire: land in Bourn, Braceby, Calthorp, Carlton Scroop, Denton, Haceby, Little Bytham, Marston, Rauceby, Scredington, Willoughby (*The Domesday Book*, ed. A. Farley (2 vols., R.C., 1783), vol. I fo. 368v).

Oxfordshire: land in Addebury, Alvescot, Dunstew, Great Rollright, Horley, Ilbury, Middle Aston, Northbrook, Stonesfield (*V.C.H. Oxford*, vol. I pp. 412–3).

Staffordshire: land in Aston by Stone, Blymhill, Bobbington, Bradeley, Brewood, Castle Church, Cheswardine, Chipnall, Church Eaton, Colton, Codsall, Croxall, Haughton, High Offley, Hopton, Ingestre, Madeley, Maer, Milwich, Norton-in-the-Moors, Patshull, Penkridge, Salt, Shareshull, Swynnerton, Tamworth, Tatenhill, Tean, Tillington, Tittensor, Walton, Wilbrighton, Wrottley (*V.C.H. Stafford*, vol. IV pp. 49–53).

Warwickshire: land in Bubbenhall, Burmington, Compton Scrofen, Compton Wyniates, Ditchford Frary, Idlicote, Morton Bagot, Tidmington, Ullenhall, Wolford, Wootton Wawen (*V.C.H. Warwick*, vol. I pp. 328–31).

2. *The Clare Inheritance Acquired in 1343* (C.P.R., 1343–5, pp. 140, 366, 384; C.47/9/23)

Bedfordshire and Buckinghamshire: the manors of Brickhill, Essington and Stewkley; a number of courts leet and small rents.

Essex: the manors of Ongar, Stapleford and Thaxted.

Gloucestershire: the manors of Campden, Rendcombe and Thornbury; a number of courts leet.

Hampshire: the manors of Cornhampton, Mapledurham, Petersfield and Upper Clatford.

Huntingdonshire: the manor of Southoe; many courts leet.

Ireland: one third of the lordship of Kilkenny.

Kent: the manors of Audley, Brasted, Dacherst, Edenbridge and Yalding; the Castle and manor of Tonbridge; holdings in Circleston, Oltham, Ormidale, Overford and Sedingdale; Northfrith Park; court of the Honour of Gloucester.

London: rents and tenements in Bread Street.

Norfolk: the manors of Cumplesham, Stafford Barningham, Warham, Wells and Wiveton.

Northamptonshire: the manors of Naseby and Whiston; the town and hundred of Rothwell.

Oxfordshire: minor judicial privileges.

Suffolk: the manors of Disining, Haverhill and Hersham; land in Cavenham.

Surrey: the manors of Effingham and Ockham; the manor and borough of Bletchingley; land and tenements in Camberwell, Chipstead, Tillingdon, Titsey and Waldingham.

Wales: the Castle, borough and lordship of Newport, comprising the manors of Dowlais, Dyffryn, Ebbw, Machen, Pencarn, Rumney and Stow; the county of Wentloog; the forest of Machen.

Wiltshire: the manors of Bedwynd, Wexcombe, Burbage Savage, Knook and Orcheston; minor judicial privileges.

3. *The Corbet Inheritance Acquired between 1347 and 1357* (*C.C.R.*, 1346–9, p. 395; *C.P.R.*, 1354–8, p. 544; see also Longleat Ms. 4010)

Shropshire: the Castle, borough and lordship of Caus, comprising the manors of Aston, 'Baghaltre', Forton, Habberley, Hope, Minsterley, Nether Gorther, Upper Gorther, Wallop, Weston and Worthen; the forests of Ponslith (Montgomery), Hayes and Habberley.

4. *Purchases Made by the Second Earl in 1383* (D.641/1/2/1 m. 3v)

Buckinghamshire: the manor of Policott.

Warwickshire: the manors of Rugby and Stangrave.

5. *The Basset Inheritance Acquired between 1390 and 1403* (D.641/1/2/4 m. 4: *C.F.R.*, 1399–1405, p. 211; see D.641/1/2/17, *passim*, for a list of these properties)

Buckinghamshire: the manor of Newton Blossomville.

Cheshire: land in Partington.

Lincolnshire: the manor of Greetwell.

Norfolk: the manor of Sheringham.

Nottinghamshire: the manors of Colston Basset and Ratcliffe on Soar; land in Milton.

Surrey: tenements in Southwark.

Warwickshire: the manor of Sheldon.

6. *The de Bohun Inheritance Acquired in 1421* (*Rot. Parl.*, vol. IV pp. 137–8; the Essex and Wiltshire manors settled by the Countess Anne

upon the sons of her third marriage to Sir William Bourchier are listed in *Feet of Fines for Essex* (4 vols., Colchester, 1899–1964), vol. IV p. 16, and are here marked *)

Buckinghamshire: the manor of Amersham.
Essex: the manors of Chignal *, East Legh *, Fobbing, Hallingbury *, Hatfield Broadoak, Haydon, Norton le Hays *, Polmarsh *, Ramsden *, Southorpe *, Wakering * and Writtle.
Gloucestershire: the manors of Arnold (already alienated by Eleanor de Bohun, *P.P.C.*, vol. II p. 294), Haresfield and Newham; the court of the Honour of Hereford.
Herefordshire: the fee of the Earldom and courts of five hundreds.
Huntingdonshire: the Castle and lordship of Kimbolton.
Kent: tenements at Greenwich.
Nottinghamshire: the manor of Kneesall.
Northamptonshire: the fee of the Earldom.
Wales: the Castles and lordships of Brecon, Hay and Huntingdon; the lordship of Talgarth; a title to the lordship of Cantref Selyf.
Wiltshire: the manors of Lillesford, Send * and Stretton.

7. *The Countess Anne's Inheritance from Thomas of Woodstock Acquired between 1414 and 1439*

Rutland: the Castle, manor and lordship of Oakham, comprising the manors of Egilton and Langham (*C.P.R.*, 1413–6, p. 269; *C.F.R.*, 1413–22, p. 286).
Yorkshire: the lordship of Holderness, comprising the manors of Barrow, Brustwick, Burton Pidsea, Elstronwick, Hedon, Keyingham, Kilnsea, Lamwath, Lelley, Preston, Skeckling, Skeffling, Skipsea, Sproatley, Tunstall and Withernsea (S.C.6/1084/3; D.641/1/2/17 mm. 20–2).

8. *Other Acquisitions and Exchanges*

(*a*) *From John, Lord Clinton, in exchange for the manor of Woodford, Northamptonshire, in May 1438:*
Warwickshire: the Castle and manor of Maxstoke (D.1721/1/11 fos. 271–4).

(*b*) *Awarded to Duke Humphrey for life by the Crown in 1438:*
Lancashire: rents from Nether Wyresdale (*C.P.R.*, 1436–41, pp. 161, 275).
Northamptonshire: the manor of Weedon Beck (granted to Eton College by the Duke in 1455, *ibid.*).
Somersetshire: rents from Westcombe (*ibid.*).
Warwickshire: the manor of Atherstone (resumed by Act of Parliament in 1451, *ibid.*; D.641/1/2/273 m. 2).
Wiltshire: rents from Great Bedwyn (*C.P.R.*, 1436–41, pp. 161, 275).

(c) *Purchased by Duke Humphrey in 1440:*
Suffolk: the manors of Hengrave and Leo's Hall (John Gage, *The History and Antiquities of Suffolk: Thingoe Hundred*, p. 178).

(d) *Awarded to Duke Humphrey by the Crown in 1447:*
Kent: the manor of Penshurst and its appurtenances (*C.P.R.*, 1446–52, p. 45).

(e) *Awarded to the Duke with effect from Oct. 1459:*
Herefordshire and Essex: the confiscated estates of Sir William Oldhall (whose attainder was reversed by the parliament of Oct. 1460; *C.P.R.*, 1452–61, p. 571; *Rot. Parl.*, vol. V pp. 349, 374).

(f) *Awarded as part of the de Bohun Estates to Duke Henry in 1478:*
Wales: the lordship of Cantref Selyf (resumed in 1483; restored to Duke Edward in 1509; *C.P.R.*, 1476–85, p. 69; *op. cit.*, 1494–1509, p. 626).

(g) *From Sir Thomas Lucas in Exchange for the Manor of Leo's Hall, Suffolk, in 1506:*
Suffolk: the manor of Helion (Gage, *op. cit.*, p. 92).

(h) *Sold to Sir Richard Sacheverell in Feb. 1520:*
Nottinghamshire: the manor of Ratcliffe on Soar (*Statutes of the Realm*, vol. III pp. 271–6).

Sold to Sir William Compton in May 1520:
Warwickshire: the manors of Tyseo, Whatcote, Wolford Magna, Wolford Parva (*ibid.*).

Sold to Sir Thomas Kitson in May 1520:
Nottinghamshire: the manor of Colston Basset (*ibid.*).
Suffolk: land at Hengrave (*ibid.*).

(i) *Surrendered as Part of an Exchange with John, Lord Berners, by 1520* (E.36/181 fos. 24, 43–4, 49):
Hampshire: the manor of Upper Clatford.
Kent: the manor of Edenbridge.
Oxfordshire: the manor of Stratton Audley.
Surrey: the manors of Chipstead, Effingham, Ockham, Titsey and Waldingham; land at Porkley and Upwood.
Wiltshire: the manor of Knook.

(j) *Surrendered as Part of an Exchange with Charles, Duke of Suffolk, by 1520* (*ibid.*):
Surrey: tenements in Southwark.

Appendix B

SENIOR HOUSEHOLD AND ESTATE STAFF

Chamberlains

By Mich. 1400	—	Roger Bradshawe (D.641/1/2/6 m. 9)
By Mich. 1445	—	Henry Hexstall (D.641/1/2/233 m. 12v)
By Mich. 1475	—	Sir Nicholas Latimer (D.641/1/2/26 m. 6)
ca. 1495/6	—	Sir Edmund Mountfort (for the Dowager Duchess Katherine) (Thomas, op. cit., p. 269)
ca. 1514	—	Sir William Knivet (E.101/518/5 pt i. m. 2)

Chancellors

— 21 Apr. 1500		Sir Richard Sackville (D.641/1/3/7 m. 2)
By ca. 1514 [1]–Apr. 1521		Robert Gilbert, clerk (E.101/518/5 pt i. m. 2; Harl. Ms. 283 fo. 70)

Cofferer

By 31 Mar. 1503–Apr. 1521	William Cholmeley (D.641/1/3/7; S.P.1/29 fo. 180)

Controllers

— ca. Mich. 1383		Nicholas Shirburne (D.641/1/2/1 m. 3v)
ca. Mich. 1383	—	John Well and Henry Sewell (ibid., passim)
— 2 Nov. 1403		William Aylesdon (C.P.R., 1401–5, p. 322)
By 23 Mar. 1431	—	William Dogett (for the Dowager Countess Anne) (D.641/1/2/12 m. 4)
By 8 Jan. 1489	—	John Tomlyn (for the Dowager Duchess Katherine) (D.641/1/2/194 m. 11v)

---

[1] An annuity of £3.6s.8d. was granted to him on 12 Dec. 1500, which suggests that he took up office at about this time (S.C.6/Hen. VII 1476 m. 2).

By Mich. 1506	—	Humphrey Bannaster (S.C.6/Hen. VII 1076 m. 15)
By May 1511	—	John Pauncefoot (S.C.6/Hen. VII 4775 m. 7)
By 14 Nov. 1517–Apr. 1521		Anthony Nowers, clerk (Longleat Misc. Ms. XIII fo. 11; E.36/220 fo. 16v)

Secretaries

28 Mar. 1500–*ca.* Mar. 1507		John Russell (D.641/1/3/6 m. 1)
By Mich. 1511–*ca.* 1514		Lawrence Stubbes, clerk (D.641/1/2/88; E.101/518/5 pt i. m. 2)
By 27 Jan. 1520	—	Thomas Moscroff, clerk (E.36/220 fo. 11v)

Stewards

By Mich. 1383–at least Mich. 1391		Nicholas de Stafford (D.641/1/2/1 m. 4v; 4 m. 3)
By Mich. 1400	—	William Conningsby (D.641/1/2/6 m. 9)
By Mich. 1409	—	Sir Roger Aston (for the Dowager Countess Anne) (D.641/1/2/9 m. 3)
By 13 Oct. 1429–at least Mich. 1433		William Minden (for Duke Humphrey) (D.641/1/2/172 m. 5; 53 mm. 5v, 7v)
By Mich. 1438	—	Humphrey Cotes (D.641/1/2/15 m. 8)
By 31 Mar. 1464–*ca.* Mich. 1474		John Heton (for the Dowager Duchess Anne) (S.C.6/1117/11 m. 6; Add. Ms. 29608 m. 1)
By Mich. 1475	—	Sir Edmund Mountfort (for Duke Henry) (D.641/1/2/26 mm. 6, 7)
By Mich. 1495	—	Richard Pole (for the Dowager Duchess Katherine) (Thomas, *op. cit.*, p. 270)
By 12 June 1502	—	Robert Turberville (D.1721/1/1 fo. 390)
By *ca.* 1514	—	Richard Pole (E.101/518/5 pt i. m. 3)

Treasurers

By Mich. 1391–at least Mich. 1399		Robert Mawesyn (D.641/1/2/40A m. 1)
By Mich. 1402	—	Sir Thomas Aston (D.641/1/2/43)
By Mich. 1405–Mich. 1406 [2]		Henry Morny (D.641/1/2/7 m. 3)
By Mich. 1412	—	Thomas Croxby (D.641/1/2/161 mm. 3, 4)

[2] From Mich. 1406 to *ca.* Mich. 1409, the treasurer's financial responsibilities were borne by John Newbury, clerk of the household (D.641/1/2/8 m. 3; 9 m. 3); from Mich. 1409 until Croxby's appointment, the steward, Sir Roger Aston, effectively acted as treasurer.

By Mich. 1430–1 Oct. 1440		Richard Donham (for the Dowager Countess Anne to 1438) (D.641/1/2/12 m. 4; Add. Ms. 2209 m. 1d)
By Mich. 1441–at least Mich. 1457		William Wistowe (D.641/1/2/168 m. 2; 23 m. 6)
By 31 Sept. 1462	—	William Fisher (Turnbull, *op. cit.*, p. 43)
By 4 Jun. 1472 [3]	—	Thomas Garth (for the Dowager Duchess Anne) (Add. Roll 22645 m. 2)
— 1 Mar. 1502		Robert Turberville (Add. Roll 40859B m. 1)
1 Mar. 1502–at least 31 Mar. 1507		Richard Mynors (*ibid.*, Longleat Misc. Ms. XII fo. 30v)
By 19 Jan. 1508	—	Humphrey Bannaster (S.P.1/22 fo. 67)
By *ca.* Mich. 1514	—	Giles Greville, clerk (E.101/518/5 pt i. m. 3; Longleat Ms. 6415 m. 2)
By 31 Mar. 1515–30 Sept. 1520		George Poley, clerk (*ibid.*, m. 7; Royal Ms. BXXXV F m. 2)
By 26 Mar. 1521	—	William Curtis, clerk (temporarily in office) (E.36/220 fo. 14)
By 7 Apr. 1521	—	William Tracy (*ibid.*, fo. 15)

Clerks of the Household

— Mich. 1400		William Stanford (D.641/1/2/6 m. 8v)
By Mich. 1400–at least Mich. 1410		John Newbury (*ibid.*, m. 9; D.641/1/2/9 m. 3)
By Mich. 1400	—	William Lyndewood (D.641/1/2/6 m. 9)
By Mich. 1402 [4]		Henry Morny (Eg. Roll 2182 mm. 1, 2)
By Mich. 1428–at least Mich. 1439		John Bullesden (D.641/1/2/231 m. 11; 15 m. 9)
By Mich. 1438	—	William Wistowe (*ibid.*, m. 6)
By Mich. 1438–at least Mich. 1451		Edward Mandby (*ibid.*; S.C.6/1305/4 m. 4)
By Mich. 1439	—	William Barber (D.641/1/2/15 m. 9)
By Mich. 1441–at least Mich. 1451		Thomas Hexstall (D. 641/1/2/168 m. 2; S.C.6/1305/4 m. 4)
By Mich. 1442	—	William Forester (D.641/1/2/54 m. 10)
By 31 Mar. 1499–at least 31 Mar. 1502		William Sharp (D.641/1/3/5; Add. Ms. 40859B)
By 31 Mar. 1499–31 Mar. 1502		William Gibbons, clerk (D.641/1/3/5)

[3] A reference to Garth's expenses in collecting money from the receiver general for the household in Oct. 1464 suggests that he may have been treasurer by this date (S.C.6/1117/11 m. 6). Similar references also occur in accounts for the lordship of Brecon for the year ending Mich. 1489 (S.C.6/Hen. VII 1651, *passim*), and Garth was probably confirmed in office by Jasper, Duke of Bedford.

[4] Morny, Wistowe and Forester were promoted to the office of treasurer within a few years of their appointment as clerks.

By 1 Apr. 1500–31 Mar. 1502	John Russell (*ibid.*)
By 31 Mar. 1506 —	John Gregory (Longleat Misc. Ms. XII fo. 30v)
ca. 1514 —	John Rosse, Richard Pooley, William Bradbolt (E. 101/518/5 pt i. m. 2)

Wardrobers

By 31 Mar. 1499 —	John Gold, clerk (D.641/1/3/9 m. 5)
— 31 Mar. 1506	William Cholmeley (Royal Ms. BXXXV F m. 1; D.641/1/3/9 m. 5)
31 Mar. 1506–at least 31 Mar. 1507	Richard Pooley, clerk (Longleat Misc. Ms. XII, *passim*)
— 31 Mar. 1509	Thomas Riche, clerk (Royal Ms. BXXXV F m. 1)
— 31 Mar. 1511	Lionel Jackson, clerk (D.641/1/3/9 m. 5)
— 31 Mar. 1512	John Landaff, clerk (*ibid.*)
— 31 Mar. 1513	Humphrey Ogull, clerk (*ibid.*, m. 6)
— 31 Mar. 1515	Henry Bullock, clerk (*ibid.*)
31 Mar. 1515–Mich. 1521	Thomas Bridges, clerk (*ibid.*, mm. 6–7; Royal Ms. BXXXV F m. 1)

Attorneys General

Aug. 1431–at least 9 Feb. 1457	John Andrews (for the Dowager Countess Anne to 1438) (D.641/1/2/13 m. 4; 1/6/3)
By Mich. 1475 —	Richard Isham (D.641/1/2/26 m. 6)
15 Jul. 1498–at least Mich. 1515	John Scott (E.13/178 rot. 13v; Longleat Ms. 6415 m. 7)
By Apr. 1521 —	Christopher Hales (S.P.1/29 fo. 179a)

Masters of the Works

| By Mich. 1514–at least Mich. 1519 | Thomas Wotton, clerk (Longleat Ms. 6415 m. 7; W.A.M. 22909) |
| By 26 Oct. 1520 | William Curtis, clerk (S.P.1/22 fo. 58) |

Auditors

By Mich. 1400–at least Mich 1411	Robert Frampton (S.C.6/924/18 m. 5; D.641/1/2/11)
By Jul. 1425–at least Aug. 1430	Henry Normanton (for Duke Humphrey) (D.641/1/2/241, 231 m. 9)
By Mich. 1430 —	Robert Quadring (for the Dowager Countess Anne) (D.641/1/2/12 m. 4)

12 Mar. 1435; auditor general from 19 Oct. 1440–at least Mich. 1467

William Weldon (D.641/1/2/15 m. 6; N.L.W. Peniarth Ms. 280 fo. 12; D.641/1/2/25 m. 1)

By 1439/40; auditor Brecon, Hay & Huntingdon 1 Jan. 1462 (for the Crown)–*d*.1464

John Harper (N.L.W. Peniarth Ms. 280 fo. 3; *C.P.R.*, 1461–7, p. 91)

By 1439/40 —

Thomas Linley (N.L.W. Peniarth Ms. 280 fo. 3)

By *ca.* Jul. 1440 —

William Lingfield (*ibid.*, fo. 10)

By *ca.* Jul. 1440 —

John Lathbury (Holderness) (*ibid.*)

By 1446/7 (Holderness); joint auditor general 17 Aug. 1457–at least Mich. 1475 (for the Dowager Duchess Anne); auditor general 29 Dec. 1485 (for the Crown) — [5]

Thomas Roger (*ibid.*, fo. 43; D.641/1/2/23 m. 6; 191 m. 3; *C.P.R.*, 1485–94, p. 48)

By *ca.* 1451/2 —

William Roucliffe (N.L.W. Peniarth Ms. 280 fo. 54)

By Mich. 1463 (for the Dowager Duchess Anne); auditor general 12 Mar. 1473–25 Sept. 1484 (for Duke Henry); Mich. 1485 (Brecon, Hay & Huntingdon; for the Crown); auditor general by 20 Oct. 1500–at least Mich. 1506 (for Duke Edward)

John Gunter (S.C.6/1117/11 m. 5; D.641/1/2/26 m. 4; *C.P.R.*, 1476–85, pp. 474–5; *ibid.*, 1485–94, p. 11; C.P.40/966, Mich. 19 Hen. VII, rot. 142v; S.C.6/Hen. VII 1076 m. 15)

— 25 Sept. 1484

Walter Gorfyn (Newport, Brecon & Hay; for the Crown) (*C.P.R.*, 1476–85, pp. 474–5; *ibid.*, 1485–94, p. 11)

29 Dec. 1485–at least Mich. 1494

John Knight (auditor general for the Crown) (*ibid.*, p. 48; Eg. Roll 2197 m. 11)

25 Sept. 1484–at least Mich. 1497

Richard Lussher (Newport, Brecon & Hay; for the Crown) (*C.P.R.*, 1476–85, pp. 474–5; *ibid.*, 1485–94, p. 11; D.641/1/2/199 m. 10v)

By Mich. 1488 —

John Donne & Richard Donne (for Lady Margaret Beaufort) (D.641/1/2/77 m. 1v)

By Mich. 1497–at least Mich. 1499

Thomas Hobart (Kent & Surrey, Caus, Staffs. & Holderness) (D.641/1/2/79 m. 9)

[5] He died in 1487 (*C.F.R.*, 1485–1509, no. 153).

199

By Mich. 1500–at least 10 Nov. 1504		Walter Thomas (D.641/1/2/201 m. 11; C.P. 40/979, Hilary 22 Hen. VII, rot. 350v)
By 20 Oct. 1500	—	William Hobson (C.P.40/966, Mich. 19 Hen. VII, rot. 142v)
By 12 Mar. 1507–Mich. 1521		William Walwyn (STA CHA 2/23/111, 26/386; S.C.6/Hen. VII 5841 m. 6v)
By Sept. 1504	—	William Reginald (S.C.6/Hen. VII 1665 m. 12v)
22 Sept. 1506–22 Sept. 1514		John Seintgeorge (Kent & Surrey, Staffs. & Holderness) (C.P.40/1012, Mich. 7 Hen. VII, rot. 262)
By Mich. 1506	—	Henry Sleford (S.C.6/Hen. VII 1844 m. 2)
By 13 Jan. 1512	—	William Becke (Add. Roll 26874 m. 1)
By 13 Jan. 1512	—	John Buttys (*ibid.*)
By 20 Feb. 1512	—	Robert Cade (K.B.27/1012, Trinity 6 Hen. VIII, rot. 61)
29 Sept. 1513–29 Sept. 1515		Edward Edgar (central circuit) (C.P.40/1012, Mich. 7 Hen. VIII, rot. 588)
By Mich. 1516	—	Richard Palmer (D.641/1/2/96 m. 4)
By Mich. 1516–Apr. 1521		David Young (D.641/1/2/92 m. 1; 96 m. 4)
By Mich. 1516	—	John Dellacourt (Eg. Roll 2200 m. 2)
By 14 Nov. 1517	—	William Sandes (Longleat Misc. Ms. XIII fo. 11)
—	at least 1519	John Snow (W.A.M. 22909)

ESTATE STAFF

Surveyors General

1 Apr. 1461	—	Sir Thomas Burgh (for the Dowager Duchess Anne) (S.C.6/1117/11 m. 5)
11 Dec. 1485–7 Mar. 1498		Sir Reginald Bray (for Lady Margaret Beaufort) (*C.P.R.*, 1485–94, p. 54)
1 Jan. 1496	—	William Bedell (Essex, Middlesex, Kent & Surrey; for the Dowager Duchess Katherine) (S.C.6/Hen. VII 1842 m. 5v)
16 Jan. 1496	—	Sir Robert Poyntz (Gloucestershire; for the Dowager) (D.641/1/2/198 m. 8)
30 Jun. 1496	—	John Wingfield (Norfolk; for the Dowager) (S.C.6/Hen. VII 1842 m. 3v)
By Mich. 1499	—	Thomas Slade (D.641/1/2/259 m. 3)
By 1501–at least Mich. 1506		Henry Sleford, clerk (W.A.M. 5470 fo. 11v; S.C.6/Hen. VIII 5803 m. 11v)

By *ca.* 1514	—	Thomas Cade, clerk (E.101/518/5 pt i. m. 2)
By 4 Mar. 1520	—	John Jennings, clerk (D.641/1/2/96 m. 4)

Receivers General

By Mich. 1383	—	Nicholas Shirburne (D.641/1/2/1 m. 1)
By Mich. 1390	—	Nicholas Bradshawe (D.641/1/2/4 m. 1)
By Mich. 1399–at least Mich. 1435		Thomas Lawrence (for the Dowager Countess Anne from Jul. 1403) (D.641/1/2/40A m. 2; S.C.11/816)
By 18 Jan. 1436–at least Mich. 1438		William Dennis (for the Dowager) (D.641/1/2/164 m. iv; 165 m. iv)
By 8 May 1425–at least 20 Dec. 1430		Thomas Barber (for Duke Humphrey) (D.641/1/2/241; 231 m. 11)
By Mich. 1432	—	Thomas Huggeford (for the Duke) (D.641/1/2/220)
21 Apr. 1437–at least Mich. 1467		John Heton (for the Dowager Duchess Anne from Jul. 1460) (D.641/1/2/15 m. 1; 25 m. 1)
By 10 May 1473–at least Mich. 1476		Thomas Garth (for the Dowager) (D.641/1/2/250 m. 4; 75 m. 3)
By 10 May 1473	—	Nicholas Gedding (for Duke Henry) (D.641/1/2/250 m. 2v)
5 Mar. 1475–at least Mich. 1477		William Fisher (for Duke Henry) (D.641/1/2/26 m. 4; 255 m. 1)
22 May 1484	—	Edmund Chaderton, clerk (for the Crown) (*C.P.R.*, 1476–85, p. 453)
7 Nov. 1485–*ca.* Mich. 1492		Richard Harper (for Lady Margaret Beaufort) (*ibid.*, 1485–94, p. 44; W.A.M. 32349)
By Mich. 1495–at least Mich. 1496		William Bedell (for Lady Margaret) (*ibid.*)
By Mich. 1495	—	Richard Pole (for the Dowager Duchess Katherine) (S.C.6/Hen. VII 1842 mm. 3v–4)
By Mich. 1497	—	William Butler, clerk (Arundel Castle Ms. A 1245)
By Mich. 1501–at least Mich. 1502		William Gibbons, clerk (D.641/1/2/28 m. 1; 202 m. 18)
By 31 May 1503–at least 18 Aug. 1508		Robert Turberville (deputy, Thomas Lambard) (D.641/1/2/267 m. 4v; S.P.1/22 fo. 85v)
By Mich. 1508–at least Mich. 1510		William Lytton (deputy, John Wheeler) (D.641/1/2/279)

10 Nov. 1511	—	Thomas Cade, clerk (C.P.40/1024, Easter 11 Hen. VIII, rot. 308v)
Before Mich. 1519	—	Thomas Moscroff, clerk (S.C.6/Hen. VIII 5807 m. 1)[6]
23 Nov. 1518	—	John Pickering, clerk (C.P. 40/1027, Hilary 11 Hen. VIII, rot. 412v)
By Mich. 1519–Apr. 1521		Thomas Cade, clerk (S.C.6/Hen. VIII 5807 m. 1v; E.36/220 fo. 14v)

Sub-Receivers of Norfolk

By Mich. 1475–Mich. 1495		William Lambkin (for the Dowager Duchess Katherine from 1485) (D.641/1/2/26 m. 2; S.C.6/Hen. VII 1842 mm. 3v–4)
Mich. 1495	—	Nicholas Gedding (for the Dowager) (*ibid.*)
Mich. 1497–Mich. 1500		William Lambkin (deputy, George Whynbergh) (S.C.6/Hen. VII 428 m. 5v)
Mich. 1500	—	Charles Knivet (deputies, George Whynbergh & from 20 May 1508 John Brown) (*ibid.*, mm. 5–5v; C.P.40/1005B, Hilary 5 Hen. VIII, rot. 148v)
Before 1518	—	John Pickering, clerk (W.A.M. 5470 fo. 35)
—	Apr. 1521	John Partesoil (S.P.1/29 fo. 177)

Stewards of the Central Circuit

(a) *Bedfordshire & Buckinghamshire*

By Mich. 1434	—	Thomas Woodville (both counties) (S.C. 11/816)
By *ca.* Dec. 1443	—	William Perkins (Bucks.) (N.L.W. Peniarth Ms. 280 fo. 31)
By Mich. 1447–at least Mich. 1452 (Bucks.); by Mich. 1454 (Beds.)		Robert Olney (*ibid.*, fo. 54; D.641/1/2/254)
By Mich. 1472	—	Richard Fowler (both counties; for the Dowager Duchess Anne) (Add. Ms. 29608 m. 3)
By Mich. 1497–at least Mich. 1503		John Mordaunt (Bucks.) (S.C.6/Hen. VII 1476 m. 4)

[6] It is possible that the term 'receiver general' is here being used in the broader sense of collector or cofferer's agent.

By Feb. 1514–Mich. 1521   Sir Andrew Windsor (both counties) (S.C.6/Hen. VIII 5841 m. 6; S.P.1/29 fo. 178)

(b) *Caliland, Cornwall*

By Mich. 1438–at least Mich. 1441 — Nicholas Ashton (D.641/1/2/15 m. 5; 17 m. 2v)

By Mich. 1447–at least Mich. 1451 — Edward Ashton (Longleat Ms. 6410 m. 2v; S.C.6/1305/4 m. 3)

ca. 1451/2–at least Mich. 1456 — John Arundel (N.L.W. Peniarth Ms. 280 fo. 53; D.641/1/2/23 m. 5)

By Mich. 1463 — John Glyn (for the Dowager Duchess Anne) (S.C.6/1117/11 m. 4)

26 Dec. 1485 — Sir Robert Willoughby (for the Crown) (*C.P.R.,* 1485–94, p. 47)

(c) *Essex*

By Mich. 1441–at least Aug. 1443 — Richard Alrede (D.641/1/2/17 m. 2v; N.L.W. Peniarth Ms. 280 fo. 30)

By Mich. 1447 — John Godmanston (Longleat Ms. 6410 m. 2v)

By Mich. 1472 — Sir Thomas Montgomery (for the Dowager Duchess Anne) (Add. Ms. 29608 m. 3)

By Mich. 1495 — John, Earl of Oxford (for the Crown) (S.C.6/Hen. VII 1842 m. 8v)

By Mich. 1499 — Robert Sapurton (D.641/1/2/259 m. 4v)

— Apr. 1521 Thomas, Duke of Norfolk (S.P.1/29 fo. 177v)

(d) *Huntingdonshire*

By Mich. 1441–at least Mich. 1447 — William Stoneham (Kimbolton) (D.641/1/2/17 m. 2v; Longleat Ms. 6410 m. 2v)

By *ca.* May 1443 — Robert Stoneham (the county) (N.L.W. Peniarth Ms. 280 fo. 30)

19 Jan. 1486–at least Mich. 1496 — Robert Partesoil (Kimbolton; for the Dowager Duchess Katherine) (S.C.6/Hen. VII 1842 m. 11)

By Mich. 1518 — William Partesoil (Swineshead) (W.A.M. 5470 fo. 38v)

By Mich. 1520 — Walter Luke (the county) (S.P.1/29 fo. 176v)

(e) *Norfolk*

By Mich. 1441 — William Rokewood (Wells & Sheringham) (D.641/1/2/17 m. 2v)

By Mich. 1447	—	John Heydon (Wells & Sheringham) (Longleat Ms. 6410 m. 2v)
8 Dec. 1485	—	Sir Thomas Lovell (Norfolk & Suffolk; for the Crown) (*C.P.R.*, 1485–94, p. 38)
15 Feb. 1493–at least Mich. 1496		Sir Henry Heydon & John Heydon (Norfolk; for the Dowager Duchess Katherine) (S.C.6/Hen. VII 1842 m. 3v)
By Mich. 1495	—	Simon Damme (Stafford Barningham; for the Dowager) (*ibid.*, m. 3)
4 May 1506		Sir Thomas Lovell (Norfolk) (S.P.1/29 fo. 177; E.36/150 fo. 9v)
By Apr. 1521	—	Sir Thomas Woodhouse (*ibid.*) [7]

(f) *Northamptonshire*

By Mich. 1405		John Mulsho (for the Dowager Countess Anne) (D.641/1/2/7 m. 3)
By Mich. 1408	—	Thomas Woodville (for the Dowager) (D.641/1/2/8 m. 3)
Aug. 1433	—	William Tresham (Rothwell; for Duke Humphrey) (D.641/1/2/15 m. 6)
By Mich. 1441–at least Mich. 1447		Richard Willoughby (Rothwell) (D.641/1/2/17 m. 2v; Longleat Ms. 6410 m. 2)
By Oct. 1483	—	William Catesby (Rothwell) (*C.P.R.*, 1485–94, p. 235)
1 Oct. 1501–at least Mich. 1506		Sir Richard Empson (Rothwell) (S.C.6/Hen. VII 455 m. 2v)
ca. 1510 [8]–Apr. 1521		Sir Andrew Windsor (Rothwell) (S.P.1/29 fo. 176v)

(g) *Nottinghamshire*

12 Jan. 1440–at least Mich. 1441		William Heton (with Rutland) (D.641/1/2/67 m. 2v; N.L.W. Peniarth Ms. 280 fo. 5)
20 Nov. 1453– at least Mich. 1457		Robert Staunton (with Leics.) (*ibid.*, fo. 54; S.C.6/954 m. 3v)
By Mich. 1472	—	William Wentworth (for the Dowager Duchess Anne) (D.641/1/2/250 mm. 1v, 2v)
30 Nov. 1485	—	Brian Sandeford (for the Crown) (*C.P.R.*, 1485–94, p. 124)

[7] Woodhouse claimed to have replaced Lovell during Duke Edward's lifetime, although both men advanced a title to the stewardship after Buckingham's death.

[8] The crown commissioners reported that Sir Andrew was appointed in 1503/4 (19 Hen. VII), but Empson was then still in office, and probably remained until his death in 1510.

By Mich 1503–at least Mich. 1505 — Simon Digby (S.C.6/Hen. VII 460 m. 2; 461 m. 1)

(h) *Rutland*

By Mich. 1437 — John Pilton (D.641/1/2/265 m. 1v)

12 Jan. 1440 — William Heton (with Notts.) (N.L.W. Peniarth Ms. 280 fo. 5)

By Mich. 1447 — Roger Brereley (Longleat Ms. 6410 m. 2v)

20 Feb. 1455—at least Mich. 1460 — Robert Fenne (D.641/1/2/266 m. 2v)

By Mich. 1472 — William, Lord Hastings (for the Dowager Duchess Anne) (Add. Ms. 29608 m. 3)

Mich. 1502 — William Rivers (D.641/1/2/267 m. 4)

(i) *Suffolk*

12 Jan. 1440 — Henry Drury (Disining) (N.L.W. Peniarth Ms. 280 fo. 5)

By Mich. 1447–at least Mich. 1472 — Thomas Higham (Disining) (Longleat Ms. 6410 m. 2v; Add. Ms. 29608 m. 3)

1509/10–Apr. 1521 — Thomas, Duke of Norfolk (S.P.1/29 fo. 177; E.36/150 fo. 10v)

(j) *Warwickshire*

15 May 1438–Mar. 1451 — Thomas Arblaster (Atherstone) (D.641/1/2/269 m. 2; 273 m. 2v)

15 Nov. 1438–at least Mich. 1457 — John Harper (Tyseo) (S.C.6/1040/15 m. 5v)

2 Sept. 1460–at least Mich. 1466 — Sir William Harcourt (Maxstoke) (D.641/1/2/274 m. 1v; 275 m. 1v)

8 Nov. 1461–at least Mich. 1472 — John Hickford (Rugby & Tyseo; for the Dowager Duchess Anne) (D.641/1/2/274 m. 4; Add. Ms. 29608 m. 3)

8 Feb. 1471–at least Mich. 1473 — Sir John Greville (Wootton Wawen; for the Dowager) (D.641/1/2/276 m. 3v)

By Mich. 1472 — Nicholas Cowley (Maxstoke; for the Dowager) (Add. Ms. 29608 m. 3)

14 Nov. 1485–Mich. 1508 — William Harper (the county; for Lady Margaret Beaufort to 1498) (*C.P.R.*, 1485–94, p. 26; S.C.6/Hen. VII 869 m. 4)

By Mich. 1496 — Sir John Cokesey (Rugby; for Lady Margaret) (D.641/1/2/251 m. 2v)

Mich. 1508–Apr. 1521 — Stewardship vacant. Deputy steward Hugh Marvyn in office (D.641/1/2/279 m. 13; S.C.6/Hen. VIII 5841 m. 4)

Receivers of Brecon, Hay & Huntingdon

By Mich. 1430	—	John Havard (D.641/1/2/12 m. 1)
By 13 Jan. 1440–at least Mich. 1448.		John Jorce (N.L.W. Peniarth Ms. 280 fo. 5; D.641/1/2/19 m. 1)
By Mich. 1449	—	John Scudamore (D.641/1/2/20 m. 1)
9 Jan. 1451–at least Mich. 1457		Thomas Vaughan (Cardiff Pub. Lib. Ms. Brecon DD 20 m. 2; D.641/1/2/23 m. 5)
14 Sept. 1461–at least Mich. 1468		Thomas ap Rosser Vaughan (for the Crown) (S.C.6/1157/9; 1236/11)
16 Nov. 1469–4 Jan. 1473		Walter Devereux (for the Crown) (*C.P.R.*, 1467–76, p. 175)
By Mich. 1475	—	Walter Vaughan (for Duke Henry) (D.641/1/2/26 m. 1)
Before Mich. 1483	—	John Bounten (for the Duke) (S.C.6/Hen. VII 1652 m. 5)
26 Nov. 1483	—	Nicholas Spicer (for the Crown) (*C.P.R.*, 1476–85, p. 437)
25 Aug. 1484–5 Jun. 1486		Walter Vaughan (Huntingdon; for the Crown) (N.L.W. Peniarth Ms. 354C fo. 70v; S.C.6/Hen. VII 1652 m. 14)
Before Mich. 1485–Mich. 1486		William Fisher (Brecon; for Lady Margaret Beaufort; deputy, John ap Griffith ap Maurice) (Eg. Roll 2192 m. 3)
5 Jun. 1486–at least Mich. 1494		Richard ap Howell (Huntingdon; for Lady Margaret; deputy, Walter Vaughan) (S.C.6/1652 m. 14)
By Mich. 1486–at least Mich. 1494		Sir Rees ap Thomas (Brecon; for Lady Margaret; deputy, John ap Griffith ap Maurice) (*ibid.*, m. 6; D.641/1/2/246 m. 1)
By Mich. 1488–at least Mich. 1494		John ap Thomas (Hay; for Lady Margaret; deputies, Rees ap Thomas ap Jankyn & Walter Vaughan) (*ibid.*, m. 2; S.C.6/Hen. VII 1652 m. 9v)
By Mich. 1497–Mich. 1499		Walter Vaughan (Hay & Huntingdon (L.R.12/9/275 m. 2)
Mich. 1498 (Brecon); Mich. 1499 (Hay & Huntingdon–at least Mich. 1501)		John Waldboeuf (*ibid.*, mm. 1, 2)
By Mich. 1507–at least Mich. 1508		Roland Bridges (S.P.1/22 fo. 61; S.C.6/Hen. VIII 4775 m. 9)
By Mich. 1510–at least Mich. 1513		Llewelyn ap Morgan ap David Gamme (*ibid.*, mm. 7–7v, 9)

| By Mich. 1514–at least Mich. 1515 | John Waldboeuf (Longleat Ms. 6415 m. 2) |
| By Mich. 1517–Mich. 1521 | Hugh Marvyn (deputy, Thomas Morgan) (S.C.6/Hen. VIII 4775 m. 9; 4776 m. 1) |

Stewards of Brecon, Hay & Huntingdon

By Mich. 1441	—	John Abrehall (D.641/1/2/17 m. 2v)
ca. Mich. 1443	—	Kynard de la Hay (N.L.W. Peniarth Ms. 280 fo. 24)
19 Sept. 1444	—	John Jorce & William John (deputies for Hay) (*ibid.*, fo. 33)
Oct. 1445–ca. Oct. 1451		Sir John Scudamore (*ibid.*, fos. 38, 50)
ca. 1445/6	—	John Jorce & Howell ap Llewelyn (deputies for Hay) (*ibid.*, fo. 41)
ca. Oct. 1451	—	Henry Griffith (*ibid.*, fo. 50)
By 14 Sept. 1461–21 Jul. 1469		William, Lord Herbert (Brecon) (S.C.6/1157/9 m. 2; G.E.C., vol. VI, p. 440)
16 Nov. 1469–4 Jan. 1473		Walter Devereux (Brecon, Hay & Huntingdon; for the Crown) (*C.P.R.*, 1467–76, p. 175)
By Mich. 1483	—	William Fisher (Brecon) (D.641/1/2/246 m. 1)
By Mich. 1484	—	Sir Thomas Vaughan (Brecon) (S.C.6/Hen. VII 1652 m. 6)
7 Oct. 1485–at least Mich. 1494		John ap Thomas (Hay) (*ibid.*)
3 Nov. 1485–at least Mich. 1494		Sir Rees ap Thomas (Brecon) (*ibid.*, m. 4v)
Mich. 1497–Mich. 1499		Walter Vaughan (Huntingdon) (L.R.12/9/275 m. 2)
—[9]	Apr. 1521	Henry, Lord Stafford & Earl of Wiltshire (E.36/150 fo. 23)

Receivers of Caus

By Mich. 1383	—	John Wyccon (D.641/1/2/1 m. 2)
By Mich. 1390	—	John Whitgreve (D.641/1/2/2 m. 2)
By Mich. 1423–ca. 1434/5		Thomas Marshall (for Duke Humphrey) (D.641/1/2/241; Longleat Ms. 4010 m. 11v)
By Mich. 1438	—	Hugh Cresset (D.641/1/2/15 m. 5)
By Mich. 1441–1444/5		Humphrey Cotes (D.641/1/2/17 m. 2v; Longleat Ms. 4010 m. 10)

[9] Probably by 1503, when he was already Steward of Newport.

ca. Oct. 1444–at least Mich. 1457		John Woderton, clerk (N.L.W. Peniarth Ms. 280 fo. 35; D.641/1/2/23 m. 5)
By Mich. 1460	—	John Knight (for the Dowager Duchess Anne) (D.641/1/2/63 m. 1v)
23 Mar. 1466	—	John Harcourt (for the Dowager) (Eg. Roll 2196 m. 12)
By Mich. 1472–at least Mich. 1476		William Lyggon (for the Dowager to Nov. 1473, then for Duke Henry) (Add. Roll 22644 m. 1; D.641/1/2/26 m. 1)
By Mich. 1485–Mich. 1491		Reginald Hassall (for Lady Margaret Beaufort; deputy, Roger Lyggon) (Eg. Roll 2197 m. 11v)
By Mich. 1492–at least Mich. 1494		Edward Hevyn (for Lady Margaret) (*ibid.*)
By Mich. 1497–Mich. 1507		Roger Lyggon (Eg. Roll 2198 m. 13; 200 m. 2v)
By Mich. 1509	—	Thomas Harcourt (*ibid.*)
By Mich. 1511–at least Mich. 1518		William Leighton (*ibid.*, Longleat Ms. 3990 m. 1)
—	Apr. 1521	John Corbet (E.36/150 fo. 51)

Stewards of Caus

By Jul. 1424	—	Cadwaller ap Owen (D.641/1/2/241)
By 1 Jul. 1441–at least Mich. 1445		William Burley (deputy, Meredith ap Cadwaller) (N.L.W. Peniarth Ms. 280 fo. 17; Longleat Ms. 4010 m. 10)
17 Mar. 1447–at least Mich. 1458		Sir John Burgh (deputy, William Lyggon) (N.L.W. Peniarth Ms. 280 fo. 42; Longleat Mss. 3847 m. 13, 3989, *passim*)
By Mich. 1465–Mich. 1466		Richard, Lord Powis (Eg. Roll 2196 m. 12; Add. Roll 22644 m. 1)
By Easter 1467–at least Mich. 1473		John, Earl of Shrewsbury (*ibid.*, m. 1)
3 Sept. 1483–at least Mich. 1494		John, Lord Powis (Eg. Roll 2197 m. 11)
Mich. 1497–20 Apr. 1500		Stewardship vacant. Deputy steward John Corbet in office (D.641/1/2/27 m. 9; Eg. Roll 2198, *passim*)
20 Apr. 1500–Apr. 1521		Henry, Lord Stafford & Earl of Wiltshire (Longleat Ms. 3701 m. 12; S.P. 1/29 fo. 173)

Senior Household and Estate Staff

Receivers of Gloucestershire, Hampshire & Wiltshire

15 Feb. 1438–Mich. 1453	Nicholas Poyntz (deputies, John Wodeford & Thomas Berkeley) (D.641/1/2/167 m. 8; 176 m. 7)
Mich. 1453–Easter 1462	Thomas Berkeley (*ibid.*; D.641/1/2/182)
5 May 1462　—	John Poyntz (for the Dowager Duchess Anne) (*ibid.*)
By Mich. 1463–at least Mich. 1465	John Burton (for the Dowager) (D.641/1/2/185 m. 10)
By Mich. 1466–25 Dec. 1470	John Drover (for the Dowager) (D.641/1/2/184 m. iv; 189 m. 7)
25 Dec. 1470–24 Jun. 1471	Thomas Roger (for the Dowager) (*ibid.*, m. 8)
Easter 1471 only　—	John Butler (for the Dowager) (*ibid.*, m. 9)
24 Jun. 1471–Mich. 1475	Christopher Cumberford (for the Dowager) (*ibid.*, m. 10; D.641/1/2/191 m. 3)
Mich. 1475 (for Duke Henry); Mich. 1485 (Hants & Wilts. only; for Lady Margaret Beaufort)–Mich. 1494	Thomas Warwyn (D.641/1/2/26 m. 3; 218 m. 4v)
Easter 1484–*ca.* Aug. 1485	Sir William Hussey, William Beverley, William Catesby, Edmund Chaderton commissioned to collect the revenues of Hants & Wilts. for 7 years to pay Duke Henry's debts (*C.P.R.*, 1485–96, pp. 497–8)
4 Dec. 1485–at least Mich. 1494	John Walshe (Glos.; for the Dowager Duchess Katherine; deputy, Thomas Picher) (D.641/1/2/182 m. 8; 197 m. 12v)
Mich. 1494　—	Nicholas Compton (Hants & Wilts.; for Lady Margaret Beaufort) (D.641/1/2/218 m. iv)
ca. Jan. 1496–13 May 1497	Richard Pole (Glos.; for the Dowager Duchess Katherine; deputy, Walter Parker) (D.641/1/2/198 m. 8; 199 m. 10)
13 May 1497–7 Mar. 1498	Thomas Lucas (Glos.; for the Crown; deputy, Walter Parker) (*ibid.*)
By Mich. 1498–Mich. 1499	John Skilling (Hants & Wilts.) (Add. Roll 26873 m. 6)
By Mich. 1498 (Glos.); Mich. 1499 (Hants & Wilts.)–Mich. 1500	Walter Parker (D.641/1/2/200 m. 7; 201 m. 10)
Mich. 1500–Mich. 1501	Richard Walworth (D.641/1/2/202 m. 19v)

Mich. 1501–at least Mich. 1504	John Russell (deputy, Walter Parker) (*ibid.*, m. 13; 204)
By 28 Mar. 1508 —	Lawrence Stubbes, clerk (S.P.1/22 fos. 65, 68)
— at least 16 Apr. 1511	Nicholas Walwyn (deputy, Walter Parker) (Add. Roll 26874 m. 1)
By 27 Jul. 1511 —	John Jennings, clerk (deputy, Walter Parker) (*ibid.*, m. 4)
By 26 Feb. 1513–at least Mich. 1518	Thomas Wotton, clerk (Longleat Ms. 6415 m. 2; Royal Ms. BXXXV F m. 2)
By Mich. 1519–at least 28 Feb. 1521	William Curtis, clerk (S.C.6/Hen. VIII 5819 m. 1; E.36/220 fo. 9v)

Stewards of Gloucestershire, Hampshire & Wiltshire

Mich. 1405–Mich. 1416	Robert Poyntz (D.641/1/2/182; 160 m. 3)
By Mich. 1433–Mich. 1435	John Greville (D.641/1/2/162 m. 2; 163 m. 7)
Mich. 1435–at least Mich. 1459	Thomas Mille (Glos.) (D.641/1/2/164 m. 6; 180 m. 1)
By Mich. 1441–at least Mich. 1448	Thomas Haydock (Hants) (D.641/1/2/17 m. 2v; Longleat Ms. 6410 m. 2v)
By Mich. 1441 —	John Bridde (Wilts.) (D.641/1/2/17 m. 2v)
By Mich. 1448–at least Mich. 1458	Sir John Stourton (Wilts.) (D.641/1/2/174 m. 7v; 179 m. 1)
By Mich. 1452 —	Thomas Uvedale (Hants) (D.641/1/2/216 m. 1)
By Mich 1460 —	Sir William Berkeley (Glos.) (D.641/1/2/181 m. 8)
4 Sept. 1462–Easter 1469	Thomas Herbert (Glos.) (D.641/1/2/187 m. 8v)
9 Jan. 1471 —	Sir John Butler (Glos.) (D.641/1/2/189 m. 10v)
8 Dec. 1472 —	William Nottingham (Glos. & Wilts.) (D.641/1/2/191 m. 3)
24 Nov. 1473–at least Mich. 1477	John Twynyho (Glos. & Wilts.) (D.641/1/2/255 mm. 3v, 4v)
By Mich. 1485–16 Jan. 1496	Sir Edmund Mountfort (Glos., deputy, Sir Robert Poyntz) (D.641/1/2/192 m. 8v; 197 m. 13)
By Mich. 1494–at least Mich. 1499	Sir Reginald Bray (Hants and Wilts.) (D.641/1/2/218 m. 1v; Add. Ch. 26873 m. 1v)
16 Jan. 1496–13 May 1497	Sir Robert Poyntz (Glos.) (D.641/1/2/198 mm. 8–8v; 199 m. 10)

By Mich. 1498	—	Thomas Smart (Glos.) (D.641/1/2/200 m. 7v)
By Mich. 1498–at least Mich. 1502		John Skilling (Wilts.) (D.641/1/2/201 m. 11v; 203)
20 Apr. 1500–at least Mich. 1504		Sir Walter Herbert (Glos.; deputy, Thomas Smart) (D.641/1/2/201 mm. 10v–11; 202 m. 2; 204)
By Mich. 1503–*ca.* 1523		Sir John Seymour (Wilts.) (*ibid.*; S.P.1/29 fo. 170)
—	1 Mar. 1504	William Tycheborne (Hants) (Add. Roll 26874 m. 2)
1 Mar. 1504–*ca.* 1523		Sir Andrew Windsor (Hants) (*ibid.*; S.P.1/29 fo. 170)
Mich. 1504–Apr. 1521		Stewardship of Glos. vacant (E.36/150 fo. 6)

Receivers of Holderness

24 Oct. 1438–19 Aug. 1439		Robert Rolleston, clerk (for the Crown) (S.C.6/1084/3)
ca. Mich. 1439–Mich. 1451		Richard Lascy, clerk (N.L.W. Peniarth Ms. 280 fo. 3; S.C.6/1305/4 m. 4)
ca. Mich. 1451	—	William Roche (N.L.W. Peniarth Ms. 280 fo. 49)
ca. Mich. 1452–at least Mich. 1457		Robert Twyer (*ibid.*, fo. 52; D.641/1/2/23 m. 5)
By Easter 1461	—	Stephen Hartfield (for the Dowager Duchess Anne) (Add. Roll 22645 m. 4)
By Mich. 1463–Easter 1470		Gilbert Standish (for the Dowager) (S.C.6/1117/11 m. 5; Add. Roll 22645 m. 3)
Easter 1470–Mich. 1470		Sir John Constable (for the Dowager) (*ibid.*)
Mich. 1470–at least Mich. 1476		John Dalkyn (for the Dowager to 1473, then for Duke Henry) (S.C.6/1084/5 m. 1; D641/1/2/26 m. 4)
24 Feb. 1484–Aug. 1485		Receivership granted to Henry, Earl of Northumberland (*C.P.R.*, 1476–85, p. 409)
By Mich. 1497	—	Robert Caterall (D.641/1/2/27 m. 3v)
By Mich. 1505–at least 24 Feb. 1508		Henry Sleford, clerk (S.C.6/Hen. VII 1028 m. 1v; S.P.1/22 fo. 84)
By 9 Jun. 1508–at least Mich. 1515		John Clapham, Abbot of Melsa (*ibid.*, fo. 77v; Longleat Ms. 6415 m. 2)
—	Apr. 1521	Henry, Earl of Northumberland (S.P.1/29 fo. 174)

Stewards of Holderness

ca. 1445/6–*ca.* 1450/1		Sir John Constable (deputy, John Ellewyn) (N.L.W. Peniarth Ms. 280 fo. 39)
ca. 1450/1–at least Mich. 1471		John Constable, jr. (S.C.6/1084/5 m. 1v)
By Mich. 1472		Sir Walter Griffith (Add. Roll 22645 m. 1)
By Mich. 1505	—	Thomas Marler (S.C.6/Hen. VII 1028 m. 6)
—	Apr. 1521	Henry, Earl of Northumberland (S.P.1/29 fo. 174)

Receivers of Kent & Surrey

By Mich. 1383–at least Mich. 1397		Nicholas Renekyn (D.641/1/2/1 m. 1; 230)
—	Mich. 1427	Richard Knighton (for Duke Humphrey) (D.641/1/2/22 m. 8; 231 m. 12)
Mich. 1427–at least Mich. 1430		John Colet (for the Duke) (*ibid., passim*)
By Mich. 1430	—	Geoffrey Young (for the Dowager Countess Anne) (D.641/1/2/12 m. 3)
28 May 1438–at least Mich. 1457		William Hexstall (D.641/1/2/233 m. 1; 23 m. 5)
By Mich. 1463	—	John Wybarne (for the Dowager Duchess Anne) (S.C.6/1117/11 m. 5)
By Mich. 1473–at least Mich. 1477		Thomas Stidolf (for Duke Henry) (D.641/1/2/255 m. 7v)
—	Mich. 1502	Henry Fane (S.C.6/Hen. VII 1076 m. 15v)
Mich. 1502–at least Mich. 1506		John Scott (*ibid., passim*)
By 4 Jan. 1508–at least 9 Jun. 1512		Thomas Topham (deputy, Thomas Stephens) (S.P.1/22 fos. 61, 76–7; Bibl. Harl. 1667 m. 7)
By 3 Nov. 1512–at least Mich. 1515		Edward Garth (*ibid.,* Longleat Ms. 6415 m. 1)
By 31 Oct. 1520–Apr. 1521		Thomas Barnswell (E.36/220 fo. 3v; 150 fo. 14)

Stewards of Kent & Surrey

By Mich. 1428–at least Mich. 1448		John Gaynesford (Surrey) (D.641/1/2/231 m. 11; Longleat Ms. 6410 m. 2v)
By Mich. 1428	—	John Bore (Kent) (D.641/1/2/231 m. 11)
By Mich. 1442–at least Mich. 1448		John Bamburgh (Kent) (D.641/1/2/17 m. 2v; Longleat Ms. 6410 m. 2v)
1 Jan. 1450–at least Mich. 1454		Richard Bruyn (Kent) (D.641/1/2/234 m. 14v)

By Mich. 1453	—	John Elynbridge (Surrey) (*ibid.*)
By Mich. 1473–at least Mich. 1477		Thomas Stidolf (Kent) (D.641/1/2/255 m. 7v)
By Mich. 1502–at least Mich. 1506		Sir Thomas Bourchier (Kent & Surrey) (D.641/1/2/235; S.C.6/Hen. VII 1076 m. 14v)
—	Mich. 1519	Charles Knivet (Kent & Surrey) (S.P.1/ 22 fo. 102)
Mich. 1519–Mich. 1521		Sir Edward Neville (S.C.6/Hen. VIII 5795 m. 2v)

Receivers of Newport

By Mich. 1383	—	John Vaughan (D.641/1/2/1 m.1)
By Mich. 1390	—	John Banham (D.641/1/2/4 m.2)
By Mich. 1400–25 Mar. 1401		John Bradley (S.C.6/924/18 mm. 1, 10)
25 Mar. 1401	—	Howell ap William (*ibid.*, m. 10)
31 Mar. 1406	—	John ap William (S.C.6/924/19 m. 1)
By Mich. 1435	—	Thomas Whitgreve (Glam. R.O., D/ DCM/45 m. 9)
By Mich. 1438–*ca.* Mich. 1446		Thomas Leny (D.641/1/2/15 m. 5; S.C.6/ 924/23 m. 11)
—	10 Dec. 1446	Howell Kemys (D.641/1/2/20 m. 5)
10 Dec. 1446–20 Feb. 1456		William Kemys (S.C.6/924/23 m. 10)
20 Feb. 1456–at least Mich. 1457		Morgan ap Jenkins ap Philip (S.C.6/924/ 25 m. 10)
4 Nov. 1460–11 May 1461		Richard, Earl of Warwick (farmer for the Crown) (*C.F.R.*, 1452–61, p. 287; *C.P.R.*, 1461–7, pp. 13, 100)
11 May 1461–27 Jul. 1469		William, Lord Herbert (farmer for the Crown; Trahagren ap Ieuan ap Meuric, receiver, Thomas Vaughan ap Rosser, deputy, Mich. 1465–6) (*ibid.*, Mon. R.O. Man/B/90/004 m. 10)
14 Feb.–14 Apr. 1471		Richard, Earl of Warwick (farmer for the Crown) (*C.F.R.*, 1461–71, p. 293)
By 7 Feb. 1476	—	Arthur Bremshot (D.641/1/2/26 m. 7)
26 Nov. 1483	—	Nicholas Spicer (for the Crown) (*C.P.R.*, 1476–85, p. 437)
ca. Mich. 1485	—	William Llewelyn (for the Crown) (Eg. Roll 2206 m. 14; *Rot. Parl.*, vol. VI p. 382)
By Mich. 1486	—	Thomas Garth (for the Dowager Duchess Katherine) (Eg. Roll 2206 m. 14)

By Dec. 1495	—	Jankyn ap John (for the Dowager) (Thomas, *op. cit.*, p. 275)
—	23 Mar. 1498	Edmund Wingfield (for the Dowager) (S.C.6/Hen. VII 1665 m. 12)
25 Mar. 1498	—	Ralph Bampton (N.L.W. Tredegar Ms. 147 m. 10)
By Mich. 1500	—	Humphrey Blount (deputy, John Richmond) (L.R. 12/9/275 m. 3)
By Mich. 1501–Mich. 1503		John Huntley (Eg. Roll 2207 m. 2; S.C.6/ Hen. VII 1665 m. 12)
Mich. 1503–Mich. 1509		William ap Howell, clerk (*ibid.*, m. 12; Eg. Roll 2207 m. 1)
Mich. 1509–at least Mich. 1515		Richard Browne (*ibid.*, mm. 1, 4; Longleat Ms. 6415 m. 1)
By Mich. 1518–Apr. 1521		Thomas ap Morgan (Add. Ms. 42066B m. 9; S.P.1/29 fo. 171)

Stewards & Sheriffs of Newport

By 31 Mar. 1406–at least 23 Feb. 1417		Sir Gilbert Denys (sheriff of Newport, steward of Machen) (S.C.6/924/20; *P.P.C.*, vol. II p. 216)
By 23 Feb. 1417	—	Morgan ap Jenan ap Jankyn (deputy sheriff) (*ibid.*)
By Mich. 1434–at least Mich. 1448		Thomas Arblaster (sheriff of Wentloog & steward of Machen) (Glam. R.O. D/DCM/45 m. 9; S.C.6/924/23 m. 10)
—	7 Nov. 1444	Morgan ap Rees (deputy sheriff of Newport) (N.L.W. Peniarth Ms. 280 fo. 34)
7 Nov. 1444–7 Nov. 1448		Howell Kemys (deputy sheriff of Newport) (Pugh, *Marcher Lordships*, p. 276)
22 Jul. 1450	—	Henry ap Griffith (sheriff of Newport & Wentloog, steward of Machen) (S.C.6/ 924/24 m. 8)
20 Oct. 1452	—	Morgan Philips (sheriff of Newport & Wentloog, steward of Machen) (N.L.W. Peniarth Ms. 280 fo. 52)
26 Oct. 1452	—	Morgan ap Jankyn (steward of Newport) (S.C.6/924/25 m. 10)
1463–1467		Sir Richard Herbert (sheriff of Wentloog & steward of Machen) (Pugh, *Marcher Lordships*, p. 180)
13 Sept. 1484	—	Sir James Tirell (sheriff of Wentloog, steward of Newport & Wentloog) (*C.P.R.*, 1476–85, p. 474)

20 Oct. 1485–*ca.* 1492	Sir John Morgan (sheriff of Newport & Wentloog, steward of Machen) (Pugh, *Marcher Lordships*, pp. 295, 262–3)
ca. 1492–*ca.* 1500	Sir Morgan John (sheriff of Newport & Wentloog, steward of Machen) (*ibid.*)
By Mich. 1502 —	David ap William (deputy steward of Newport) (Eg. Roll 2207 m. 2)
By Mich. 1503–Apr. 1521	Henry, Lord Stafford & Earl of Wiltshire (sheriff of Newport, Wentloog & Machen) (S.C.6/Hen. VII 1665 m. 12)
By Mich. 1510–at least Mich. 1512	John ap Morgan (deputy steward of Newport) (Eg. Roll 2207 m. 1)
— Apr. 1521	Thomas ap Morgan (deputy steward of Newport) (S.P.1/29 fo. 171)

Receivers of Staffordshire

By Mich. 1383–at least Mich. 1390	John Bradley (D.641/1/2/1 m. 2; 4 m. 2)
ca. 1395 —	Thomas Davy (D.641/1/2/43; 45)
By Mich. 1399–Mich. 1428	Hugh Stanford (for the second Earl of Stafford's feoffees from Jul. 1403; for Duke Humphrey from Feb. 1423) (D.641/1/2/40A m. 1; 45; 53 m. 5v)
19 Nov. 1405 —	John Bradley (for the Crown) (D.641/1/2/48)
By Mich. 1433–at least Mich. 1434	Humphrey Cotes (D.641/1/2/53, *passim*)
— at least Mich. 1438	Thomas Barber (D.641/1/2/54 m. 10v)
4 Jun. 1439–Mich. 1450	Humphrey Cotes (D.641/1/2/55 m. 9; 57 m. 11v)
Mich. 1450–at least Mich. 1461	Roger Draycote (*ibid.*, m. 10; D.641/1/2/63 m. 11)
1 May 1462–at least Mich. 1464	John Burton (for the Dowager Duchess Anne) (D.641/1/2/65 m. 10; S.C.6/1117/11 m. 4)
13 Feb. 1465–at least Mich. 1476	John Harcourt (for the Dowager) (D.641/1/2/68 m. 10; 75 m. 1v)
By Mich. 1475 —	William Harper (for Duke Humphrey) (D.641/1/2/26 m. 1)
By Mich. 1484–at least Mich. 1489	William Colwiche (for the Crown; from Mich. 1485 for Lady Margaret Beaufort) (Harl. Ms. 433 fo. 328; D.641/1/2/76 m. 10v; 77 m. 10)

By Mich. 1494	—	Ralph Agarde (for Lady Margaret) (D.641/ 1/2/78 m. 10)
By Mich. 1497–Mich. 1502		William Gibbons, clerk (Thomas Robyns, deputy) (D.641/1/2/79 m. 9; 82 m. 3v)
Mich. 1502–May 1507		Thomas Robyns (D.641/1/2/83; S.C.6/ Hen. VII 1844 m. 1v)
18 May 1507–*ca*. Mich. 1510		Thomas Harcourt (*ibid.*)
Mich. 1510 only		John, son and executor of Thomas Harcourt (S.C.6/Hen. VIII 5803)
Mich. 1510–Mich. 1511		Robert Whitgreve (D.641/1/2/88)
Mich. 1511–Mich. 1512		James Newell (D.641/1/2/87 m. 4v)
Mich. 1512–at least Mich. 1515		Thomas Cade, clerk (James Newell as acting receiver by Mich. 1514) (D.641/ 1/2/89 m. 3v; 90; Longleat Ms. 6415 m. 2)[10]
—	Apr. 1521	James Newell (S.P.1/29 fo. 174)

Stewards of Staffordshire

By Mich. 1399–at least Mich. 1406		John Knightley (confirmed in office by the Crown, Nov. 1405) (D.641/1/2/40A; 48 m. 1)
15 Jul. 1428	—	John Harper (for the Dowager Countess Anne) (Add. Ch. 19858)
By Mich. 1442–Easter 1451		Hugh Erdswyck (D.641/1/254 m. 6; 57 m. 10)
Easter 1451–Mich. 1463		Stewardship vacant. Clerk of the court, Roger Clerk, in office (appointed 20 Oct. 1439) (D.641/1/2/54 m. 6; 57–65; 68 m. 10v)
Mich. 1463	—	William Cumberford (D.641/1/2/66 m. 1v)
By Mich. 1472–*ca*. Mich. 1483		William Harper (for the Dowager Duchess Anne to 1480, then for Duke Henry) (Add. Ms. 29608 m. 3; Harl. Ms. 433 fo. 328)
7 Mar. 1484	—	Thomas Wrotley (for the Crown) (*C.P.R.*, 1476–85, p. 437)
22 Sept. 1485–at least Mich. 1495		Sir Humphrey Stanley (deputy, Humphrey Barber) (D.641/1/2/76 m. 10v; 78 m. 9v)
Mich. 1497–Mich. 1510		Stewardship vacant. A deputy in office (D.641/1/2/79 m. 9–81 fo. 16v)

---

[10] Both Cade and Newell were described as receivers of Staffordshire in 1515, the former in the account of his colleague, the cofferer, and the latter in returns made locally by Duke Edward's bailiffs.

By Mich. 1502   —   Richard Littleton (deputy, Nicholas Wescott) (D.641/1/2/83)

By Mich. 1509–Apr. 1521   George, Earl of Shrewsbury (deputy, John Slater) (S.C.6/Hen. VIII 5810³ m. 11; S.P.1/29 fo. 174)

Appendix C

COUNCILLORS RETAINED BY THE THREE DUKES AND ANNE, DUCHESS OF BUCKINGHAM

This appendix is intended to provide evidence of the connexion between the Staffords and those known to have served on their council over the years *ca.* 1423–1521. Most of the men listed below possessed considerable influence in their own right, and the factor of space alone makes it impossible to embark upon a fuller discussion of their careers. Further information about specific individuals is available in a number of printed sources; those most frequently cited have been abbreviated as follows:

B.R.C.	*A Biographical Register of the University of Cambridge to 1500*, ed. A. B. Emden (Cambridge, 1963).
B.R.O.	*A Biographical Register of the University of Oxford to 1500*, ed. A. B. Emden (3 vols., Oxford, 1957–9).
Commons & Speakers	J. S. Roskell, *The Commons and their Speakers in English Parliaments, 1375–1523* (Manchester, 1965).
Commons of 1422	J. S. Roskell, *The Commons in the Parliament of 1422* (Manchester, 1954).
D.L.	Sir Robert Somerville, *The Duchy of Lancaster* (2 vols., London, 1953–70), vol. I.
D.N.B.	*The Dictionary of National Biography.*
H.P.B.	*History of Parliament: Biographies of the Members of the Commons House, 1439–1509*, ed. J. C. Wedgwood (London, 1936).
Return	*Return of Members of Parliament, England 1213–1702* (London, 1878).
Pugh	*The Marcher Lordships of South Wales 1415–1536*, ed. T. B. Pugh (Univ. of Wales, 1963).
S.P.H.	*A Parliamentary History of Stafford*, ed. J. C. Wedgwood (2 vols., William Salt Archaeological Society, 1917–8), vol. I.

It has not been considered necessary to provide detailed references to royal commissions or senior judicial appointments held by the more important councillors, as these may be found in the relevant volumes of the *Calendars* *of Patent Rolls.* A number of councillors occupied senior administrative posts on the Stafford estates—offices marked * are documented in Appendix A, while details of annuities (marked †) follow in Appendix D.

Jasper, Duke of Bedford, seems to have relied heavily upon the advice of the Stafford family retainers still in the services of his wife, the Dowager Duchess Katherine, but since the membership of his council remains largely a matter of conjecture, it has not been touched on here.

The abbreviation 'i.j.' denotes a ducal commission to act as an itinerant justice in the Welsh Marcher lordships.

PART I

DUKE HUMPHREY'S COUNCILLORS

(a) *Lawyers and Administrators of Justice*

John Andrews (*ca.* 1410–60): attorney general 1431/57 *; farmer of Stratton St Margaret, Wilts., & bailiff of the Liberty of Hereford in Glos., 1439 (D.641/1/2/167 m. 8v); i.j. Brecon, 1445/6 (N. L. W. Peniarth Ms. 280 fos. 34, 40); involved in Buckingham's transactions as Constable of Dover, 1451, & Calais, 1453 (S.C.6/1305/4 m. 5; E.101/54/12); his attorney in the Common Pleas, 1456 (C.P.40/781, Easter 34 Hen. VI, rot. 340v), and Exchequer of Pleas, 1458 (D.641/1/6/3); his feoffee & mainpernor (*C.P.R.*, 1446-52, p. 78; *C.F.R.*, 1445-52, p. 115); shire kt for Glos., also returned for Buckingham's mesne borough of Bletchingley, 1449/50 (*H.P.B.*, p. 11).

Piers Ardern (*d.* 1467): retained 1443 as a serjeant at law †; Chief Baron of the Exchequer and Justice of the Common Pleas, 1448; mainly employed by the Crown (*D.L.*, pp. 452–53, 469, 472, 484).

Nicholas Ashton (1395-1466): retained 1438 †, being also employed by the Crown (*D.L.*, p. 451); serjeant at law, 1443; Justice of the Common Pleas, 1444; Cornish landowner & shire kt (*H.P.B.*, p. 25).

John Bamburgh: retained 1438 †; steward of Kent and Surrey, 1442 *; prominent local landowner & commissioner; steward of the Archbishop of Canterbury's liberties in Kent.

Thomas Bate (1400–59): retained 1447 †; Warwicks. landowner and shire kt (*H.P.B.*, p. 50).

Thomas Burgoyne (1405-70): retained as 'our good and well-loved friend', 1446 †; influential in Cambs., and as under-sheriff of London (*H.P.B.*, pp. 137–8).

Richard Chokke (*d.*1483): retained 1453/61 †, while employed successively as apprentice and serjeant at law by the Crown (*D.L.*, p. 431); Justice of the Common Pleas, 1461; Duke Henry's feoffee, 1478 (*C.P.R.*, 1475-85, p. 257; *Stats. of the Realm*, vol. III p. 271).

William Cumberford (1410–72): retained 1442/67 †; feoffee for Buckingham & his son, John, & Duke Henry (C.66/486 m. 14, 494 m. 8; W.A.M. 15195; Northants. R.O. SS 4254; *C.P.R.*, 1467-77, p. 158; *Stats. of the*

Realm, vol. III p. 273); i.j. Brecon, 1443/6 (N.L.W. Peniarth Ms. 280 fos. 24-5, 34, 40); awarded £10 *p.a.* for life by the Dowager Duchess Anne, 1460 (S.C.6/1117/11 m. 6); steward of Staffs., 1463 *; also retained by the Crown (*D.L.*, p. 457); influential in Staffs. & as protonotary of the Common Pleas (*H.P.B.*, p. 244).

Robert Danby (*d.ca.* 1473): retained 1441 as a serjeant at law †; also employed by the Crown (*D.L.*, p. 451); Justice of the Common Pleas, 1452; Chief Justice, 1461.

Thomas Dencalf: retained 1444/6 to assist in Buckingham's suit for the manor of Bosley, Cheshire (Chester 29/149 rot. 16-16v; 151 rot. 24; D.641/1/2/56 m. 11).

William Denteth: retained 1439 †; still being paid at Mich. 1456 (D.641/1/2/56 m. 10v); probably a local Staffs. attorney.

Thomas Higham: retained 1441 †; steward of Disining, Suffolk 1447/72 *; granted the wardship of John Forster by Buckingham, 1445 (N.L.W. Peniarth Ms. 280 fo. 35); a supporter of the court party with great influence in Suffolk (*C.P.R.*, 1452-61, *passim*).

John Hody (*d.*1441): retained 1437 †; employed successively as apprentice & serjeant at law by the Crown (*D.L.*, p. 451); Chief Justice of the King's Bench, 1440; m.p. for Shaftesbury & later shire kt for Som. & Dorset (*Return*, pp. 302-30).

John Holme (*d.ca.* 1449): retained 1440 as Buckingham's attorney at the Exchequer (D.641/1/2/15 m. 7); Chief Baron of the Exchequer, 1446; royal commissioner in Yorks. & Lincs.

Richard Hotoft (1410-*ca.* 1470): retained 1440 †; also employed by the Crown (*D.L.*, p. 569); shire kt for Leics., with influence throughout the central Midlands (*H.P.B.*, p. 472).

William Lacon (1410-75): retained 1453 while a serjeant at law †; Justice of the King's Bench, 1465; Salop. landowner & shire kt (*H.P.B.*, pp. 52-3).

Thomas Littleton (1415-81): retained 1453/63 †; feoffee for Dukes Humphrey and Henry (W.A.M. 15195; Northants. R.O. SS4254; *Feet of Fines for Essex*, vol. IV no. 431; *Stats. of the Realm*, vol. III pp. 271, 273, 276); Justice of the Common Pleas, 1466, King's Bench, 1475; often employed by the Crown (*D.L.*, pp. 451, 472); influential throughout the N. Midlands & eminent as a jurist (*D.N.B.*, vol. XXXIII p. 373).

John Markham (*d.*1475): retained 1440, while a serjeant at law †; Justice of the King's Bench, 1446, Chief Justice, 1461; a Lincs. landowner & local commissioner.

Walter Moyll (1405-71): retained 1442 †; chiefly connected with Ralph, Lord Cromwell, & Earls of Devon (*C.C.R.*, 1441-7, pp. 222-3; 1454-61, p. 357); Chief Justice of the Common Pleas, 1454; Cornish landowner & m.p. (*H.P.B.*, p. 617).

John Needham (1415-80): retained 1453 †; common serjeant of London, 1449; Justice of the Common Pleas, 1457, King's Bench, 1471; often employed by the Crown (*D.L.*, pp. 225, 469, 472); influential in Staffs. & as a London m.p. (*H.P.B.*, p. 624).

Ralph Pole (*d.ca.* 1459): retained 1443 †; already one of the Queen's councillors & active in the King's service (A. R. Myers, 'The Household of Queen Margaret of Anjou', *B.J.R.L.*, L(1967/8), p. 416; *D.L.*, pp. 451, 469); Justice of the King's Bench, 1453.

John Portington (*d.*1455): retained 1441 †; i.j. Brecon, 1440 (N.L.W. Peniarth Ms. 280 fo. 3): Justice of the Common Pleas, 1443/54.

Nicholas Radford (1390–1455): retained 1438 †; eminent Devon shire kt & landowner, employed by William, Lord Bonville; his murder by the followers of Sir Thomas Courtenay, the son of Bonville's great enemy, Thomas, Earl of Devon, was followed by a protracted outbreak of violence in the South West (*D.L.*, p. 453; *H.P.B.*, p. 707; R. Storey, *The End of the House of Lancaster* (London, 1966), pp. 168–70).

Miles Scull: retained 1440, while a serjeant at law †; Herefs. landowner, i.j. Brecon & Huntington, 1440/6 (N.L.W. Peniarth Ms. 280, fos. 3, 24, 32, 34, 40).

William Tresham (1400–52): retained 1430, while an apprentice at law †; influential Crown servant (*D.L.*, pp. 194, 454, 210–11, 476, 586); Northants. landowner & shire kt, four times speaker of the Commons (*Commons & Speakers*, pp. 218–30).

John Vampage (*d.*1452): retained 1441 †; extensively employed by the Crown (*D.L.*, p. 454), & also as a feoffee by Richard Beauchamp, Earl of Warwick; shire kt for Worcs., with great influence in that area (*Commons of 1422*, pp. 230–1).

Robert Whitgreve (1385–1452): i.j. Newport, 1432 (Pugh, p. 299); parker & keeper of Staffs. Castle, 1433 (D.641/1/2/59 m. 1); Buckingham's attorney in his suit for the lordship of Holderness, 1438 (D.1721/1/11 fo. 124); his councillor by 1443 (D.641/1/2/54 m. 10), mainpernor & feoffee (C.66/494 m. 8; *C.P.R.*, 1446–52, p. 78); rewarded with an annuity, 1431 †, a coat of arms, 1442, and land in Stafford, 1451 (D.1721/1/1 fo. 391v; N.L.W. Peniarth Ms. 280 fo. 51); also retained by the Crown (*D.L.*, p. 543); teller of the Exchequer, 1428/50, & experienced parliamentarian (*Commons of 1422*, pp. 84–5, 236).

William Yelverton (*d.ca.* 1471): retained 1442 †; also employed by the Crown (*D.L.*, pp. 451, 598); Justice of the King's Bench, 1443; influential Norfolk landowner, being m.p. for Yarmouth & recorder of Norwich 1433/50 (*H.P.B.*, p. 978).

Thomas Young (1415–77): retained 1446 †; employed by the Crown (*D.L.*, p. 452), but was imprisoned in 1451 for presenting a bill in parliament which asked Henry VI to recognise the Duke of York as his heir; frequently elected m.p. for Bristol (Storey, *op. cit.*, p. 81; *H.P.B.*, p. 981).

(b) *Administrative Staff*

John Abrehall (*d*.1443): i.j. Brecon, 1440/3 (N.L.W. Peniarth Ms. 280 fos. 3, 24); steward of Brecon, 1441/2 *; joint farmer of Cantref Selyf, 1439/43 (*C.P.R.*, 1436–41, p. 288; E.368/233 rot. 109); influential Herefs. landowner, administrator & shire kt (*D.L.*, p. 650; *H.P.B.*, p. 1).

Thomas Arblaster (1400–63): councillor by 1443 (D.641/1/2/54 m. 10); active as an administrator in Wales (Pugh, p. 287) & an i.j. Brecon, 1440/6 (N.L.W. Peniarth Ms. 280 fos. 3, 34, 40); Buckingham's feoffee (*C.P.R.*, 1429–36, p. 466; *C.C.R.*, 1429–35, pp. 357–8); shire kt for Staffs. (*H.P.B.*, p. 17).

Thomas Berkeley (*d.ca.* 1462): present at many council meetings while receiver of Glos., Hants & Wilts., 1453/62 *; party to suits for debt brought by Buckingham, 1458 (C.P.40/791, Mich. 37 Hen. VI, rot. 62, 544).

Humphrey Cotes: councillor by 1443 (D.641/1/2/54 m. 10); steward of the Countess Anne's household to 1438; receiver of Staffs., 1433/4 *, Caus, 1441/5 *; involved in Buckingham's suit for the manor of Bosley, 1442/6 (D.641/1/2/55, 56).

Henry Drury (*d.ca.* 1444): councillor by 1443 (D.641/1/2/54 m. 10); steward of Suffolk, 1440 *; i.j. Brecon, 1440 (N.L.W. Peniarth Ms. 280 fo. 3); Buckingham's feoffee & mainpernor (*ibid.*, fos. 8, 13, 16; *C.C.R.*, 1422–9, pp. 318, 321–2, 344; *C.P.R.*, 1436–41, pp. 527–8); granted the farm of Stafford Barningham, Norfolk, 1438 (D.641/1/2/15 m. 4); Suffolk landowner & shire kt (*Return*, pp. 325, 327).

Hugh Erdswyck (1380–1443): witnessed Buckingham's ratification of the Newport borough charter, 1427 (*Archaeologia*, XLV pt. ii (1885), p. 450); steward of Staffs., 1442/51 *; Buckingham's feoffee (*C.C.R*, 1422–9, p. 318); influential Staffs. landowner & shire kt (*S.P.H.*, pp. 177–9).

John Harper (1395–1464): councillor by 1443 (D.641/1/2/54 m. 10); auditor, 1439/64, & holder of many posts in the Midlands *; i.j. Newport, 1432, & Brecon, 1440/5 (Pugh, p. 291; N.L.W. Peniarth Ms. 280 fos. 3, 24); Buckingham's feoffee (W.A.M. 15195; *C.P.R.*, 1429–36, p. 466; 1436–41, p. 527; 1446–52, p. 78; *C.C.R.*, 1422–9, p. 318; 1429–35, pp. 357–9); crown auditor for S. Wales, 1459 (*C.P.R.*, 1452–61, p. 527); influential Staffs. landowner & parliamentarian (*Commons of 1422*, p. 189).

John Heton (*d*.1469): receiver general, 1437/67 *; steward of the household, 1464/74 *; Buckingham's mainpernor & feoffee (W.A.M. 15195; C.66/494 m. 8; *Stats. of the Realm*, vol. III p. 273; N.L.W. Peniarth Ms. 280 fos. 13, 15–6, 44, 47–8; *C.F.R.*, 1445–52, p. 115); Bucks. landowner & shire kt (*H.P.B.*, p. 440).

William Hexstall (1405–70): receiver of Kent & Surrey, 1438/57 *; Buckingham's attorney, mainpernor & feoffee (N.L.W. Peniarth Ms. 280 fos. 14, 21; *C.C.R.*, 1422–9, p. 318; C.66/486 m. 14); teller of the Exchequer, 1456, & m.p. for Midland & Southern seats (*S.P.H.*, pp. 208–9).

William Minden: steward of the household, 1429/33 *; i.j. Brecon, 1432 (Pugh, p. 295); conciliar commissioner, Newport, 1450/1 (S.C. 6/924/24 m. 3).

Nicholas Poyntz (d.1460): retained 1435 †; Buckingham's attorney in his suit for the lordship of Holderness, 1438 (D.1721/1/11 fo. 124); i.j. Brecon, 1440 (N.L.W. Peniarth Ms. 280 fo. 40); farmer of Cantref Selyf, 1440/53 (C.P.R., 1436–41, p. 491; E.368/225 rot. 40–1, 66–6v); parker of Eastwood, Glos., 1441 (D.641/1/2/17 m. 3v); influential Glos. landowner & shire kt (J. Maclean, *A Historical Memoir of the Family of Poyntz* (Exeter, 1886), pp. 53–7; *Return*, p. 318).

William Weldon: councillor by 1443 (D.641/1/2/54 m. 10); auditor, 1433/67 *; i.j. Brecon, 1443 (N.L.W. Peniarth Ms. 280 fo. 34); supervised Buckingham's finances as Constable of Calais & his dealings in the Exchequer, 1451/7 (*ibid.*, fo. 53; D.641/1/2/23 m. 7); his feoffee & executor (W.A.M. 15195; *Stats. of the Realm*, vol. III p. 273); crown auditor in S. Wales (Pugh, p. 298).

Richard Witherton: involved in Buckingham's legal affairs from 1440 (N.L.W. Peniarth Ms. 280 fos. 3, 8, 47–8); his deputy as Captain of Calais, 1441, & as Warden of the Cinque Ports, 1452 (*ibid.*, fos. 17, 21, 52); retained 1441 †; councillor by 1443 (D.641/1/2/64 m. 10); i.j. Brecon, 1443 (N.L.W. Peniarth Ms. 280 fo. 24).

(c) *Justices Itinerant, Gentlemen & Yeomen, Probably of Conciliar Rank*

James, Lord Audley (d.1459): i.j. Brecon, 1443/5 (N.L.W. Peniarth Ms. 280 fos. 24, 34).

John, Lord Berners (d.1474): Buckingham's half-brother; retained 1441 *; i.j. Brecon, 1448 (*ibid.*, fo. 40); the Duke's feoffee (C.66/494 m. 8; W.A.M. 15195; *Stats. of the Realm*, vol. III p. 273; G.E.C., vol. II p. 153).

William Burley (d.1459): i.j. Brecon 1440/6 (N.L.W. Peniarth Ms. 280 fos. 3, 11, 24, 34, 40); steward of Caus, 1442/7 *; a man of great legal, political and administrative experience (J. S. Roskell 'William Burley, Speaker for the Commons in 1437, 1445–6', *Shrops. Arch. & Nat. Hist. Trans.*, 4th series LVI (1960), pp. 263–72).

Sir Kinard de la Bere (d.1445): i.j. Brecon & Huntington, 1443/5 (N.L.W. Peniarth Ms. 280 fos. 24, 32, 34); influential Herefs. landowner & shire kt (*Return*, p. 326).

Thomas Fitzhenry (1415–75): i.j. Huntington, 1446 (N.L.W. Peniarth Ms. 280 fo. 32); Herefs. lawyer, administrator & shire kt (*D.L.*, p. 454; *H.P.B.*, pp. 331–2).

William, Lord Fitzwarren (d.1469): Buckingham's half-brother; i.j. Brecon, 1443 (N.L.W. Peniarth Ms. 280 fo. 40); the Duke's feoffee (C.66/949 m. 8).

Sir John Gresley (d.1449): witnessed Buckingham's confirmation of the Newport borough charter, 1427 (*Archaeologia, loc. cit.*); i.j. Newport, 1432

(Pugh, p. 291); Glos. landowner & shire kt, with property in Wilts. & the Marches (*Return*, pp. 289–324; *C.F.R.*, 1437–48, p. 274).

Richard Heton: brother of John Heton (*q.v.*); retained 1454/63 †; involved in the property transactions of John, Earl of Wiltshire, and Duke Henry (*C.P.R.*, 1467–77, p. 158; *C.C.R.*, 1476–85, no. 1210).

John Jorce (*d.ca.* 1450): i.j. Brecon & Huntington, 1440/50 (N.L.W. Peniarth Ms. 280 fos. 3, 13, 32, 34); held various posts in the Brecon area, 1440/8; also left a sizeable estate in the Midlands (C.1/24/27).

William Lee (*d.ca.* 1444): i.j. S. Wales for the Crown, 1431, for Newport, 1432 (Pugh, p. 294); Staffs. lawyer, landowner & shire kt (*S.P.H.*, vol. I pp. 168–9).

Sir John Mainwaring: i.j. Brecon, 1443 (N.L.W. Peniarth Ms. 280 fo. 24); advanced 100 marks by Duke Humphrey, 1454, probably as a dowry for his wife, Lord Dudley's daughter (*ibid.*, fo. 55; D.641/1/2/60 m. 11); Buckingham's deputy as steward of Congleton, Cheshire, 1451/4 (*D.L.*, p. 513).

John Merbury: witnessed Buckingham's confirmation of the Newport borough charter, 1427 (*Archaeologia, loc. cit.*); steward of Brecon, 1415/21, & holder of other royal offices in Wales (*D.L.*, p. 639; *C.P.R.*, 1416–22, pp. 253, 368); farmer of Cantref Selyf, 1421 (*C.F.R.*, 1413–22, p. 400); Herefs. landowner & shire kt (*Return*, pp. 292–313).

Thomas Mille (1400–60): i.j. Brecon, 1440/6 (N.L.W. Peniarth Ms. 280 fo. 3); steward of Glos., Hants & Wilts., 1435/59 *; parker of Haresfield, Glos., 1453 (*ibid.*, fo. 54); shire kt for Glos. (H.P.B., p. 595).

Thomas Mollesley: i.j. Brecon, 1440 (*ibid.*, fo. 3); involved in the affairs of the first & second Dukes of Suffolk (*C.P.R.*, 1446–52, p. 150; 1452–61, p. 199).

John Pympe: Buckingham's agent at the Maidstone sessions, 1446 (D.641/1/2/233B m. 12v); held the manor of Nettlestead, Kent, of the Staffords from 1440 (N.L.W. Peniarth Ms. 280 fo. 21).

John Russell (*d.*1437): witnessed Buckingham's confirmation of the Newport borough charter, 1427 (*Archaeologia, loc. cit.*); i.j. Newport, 1432 (Pugh, p. 296); retained as a lawyer by the Crown (*D.L.*, pp. 184, 453); Herefs. landowner & shire kt (*Commons of 1422*, pp. 214–5).

Sir John Scudamore (1385–1461): i.j. Huntington & Brecon, 1444/6 (N.L.W. Peniarth Ms. 280 fos. 32, 40); retained 1443 †; steward of Brecon, 1445/51, receiver, 1449 *; Herefs. landowner & shire kt (H.P.B., p. 753).

Sir Robert Stilley (*d.*1438): witnessed Buckingham's confirmation of the Newport borough charter, 1427 (*Archaeologia, loc. cit.*); landowner in the N. Midlands & shire kt for Derbs. (*Return*, p. 271).

Sir William ap Thomas (*d.*1445): witnessed Buckingham's confirmation of the Newport borough charter, 1427 (*Archaeologia, loc. cit.*); a Marcher landowner employed by the Crown in S. Wales & by Richard, Duke of York (Pugh, p. 293; *D.L.*, pp. 644, 646–7).

Sir Richard Vernon (*d.*1451): i.j. Brecon, 1440/5 (N.L.W. Peniarth Ms.

280 fos. 3, 24, 34); retained 1441 †; treasurer of Calais & joint warden of the mint during Buckingham's constableship (*ibid.*, fo. 48); wealthy Staffs. landowner & crown servant with many influential connexions (*D.L.*, pp. 550–6; *Commons of 1422*, p. 231).

Thomas Whitgreve: i.j. Newport, 1432; receiver there, 1435 *; former servant of Edmund, Earl of March (Pugh, p. 299).

Thomas Willoughby: yeoman of the household retained to give counsel, 1438 †.

PART II

THE DOWAGER DUCHESS ANNE'S COUNCILLORS

Sir Thomas Burgh (1430–96): a member of the household at 10 marks *p.a.*, 1456/7 (D.641/1/2/23 m. 6); Buckingham's feoffee (W.A.M. 15195; *C.P.R.*, 1452–61, p. 469); surveyor general, 1462 *; the Dowager's executor, 1480 (P.C.C. Logge 2); Duke Henry's feoffee (*C.C.R.*, 1476–85, p. 257; *Stats. of the Realm*, vol. III pp. 271, 273, 276); influential Lincs. shire kt, crown servant & courtier (*H.P.B.*, p. 136; *D.L.*, pp. 240, 576).

Sir John Clay (1415–64): awarded £10 *p.a.* from Amersham, Bucks., in return for past & future services, May 1461 (S.C.6/1117/11 m. 5); shire kt for Herts. & prominent Yorkist (*H.P.B.*, p. 187).

William Eland (1415–88): retained as a councillor at 26s.8d. *p.a.*, payable from Holderness by 1463 (Add. Ch. 22645 m. 3); m.p. & citizen of Hull (*H.P.B.*, p. 294).

Thomas Garth (1445–1505): attorney for Buckingham's feoffees, 1462 (W.A.M. 15195); receiver general & treasurer of the Dowager's household, 1473/6 *; her feoffee, 1480 (P.C.C. Logge 2), involved in her property transactions & those of Duke Henry (*C.C.R.*, 1476–85, pp. 89, 208–9); bailiff & parker of Penshurst, Kent, *ca.* 1483/1505 (D.641/1/2/235 m. 2); receiver of Newport, 1486 *; held many crown offices, especially under Henry VII (*H.P.B.*, p. 363).

William, Lord Hastings (*d.*1483): retained as constable & steward of Rutland at 20 marks *p.a.* in return for his counsel, Nov. 1461 (S.C.6/1117/11 m. 5); the Dowager's executor, 1480 (P.C.C. Logge 2); one of Edward IV's most powerful supporters (W. H. Dunham, *Lord Hastings' Indentured Retainers, 1461–1483, Trans. of the Connecticut Academy of Arts and Sciences*, XXXIX (1955), *passim*).

Thomas Herbert (1430–69): William, Lord Herbert's brother; steward of Glos., 1462 *; joined the council at £5 *p.a.*, assigned from Thornbury, May 1464; parker of Eastwood, Glos. (D.641/1/2/85 m. 8v); shire kt for Glos. (*H.P.B.*, p. 433).

Richard Heton: see part I (c).

John Hickford (1425–85): made both steward of Rugby & Tyseo, Warwicks., & councillor, Nov. 1461/72 *; shire kt for Warwicks.; helped to suppress Buckingham's rebellion, 1483 (*H.P.B.*, p. 478).

Sir William Nottingham (1415–83) steward of Glos. & Wilts.*; master of Haresfield Park, Glos., & councillor at law, Dec. 1472 (D.641/1/2/191 mm. 3–3v); crown servant & shire kt for Glos. (*D.L.*, p. 454); Chief Baron of the Exchequer, 1479/83; councillor to Edward IV (*H.P.B.*, p. 642).

Robert Sheffield (1430–1502): retained as a councillor at law, at 26s.8d. p.a. assigned from Holderness by Mich. 1463 (Add. Ch. 2264 m. 3); party to Duke Edward's property transactions, 1502 (*Feet of Fines for Essex*, vol. IV no. 112); Lincs. landowner, commissioner & crown attorney (*H.P.B.*, p. 759; *D.L.*, p. 454).

PART III

DUKE HENRY'S COUNCILLORS

Thomas Bridges (*d.*1493): i.j. Newport, 1476 (Pugh, p. 289); serjeant at law 1478/83; shire kt for Glos. & Herefs. (*H.P.B.*, p. 111).

William Catesby (1450–85): i.j. Newport, 1476 (Pugh, p. 289); steward of Rothwell, Northants., by 1483 *; Duke Henry's feoffee (*Stats. of the Realm*, vol. III p. 273); purchased Tilbrook, Beds., with him, 1477/8 (*V.C.H. Bucks.*, vol. III pp. 172–3); commissioned to settle his debts, 1483 (*C.P.R.*, 1476–85, pp. 497–8); one of Richard III's senior advisers (J. S. Roskell, 'William Catesby, Counsellor to Richard III', *B.J.R.L.*, XLII (1959), pp. 145–74).

Thomas Cheyne: i.j. Newport, 1476 (Pugh, p. 289); then a member of Buckingham's household (D.641/1/2/26 m. 5).

Sir Richard Darrell (*d.*1489): i.j. Newport, 1476 (Pugh, p. 290); Buckingham's step-father.

Guy Fairfax (*d.*1495): retained as a councillor & attorney at Westminster by 1475 (D.641/1/2/26 m. 6); Buckingham's feoffee (*C.P.R.*, 1476–85, p. 275; *Stats. of the Realm*, vol. III pp. 271, 273, 276); recorder of York, 1476; Justice of the King's Bench, 1477/95; lawyer & administrator for the Crown (*D.L.*, pp. 250–2, 454, 473).

William Fisher (*d.*1497): treasurer of the Dowager's household, 1462 *; Duke Henry's receiver general, 1475 *; his feoffee (*Stats. of the Realm*, vol. III p. 276); i.j. Newport, 1476; steward, receiver & constable of Brecon to 1485 *; a lawyer; councillor to Jasper, Duke of Bedford & cofferer to Henry VII, 1491/5 (*H.P.B.*, p. 329; Pugh, p. 290).

John Gunter (*d.*1511): a member of the Dowager's household, 1461 (D.641/1/2/276 m. 6); attorney for Duke Humphrey's feoffees, 1462 (W.A.M. 15195) & auditor, 1463/*ca.* 1511 *; i.j. Newport, 1476 & 1503 (Pugh, p. 290; Eg. Roll 2203); involved in cases of debt brought on Duke Edward's behalf, 1504/8 (see Appendix E).

William Hussey (*d.ca.* 1495): retained to give counsel at 26s.8d. p.a. by 1475 (D.641/1/2/26 m. 6); the Dowager's executor, 1480 (P.C.C. Logge

22); attorney general, 1471; Chief Justice of the King's Bench, 1481/95; m.p. for Bramber & Grantham when young (*H.P.B.*, p. 489).

Richard Isham (*d*.1491/2): Duke Henry's attorney general, 1475 *; his feoffee (*C.P.R.*, 1476–85, p. 257; *Stats. of the Realm*, vol. III p. 271); attorney general to the Crown, 1483 (*C.C.R.*, 1476–85, no. 1188).

Sir William Knivet (1440–1515): Duke Henry's uncle by marriage (G.E.C., vol. II p. 63); his feoffee (*C.P.R.*, 1476–85, p. 257; *Stats. of the Realm*, vol. III pp. 271, 273); took part in the rebellion of 1483 & allegedly saved Duke Edward from capture (*Rot. Parl.*, vol. VI p. 245; D.1721/1/11 fos. 241–2); the latter's chamberlain & councillor at £36.10s. *p.a.* by 1514 *; influential Norfolk landowner & shire kt (*H.P.B.*, p. 520).

Sir Nicholas Latimer (*d*.1505): Duke Henry's chamberlain, 1475 *; his feoffee (*Stats. of the Realm*, vol. III pp. 271, 276); i.j. Brecon, 1476 (Pugh, p. 293); attainted for his part in the rebellion of 1483 (*Rot. Parl.*, vol. VI p. 245); wealthy Dorset landowner & shire kt (*H.P.B.*, p. 527).

Thomas Limerick (*d*.1486): i.j. Brecon, 1476 (Pugh, p. 294); Glos. lawyer & shire kt (*H.P.B.*, pp. 544–5).

Sir William Mountfort (*d*.1494): acquired his Warwicks. estates through Duke Humphrey's patronage (see p. 80); Duke Henry's steward, 1475 *; i.j. Brecon, 1476 (Pugh, p. 295); the Dowager Katherine's chamberlain, 1495/6 *; while young he supported Margaret of Anjou & was a shire kt for Warwicks.; he later became influential in the Glos. area (*H.P.B.*, p. 602).

Thomas Nandick, clerk: Cambridge scholar, 1476 (*B.R.C.*, p. 418); present at Brecon during the rebellion of 1483 & attainted as 'late of Cambridge, Nigromansier'; pardoned, 1485 (*Rot. Parl.*, vol. VI pp. 245, 273).

Sir Roger Townsend (*d*.1493): paid £2 *p.a.* as Buckingham's attorney at Westminster by 1475 (D.641/1/2/26 m. 6); his feoffee (*Stats. of the Realm*, vol. III p. 276); Justice of the Common Pleas, 1484/93; Norfolk landowner & administrator (*H.P.B.*, p. 864).

John Twynyho (1440–85): steward of Glos. & Wilts., 1473/7 *; Buckingham's attorney at the Exchequer by 1475 (D.641/1/2/255 m. 7); i.j. Brecon, 1476 (Pugh, p. 297); recorder & m.p. for Bristol (*H.P.B.*, p. 886).

PART IV

DUKE EDWARD'S COUNCILLORS

(a) *Lawyers and Administrators of Justice*

John Brooke: awarded Stafford livery, 1503 (D.641/1/3/9 m. 33v); i.j. Brecon, 1508 (S.P. 1/22 fo. 77); involved in various collusive suits as Buckingham's feoffee, 1513 (C.P.40/1003, Easter 5 Hen. VIII, rot. 346v, 441, 453–3v); steward of Bedminster, Wilts., 1519 *; in attendance at Thornbury to give counsel, 1521 (E.36/220 fo. 6).

Richard Brooke (*d*. 1529): councillor by 1508 (S.P.1/22 fo. 81); Buckingham's feoffee, 1513/4 (C.P. 40/1003, Easter 5 Hen. VII, rot. 445, 448–9; 1008, Mich. 6 Hen. VII, rot. 555, 558–8v); recorder & m.p. for London, 1510/15; Justice of the Common Pleas, 1520; Chief Baron of the Exchequer, 1526.

John Carter: Buckingham's attorney at the Exchequer 1498/1509 (E.13/ 178–185); farmer of Amersham, Bucks., by 1521 (*L. & P. Henry VIII*, vol. III, pt ii., no. 2994 (25)).

Humphrey Conningsby (*d*.1532): retained 1500 † when already involved in Buckingham's affairs (*C.C.R.*, 1485–1500, no. 1219); also employed by the Crown (*D.L.*, p. 452); Justice of the King's Bench, 1509.

Edmund Dudley (*d*.1510): a councillor by 1498/9 (D.641/1/2/200 m. 7); Buckingham's feoffee, 1501 (C.P. 40/957, Trinity 16 Hen. VII, rot. 358v); one of Henry VII's most influential advisers (D. M. Brodie, 'Edmund Dudley, Minister of Henry VII ', *T.R.H.S.*, 4th series XV (1932)).

John Estrange: received £9 as a 'learned man' attending the Brecon sessions and recording the proceedings, 1520 (E.36/220 fo. 16).

Sir Thomas Frowyck (*d*.1506): retained by 1502 † when he became a Justice of the Common Pleas; member of an influential Middx. family.

William Greville (*d*.1513): retained 1504 †; feoffee for Buckingham's sister, 1505 (*C.C.R.*, 1500–9, no. 435); Justice of the Common Pleas, 1509.

Christopher Hales (*d*.1541): Buckingham's attorney general by 1521 *; Henry VII's solicitor general, 1525, attorney general, 1529; Master of the Rolls, 1536.

Humphrey Hervey: retained by 1503 †; in attendance at Thornbury, 1508 (S.P. 1/22 fo. 64); royal commissioner in the S.W.

Thomas Jubbes: awarded the Stafford livery, 1503 (D.641/1/3/9 m. 31v); involved in collusive suits as Buckingham's feoffee, 1512/4 (C.P. 40/1001, Mich. 4 Hen. VIII, rot. 546, 555–5v, 559v, 560v; 1003, Easter 5 Hen. VIII, rot. 346v, 441, 453–3v; 1008, Mich. 6 Hen. VIII, rot. 555, 558–8v); in attendance at Thornbury, 1521 (E.36/220 fo. 3); influential in Glos. as recorder & m.p. for Bristol (*Return*, p. 369).

Richard Littleton (1455–1516): son of Thomas Littleton (*q.v.*); steward of Staffs., 1502 *; i.j. Brecon, 1503 (Pugh, p. 294); owned property in Staffs., Warwicks. & the Marches (*H.P.B.*, p. 54).

Sir Walter Luke (*d*.1544): steward of Hunts. by 1520 *; serjeant at law, 1531; Justice of the King's Bench, 1532.

Thomas Matston (*d*.1541): retained 1517 †; present at Thornbury, 1521 (E.36/220, *passim*); also employed by the Crown (*D.L.*, p. 639).

John Scott (*d*.1532): Buckingham's attorney general, 1498/1515 *; receiver of Kent & Surrey, 1502/6 *; i.j. Brecon & Newport, 1503 (Pugh, p. 296; Eg. Roll 2203); represented Buckingham in his suits against his brother, 1504, and for the constableship, 1515 (*Year Book*, Mich. 20 Hen. VII, fos. 10–11; D.1721/1/11 fo. 139); involved in actions for debt & collusive suits on his behalf, 1501/14 (*Stats. of the Realm*, vol. III p. 277; *Feet of Fines for Essex*, vol. IV p. 107; C.P. 40/957, Trinity 16 Hen. VII, rot. 358v;

1001, Mich. 4 Hen. VIII, rot. 546, 555–5v, 559–60; 1003, Easter 4/5 Hen. VIII, rot. 246, 442–2v, 446, 449, 456, 458; see also Appendix E); parker of Bletchingley, Surr., 1506 (S.C.6/Hen. VII 1076 m. 15); Chief Baron of the Exchequer, in reversion, 1513, appointed, 1528.

(b) *Administrative Staff*

Sir Humphrey Bannaster (*d.*1523): i.j. Brecon, 1503 (Pugh, p. 288); Councillor by 1505 (S.C.6/Hen. VII 1076 m. 15); controller of the household, 1506 *; treasurer, 1508 *; involved in many suits for debt on Buckingham's behalf, 1506/11 (see Appendix E); himself sued for debt, 1511 (*ibid.*), but had then joined the household of Charles Brandon, Duke of Suffolk.

Thomas Cade, clerk : awarded Stafford livery, 1503 (D.641/1/3/19 m. 31v); receiver general, 1511 *; receiver of Staffs., 1512/15 *; Buckingham's feoffee, 1513 (C.P.40/1003, Easter 4/5 Hen. VIII, rot. 445, 448–9); surveyor & councillor by 1514 *; sued for breaking his contract, 1514 (see Appendix E); but reappointed as receiver general, 1519 *; steward of Cardinal Wolsey's household, 1528 (*L. & P. Henry VIII*, vol. IV, pt ii., no. 3807).

William Curtis, clerk : receiver of Glos., Hants & Wilts., 1519/21 *; master of the works *, treasurer * & councillor, 1521 (S.P.1/22 fo. 58).

John Dellacourt, clerk : wore Stafford livery by 1515 (E.101/631/20 m. 18v); auditor, 1516 *; councillor by 1520 (S.P.1/22 fo. 58); testified against Duke Edward, 1521 (K.B. 8/5 mm. 3v–4v); distinguished fellow of Magdalen College (*B.R.O.*, vol. I p. 557).

William Gibbons, clerk (*d.ca.* 1502): clerk of the household, 1497 *; receiver of Staffs., 1497/1502 *; receiver general, 1499/1502 *; served on many conciliar commissions (D.641/1/2/200 m. 7v; 267 m. 3); Buckingham's feoffee, 1501 (C.P. 40/957, Trinity 16 Hen. VII, rot. 358v); Oxford scholar, 1400 (*B.R.O.*, vol. II p. 839).

Robert Gilbert, clerk : scholar & fellow of Magdalen College (*B.R.O.*, vol. II p. 767); retained 1500 †; Buckingham's surety in his dealings with the Crown, 1507/21 (*C.C.R.*, 1500–9, no. 822; *L. & P. Henry VIII*, vol. I, pt i., no. 357 (41); Royal Ms. BXXXV A 1–11); brought many actions for debt on his behalf, 1507/18 (see Appendix E); his feoffee, 1512/14 (C.P. 40/1001, Mich. 4 Hen. VIII, rot. 546, 555–5v, 559–60; 1003, Easter 5 Hen. VIII, rot. 445, 448–9; 1008, Mich. 6 Hen. VIII, rot. 555, 558–8v); his chancellor by 1514 *; testified against him, 1521 (Harl. Ms. 283 fo. 70).

Giles Greville: sued for failing to present his accounts, 1512 (Appendix E); but still made treasurer by 1514 *; then a councillor (E.101/518/5 pt i. m. 3); held many commissions in the Glos. area.

Dr John Jennings (*d.* 1523): receiver of Glos., Hants & Wilts., 1511 *; surveyor general & councillor by 1520 (S.P.1/22 fo. 58); Doctor of civil laws, 1499 (*B.R.O.*, vol. II pp. 1015–6); practising attorney in the Court of Arches, 1510 (*L. & P. Henry VIII*, vol. I, pt i., no. 1803).

Sir William Knivet: see part III.

Richard Mynors (*d*.1524): treasurer, 1502/7 *; conciliar commissioner, 1505 (S.C.6/Hen. VIII 4775 m. 6); brought many actions for debt on the Duke's behalf, 1505/11 (see Appendix E); sued for failing to account for receipts of £1,562, 1507/12 (*ibid.*); had joined the Earl of Shrewsbury's retinue by 1513 (*L. & P. Henry VIII*, vol. I, pt iii., no. 2392).

Thomas Moscroff, clerk: an Oxford scholar & physician; retained & made receiver general, 1519 *; secretary & councillor by 1520 (S.P.1/22 fo. 58).

John Pauncefoot: conciliar commissioner, 1511 (S.C.6/Hen. VIII 4775 m. 7); controller of the household by 1514 *; Glos. landowner and crown administrator.

Richard Pole (*d*.1517): receiver general & steward of the household, 1495 *; reappointed steward & made councillor by 1514 (E.101/518/5 pt 1. m. 3); influential courtier & Herefs. shire kt (*H.P.B.*, pp. 690–1).

George Poley, clerk (*d*.1538): Cambridge scholar, 1500; university preacher, 1509 (*B.R.C.*, p. 457); treasurer, 1515/20 *; keeper of the jewels, 1515/17 (E.101/631/20 m. 12; D. 641/1/3/9 m. 31v); sued for debt, 1516 (Appendix E); but still made almoner & councillor by 1520 (S.P.1/22 fo. 58).

Sir John Russell (*d*.1556): clerk of the kitchens, 1495 (S.C.6/Hen. VII 1842 m. 6); secretary, 1499/1507 *; receiver of Glos., Hants & Wilts., 1501/4 *; Buckingham's feoffee, 1501 (C.P.40/957, Trinity 16 Hen. VII, rot. 358v); i.j. Newport & Brecon, 1503 (Eg. Roll 2203; Pugh, p. 296); brought many suits for debt on the Duke's behalf, 1505/11 (see Appendix E); sued for embezzlement, 1508/11 (STA CHA 2/23/11); but prospered under royal patronage, becoming secretary to Princess Mary, 1525, & a wealthy Worcs. landowner & shire kt (*Return*, p. 371).

Henry Sleford, clerk (*d.ca.* 1518): Cambridge scholar in canon law (*B.R.C.*, p. 533); surveyor general, 1501/6 *; councillor by 1505 (S.C.6/Hen. VII 1076 m. 15); receiver of Holderness, 1505/8 *.

Henry, Lord Stafford & Earl of Wiltshire (*d*.1523): Buckingham's younger brother; toured the Marcher Lordships, 1500 (Pugh, p. 262); steward of Brecon, Caus & Newport, *ca.* 1500/21 *.

Thomas Stephens: a lawyer; i.j. Brecon, 1508 (S.P. 1/22 fo. 77); then deputy receiver of Kent & Surrey.

Laurence Stubbes, clerk (*d.ca.* 1536): distinguished fellow of Magdalen College (*B.R.O.*, vol. II p. 1809); member of the household, 1507 (D.1721/1/5); conciliar commissioner, 1508 (S.C.6/Hen. VIII 4775 m. 6); then receiver of Glos., Hants & Wilts.*; secretary, 1511/14 *; joined Cardinal Wolsey's household by 1515 (*L. & P. Henry VIII*, vol. II, pt. i., no. 1369).

Robert Turberville (*d.ca.* 1529): treasurer of the household to 1502 *; then steward *; receiver general 1503/8 *; i.j. Brecon & Newport, 1503 (Pugh, p. 297; Eg. Roll 2203); involved in many suits for debt on Buckingham's behalf, 1505/20 (see Appendix E); annuitant, 1509/21 †; influential Herts. landowner, lawyer & shire kt (*H.P.B.*, p. 885).

William Walwyn : auditor general, 1507/21 *; Buckingham's surety in his dealings with the Crown, 1507 (*C.C.R.*, 1500–9, no. 822); brought actions for debt on his behalf, 1507/20 (see Appendix E); crown auditor for S. Wales (*L. & P. Henry VIII*, vol. I, pt i., no. 1802).

Thomas Wotton, clerk : receiver of Glos., Hants & Wilts., 1513/18 *; master of the works, 1514/19 *; sued for debt, 1516 (see Appendix E); but appears as a chaplain & councillor, 1520 (S.P.1/22 fo. 38).

Appendix D

FEES AND ANNUITIES AWARDED BY THE FIRST AND THIRD DUKES OF BUCKINGHAM

Where possible a brief indication of each recipient's social position has been given, together with the size and provenance of his or her fee and the reason why it was awarded. Members of the ducal council are marked * and are more fully documented in Appendix C. Many other annuitants were senior household and estate staff; their appointments are noted briefly here, and at greater length in the appropriate sections of Appendix B. Unless otherwise stated fees were awarded by letters patent under the Stafford seal.

PART I

(a) *Annuities Paid by Duke Humphrey during the Years 1442 and 1447*

The two annuity lists for the years ending Mich. 1442 and 1447 (D.641/1/ 2/17 mm. IV–2V and Longleat Ms. 6410 mm. 2V–3V) have here been combined. Names which appear in both accounts are marked (1442–7), while those occurring in one but not the other are designated either (1442) or (1447) accordingly.

(1) *Knights*

John Astley (1442–7): awarded 20 marks *p.a.* for life from Amersham, Bucks., in Nov. 1441 (N.L.W. Peniarth Ms. 280 fo. 20).

John Bourchier * (esquire 1442, knight 1447): Buckingham's half-brother; awarded £26.13s.4d. *p.a.* from Writtle, Essex, before Mich. 1441, but not paid until 1443 (*ibid.*, fo. 24).

John Burgh (esquire 1442, knight 1447): steward of Caus 1447–58; awarded 10 marks *p.a.* for life from Caus, Salop., by indentures of Sept. 1441; to provide armed men as required & serve the Duke before all others in England (*ibid.*, fo. 18).

John Constable (1442–7): steward of Holderness 1445–50; awarded £20 *p.a.*; terms unknown.

Kinard de la Bere * (1442): awarded 10 marks *p.a.*; terms unknown.

Edward Grey (1442): awarded £40 *p.a.* until becoming a banneret & then 100 marks *p.a.* for life from Rutland & Tyseo, Warwicks., by indentures of Apr. 1440; to serve at home & abroad, in peace & war, with 14 mounted men (*ibid.*, fos. 6–7); last recorded payment Mich. 1445 (D.641/1/2/271 m. 4v).

John Hanford (1442–7): awarded £10 *p.a.* for life from Rothwell, Northants., by indentures of Sept. 1441; to serve at home & abroad, in peace & war, with men as required (N.L.W. Peniarth Ms. 280 fo. 18).

Nicholas Longford (1447): awarded £10 *p.a.* from Staffs., by indentures of 1444; to serve at home & abroad (*ibid.*, fo. 31).

John Mainwaring * (1442–7): awarded £10 *p.a.* for life from Rothwell, Northants., by indentures of Sept. 1441; to provide men as required & serve the Duke before all others, at home & abroad, in peace & war (*ibid.*, fo. 24).

John Scudamore * (esquire 1442, knight 1447): awarded 10 marks *p.a.* from Brecon by indentures of *ca.* 1443; to provide men as required (*ibid.*, fo. 25).

Griffith Vaughan (1442): awarded 5 marks *p.a.* until his rebellion & death in 1447; terms unknown.

Richard Vernon * (1442–7): awarded £20 *p.a.* for life from Rugby, Warwicks., by indentures of Oct. 1440; to serve in peace & war with six mounted men (*ibid.*, fos. 11–12).

Geoffrey Warburton * (1442–7): awarded £10 *p.a.* for life from Rothwell, Northants., by indentures of Sept. 1441; to serve at home & abroad (*ibid.*, fo. 18).

(2) *Esquires*

Thomas Arblaster * (1442–7): awarded £5 *p.a.*; terms unknown.

Ralph Basset (1447): awarded 10 marks *p.a.* from Norton-in-the-Moors, Staffs., by indentures of Oct. 1444 (*ibid.*, fo. 35).

Henry Bradburne (1447): retained on the same date & terms as Basset.

John Carson (1442–7): awarded £10 *p.a.* from Naseby, Northants., by indentures of Oct. 1440; to serve in England with three mounted men, or men as required (*ibid.*, fo. 11).

John Constable (1447): son of Sir John (*q.v.*); awarded £10 *p.a.*; terms unknown.

Richard Culpepper (1442–7): awarded £5 *p.a.* from Tonbridge, Kent, in Sept. 1440 (D.641/1/2/233A m. 11).

John Dawnport (1442–7): awarded 10 marks *p.a.* for life from Naseby, Northants., by indentures of Sept. 1441; to serve the Duke before all others in England with men as required (N.L.W. Peniarth Ms. 280 fo. 18).

Robert de Lye (1442–7): member of Buckingham's household 1438/9 & parker of Disining, Suffolk, 1444 (*ibid.*, fo. 32; D.641/1/2/15 m. 6); awarded 10 marks *p.a.* for life from Colston Basset, Notts., by indentures of Sept. 1441; to serve the Duke before all others in England with men as required (N.L.W. Peniarth Ms. 280 fo. 32).

Richard Donham (1442, esquire 1447): treasurer of the household 1430/40;

awarded 10 marks *p.a.* as a pension for life from Ongar, Essex, in May 1439 (D.641/1/2/18 m. 6).

John Downe (1442–7): steward of Halton, Cheshire, 1448 (N.L.W. Peniarth Ms. 280 fo. 18); awarded 10 marks *p.a.* for life from Wolford, Warwicks., by indentures of Sept. 1441; to serve the Duke before all others in England with men as required (*ibid.*, fo. 18).

William Draycote (1442–7): constable of Maxstoke Castle 1439; steward of Maxstoke 1445 (S.C.6/1040/15 m. 1v; N.L.W. Peniarth Ms. 280 fo. 38); awarded 5 marks *p.a.*

John Dutton (1442): awarded 10 marks *p.a.* for life from Caus, Salop., by indentures of Sept. 1441; to serve the Duke before all others in England with men as assigned (*ibid.*, fo. 18).

Ralph Egerton (1442–7): retained on the same date & terms as Dutton; paid from Bradeley, Staffs. (*ibid.*).

Robert Grey (1447): awarded 20 marks *p.a.* from Oakham, Rutland, by indentures of 1445/6 (*ibid.*, fo. 38).

Robert Grovenor (1442–7); retained on the same date & terms as Dutton; paid from Thornbury, Glos. (*ibid.*, fo. 18).

Walter Hakeluyt (1442): awarded 10 marks *p.a.* from Brecon, by indentures of Mar. 1443; to present men as required (*ibid.*, fo. 25).

John Hampton (1442–7): awarded 10 marks *p.a.* for life from Staffs. in Nov. 1441; raised to £10 *p.a.* in 1445 (*ibid.*, fo. 20; D.641/1/2/56 m. 10).

Richard Hotoft * (1442–7): a lawyer; originally awarded £2 *p.a.* from Lalleford, Warwicks., in 1440; given an additional £5 *p.a.* in 1442 (D.641/1/2/17 m. 3v).

Thomas Mille * (1442–7): awarded 10 marks *p.a.*; probably from Glos.

Reginald Morton (1442): awarded £10 *p.a.* for life from Oakham, Rutland, by indentures of *ca.* Oct. 1440; to serve in England with six mounted men, or men as assigned (N.L.W. Peniarth Ms. 280 fo. 12).

William Palmer (1442–7): one of the Dowager Countess Anne's executors (*ibid.*, fo. 8); awarded 10 marks *p.a.* from Lillesford, Wilts., in May 1439 (D.641/1/2/167 mm. 8v–9).

Walter Percival (1447): Buckingham's deputy as constable of Calais, Aug. 1442; awarded £10 *p.a.* from Tonbridge, Kent, in *ca.* 1445/6 (*ibid.*, fos. 21, 41).

William Perkins (1442): steward of Bucks, 1443; awarded 10 marks *p.a.*

Nicholas Poyntz * (1442–7): awarded 10 marks *p.a.* from Send, Wilts., by the Countess Anne before Mich. 1435 (S.C.11/816).

William Rokewood (1442–7): steward of Wells & Sheringham, Norfolk, 1441/2; awarded 10 marks *p.a.*

John Savage (1442): awarded 10 marks *p.a.* for life from Thornbury, Glos., by indentures of Sept. 1441; to serve the Duke before all others in England with men as required (N.L.W. Peniarth Ms. 280 fo. 18).

Clement Spicer (1447): a member of the household during the 1450s (D.641/1/2/57 m. 11; 58 m. 11); awarded 10 marks *p.a.* from Haverhill,

Suffolk, for loyal service past & future in Feb. 1440 (N.L.W. Peniarth Ms. 280 fo. 5).

William Stanley (1442–7): awarded 10 marks *p.a.* for life from Caus, Salop., by indentures of Sept. 1441; to serve the Duke before all others in England with men as required (*ibid.*, fo. 18).

John Trevelyan (1447): awarded 10 marks *p.a.*; terms unknown.

Thomas Trussell (1442–7); awarded 10 marks *p.a.* for life from Oakham, Rutland, by indentures of Oct. 1440; to serve the Duke before all others in England with six armed men (*ibid.*, fo. 12).

Hugh Venables (1442–7): awarded 10 marks *p.a.* for life from Thornbury, Glos., by indentures of Sept. 1441; to serve the Duke before all others in England with men as required (*ibid.*, fo. 18).

Richard Witherton * (1442–7): awarded £20 *p.a.* for life (£10 by indentures, £10 by letters patent in return for past services) from Suffolk, in June 1441 (*ibid.*, fo. 16).

(3) *Other annuitants*

Anne, Duchess of Buckingham (1442–7): awarded £100 *p.a.*

John Andrews * (1442–7): attorney general to the Staffords 1431/57; awarded 5 marks *p.a.* by the Dowager Countess Anne in 1431 (D.641/1/2/13 m. 4); increased to 10 marks *p.a.* by Duke Humphrey before 1441.

Nicholas Ashton * (1442): a lawyer; awarded £2 *p.a.* from Caliland, Cornwall, in May 1438 (D.641/1/2/15 m. 6).

William Bamburgh * (1442–7): entry probably refers to John Bamburgh, a lawyer; awarded £2 *p.a.* from Kent in *ca.* 1428 (D.641/1/2/231 m. 11).

John Barber (1442–7): a yeoman of the household 1438/9 (D.641/1/2/15 m. 6); awarded 5 marks *p.a.* from Stafford in Mar. 1441 (N.L.W. Peniarth Ms. 280 fo. 14).

William Barber (1442–7): John's father; clerk of the household 1439; yeoman of the stables 1446 (D.641/1/2/56 m. 11); awarded 5 marks *p.a.* from Staffs. in March 1441 (D.641/1/2/54 m. 9).

Cadwaller Barclagh (1447): awarded 24*s*.5*d*. *p.a.* for life in Apr. 1447 (Eg. Roll 2196 m. 12v).

Thomas Barston (1442–7): awarded 5 marks *p.a.*; terms unknown.

Katherine Basset (1447): a lady-in-waiting 1438/9 (D.641/1/2/15 m. 6); awarded £5 *p.a.*, above her wage of 53*s*.4*d*. *p.a.*

Thomas Bate * (1447): a lawyer; awarded £2 *p.a.* from Atherstone, Warwicks., in *ca.* 1446/7 (N.L.W. Peniarth Ms. 280 fo. 46).

William Bere (1442–7): a trumpeter; awarded £2 *p.a.* from Staffs. in Sept. 1439 (D.641/1/2/55 m. 9v).

John Browood (1442–7): a trumpeter; awarded 4 marks *p.a.* from Staffs. in Nov. 1430 (*ibid.*, m. 9).

William Brugges (1442–7): Garter King of Arms; awarded £2 *p.a.* from Tonbridge, Kent, in May 1430 (D.641/1/2/231 m. 11).

Richard Buryell (1442–7): a minstrel; awarded £2 *p.a.* from Staffs. in Jan. 1441 (D. 641/1/2/54 m. 9v).

John Carbonell (1442): a furrier from Coventry; awarded 60s.8d. *p.a.* for life from Wootton Wawen, Warwicks., in Apr. 1428 (D.641/1/2/15 m. 6).

Humphrey Clerkson (1442–7): awarded 4 marks *p.a.* for life from Rugby, Warwicks., in return for past & future service in June 1433 (D.641/1/2/269 m. 4).

William Cook (1442): a yeoman of the household, 1438 (D. 641/1/2/15 m. 6); awarded 5 marks *p.a.*

William Cumberford * (1447): a lawyer; awarded £2 *p.a.* from Staffs. in Apr. 1442; still being paid at Mich. 1467 (D.641/1/2/59 m. 10; 25 m. 1).

John Curray (1442–7): a trumpeter; awarded 4 marks *p.a.*

Robert Danby * (1447): a lawyer; awarded £2 *p.a.* in 1441 (N.L.W. Peniarth Ms. 280 fo. 31).

Andrew Danyell (1442–7): awarded £5 *p.a.*; terms unknown.

Edmund de la Bere (1447); keeper of Hay Castle & one of Buckingham's esquires; awarded 61s.4d. *p.a.* as master of the lordship of Hay in 1447 (*ibid.*, fo. 44).

Gerard de la Hay (1447): Buckingham's attorney at the Exchequer 1445; then awarded £2 *p.a.* (*ibid.*, fo. 35).

Elizabeth Drury (1442–7): widow of Henry Drury, a Stafford family retainer; awarded a pension of 20 marks *p.a.* for life in 1441 (*ibid.*, fo. 22).

John Enderby (1447): awarded £2 *p.a.* from Kimbolton, Hunts., in 1443 (*ibid.*, fo. 30).

Beatrice Fowne (1447): a lady-in-waiting 1438/9 (D.641/1/2/15 m. 6); awarded an additional 5 marks *p.a.*, above her wage of 26s.8d. *p.a.*

Robert Frampton (1442): chief Baron of the Exchequer; attorney, auditor, feoffee & executor for the Dowager Countess Anne (*C.F.R.*, 1399–1405, pp. 70, 72, 99; *C.C.R.*, 1415–19, pp. 46, 270; *Testamenta Vetusta*, p. 238); awarded £10 *p.a.* by Duke Humphrey before 1441.

David Geffrey (1447): awarded £4 *p.a.*; terms unknown.

John Grymmesby (1442–7): a harpist; awarded £2 *p.a.* for life from Stafford in Dec. 1430 (D.641/1/2/54 m. 9).

Hans of the Stable (1442–7): a yeoman groom of the stable 1445/6 (D.641/1/2/223A m. 11); awarded £2 *p.a.* for life from Bletchingley, Surrey, in Oct. 1434 (N.L.W. Peniarth Ms. 280 fo. 2).

William Harpe (1447): awarded £1 *p.a.*; terms unknown.

John Harper * (1442–7): awarded 10 marks *p.a.* by 1441.

Thomas Higham * (1442–7): a lawyer; awarded £2 *p.a.* from Disining, Suffolk, in Mar. 1441 (*ibid.*, fo. 14).

John Holme * (1442): a lawyer, awarded £2 *p.a.* as Buckingham's attorney in the Exchequer by 1441 (*ibid.*, fo. 9).

John Hunte (1447): one of the King's chaplains; awarded £2 *p.a.* from Stanford Rivers, Essex, in 1439/40 (*ibid.*, fo. 8).

John Kynge (1442): awarded 5 marks *p.a.*; terms unknown.

John Markham * (1442): a lawyer; awarded £2 *p.a.*, from Kneesall, Notts., in Apr. 1440 (*ibid.*, fo. 6).

Richard Moldeworth (1442–7): a yeoman of the household 1438/9 (D.641/1/2/15 m. 6); awarded 5 marks *p.a.* from Stafford in Mar. 1441, in return for past & future services (N.L.W. Peniarth Ms. 280 fo. 14).

Richard Moygne (1442–7): awarded £2 *p.a.* from Hatfield Broadoak, Essex, in Dec. 1440 (*ibid.*, fo. 13).

John Parker (1442): Buckingham's yeoman cook; awarded 4 marks *p.a.* for life from Stafford in Nov. 1441 (*ibid.*, fo. 19).

Nicholas Parker (1442): one of Earl Edmund's yeomen grooms; confirmed in the 5 marks *p.a.* awarded to him for life from Staffs. before 1403 (D.641/1/2/48).

Philippa Peshale (1442): a lady-in-waiting, probably widow of Sir Adam de Peshale, one of Earl Edmund's tenants (D. 641/1/2/44); awarded 5 marks *p.a.*

Ralph Pole * (1447): a lawyer; awarded £2 *p.a.* from Staffs. in July 1443 (D.641/1/2/56 m. 10v).

John Portington * (1442): a lawyer; awarded £2 *p.a.* from Holderness in Apr. 1440 (N.L.W. Peniarth Ms. 280 fo. 6).

Nicholas Radford * (1442–7): a lawyer; awarded £2 *p.a.* from Caliland, Cornwall, in Nov. 1438 (D.641/1/2/15 m. 6).

James Romayne (1442): a member of the retinue in 1445/6 (D. 641/1/2/233B m. 12); awarded £4 *p.a.*

William Sandebach (1442): awarded £2 *p.a.* for life from Rugby, Warwicks., at Mich. 1433 (D.641/1/2/269 m. 4).

Miles Scull * (1442–7): a lawyer; awarded £2 *p.a.* from Brecon in 1439/40 (N.L.W. Peniarth Ms. 280 fo. 8).

William Slyherst (1442): awarded £2 *p.a.*; terms unknown.

William Smert (1442–7): one of Earl Edmund's retainers; confirmed in the 5 marks *p.a.* awarded to him for life from Stafford before 1403 (D.641/1/2/48).

Richard Spenser (1442–7): a carpenter; awarded £2 *p.a.* in Sept. 1440 (N.L.W. Peniarth Ms. 280 fo. 11).

William Tresham (1442–7): a lawyer; awarded £2 *p.a.* by the Countess Anne in Feb. 1430; fee paid from Rothwell, Northants., after 1438 (D.641/1/2/12; 15 m. 6).

Thomas Tyler (1447): a carpenter (N.L.W. Peniarth Ms. 280 fo. 47); awarded £2 *p.a.*

John Vampage * (1442–7): a lawyer; awarded £2 *p.a.* from Wootton Wawen, Warwicks., in 1441/2 (*ibid.*, fo. 21).

Isabel Verney (1442–7): awarded £5 *p.a.* from Sheldon, Warwicks., in June 1441 (*ibid.*, fo. 16), above a fee of £5 marks *p.a.* granted to her as the widow of Walter Verney from Wootton Wawen in Apr. 1438 (D.641/1/2/15 m. 6).

Ralph Vyckers (1442): awarded £2 *p.a.* for life from Norton-in-the-Moors, Staffs., for past & future services in Feb. 1441 (D.641/1/2/54 m. 9v).

Robert Whitgreve * (1442–7): a lawyer; awarded 10 marks *p.a.* from Newport in May 1431 (S.C.6/924/23 m. 10).

Thomas Willoughby (1442–7): a yeoman of the household; awarded 4 marks *p.a.* for life from Kent in April 1438 (D.461/1/2/231 m. 11).

Edward Wynter (1442–7): a trumpeter; awarded 4 marks *p.a.*

William Yelverton * (1442): a lawyer; awarded £2 *p.a.* from Wells, Norfolk, in Apr. 1442 (N.L.W. Peniarth Ms. 280 fo. 6).

Thomas Young * (1447): a lawyer; awarded £2 *p.a.* from Thornbury, Glos., in Oct. 1446 (D.641/1/2/174 m. 7v).

(b) *Other Annuities Awarded by Duke Humphrey between 1438 and 1447*

Piers Ardern *: a lawyer; awarded £2 *p.a.* from Hatfield Broadoak, Essex, in *ca.* Jul. 1443 (N.L.W. Peniarth Ms. 280 fo. 30).

Thomas Burgoyne *: a lawyer; awarded £2 *p.a.* in *ca.* 1446 (*ibid.*, fo. 41).

Kynard de la Hay: steward of Brecon, Hay & Huntingdon; awarded 10 marks *p.a.* by indentures of 1443; to present men as required (*ibid.*, fo. 25).

William Denteth *: a lawyer; awarded £2 *p.a.* from Staffs. in Sept. 1439 (D.641/1/2/54 m. 9).

William Garnet: awarded 5 marks *p.a.* from Staffs. in Mar. 1441; fee paid in 1446, but cancelled by Mich. 1450 (D.641/1/2/54 m. 9v; 56 m. 10v; 57 mm. 10–10v).

Mathew Gough: awarded £20 *p.a.* from the County of Perche, France, in 1445, as Buckingham's bailiff (N.L.W. Peniarth Ms. 280 fo. 36).

Lawrence Kay: awarded £2 *p.a.*, paid by the auditor general from *ca.* 1445 (*ibid.*, fo. 39).

Walter Moyll *: a lawyer; awarded £2 *p.a.* from Caliland, Cornwall, in 1443 (*ibid.*, fo. 30).

William Rukke: awarded 10 marks *p.a.*, from Wells, Norfolk, in Jan. 1440; terms unknown (*ibid.*, fo. 4).

Thomas Vaughan: receiver of Brecon 1451/7; awarded 6 marks *p.a.* in 1444/5, above his fee of £5 *p.a.* as constable of Huntington Castle from 1446 onwards (*ibid.*, fos. 33, 41).

William Walleton: probably one of Buckingham's esquires; awarded 5 marks *p.a.* from Holderness in 1445; terms unknown (*ibid.*, fo. 39).

John Woodstock: awarded £1 *p.a.* from Holderness in 1443; terms unknown (*ibid.*).

(c) *Other Annuities Awarded by Duke Humphrey between 1448 and 1460*

Richard Bagot, esq.: awarded 10 marks *p.a.* from Norton-in-the-Moors, Staffs., by indentures of Sept. 1445 (D.641/1/2/60 m. 9v).

Richard Chokke: a lawyer; awarded £2 *p.a.* from Thornbury, Glos., in May 1453; fee paid until Mich. 1461 (N.L.W. Peniarth Ms. 280 fo. 53; S.C.6/1117/11 m. 6).

John Cockayn, esq.: steward of Ashbourne, Derbs., 1453 (N.L.W. Peniarth Ms. 280 fo. 53); awarded 10 marks *p.a.* for life from Staffs. by indentures of Aug. 1453 (D.641/1/2/59 m. 10).

William Corall: awarded £2 *p.a.* from Tonbridge, Kent, in 1447/8; terms unrecorded (N.L.W. Peniarth Ms. 280 fo. 47).

William Crowland: awarded £2 *p.a.* from Disining, Suffolk, in Sept. 1453; terms unrecorded (*ibid.*, fo. 54).

Thomas de la Mere: awarded £5 *p.a.* from Westcombe, Somerset, in return for past & future services in Jan. 1452 (D.641/1/2/176 m. 7v).

Thomas Edmund: Buckingham's physician; awarded 10 marks *p.a.* for life from Thornbury, Glos., by indentures of Jan. 1449; to attend the Duke before all others in England and abroad (D.641/1/2/174 m. 7v).

Hugh Egerton, esq.: awarded 10 marks *p.a.* from Bradeley, Staffs., in Feb. 1454; terms unknown (D.641/1/2/59 m. 10v).

William Fiennes, Lord Saye & Sele: awarded £10 *p.a.* for life from Buckingham's revenues as Warden of the Cinque Ports by indentures of 1450/1; to serve the Duke before all others in England with 'a competent fellowship' as required (N.L.W. Peniarth Ms. 280 fo. 49); cancelled by Mich. 1454 (D.641/1/2/22 m. 9).

Sir Thomas Findern: awarded £10 *p.a.* for life from Disining, Suffolk, by indentures of 1447/8; probably to serve Buckingham in England with men as required (N.L.W. Peniarth Ms. 280 fo. 46).

William Forth: awarded 5 marks *p.a.* for life from Tonbridge, Kent, in *ca.* 1455; terms unknown (*ibid.*, fo. 56).

William Frere: awarded 10 marks *p.a.* for life from Tyseo, Warwicks., in May 1455 (S.C.6/1040/15 m. 5v).

Richard Furbour: awarded £1 *p.a.* from Norton-in-the-Moors, Staffs., in return for past & future services in Oct. 1455 (D.641/1/2/60 m. 9v).

John Gresley, esq.: awarded £10 *p.a.* for life by indentures of *ca.* 1451/2; to serve with five mounted men in England & men as required when abroad (N.L.W. Peniarth Ms. 280 fo. 49).

Richard Heton, esq.*: awarded £2 *p.a.* from Oakham, Rutland, in 1454/5 (*ibid.*, fo. 56); still being paid in 1463 (S.C.6/1117/11 m. 6).

Richard Houghton: awarded 5 marks *p.a.* for life from Tonbridge, Kent, in *ca.* 1455; terms unknown (*ibid.*).

Richard Kyndeskelth: awarded £2 *p.a.* from Brustwick, Holderness, in 1451/2; terms unknown (*ibid.*, fo. 52).

William Lacon*: a lawyer; awarded £2 *p.a.* from Caus, Salop., in May 1453 (*ibid.*, fo. 53).

Thomas Littleton*: a lawyer; awarded £2 *p.a.* from Tyseo, Warwicks., in May 1453; still being paid at Mich. 1463 (*ibid.*, D.641/1/2/66 m. 2).

Henry Makworth: Buckingham's constable of Calais Castle 1449; then awarded an additional fee of £2 *p.a.* (N.L.W. Peniarth Ms. 280 fo. 47).

John Needham *: a lawyer; awarded £2 *p.a.* from Maxstoke, Warwicks., in May 1453 (*ibid.*, fo. 53).

Lady Mary Neville: one of the Duchess Anne's kinswomen; awarded £5 *p.a.* from the central circuit in Sept. 1451 (D.641/1/2/23 m. 7).

Richard Rose: awarded 5 marks *p.a.* from Holderness in 1451/2; terms unknown (N.L.W. Peniarth Ms. 280 fo. 48).

Humphrey, Lord Stafford: Buckingham's eldest son; awarded £40 *p.a.* from the central circuit in Mar. 1455 (D.641/1/2/23 m. 7).

Sir Humphrey Stafford of Grafton: Buckingham's distant kinsman, he could himself muster a following of over 200 men; awarded 40 marks *p.a.* by Mich. 1448, terms unknown; he was killed by Cade's rebels in 1450 (K. B. McFarlane, *Nobility of Later Medieval England*; Storey, *op. cit.*, pp. 57–8).

Sir William Vernon: awarded £10 *p.a.* from Rugby, Warwicks., by Lord Stafford's indentures of Aug. 1454; to serve in peace & war (S.C.6/1040/15 m. 3).

John Wingford *: a lawyer; awarded £2 *p.a.* from Tonbridge, Kent, in 1450/1 (N.L.W. Peniarth Ms. 280 fo. 48).

PART II

(a) *Annuities Awarded by Duke Edward, and Listed in the Royal Commissioners' Report of 1523*

Unless otherwise stated the information provided here derives from S.P.1/29 fo. 180.

John Bordesley: awarded 5 marks *p.a.* from the Glos. area before Mich. 1519 (S.C.6/Hen. VIII 5819 m. 4v); terms unknown.

John Borell: keeper of Hatfield Park, Essex; awarded £2 *p.a.*, & considered 'a very hardy substancyall man' by the commissioners (S.P.1/29 fo. 78).

Margaret Borell: probably the former's wife; awarded £2 *p.a.*

John Carter *: a lawyer; awarded 5 marks *p.a.*

William Cholmeley: Buckingham's cofferer 1503/21; awarded 5 marks *p.a.* by Mich. 1511; doubled before Mich. 1518 (D.641/1/2/88; 96 m. 3v).

Thomas Denton: awarded £10 *p.a.* for life from Maxstoke, Warwicks., in Jul. 1517; terms unknown (S.C.6/Hen. VIII 5841 m. 4v).

John Fraunces: Buckingham's physician; awarded 5 marks *p.a.* from the receivership of Kent & Surrey (S.C.6/Hen. VIII 5795 m. 3).

John Haslewood: a London draper; awarded £10 *p.a.* for life from Writtle, Essex, in Nov. 1519 (S.C.6/Hen. VIII 5841 m. 5); shared a second annuity of 10 marks *p.a.* with Mistress Philipps (*q.v.*) & was made parker of Writtle (S.P.1/29 fo. 177).

William Hasynge: Buckingham's herald at arms; awarded £10 *p.a.* from Burton, Bucks., by Mich. 1520 (S.C.6/Hen. VIII 5841 m. 5).

Sir John Grey: younger brother of Thomas, Marquess of Dorset; awarded 10 marks *p.a.* from Rothwell, Northants., before Mich. 1520 (*ibid.*, m. 4v).

Thomas Jubbes *: a lawyer; awarded £2 *p.a.* from the Glos. area by Mich. 1519 (S.C.6/Hen. VIII 5819 m. 4v).

Thomas Kemys: keeper of the cellar 1506 (Longleat Misc. Ms. XII fo. 30v); gentleman of the household *ca.* 1514 (E.101/518/5 pt i, m. 2); awarded 10 marks *p.a.* by Mich. 1519 (S.C.6/Hen. VIII 5841 m. 4v).

John Kyrke: a gentleman of the household 1520 (E.36/220 fo. 2v); awarded £10 *p.a.* from the Glos. area by Mich. 1519 (S.C.6/Hen. VIII 5819 m. 4v).

Richard Langhurst: yeoman of the household 1506 (Longleat Misc. Ms. XII fo. 30); awarded £2 *p.a.* as keeper of the robes from the Glos. area by Mich. 1519 (*ibid.*, m. 2).

Thomas Moscroff *: awarded £10 *p.a.* from Amersham, Bucks., as an exhibitioner at Oxford in June 1519 (S.C.6/Hen. VIII 5841 m. 5).

Sir Edward Neville: brother of George, Lord Bergavenny: awarded £5 *p.a.* from the receivership of Kent & Surrey, above a similar salary as chief steward there from 1519.

William Norris: awarded £2 *p.a.* from the receivership of Kent & Surrey by Mich. 1520 (S.C.6/Hen. VIII 5795 m. 3).

Mistress Philipps: an embroideress 1517/8 (Longleat Misc. Ms. XIII); shared an annuity of 10 marks *p.a.* from Writtle, Essex, with John Haslewood.

John Pierson: awarded 5 marks *p.a.* from Burton, Bucks., as an Oxford scholar in Oct. 1518 (S.C.6/Hen. VIII 5841 m. 5).

Thomas Rowse: the Duke's barber; awarded 17s.4d. *p.a.* from the Glos. area by Mich. 1519 (S.C.6/Hen. VIII 5819 m. 4v).

Ambrose Skelton: gentleman of the chamber 1506 (Longleat Misc. Ms. XII fo. 30); awarded 10 marks *p.a.*, above a salary of £4.11s.0d. *p.a.* as parker of Bletchingley, Surrey, from 1512 (Harleian Ms. 1667 m. 11v).

Richard Stubbes: awarded 5 marks *p.a.* from Pollicott, Bucks., as an Oxford scholar by Mich. 1520 (S.C.6/Hen. VIII 5841 m. 5).

Robert Walhead: awarded 60s.11d. *p.a.* 'for kepyng Crawld'; post unidentified – probably a parker.

Robert Whiteoak: awarded £2 *p.a.* as keeper of the woods at Bedminster, Som.

Sir Thomas Woodhouse: steward of Norfolk; awarded £20 *p.a.* from Norfolk in May 1516 (S.C.6/Hen. VIII 5841 m. 4v).

Thomas Wrottesley: Garter King of Arms; awarded £4 *p.a.* from Burton, Bucks., by Mich. 1519 (*ibid.*, m. 5).

(b) *Other Annuities Awarded by Duke Edward between 1500 and 1521.*

William Bedell: one of Buckingham's esquires; awarded 5 marks *p.a.* from Tyseo, Warwicks., in Feb. 1504 (S.C.6/Hen. VII 868 m. 3v).

Robert Brook: master of the henchmen; awarded 5 marks *p.a.* direct from the coffers as an exhibitioner at Oxford by Mich. 1520 (E.36/220 fo. 10v).

Humphrey Conningsby *: a lawyer, awarded £2 *p.a.* from Little Brickhill, Bucks., in June 1500 (S.C.6/Hen. VII 1476 m. 2).

Elizabeth Deton: probably a lady-in-waiting; her annuity of 5 marks, awarded from the receivership of Kent & Surrey, was unpaid in 1502/3 (D.641/1/2/235 m. 1).

Thomas Frowyck *: a lawyer; awarded £2 *p.a.* from the receivership of Kent & Surrey by Mich. 1502 (*ibid.*).

Margaret Gedding: nurse to Buckingham's children and lady-in-waiting to the Duchess Eleanor until her dismissal in *ca.* 1520 (E.101/518/5 pt i. m. 1; Cottonian Ms. Titus B1 fo. 174); awarded 10 marks *p.a.* from the receivership of Kent & Surrey by Mich. 1502 (*ibid.*).

Robert Gilbert *: awarded £5 *p.a.* from Little Brickhill, Bucks., as ' scholar and chaplain ' in Dec. 1500 (S.C.6/Hen. VII 1476 m. 2).

Thomas Gower: bailiff of Kinwardstone Hundred, Wilts., 1520; awarded £10 *p.a.* from that area by Mich. 1520 (S.C.6/Hen. VIII 5819 mm. iv, 5).

William Greville *: a lawyer; awarded £2 *p.a.* from Tyseo, Warwicks., in Sept. 1504 (S.C.6/Hen. VII 868 m. 3v).

John Gunter *: awarded £5 *p.a.* from the receivership of Kent & Surrey by Mich. 1505 (S.C.6/Hen. VII 1076 m. 15).

Humphrey Hervey *: a lawyer; awarded £2 *p.a.* from Glos. by Mich. 1503 (D.641/1/2/204 m. 1).

Thomas Leukenor: Kentish landowner; awarded £5 *p.a.* from the receivership of Kent & Surrey by Mich. 1502 (D.641/1/2/235 m. 1).

Thomas Matston *: a lawyer; awarded £2 *p.a.* from the Glos. area in Dec. 1517 (S.C.6/Hen. VIII 5819 m. 4v).

The Priors of Tonbridge: awarded £9.4s.9½d. *p.a.* according to a long-standing grant of alms from the receivership of Kent & Surrey confirmed by Mich. 1502 (D.641/1/2/235 m. 1).

Robert Turberville *: awarded 5 marks *p.a.* from the central circuit before Apr. 1509 & still being paid in 1521 (S.C.6/Hen. VIII 5841 m. 5).

Baldwin Tynby: clerk of the signet; awarded £2 *p.a.* from the Glos. area by Mich. 1520 (S.C.6/Hen. VIII 5819 m. 4v).

William Wroughton: awarded 5 marks *p.a.* from Thornbury, Glos., in return for past & future services in Apr. 1502, but no longer being paid by Mich. 1519 (S.C.6/Hen. VII 1075 m. 12v; Hen. VIII 5819 mm. 4v–5).

Appendix E

CASES BROUGHT BY EDWARD, DUKE OF BUCKINGHAM, AND OFFICIALS ACTING ON HIS BEHALF IN THE COURTS OF THE KING'S BENCH AND THE COMMON PLEAS BETWEEN MICHAELMAS 1498 AND EASTER 1521

PART I

THE COURT OF THE KING'S BENCH

(All references are to King's Bench rolls, class K.B.27 in the Public Record Office.)

1498   Gregory Cheneley, John Alyston, James Stryicheley (trespass), Essex (949, Mich. 14 Hen. VII, rot. 14v).

1501   Richard Robyns (trespass), Glos. (958, Hilary 16 Hen. VII, rot. 1v).

1501   Thomas Eylond, Robert Cotell, Thomas Roos (trespass), Notts. (960, Trinity 16 Hen. VII, rot. 14).

1501   Thomas Sevenoak, James Outryde (trespass), Kent (*ibid.*, rot. 56).

1505   Reginald Pecham, Henry Fane, John Malle (trespass), Kent (975, Easter 20 Hen. VII, rot. 18).

1505   Thomas Fane & Paul Eden (trespass), Kent (*ibid.*).

1506   Edward Legh, Richard & William Bavell, Nicholas Basset, Richard Dean, John Granger (trespass), Kent (980, Trinity 21 Hen. VII, rot. 10v).

1507   Sir Thomas Blount (abducting a ward), Salop. (985, Mich. 23 Hen. VII, rot. 44).

1507   Wistann Broun (abducting a ward), Essex (*ibid.*, rot. 53).

1507   Thomas Fane (two separate cases of trespass), Kent (*ibid.*, rot. 50).

1508   Henry Fane (trespass), Kent (989, Mich. 24 Hen. VII, rot. 52v).

1509   John Broket (abducting a ward), Essex (993, Mich. 1 Hen. VIII, rot. 90v).

1510   Thomas Lucas (fraud), Norfolk (996, Trinity 2 Hen. VIII, rot. 63-3v).

1514   John Richard & Alfred Palley (trespass), Kent (1010, Hilary 5 Hen. VIII, rot. 3).

PART II

THE COURT OF COMMON PLEAS

(All references are to Common Plea rolls, class C.P.40 in the Public Record Office.) Cases which reached a successful conclusion are marked *.

Suits for debt against:

1503	Edmund Vaux (100 marks on a bond), Surrey (965, Trinity 18 Hen. VII, rot. 100v; 968, Easter 19 Hen. VII, rot. 150).
1505	William Welham, Robert Sparowe (£8 jointly), Surrey (972, Easter 20 Hen. VII, rot. 94v; 973, Trinity 20 Hen. VII, rot. 61).*
1505	John Dance (£9), Glos. (974, Mich. 21 Hen. VII, rot. 238v).
1506	Richard Leukenor (64s.), Kent (975, Hilary 21 Hen. VII, rot. 193v).
1506	Thomas Wyther, chaplain of the College of Plesshey (£21), London (977, Trinity 21 Hen. VII, rot. 14v).
1507	Thomas Smart (£30 on a bond), London (980, Easter 22 Hen. VII, rot. 184v; 984, Easter 23 Hen. VII, rot. 355v).
1508	Christopher Throkmorton, Anthony Poyntz, Anthony Bradshaw (£40 each), London (983, Hilary 23 Hen. VII, rot. 44v).
1508	Gilbert Comyn (£60), London (984, Easter 23 Hen. VII, rot. 373).
1508	Nicholas Burstow (£40), Surrey (*ibid.*, rot. 86).
1508	Sir Nicholas Vaus, George Boyvyll (£40 each, on a bond), London (985, Trinity 23 Hen. VII, rot. 37; 986, Mich. 24 Hen. VII, rot. 680).
1510	Sir William Sandys (500 marks on a bond), London (990, Hilary 1 Hen. VIII, rot. 455v; 993, Mich. 2 Hen. VIII, rot. 551).
1510	Roger Lyngham, Thomas Clogh, Hugh Meredyth, John Lawrence, Roger ap John (£40 each), London (992, Trinity 2 Hen. VIII, rot. 95v).
1510	Richard Cornwall, Giles Strangeways, John Dansey (£40 each), London (*ibid.*, rot. 466).
1510	William Herbert (£100 on a bond), London (*ibid.*, rot. 87; 994, Hilary 2 Hen. VIII, rot. 349v).
1512	Thomas Matlar (£86.11s.1d.), London (999, Easter 4 Hen. VIII, rot. 464v).
1512	Christopher Baynam (two actions for £30.11s.4½d. & £28.13s.2d.), Glos. (1001, Mich. 4 Hen. VIII, rot. 710).
1512	Thomas [–] (£46.11s.), London (*ibid.*, rot. 23).
1512	John Blount (£20), London (*ibid.*, rot. 71).
1512	Alice Cornwall & John Barnes, the executors of Robert Cornwall (£8.10s.10d.), Suffolk (*ibid.*, rot. 250).
1512	Richard Fane (£100), London (*ibid.*, rot. 71).
1513	Thomas Barchard (49s.4d.), John Roche (40s.), Yorks. (1002, Hilary 4 Hen. VIII, rot. 269v).

1513   Thomas Tyvett, John ap Morgan, John Hardynge (£100 each as sureties for Thomas ap Owen (*q.v.*), bailiff of Little Brickhill, Bucks.), Bucks. (1005, Mich. 5 Hen. VIII, rot. 73).

1514   Henry & John Smith (£7.10s. each), Yorks. (1005B, Hilary 5 Hen. VIII, rot. 201v).

1514   Sir Edward Darrell (500 marks on a bond), Glos. (*ibid.*, rot. 221; 1007, Trinity 6 Hen. VIII, rot. 353; 1008, Mich. 6 Hen. VIII, rot. 450–450b).

1515   James Strangeways (£200), Yorks. (1010, Easter 7 Hen. VIII, rot. 33).

1515   Fulk Walwyn (no sum given), Herefs. (1011, Trinity 7 Hen. VIII, rot. 181).

1517   William Herbert, Howell Gunter, John ap Howell (£100 each), Glos. (1017, Hilary 8 Hen. VIII, rot. 492).

1518   The Abbot of Llanthony, Thomas ap Roberts, George Lewes (£100 each on bonds), Glos. (1021B, Trinity 10 Hen. VIII, rot. 586; 1023, Hilary 10 Hen. VIII, rot. 306v).

1518   Thomas Gamage, Howell Carne, John & Howell Kemys (£100 each), Glos. (1021B, Trinity 10 Hen. VIII, rot. 624v).

1518   James Baskerville (£40 on a bond as surety for Jankyn ap Thomas Havard (*q.v.*), constable of Brecon), Glos. (*ibid.*, rot. 625).

1518   James Bromwych (same), Glos. (*ibid.*, rot. 625v).

1518   Jankyn ap Hopkyn (£20, same), Glos. (*ibid.*, rot. 586v).

1518   Thomas ap William (same), Glos. (*ibid.*, rot. 625v).

1518   John Walwyn (£40, same), Glos. (*ibid.*, rot. 586v).

1518   Thomas Gylle, Richard Fletcher (£5 each), Essex (1022, Mich. 10 Hen. VIII, rot. 311v).

1519   William Baskerville, Thomas Blount (£50 each), Glos. (1023, Hilary 10 Hen. VIII, rot. 177).

1521   Humphrey Fowke (£100 on a bond), Glos. (1031, Hilary 12 Hen. VIII, rot. 419).

1521   William Leighton (£100), Glos. (*ibid.*, rot. 249).

Suits for Trespass in the Duke's Parks and Closes against:

1501   Thomas Humphrey; Tyseo, Warwicks. (956, Easter 16 Hen. VII, rot. 167).

1503   Richard Stephen; Amersham, Bucks. (963, Hilary 18 Hen. VII, rot. 298).

1503   John Reynold; Haverhill, Suffolk (*ibid.*).

1503   Walter Apilthorp, John Chaweler; Gazeley, Suffolk (*ibid.*, rot. 384v).

1506   Henry Fane (receiver of Kent & Surrey), Paul Eden; Tonbridge, Kent (976, Easter 21 Hen. VII, rot. 60).

1507   Nicholas Burstow; Bletchingley, Surrey (982, Mich. 23 Hen. VII, rot. 724).

1507   Sir John Constable, Thomas Missenden, Thomas Rowlyns, Thomas Smith, Ralph de la Stable; Brustwick, Holderness (*ibid.*, rot. 671).

1507   William Cotton; Gazeley, Suffolk (*ibid.*, rot. 653).

1507   Thomas Ealing; Bletchingley, Surrey (*ibid.*, rot. 724).

1507   George Newborough, Edward Wattes; Penshurst, Kent (*ibid.*, rot. 200v).

1507   William & Simon Reigate, William Affene, John Erwell; Bletchingley, Surrey (*ibid.*, rot. 724).

1507   Thomas Smith; Brustwick, Holderness (*ibid.*, rot. 671).

1508   Thomas Gylmyn; Bletchingley, Surrey (983, Hilary 23 Hen. VII, rot. 250).

1508   Lewis Bagot; Stafford (984, Easter, 23 Hen. VII, rot. 296).

1509   Thomas Fane; Penshurst, Kent (989, Mich. 1 Hen. VIII, rot. 556).

1509   Thomas Fane; Tonbridge, Kent (*ibid.*, rot. 620).

1509   Thomas Fane, Paul Eden; Penshurst, Kent (*ibid.*, rot. 556).

1509   Edward Legh, Richard & William Bavell, Nicholas Basset, Richard Dean, John Granger; Brastead, Surrey (*ibid.*, rot. 61).

1509   Reginald Pecham, Henry Fane, John Malle; Tonbridge, Kent (*ibid.*, rot. 620).

1511   Thomas Eyes; Haresfield, Glos. (995, Easter 3 Hen. VIII, rot. 397v).

1514   Thomas Lattar; Tonbridge, Kent (1005B, Hilary 5 Hen. VIII, rot. 33v).

1514   Thomas Webb, snr., Thomas Webb, jr., Robert Webb, Robert Kent; Disining, Suffolk (1006, Easter 6 Hen. VIII, rot. 489v).

1514   John Harvy; the same (*ibid.*).

1514   John Eyes, John Nasshe, Richard Wyman; Haresfield, Glos. (1007, Trinity 6 Hen. VIII, rot. 552).

1514   John Pauncefoot; the same (*ibid.*).

1514   John Tyherst, Thomas Childryn, John Mills, John & Thomas Hasden, Thomas Kent; Hadlow, Kent (*ibid.*, rot. 66v).

1516   Richard Somer, John Sedger, Thomas Joyner; Northleigh, Kent (1015, Trinity 8 Hen. VIII, rot. 600v).

1516   William & Henry Game, John & William Swayne, Henry Francys; Kempston, Beds. (*ibid.*, rot. 459).

1519   John Huntley; Haresfield, Glos. (1023, Hilary 10 Hen. VIII, rot. 249).

Suits for theft against:

1501   Richard Robyns, John George, John Gasard (sheep stealing), Glos. (955, Hilary 16 Hen. VII, rot. 195).

1501   John Fowler, Henry Ball (same), Hunts. (957, Trinity 16 Hen. VII, rot. 30).

1501   Thomas Callys (theft of crops), Northants (*ibid.*, rot. 250).

1502   Robert Mitton (theft of timber), Rutland (962, Mich. 18 Hen. VII, rot. 175).

1503   Robert Poyser, John Briggeshill (same), Surrey (966, Mich. 19 Hen. VII, rot. 356).

1505   Henry Fane (theft of goods & chattels), Kent (972, Easter 20 Hen. VII, rot. 91v).

1506   Richard Horne, William Walter (theft of timber), Kent (977, Trinity 21 Hen. VII, rot. 40v).

1507   John Corbet, Thomas Knight, Richard Mitton, Thomas Screvyn, Roger Glasse (theft of crops), Salop. (981, Trinity 22 Hen. VII, rot. 561v).

1507   Robert ap David Lloyd, William Leighton, William & Richard Mitton, William & Richard Corbet, Richard Lynghyn, Reginald ap David, Griffith Blotyk, Richard Wythesade, Thomas Kynaston (sheep stealing), Salop. (*ibid.*, rot. 61).

1507   John Hows (sheep stealing), Essex (982, Mich. 23 Hen. VII, rot. 643).

1507   Richard Elf, William Tranter (stealing crops), Glos. (*ibid.*, rot. 351v).

1507   Robert Cotton (stealing crops), Essex (*ibid.*, rot. 641–3v).

1507   Robert Cotton, William Basset (stealing crops), Essex (*ibid.*, rot. 641).

1507   John Pecok, William Harwell (sheep stealing), Essex (*ibid.*, rot. 643).

1510   Roger Legh, John Basyngden, William Pilkington, Thomas Darcy (stealing timber), Surrey (991, Easter 2 Hen. VIII, rot. 69v).

1512   Roland Gravenor (stealing crops), Salop. (1001, Mich. 4 Hen. VIII, rot. 212).

1516   William Dee, Richard Vampage, Laurence Wolle (theft of goods & chattels), Glos. (1015, Trinity 8 Hen. VIII, rot. 491).

1517   John Cockes (same), Surrey (1019, Trinity 9 Hen. VIII, rot. 575).

1519   William Lessyn (stealing a horse), Hunts. (1025, Mich. 11 Hen. VIII, rot. 693).

Suits against Household and Estate Staff:

1501   Thomas Holand, Henry Grafton, David ap Rees, Miles Clark, William Morys (failure to render accounts: offices unspecified), Herefs. (955, Hilary 16 Hen. VII, rot. 354).

1501   Richard Boteler (failure to account as bailiff of Wootton Wawen), Warwicks. (958, Mich. 17 Hen. VII, rot. 285).

1502   William Dalby (same, as bailiff of Fobbing), Essex (960, Easter 17 Hen. VII, rot. 170).

1505   Henry Fane (£20.7s.1d. arrears as receiver of Kent & Surrey), Kent (972, Easter 20 Hen. VII, rot. 91v; 995, Easter 3 Hen. VIII, rot. 349v).

1505   John Hyll (failure to account as reeve of Newenham), Glos. (974, Mich. 21 Hen. VII, rot. 238v).

1506   Richard Egerton, clerk (£115 received on Buckingham's behalf), Glos. (975, Hilary 21 Hen. VII, rot. 447; 978, Mich. 22 Hen. VII, rot. 347).*

1506   Richard Ryvers (failure to account, probably as bailiff of Penshurst), Kent (975, Hilary 21 Hen. VII, rot. 220).

1506   William Sharpe (failure to account, probably as feodary of the Honour of Glos. in Beds.), London (*ibid.*, rot. 42).

1506   John Moryce (£28.10s. arrears as feodary of the Honour of Glos. in Northants.), Northants. (976, Easter 21 Hen. VII, rot. 390; 979, Hilary 22 Hen. VII, rot. 350v).*

1506   Eusebius Catesby (failure to account, probably as one of the Duke's bailiffs in Northants.), Glos. (978, Mich. 22 Hen. VII, rot. 633v).

1507-8 Richard Mynors (eight separate actions for a total of £1,561.18s.9½d. arrears as treasurer), various counties (980, Easter 22 Hen. VII, rot. 185v; 984, Easter 23 Hen. VII, rot. 451; 986, Mich. 24 Hen. VII, rot. 6, 342, 344v, 557, 560v; 988A, Easter 1 Hen. VIII, rot. 91; 989, Mich. 1 Hen. VIII, rot. 447).

1511   Humphrey Bannaster (£38.7s.4d. arrears as treasurer), Kent (994, Hilary 2 Hen. VIII, rot. 499).

1511   Robert Turberville (£21.17s.4¾d. arrears as receiver general), London (*ibid.*, rot. 16).*

1512   Giles Greville (failure to account, probably as treasurer), Glos. (999 Easter, 4 Hen. VIII, rot. 36v).

1512   Robert Whitgreve (£12.4s. arrears, probably as receiver of Staffs.), Staffs. (1001, Mich. 4 Hen. VIII, rot. 357).

1513   Hugh Hankyn, executor of Ralph Cholmeley, bailiff of Macclesfield, Cheshire (D.641/1/2/84 mm. 8-8v) (arrears of £34.7s.7d.), Staffs. (1002, Hilary 4 Hen. VIII, rot. 266).

1513   Thomas ap Owen (failure to account as bailiff of Little Brickhill), Bucks. (1003, Easter 5 Hen. VIII, rot. 52v).

1513   Henry Spencer (failure to account as bailiff of Hackleton & Peddington), Northants. (*ibid.* rot. 19v).

1513   Richard Archer (same), Northants. (*ibid.*).

1513   John Harcourt (two actions for arrears of £39.4s.4d. & £24.3s.4d., probably as receiver of Staffs.), Staffs. (*ibid.*, rot. 165v).

1513   Thomas ap Owen (£60, probably on a bond entered as bailiff of Little Brickhill), Bucks. (1005 Mich. 5 Hen. VIII, rot. 73).

1514   Nicholas Walwyn (£60 on a bond entered as receiver of the S.W. estates), London (1005B, Hilary 5 Hen. VIII, rot. 346v).*

1514   John Buttys (200 marks on a bond entered as auditor), Norfolk (1007, Trinity 6 Hen. VIII, rot. 466).

1515   John Seintgeorge (failure to perform his duties as auditor), Glos. (1012, Mich. 7 Hen. VIII, rot. 262; 1013, Hilary 7 Hen. VIII, rot. 354).

1515   Edward Edgar (same), London (1012, Mich. 7 Hen. VIII, rot. 588).

1516   Henry Bullock (wardrober), Thomas Wotton (master of the works), George Poley (jeweller), Thomas Bridges (wardrober) (100 marks each on bonds), Glos. (1016, Mich. 7 Hen. VIII, rot. 588).

1518   Jankyn ap Thomas Havard (six actions for a total of £200 on bonds entered as constable of Brecon), Glos. (1021B, Trinity 10 Hen. VIII, rot. 625-625v, 586v).

1518   Thomas Cade (£1,200 on a bond entered as receiver general), Glos. (*ibid.*, rot. 625; 1024, Easter 11 Hen. VIII, rot. 308v).

1518   Thomas Predyth (100 marks on a bond entered as bailiff of Little Brickhill, Bucks.), Glos. (1021B, Trinity 10 Hen. VIII, rot. 612).

1519   John Pickering (£1,200 on a bond entered as receiver general), London (1026, Mich. 11 Hen. VIII, rot. 97; 1027 Hilary 11 Hen. VIII, rot. 412v).

1519   Baldwin Tynby (theft of goods worth £20, probably as clerk of the signet), Glos. (1026, Mich. 11 Hen. VIII, rot. 490v).

Suits concerning Damage to Property and Infringement of Buckingham's Rights by:

1499   Matilda Staunton (abducting a ward), Northants. (947, Hilary 14 Henry VII, rot. 244).

1501   William Brigge (failure to effect repairs at Haverhill), Suffolk (956, Easter 16 Hen. VII, rot. 5).

1501   Gilbert Ipsewell (damage to woods at Little Brickhill), Bucks. (957, Trinity 16 Hen. VII, rot. 145).

1506   Abbot of St Peter's Westminster (abducting a ward), Kent (975, Hilary 21 Hen. VII, rot. 356).*

1508   John Sherman (marrying a villein from Thornbury without permission), Glos. (983, Hilary 23 Hen. VII, rot. 282).

1508   William Chamber (same), Glos. (984, Easter 23 Hen. VII, rot. 389).

1511   Richard Humphrey (evading marriage obligations), Glos. (995, Easter 3 Hen. VIII, rot. 397).

1514   William Holand (obstructing a water course at Thornbury), Glos. (1006, Easter 6 Hen. VIII, rot. 459).

1514   John Cambridge (marrying a villein from Thornbury without permission), Glos. (1008, Mich. 6 Hen. VIII, rot. 6v).

1516   William Keddy (same), Glos. (1014, Easter 8 Hen. VIII, rot. 218).

1520   Sir Thomas Berkley & his wife (abducting a ward), Glos. (1029, Trinity 12 Hen. VIII, rot. 650v).

Other cases against:

1512   Sir Thomas Lucas (slander), Suffolk (1001, Mich. 4 Hen. VIII, rot. 659).*

1512   Sir Amyas Paulet (fraud), Som. (*ibid.*, rot. 206).

1514   The Abbey & Convent of the Blessed Mary of Combe (ownership of land in Naseby, Northants.) (1008, Mich. 6 Hen VIII, rot. 23).

Debts claimed by the Duke's Senior Ministers, either on his Behalf or in an Official Capacity, from:

1502   William Cole (£77.12s.5d.), Glos. (959, Hilary 17 Hen. VII, rot. 347v).

1502   William Creik (£16 on a bond), Surrey (962, Mich. 18 Hen. VII, rot. 348v).

1502   Robert Broke, salter (£20 on a bond), Surrey (*ibid.*, rot. 446v).

1505   John & Richard Symkynson (£6 jointly), Surrey (973, Trinity 20 Hen. VII, rot. 55).

1505   Thomas Agard (10 marks), Surrey (*ibid.*, rot. 62).

1505   William Betson (£5 on a bond), Glos. (974, Mich. 21 Hen. VII, rot. 352v).

1505   Richard Dyke (same), Glos. (*ibid.*, rot. 152v).

1505   Walter Fowke (£10), Kent (*ibid.*, rot. 75v).

1505   Thomas & Richard Butler (£28), Surrey (*ibid.*, rot. 537).

1505   Thomas & Richard Cornwall, Christopher Throckmorton (£40 each on bonds), Surrey (*ibid.*, rot. 584).

1505   Thomas Hardgery (£8), Surrey (*ibid.*, rot. 537).

1506   William Angewyn (10 marks), London (976, Easter 21 Hen. VII, rot. 148v).

1506   John Alyn (same), London (*ibid.*, rot. 447v).

1506   Roger, Thomas & Robert Jeffreyson (£100 jointly on a bond), London (977, Trinity 21 Hen. VII, rot. 14v).

1506   John Huntley (50 marks, perhaps owed as receiver of Newport), London (*ibid.*, rot. 479v).

1506   Edmund Pesshey (100 marks), London (978, Mich. 22 Hen. VII, rot. 578).

1506   John Chokke (20 marks), London (*ibid.*, rot. 567).

1507   Francis Forster (£100), London (979, Hilary 22 Hen. VII, rot. 16v).

1507   William Gallone, Robert Billope, John Neuton, John Martyn, Thomas Baker (£40 jointly on a bond), Yorks. (*ibid.*, rot. 487v).

1507   William Pakker, John Edward, William Maudesley, Edmund Pers (40s. each), Essex (*ibid.*, rot. 550).

1507   John Gregory (£40), London (980, Easter 22 Hen. VII, rot. 185).

1507   Thomas Clogh, Hugh Meredyth, Roger ap John, Roger Lyngham, John Lawrence (200 marks each), London (981, Trinity 22 Hen. VII, rot. 31v).

1507   George Whynbergh (£6.11s. as executor of William Lambkin, sub-receiver of Norfolk), London (*ibid.*, rot. 31v).

1507   John Hulle, Thomas Kynge (£10 each), London (982, Mich. 23 Hen. VII, rot. 6v).

1508	John Griffyn, Richard Graunte (£12 each), London (984, Easter 23 Hen. VII, rot. 377).
1508	William Henson, William Mosse, Robert Parmyter (£40 each), London (*ibid.*, rot. 373v).
1509	Robert Boughey, Robert Mascy, Thomas Robyns (receiver of Staffs.) (£300 each), Surrey (988B, Trinity 1 Hen. VIII, rot. 199v).
1509	John & Thomas Dobbys, Robert Baynbrygge, William Croskeyll (£100 each), Surrey (*ibid.*).
1509	Roger & Alice Cowper, John Smert, Robert Belle (£20 each), Surrey (*ibid.*).
1509	Roland Bridges (receiver of Brecon), James Scudamore, James Bridges, John Dansey (£50 each), Surrey (*ibid.*).
1510	John ap William Hopkyn, Henry Myle, Robert Hargast, John Dansey, Thomas Wynston (40 marks each), London (991, Easter 2 Hen. VIII, rot. 95).
1510	Thomas Bryan (£10), London (993, Mich. 2 Hen. VIII, rot. 689).
1511	John Vaughan, John Waldboeuf (receiver of Brecon) (£40 each), London (994, Hilary 2 Hen. VIII, rot. 16).
1512	John Wood (£160 on a bond), London (1001, Mich. 4 Hen. VIII, rot. 66ov).
1512	John Sewall, John Wood, John Clement (same on bonds for the farm of Writtle manor), London (*ibid.*, rot. 81, 451v).
1512	Richard Lane, James Newell (receiver of Staffs.), William Chetwyn (40 marks each), London (*ibid.*, rot. 81v).
1512	The same (50 marks each), London (*ibid.*, rot. 488).
1512	John Clement (£160 on a bond), London (*ibid.*, rot. 543v).
1514	John Brown (£100 on a bond entered as deputy to the sub-receiver of Norfolk), London (1005B, Hilary 5 Hen. VIII, rot. 148v).
1514	Roger Porter (20 marks), Glos. (1007, Trinity 6 Hen. VIII, rot. 222v).
1518	Thomas Bussher, Robert Jordan, John Hystoke, Thomas Coterell (£40 each), Glos. (1021B, Trinity 10 Hen. VIII, rot. 586).
1520	Robert Mosse (£40), Kent (1030, Mich. 12 Hen. VIII, rot. 99).
1520	John and Robert Parmyter, William Hynson, Robert Mosse (£40 each), Kent (*ibid.*).

MANUSCRIPT SOURCES

(1) THE PUBLIC RECORD OFFICE

Manuscripts from the following classes of documents have been cited in the text

C.1	Early Chancery Proceedings, Series I.
C.47	Chancery Miscellanea.
C.66	Patent Rolls.
C.115	Duchess of Norfolk Deeds: Llanthony Cartulary.
C.135	Inquisitions Post Mortem, Edward III.
C.139	Inquisitions Post Mortem, Henry VI.
Chester 29	Palatinate of Chester, Plea Rolls.
C.P.40	Common Pleas, *Placito de Banco* Rolls.
D.L.41	Duchy of Lancaster Miscellanea.
E.13	Exchequer of Pleas, Plea Rolls.
E.28	Council and Privy Seal Records.
E.36	Exchequer (Treasury of Receipt) Miscellaneous.
E.101	Exchequer (King's Remembrancer) Accounts, various.
E.356	Customs Accounts, Edward I to Elizabeth I.
E.359	Accounts of Subsidies and Aids.
E.368	Memoranda Rolls (Lord Treasurers' Remembrancer).
E.404	Exchequer of Receipts, Warrants for Issue.
K.B.8	King's Bench, *Baga de Secretis*.
K.B.27	King's Bench, *Coram Rege* Rolls.
L.R.12	Exchequer (Land Revenue) Receivers' Accounts, Series III.
S.C.6	Ministers' and Receivers' Accounts.
S.C.8.	Ancient Petitions.
S.C.11	Rentals and Surveys (general Series) Rolls.
S.P.1	State Papers.
STA CHA 2	Star Chamber Proceedings, Henry VIII.

(2) THE BRITISH LIBRARY

Additional Charters and Rolls	19858, 22644–5, 26874.
Additional Mss.	19398, 26873, 29608, 34213, 36542, 40859B, 42066B.
Arundel Ms.	318.

Manuscript Sources

Cottonian Mss.	Galba B III, Titus BI.
Egerton Rolls	200, 2192–3, 2195–8, 2200, 2203, 2206–9.
Harleian Mss.	283, 433, 4181.
Bibl. Harl.	1667.
Royal Mss.	14B XXXV A–F; 7F XIV.
Stowe Ms.	795.

(3) OTHER REPOSITORIES

(a) *Arundel Castle* (Mss. in the Custody of the late Duke of Norfolk)
Ms. A 1245.

(b) *Cardiff Public Library*
Ms. Brecon DD 20.

(c) *Corporation of London Record Office*
Husting Book 11 (1506–37); Repertory of the Court of Aldermen, vol. V.

(d) *Glamorgan County Record Office*
Ms. D/DCM/45.

(e) *Longleat House* (Mss. in the Custody of the Marquess of Bath)
Mss. 345, 455, 457, 639, 3701, 3847, 3988–90, 4010, 6410, 6415.
Misc. Mss. XII, XIII.

(f) *Magdalene College, Cambridge*
The Old Book of Magdalene College.

(g) *Monmouth County Record Office*
Ms. MAN/B/90/004.

(h) *National Library of Wales*
Peniarth Mss. 280 (the Redd Booke of Caures Castle), 354C.
Tredegar Park Ms. 147.

(i) *Northamptonshire County Record Office*
Ms. SS 4254.

(j) *Staffordshire County Record Office*
Lord Stafford's Mss., class no. D. 641; Lord Bagot's Mss. D.1721/1/1, 5, 6, 11 (volumes of Mss. relating to the Stafford estates).

(k) *Westminster Abbey*
Muniments: 4532, 4538, 4542, 4555, 5470, 12187, 15195, 22909, 32348–9.

PRINTED SOURCES

(1) CALENDARS, CATALOGUES AND TEXTS OF OFFICIAL RECORDS

Calendar of Charter Rolls (6 vols., H.M.S.O., 1903–27).

Calendar of Close Rolls (61 vols., H.M.S.O., 1892–1963).

Calendar of Entries in the Papal Registers Relating to Great Britain and Ireland (14 vols., H.M.S.O., 1894–1961).

Calendar of Fine Rolls (22 vols., H.M.S.O., 1911–63).

Calendar of Patent Rolls (54 vols., H.M.S.O., 1891–1916).

The Domesday Book, ed. A. Farley (2 vols., R.C., 1783).

Feet of Fines for Essex (4 vols., Colchester, 1899–1964).

Foedera, Conventiones, Litterae et cuiuscunque Generis Acta Publica, ed. T. Rymer (20 vols., The Hague, 1704–35).

Grants from the Crown during the Reign of Edward V, ed. J. G. Nichols (C.S., 1st series vol. LX, 1854).

Historical Manuscripts Commission, *Fourth Report* (H.M.S.O., 1874).

—— *Sixth Report* (H.M.S.O., 1877–8).

—— *Seventh Report* (H.M.S.O., 1879).

—— *Report of the Hastings Mss.* (4 vols., H.M.S.O., 1928–47).

The Household of Edward IV, The Black Book and the Ordinances of 1478, ed. A. R. Myers (Manchester, 1959).

Issues of the Exchequer, ed. J. Devon (R.C., 1847).

Letters and Papers, Foreign and Domestic, of the Reign of Henry VIII, ed. J. S. Brewer (vols. I–IV, H.M.S.O., 1864–1920).

Letters and Papers Illustrative of the Reigns of Richard III and Henry VII, ed. J. S. Gairdner (2 vols., R.S., 1861–3).

Letters and Papers Illustrative of the Wars of the English in France during the Reign of King Henry VI, ed. J. Stevenson (2 vols., R.S., 1861–4).

Letters, Despatches and State Papers relating to the Negotiations between England and Spain (vols. I, II and Supplement, ed. G. A. Bergenroth, H.M.S.O., 1862–8).

Materials for a History of the Reign of Henry VII, ed. W. W. Campbell (2 vols., R.S., 1873–7).

Proceedings and Ordinances of the Privy Council, ed. N. H. Nicholas (7 vols., R.C., 1843–7).

Procès de Condamnation et de Réhabilitation de Jeanne d'Arc, ed. J. Quicherat (5 vols., Paris, 1841–9).

Reports d'Ascuns Cases qui Ont Evenues au Temps du Roy Henry VII et du Roy Henry VIII, ed. R. Keilway (London, 1688).

Les Reports des Cases en les Ans des Roys Edward V, Richard III, Henrie VII et Henri VIII (London, 1679).

Les Reports des Divers Selects Matters et Resolutions des Reverend Judges et Sages del Ley, ed. J. Dyer (London, 1678).

Return of Members of Parliament, England 1213–1702 (London, 1878).

Rotuli Parliamentorum, ed. J. Strachey & others (6 vols., London, 1767–77).

State Papers and Manuscripts relating to English Affairs, existing in the Archives and Collections of Venice (vols. I to III, ed. R. Brown, H.M.S.O., 1864–9).

Statutes of the Realm (large folio), ed. A. Luders & others (11 vols., R.C., 1810–28).

(2) CHRONICLES AND LITERARY SOURCES

A Collection of All the Wills now known to be Extant of all the Kings and Queens of England from William I to Henry VII, ed. J. Nichols (Society of Antiquaries, London, 1780).

Collections of a Citizen of London, ed. J. Gairdner (C.S., 2nd series vol. XVII, 1876).

Compota Domestica Familiarum de Buckingham et d'Angoulême, ed. W. B. D. D. Turnbull (Roxburghe Club, Edinburgh, 1836).

An English Chronicle, ed. J. S. Davies (C.S., 1st series vol. LXIV, 1856).

'Extracts from the Household Book of Edward, Duke of Buckingham, 1508–9', ed. J. Gage, *Archaeologia* XXV (1834).

Fortescue, Sir John, *De Laudibus Legum Angliae*, ed. S. B. Chrimes (Cambridge, 1942).

—— *The Governance of England*, ed. C. Plummer (Oxford, 1885).

Froissart, Jean, *Chroniques de Jean Froissart*, ed. S. Luce & others (14 vols., Société de l'Histoire de France, Paris, 1869–1966).

The Great Chronicle of London, ed. A. H. Thomas and I. D. Thornley (London, 1938).

Hall, Edward, *Edward Hall's Chronicle*, ed. H. Ellis (London, 1809).

Hardyng, John, *The Chronicle of John Hardyng . . . with the Continuation by R. Grafton*, ed. H. Ellis (London, 1812).

Henrici Quinti Angliae Regis Gesta, ed. B. Williams (London, 1850).

Higden, Ralph, *Polychronicon Ranulphi Higden*, ed. J. Lumby & C. Babington (9 vols., R.C., 1865–6).

Historiae Croylandensis Continuatio, ed. W. Fulman in *Rerum Anglicarum Scriptorum Veterum* (Oxford, 1684), vol. I.

Johnson, Richard, 'A Crowne Garland of Golden Roses', ed. W. Chappel in *Early English Poetry, Ballads and Popular Literature in the Middle Ages* (Percy Society, London, 1842).

Leland, John, *The Itinerary of John Leland*, ed. L. Toulmin Smith (5 vols., London, 1906–10).

Printed Sources

Macquereau, Robert, *Histoire Générale de L'Europe Depuis La Naissance de Charle-Quint Jusqu'au Cinq Juin MDXXVII* (Louvain, 1765).

Mancini, Dominic, *The Usurpation of Richard III*, ed. C. A. J. Armstrong (Oxford, 1969).

The Marcher Lordships of South Wales, 1415-1536, ed. T. B. Pugh (Cardiff, 1963).

More, Sir Thomas, *The History of Richard III*, ed. R. S. Sylvester in *The Complete Works of St Thomas More* (5 vols., Yale University Press, 1963–).

—— *The Workes of Sir Thomas More Knyght, sometyme Lorde Chauncellour of England, wrytten by him in the Englysh tonge*, ed. W. Rastell (London, 1557).

Old English Ballads, 1553-1625, ed. H. E. Rollins (Cambridge, 1920).

Original Letters Illustrative of English History, ed. H. Ellis (3rd series in 11 vols., London, 1824–46).

The Paston Letters, 1422-1509, ed. J. Gairdner (4 vols., London, 1900–1).

'*Registrum Annalium Collegii Mertonensis, 1483-1521* ', ed. H. E. Salter, *Oxford Historical Society*, LXXVI (1921).

Ross, John, *Historia Regum Angliae*, ed. T. Hearne (Oxford, 1745).

Six Town Chronicles of England, ed. R. Flenley (Oxford, 1911).

' Some Ancient Indictments in the King's Bench referring to Kent, 1450–1452 ', ed. R. Virgoe, *Kent Records*, vol. XVIII (1964).

The Stonor Letters and Papers, 1290-1483, ed. C. L. Kingsford (C.S., 3rd series vols. XXIX & XXX, 1919).

The Story of Helyas, Knight of the Swan, trans. R. Copland (Facsimile of the 1512 edition, published by the Grolier Club, New York, 1901).

Testamenta Vetusta, ed. N. H. Nicholas (2 vols., London, 1826).

Three Fifteenth Century Chronicles, ed. J. Gairdner (C.S., 2nd series vol. XXVIII, 1880).

Vergil, Polydore, *English History*, ed. H. Ellis (C.S., 1st series Vol. XXX, 1844).

—— *The Anglica Historia of Polydore Vergil*, ed. D. Hay (C.S., 3rd series vol. LXXIV, 1950).

Waurin, Jehan de, *Recueil des Croniques et Anchiennes Istories de la Grant Bretaigne, a Present Nomine Engleterre*, ed. W. Hardy (5 vols., R.S., 1864–91).

Worcester, William, *Itineraries*, ed. J. H. Harvey (Oxford, 1969).

(3) SECONDARY WORKS AND WORKS OF REFERENCE

Allmand, C. T., ' The Anglo-French Negotiations of 1439 ', *B.I.H.R.*, XL (1967).

Altschul, M., *A Baronial Family in Medieval England: The Clares 1217-1314* (Johns Hopkins University Press, 1965).

Printed Sources

Anglo, S., *A Historical Introduction to the Great Tournament Roll of Westminster* (Oxford, 1968).

Armstrong, C. A. J., 'Politics and the Battle of St. Albans', *B.I.H.R.*, XXXIII (1960).

Bacon, F., *The History of Henry VII*, in *The Works of Francis Bacon*, ed. J. Spedding & others (14 vols., London, 1857–74).

Batho, G. R., 'The Finances of an Elizabethan Nobleman; Henry Percy, Ninth Earl of Northumberland', *Econ. H.R.*, 2nd Series, IX (1956–7).

Baugh, A. C., 'Documenting Sir Thomas Malory', *Speculum*, VIII (1933).

Bean, J. M. W., *The Estates of the Percy Family* (Oxford, 1958).

Brodie, D. M., 'Edmund Dudley, Minister of Henry VII', *T.R.H.S.*, 4th series, XV (1932).

Bruce, J., 'The History of the Star Chamber', *Archaeologia*, XXVIII (1834).

Cockayne, G. E., *The Complete Peerage*, ed. V. Gibbs & others (12 vols., 1910–59).

Compton, R., *L'Authorite et Iurisdiction des Courts de la Maiestie de la Roygne* (London, 1594).

Compton Reeves, A., 'Some of Humphrey Stafford's Military Indentures', *Nottingham Medieval Studies*, XVI (1972).

Conway, A. E., 'The Maidstone Sector of Buckingham's Rebellion', *Archaeologia Cantiana*, XXXVII (1925).

Cooper, C. H., *Annals of Cambridge* (5 vols., Cambridge, 1842–1908).

Davies, R. R., 'Baronial Accounts, Incomes and Arrears in the Later Middle Ages', *Econ. H.R.*, XXI (1968).

Denholm-Young, N., *Seignorial Administration in England* (Oxford, 1937).

The Dictionary of National Biography.

Dodds, M. H., and Dodds, R., *The Pilgrimage of Grace 1536–1537 and the Exeter Conspiracy 1538* (2 vols., Cambridge, 1915).

Douglas-Simpson, W., 'Bastard Feudalism and the Later Castles', *Antiquaries Journal*, XXVI (1946).

Du Boulay, F. R. H., *The Lordship of Canterbury* (London, 1966).

Du Fresne Beaucourt, *Histoire de Charles VII* (6 vols., Paris, 1881–91).

Dugdale, W., *The Antiquities of Warwickshire* (2 vols., London, 1730).

—— *The Baronage of England* (2 vols., London, 1675).

Dunham, W. H., *Lord Hastings' Indentured Retainers, 1461–1483* (*Trans. of the Connecticut Academy of Arts and Sciences*, XXXIX (1955)).

—— 'Wolsey's Rule of the King's whole Council', *American History Review*, XLIX (1944).

Emden, A. B., ed., *A Biographical Register of the University of Cambridge* (Cambridge, 1963).

—— *A Biographical Register of the University of Oxford* (3 vols., Oxford, 1957–9).

Evans, H. T., *Wales and the Wars of the Roses* (Cambridge, 1920).

Field, P. J. C., 'Sir Thomas Malory, M.P.', *B.I.H.R.*, XLVII (1974).

Flenly, R., 'London and Foreign Merchants in the Reign of Henry VI', *E.H.R.*, XXV (1910).

Gage, J., *The History and Antiquities of Hengrave in Suffolk* (London, 1822).

—— *The History and Antiquities of Suffolk: Thingoe Hundred* (London, 1838).

Gairdner, J., *Richard III* (Cambridge, 1898).

Griffiths, R. A., 'Duke Richard of York's Intentions in 1450 and the Origins of the Wars of the Roses', *Journal of Medieval History*, I (1975).

Hanham, A., *Richard III and the Early Historians* (Oxford, 1975).

Harris, B. J., 'Landlords and Tenants in England in the Later Middle Ages: The Buckingham Estates', *Past and Present*, XLIII (1969).

Harriss, G. L., 'The Struggle for Calais', *E.H.R.*, LXXV (1960).

Hastings, M., *The Court of Common Pleas in Fifteenth Century England* (Cornell University Press, 1947).

Ives, E. W., 'Andrew Dymmock and the Papers of Antony, Earl Rivers, 1482–3', *B.I.H.R.*, XLI (1968).

Jack, R. I., 'The Ecclesiastical Patronage Exercised by a Baronial Family in the Later Middle Ages', *Journal of Religious History*, III (1964–5).

Jones, T., *A History of the County of Brecknock*, enlarged by Sir Joseph Burley (4 vols., Brecon, 1909–30).

Lambert, U., *Blechingley* (2 vols., London, 1921).

Lander, J., 'Marriage and Politics in the Fifteenth Century: the Nevilles and the Wydevilles', *B.I.H.R.*, XXXVI (1963).

—— 'Bonds, coercion and fear: Henry VII and the peerage', *Florilegium Historiale: Essays presented to Wallace K. Ferguson*, ed. J. G. Rowe and W. H. Stokdale (Toronto, 1971).

Leadam, I. S., 'The Inquisition of 1517: Inclosures and Evictions', *T.R.H.S.*, new series VI (1892).

Levett, A. D., *Studies in Manorial History* (Oxford, 1938).

Levine, M., 'The Fall of Edward, Duke of Buckingham', *Tudor Men and Institutions*, ed. A. J. Flavin (Louisiana, 1972).

McFarlane, K. B., 'The Investment of Sir John Fastolf's Profits of War', *T.R.H.S.*, 5th series VII (1957).

—— *The Nobility of Later Medieval England* (Oxford, 1973).

—— 'Parliament and Bastard Feudalism', *T.R.H.S.*, 4th series XXVI (1944).

—— 'The Wars of the Roses', *Proceedings of the British Academy*, L (1964).

Maclean, J., *A Historical Memoir of the Family of Poyntz* (Exeter, 1886).

Mazzinghi, T. J., 'Castle Church', *William Salt Archaeological Society*, VIII (1887).

Mullinger, J. B., *The University of Cambridge, from the Royal Injunctions of 1535 to the Accession of Charles I* (Cambridge, 1884).

Myers, A. R., 'The Household of Queen Elizabeth Woodville, 1466-7 ', *B.J.R.L.*, L (1967-8).

—— 'The Household of Queen Margaret of Anjou, 1452-3 ', *B.J.R.L.*, L (1957-8).

Owen, H. and Blakeway, J. B., *A History of Shrewsbury* (2 vols., London, 1825).

Pugh, T. B., 'The Indenture of the Marches between Henry VII and Edward Stafford, Duke of Buckingham ', *E.H.R.*, LXXI (1956).

—— 'The magnates, knights and gentry ', *Fifteenth Century England*, ed. S. B. Chrimes & others (Manchester, 1972).

Rawcliffe, C., 'The Papers of Edward, duke of Buckingham ', *Journal of the Society of Archivists*, V (1976).

Rees, W., *South Wales and the March, 1284-1415. A Social and Agrarian Study* (Oxford, 1924).

Rosenthal, J. T., 'The Estates and Finances of Richard, Duke of York (1411-60) ', *Studies in Medieval and Renaissance History* (University of Nebraska), II (1965).

Roskell, J. S., *The Commons and their Speakers in English Parliaments, 1375-1523* (Manchester, 1965).

—— *The Commons in the Parliament of 1422* (Manchester, 1954).

—— 'The Problem of the Attendance of the Lords in Mediaeval Parliaments ', *B.I.H.R.*, XXIX (1956).

—— 'William Burley, Speaker for the Commons in 1437, 1445-6 ', *Shropshire Archaeological and Natural History Society Transactions*, 4th series, LVI (1960).

—— 'William Catesby, Counsellor to Richard III ', *B.J.R.L.*, XLII (1959).

Ross, C. D., *Edward IV* (London, 1975).

—— 'The Estates and Finances of Richard Beauchamp, Earl of Warwick ', *Dugdale Occasional Papers*, XII (1956).

Ross, C. D. and Pugh, T. B., 'Materials for the Study of Baronial Incomes in Fifteenth Century England ', *Econ. H.R.*, 2nd series, VI (1953).

Round, J. H., *Peerage and Pedigree* (2 vols., London, 1910).

Russell, J. G., *The Field of the Cloth of Gold* (London, 1969).

Searle, W. G., 'The History of the Queen's College of St Margaret and St Bernard in the University of Cambridge, 1446-1560 ', *Cambridge Antiquarian Society*, IX (1867).

Somerville, R., *The Duchy of Lancaster* (2 vols., London, 1953-70).

—— 'The Duchy of Lancaster Council and the Court of the Star Chamber ', *T.R.H.S.*, 4th series, XXIII (1941).

Storey, R. L., *The End of the House of Lancaster* (London, 1966).

Victoria History of the County of Buckinghamshire.

—— *Oxford.*

—— *Shropshire.*

—— *Stafford.*

—— *Warwick.*

Virgoe, R., 'The Death of William de la Pole, Duke of Suffolk ', *B.J.R.L.*, XLVII (1965).

Wagner, A., 'The Swan Badge and the Swan Knight', *Archaeologia*, XCVII (1959).

Wedgwood, J. C., ed., *History of Parliament. Biographies of the Members of the Commons House, 1439–1509* (H.M.S.O., 1936).

—— *A Parliamentary History of Stafford* (2 vols., for the William Salt Archaeological Society, 1917–18).

Wernham, R. B., *Before the Armada* (London, 1966).

Wolffe, B. P., *The Crown Lands* (London, 1970).

Wood, M., *The English Medieval House* (London, 1965).

INDEX

Persons holding offices on the Stafford estates or in the ducal household are entered in the index in capital letters. Those who did not hold offices, but who are known, in common with many of the Staffords' employees, to have been members of the ducal council or to have received regular fees are described as annuitants and/or councillors.

Index

Index

Index

Index

Index

Index

Index

Normandy, France, lieutenant generalship of, 20

NORMANTON, HENRY, 198

Norris, William, annuitant, 101–2, 241

Northampton
Battle of, 19, 27
borough of, 27, 29
earldom of, 7, 17, 176–7, 193

Northbrook, co. Oxon., 191

Northumberland, earls of, see Percy

Norton in the Moors, co. Staffs., 191

Norton le Hays, co. Essex, 193

NOTTINGHAM, WILLIAM, 210, 226

NOWERS, ANTHONY, 196

Oakham, co. Rutland, Castle and lordship of, 17–18, 193; profits, 108

Ockham, co. Surrey, 192, 194

OGULL, HUMPHREY, 198

Oldhall, Sir William, 26, 194

OLNEY, ROBERT, 202

Ongar, co. Essex, 191

Orcheston, co. Wilts., 192

Ormonde, earl of, see Botiller, Thomas le

Outryde, James, 243

Oxford, earls of, see de Vere

Oxford, University of, 90, 92, 94, 172; Merton College in, 97

Pakker, William, 250

Palley, Alfred, 243

PALMER, RICHARD, 200

Palmer, William, annuitant, 234

Paris, governorship of, 20

PARKER, JOHN, 237

PARKER, NICHOLAS, 237

PARKER, WALTER, 209 (ter), 210 (ter)

Parliament, 11, 15, 16, 26, 117, 118, 144; patronage of m.p.s by the Staffords, 80–2

Parmyter, John, 251

Parmyter, Robert, 251 (bis)

PARTESOIL, JOHN, 202

PARTESOIL, ROBERT, 203

PARTESOIL, WILLIAM, 203

Patshull, co. Staffs., 191

Paulet, Sir Amyas, 249

PAUNCEFOOT, JOHN, 196, 230, 246

Payne, William, 172

Pecham, Reginald, 243, 246

Pecok, John, 247

Pembroke, earls of, see Herbert; Tudor

Pencarn, co. Mon., 192

Penkelly, co. Brecon, lordship of, 170

Penkridge, co. Staffs., 191

Penshurst, co. Kent, manor of, 21, 41, 68, 87, 100, 111, 134, 138, 139, 154, 156, 193

Penshurst, park at, attack on, 178; enclosures, 64

Perche, County of, France, 20, 109, 111, 114–15

Percival, Walter, annuitant, 234

Percy, earls of Northumberland, imposition of entry fines, 62; manuscripts, 4; retinue, 76

Percy, Henry, earl of Northumberland (d. 1461), retinue, 76

Percy, Henry, earl of Northumberland (d. 1489), farmer of Holderness, 211; his daughter, Eleanor, marries Edward, duke of Buckingham, 35–6

PERCY, HENRY, EARL OF NORTHUMBERLAND (d. 1527), 39, 41, 142, 183, 185; litigation, 174–6; offices, 102, 211, 212

Percy, Henry, earl of Northumberland (d. 1585), 138

Perendon, co. Essex, 120 n. 54

PERKINS, WILLIAM, 202, 234

Pers, Edmund, 250

PESHALE, PHILIPPA, 237

Pesshey, Edmund, 250

Petersfield, co. Hants., 191

Philipps, Mistress, embroideress, annuitant, 241

PHILIPS, MORGAN, 214

PICHER, THOMAS, 209

PICKERING, JOHN, 168, 202 (bis), 249; his report on the Stafford estates, 56–7, 60–3, 98, 156

Pierson, John, annuitant, 241

Pilkington, William, 247

PILTON, JOHN, 205

Plantagenet, Edward, earl of Rutland and duke of York (d. 1415), 17–8; farmer of Newport, 107

Plantagenet, George, duke of Clarence (d. 1478), trial of, 28

Plantagenet, Richard, duke of York (d. 1460), 4, 16, 19, 80–1, 159; estates, 45; finances, 104, 114, 121; relations with Humphrey, duke of Buckingham, 24–7, 46, 48; relations with Henry VI, 24–7, 188–9

Plantagenet, Richard, duke of York (d. ?1483), 29, 32

Pleshey, co. Essex, 14
College, 84

Index

Index

Index

Index

Index

WELDON, WILLIAM, 51, 199, 223
Welham, William, 244
WELL, JOHN, 195
Wells, co. Norfolk, 192, 203-4
Wentloog, co. Mon., coroner of, 154 n. 25
Wentloog, county of, 192
WENTWORTH, WILLIAM, 204
Westcombe, co. Somerset, 193
WESTCOTT, NICHOLAS, 217
Westminster, abbot of, 249
Westmorland, earls of, see Neville
Weston, co. Salop., 192
Wexcombe, co. Wilts., 192
Whatcote, co. Warwicks., 194
Wheatenhurst, co. Glos., 37-9
WHEELER, JOHN, 169-70, 201
Whiston, co. Northants., 192
Whiteoak, Robert, annuitant, 241
Whitgreve, family of, influence in Stafford, 81-2
WHITGREVE, JOHN, 207
WHITGREVE, ROBERT (d. 1452), 80-2, 157, 159, 221, 238
WHITGREVE, ROBERT (fl. 1510/11), 216, 248
WHITGREVE, THOMAS, 213, 225
WHYNBERGH, GEORGE, 202, 250
Wilbrighton, co. Staffs., 191
William I, 7
WILLIAM AP HOWELL, 214
William ap Thomas, Sir, councillor, 224
Willoughby, co. Lincs., 191
Willoughby, John, 176
WILLOUGHBY, RICHARD, 204
WILLOUGHBY, SIR ROBERT, 203
WILLOUGHBY, THOMAS, 153, 225, 238
Willoughby, William, lord (d. 1526), litigation, 175
Willoughby de Brooke, Robert, lord (d. 1521), 141; litigation, 175
Wiltshire, earls of, see Botiller; Stafford
Winchester, bishop of, see Beaufort, Henry
WINDSOR, SIR ANDREW, 102, 203, 204, 211
WINGFIELD, EDMUND, 214
WINGFIELD, JOHN, 56, 200
Wingford, John, annuitant, 240
WISTOWE, WILLIAM, 71, 197 (bis)
Withernsea, co. Yorks., 193
Witherton, Richard, councillor and annuitant, 223, 235
Wiveton, co. Norfolk, 192
WODEFORD, JOHN, 47, 209
WODERTON, JOHN, 48, 83, 208
Woderton, Walter, 84
Wolford Magna, co. Warwicks., 191, 194
Wolford Parva, co. Warwicks., 194
Wolle, Laurence, 247

Wolsey, Thomas, cardinal, archbishop of York (d. 1530), 90, 91, 151; litigation, 175; relations with Edward, duke of Buckingham, 40-4, 100, 136, 167, 170-1
Wood, John, 251 (bis)
Woodford, co. Northants., 193
WOODHOUSE, JOHN, 110 n. 18
WOODHOUSE, SIR THOMAS, 204, 241
Woodstock, John, annuitant, 238
Woodstock, Thomas of, duke of Gloucester (d. 1397), arms of, 31; inheritance of his wife, Eleanor de Bohun, 12-6, 193; her library, 95; his daughter, Anne, marries Thomas and Edmund Stafford, 12; her inheritance, 17-18, 108, 193
WOODSTOCK, SIR THOMAS, 101-2
WOODVILLE, THOMAS, 202, 204
Wootton Wawen, co. Warwicks., 191, 205
Worcester, earls of, see Tiptoft; Herbert
Worcester, William, 26; Pseudo-, 28
Worde, Wynkin de, 96
Worthen, co. Salop., advowson of, 83
Worthen, bailiff and manor of, 149, 192
WOTTON, THOMAS, 151, 198, 210, 231, 249
Writtle, co. Essex, 25, 47, 66, 67, 87, 193; an administrative centre, 54
WROTLEY, THOMAS, 216
Wrottesley, Thomas, annuitant, 241
Wrottley, co. Staffs., 191
Wroughton, William, annuitant, 242
WYBARNE, JOHN, 212
WYCCON, JOHN, 207
Wydeville, family of, 186-7; relations with Henry, duke of Buckingham, 28-33
Wydeville, Anthony, earl Rivers (d. 1483), 28, 37, 187; a landlord, 65, 161
Wydeville, Richard, earl Rivers (d. 1469), 77, 187
Wyman, Richard, 246
Wynch, John, prior of Llanthony, 84
Wynston, Thomas, 251
WYNTER, EDWARD, 238
Wyther, Thomas, 244
Wythesade, Richard, 247

Yalding, co. Kent, 191
Yelverton, William, councillor, 221, 238
York, dukes of, see Plantagenet
York, archbishops of, see Rotherham; Wolsey
YOUNG, DAVID, 200
YOUNG, GEOFFREY, 212
Young, Thomas, councillor, 221, 238

Zouche, John, lord (d. 1526), 185

279